The Memoirs of
AGA KHAN

WORLD ENOUGH AND TIME

BY

HIS HIGHNESS
THE AGA KHAN,

P.C., G.C.S.I., G.C.V.O., G.C.I.E.

Sultan Muhammad Shah

19 54

Simon and Schuster, New York

First Printing
Library of Congress Catalog Card Number: 54-8644
Dewey Decimal Classification Number: 92
MANUFACTURED IN THE UNITED STATES OF AMERICA
BY H. WOLFF BOOK MFG. CO., NEW YORK, N. Y.

~§ "Life is a great and noble calling, not a mean and groveling thing to be shuffled through as best we can, but a lofty and exalted destiny."

CONTENTS

PREFACE
by W. Somerset Maugham

I HAVE KNOWN the Aga Khan for many years. He has been a kind and helpful friend. The introductions he gave me when I spent a winter in India enabled me to profit by the rich experience of my sojourn in that wonderful country as otherwise I could never have done, so that when he paid me the compliment of asking me to write a preface to his autobiography I was glad to be given the opportunity to do him this small, and really unnecessary, service. For the book speaks for itself. It was not till I had read it that it was borne upon me how difficult a task I was undertaking. The Aga Khan has led a full life. He has been a great traveler and there are few parts of the world that he has not visited either for pleasure or because his political and religious interests made it necessary. He has been a great theater goer; he has loved the opera and the ballet. He is an assiduous reader. He has been occupied in affairs in which the fate of nations was involved. He has bred horses and raced them. He has been on terms of close friendship with kings and princes of the blood royal, maharajahs, viceroys, field marshals, actors and actresses, trainers, golf professionals, society beauties and society entertainers. He has founded a university. As head of a widely diffused sect, the Ismailis, he has throughout his life sedulously endeavored to further the welfare, spiritual and material, of his countless followers. Toward the end of this autobiography he remarks that he has never once been bored. That alone is enough to mark the Aga Khan out as a remarkable man.

I must tell the reader at once that I am incompetent to deal with some of his multifarious activities. I know nothing of racing. I am so little interested in it that one day when I was lunching with the Aga Khan just

*before Tulyar won the Derby we talked only of India and I never thought
of asking him whether his horse had a chance of winning. I know no more
of politics than the ordinary newspaper reader. For long years the Aga
Khan was intimately concerned with them. His advice was constantly
sought, and it was generally sound. He believed in moderation: "Of one
fact," he writes, "my years in public life have convinced me; that the value
of a compromise is that it can supply a bridge across a difficult period, and
later having employed it it is often possible to bring into effect the full-
scale measures of reform which, originally, would have been rejected out
of hand." He knew well the statesmen on whose decisions during the last
fifty years great events depended. It is seldom he passes a harsh judgment
on them. He pays generous tribute to their integrity, intelligence, patriotism, wide knowledge and experience. It seems strange that with these
valuable qualities they should have landed us all in the sorry mess in
which we now find ourselves.*

*The Aga Khan is a charitable man, and it goes against his grain to speak
ill of others. The only occasion in this book of his on which he betrays
bitterness is when he animadverts on the behavior of our countrymen in
their dealings with the inhabitants of the countries in which in one way
and another they held a predominant position, in Egypt and India and
in the treaty ports of China. During the eighties relations between British
and Indians were in general easy, amiable and without strain, and had
they continued to be as they were then, "I greatly doubt," he writes,
"whether political bitterness would have developed to the extent it did,
and possibly something far less total than the severance of the Republic
of India from the Imperial connection would have been feasible." It is
a disquieting thought. He goes on as follows: "What happened to the
Englishman has been to me all my life a source of wonder and astonishment. Suddenly it seemed that his prestige as a member of an imperial,
governing race would be lost if he accepted those of a different color as
fundamentally his equals. The color bar was no longer thought of as a
physical difference, but far more dangerously—in the end disastrously—
as an intellectual and spiritual difference. . . . The pernicious theory
spread that all Asiatics were a second-class race, and 'white men' possessed some intrinsic and unchallengeable superiority." According to the
Aga Khan the root-cause of the attitude adopted by the ruling class was
fear and a lack of inner self-confidence. Another was the presence in in-*

creasing numbers of British wives with no knowledge of or interest in the customs and outlook of Indians. They were no less narrow and provincial when forty years after the time of which the Aga Khan writes I myself went to India. These women who for the most part came from modest homes in the country and, since taxation was already high, had at the most a maid of all work to do the household chores found themselves in spacious quarters, with a number of servants to do their bidding. It went to their heads. I remember having tea one day with the wife of a not very important official. In England she might have been a manicurist or a stenographer. She asked me about my travels and when I told her that I had spent most of my time in the Indian States, she said: "You know, we don't have anything more to do with Indians than we can help. One has to keep them at arm's length."

The rest of the company agreed with her.

The clubs were barred to Indians till by the influence of Lord Willingdon some were persuaded to admit them, but so far as I could see, it made little difference since even in them white and colored kept conspicuously apart.

When I was in Hyderabad the Crown Prince asked me to lunch. I had spent some time in Bombay and was then on my way to Calcutta.

"I suppose you were made an honorary member of the Club when you were in Bombay," he said, and when I told him I was, he added: "And I suppose you'll be made an honorary member of the Club at Calcutta?"

"I hope so," I answered.

"Do you know the difference between the Club at Bombay and the Club at Calcutta?" he asked me. I shook my head. "In one they don't allow either dogs or Indians; in the other they do allow dogs."

I couldn't for the life of me think what to say to that.

But it was not only in India that these unhappy conditions prevailed. In the foreign concessions in China there was the same arrogant and hidebound colonialism and the general attitude toward the Chinese was little short of outrageous. "All the best hotels refused entry to Chinese, except in wings specially set aside for them. It was the same in restaurants. From European clubs they were totally excluded. Even in shops a Chinese customer would have to stand aside and wait to be served when a European or an American came in after him and demanded attention." Lord Cromer was the British Resident when the Aga Khan went to Egypt.

He found the British were not merely in political control of the country, but assumed a social superiority which the Egyptians appeared humbly to accept. "There was no common ground of social intercourse. Therefore inevitably behind the façade of humility there developed a sullen and brooding, almost personal, resentment which later on needlessly, bitterly, poisoned the clash of Egyptian nationalism with Britain's interests as the occupying power." Now that the foreign concessions in China exist no more, now that the last British soldiers are leaving Egypt, now that, as the Aga Khan puts it, British rule in India has dissolved and passed away like early morning mist before strong sunlight, the British have left behind them a legacy of hatred. We too may ask ourselves what happened to Englishmen that caused them so to act as to arouse an antagonism which was bound in the end to have such untoward consequences. I am not satisfied with the explanation which the Aga Khan gives. I think it is to be sought rather in that hackneyed, but consistently disregarded aphorism of Lord Acton's: Power corrupts and absolute power corrupts absolutely.

It is no good crying over spilt milk, so the determinists tell us, and if I have dwelt on this subject it is with intention. In the world of today the Americans occupy the position which the British so long, and for all their failings not ingloriously, held. Perhaps it would be to their advantage to profit by our example and avoid making the errors that have cost us so dearly. A brown man can fire a Sten gun and shoot as straight as a white man; a yellow man can drop an atom bomb as efficiently. What does this mean but that the color bar is now a crass absurdity? The British wanted to be loved and were convinced that they were; the Americans want to be loved too, but are uneasily, distressingly, conscious that they are not. They find it hard to understand. With their boundless generosity they have poured money into the countries which two disastrous wars have reduced to poverty and it is natural that they should wish to see it spent as they think fit and not always as the recipients would like to spend it. It is true enough that the man who pays the piper calls the tune, but if it is a tune the company finds it hard to dance to, perhaps he is well-advised to do his best so to modify it that they find it easy. Doubtless it is more blessed to give than to receive, but it is also more hazardous, for you put the recipient of your bounty under an obligation and that is a condition that only the very magnanimous can accept with good will. Gratitude is not a virtue that comes easily to the human race. I do not think it can be denied that the British conferred great benefits on the peoples over which they ruled; but they humiliated them and so earned their hatred. The Americans would do well to remember it.

But enough of that. The Aga Khan is descended from the Prophet Mohammed through his daughter Fatima and is descended also from the Fatimite Caliphs of Egypt. He is justifiably proud of his illustrious ancestry. His grandfather, also known as Aga Khan, by inheritance spiritual head of the Ismailis, was a Persian nobleman, son-in-law of the powerful monarch, Fateh Ali Shah and hereditary chieftain of Kerman. Smarting under an insult that had been put upon him he took up arms against a later Shah, Mohammed by name, was worsted and forced to make his escape, attended by a few horsemen, through the deserts of Baluchistan to Sind. There he raised a troop of light horse and after various vicissitudes eventually reached Bombay with his two hundred horsemen, his relations, clients and supporters. He acquired a vast estate upon which he built palaces, innumerable smaller houses for his dependents and outbuildings, gardens and fountains. He lived in feudal state and never had less than a hundred horses in his stables. He died when the author of this book was a child and was succeeded by his son who, however, only survived him a short time, upon which the Aga Khan whom we know, at the age of eight, inherited his titles, wealth and responsibilities, spiritual and temporal. His education was conducted to prepare him for the sacred charge to which he was born. He was taught English, French, Arabic and Persian. Religious instruction was imparted to him by a renowned teacher of Islamic lore. No holidays were allowed him. The only relief from work was on Saturdays and feast days when he received his followers who came to offer gifts and do him homage.

The Aga Khan, raised to such eminence at so early an age, was fortunate in that his mother was a highly cultivated woman. She was deeply versed in Persian and Arabic poetry, as were several of her ladies in waiting, and at mealtimes at her table "our conversation was of literature, of poetry; or perhaps one of the elderly ladies who traveled to and from Teheran a great deal would talk about her experiences at the Court of the Shah." The Begum was a mystic and habitually spent a great deal of time in prayer for spiritual enlightenment and union with God. "I have, in something near ecstasy," he writes, "heard her read perhaps some verses by Roumi or Hafiz, with their exquisite analogies between man's beatific vision of the Divine and the temporal beauty and colors of flowers, the music and magic of the night, and the transient splendors of the Persian dawn." The Aga Khan is a deeply religious man. One of the most interesting chapters in this book is that in which after telling of his personal beliefs, he gives a concise exposition of Islam as it is understood and practiced today. It is there for the reader to read and I will say no more about it than that it is sympathetic and persuasive. It may be that it will occur to him that the duties of man as he may learn them from the verses of the Koran and the Traditions of the Prophet are not very different from those he may learn from the Sermon on the Mount. But man is an imperfect creature, at the mercy of his passions, and it should surprise no one that too often these duties are no more practiced by Muslim than by Christian.

The general public knows the Aga Khan chiefly as a racing man and it is not unlikely that the reader of the book, remembering pages in which he narrates his experiences as a breeder of bloodstock and the happy winner of many classical events, will be a trifle taken aback by this moving, thoughtful and sincere chapter. There is no reason why he should be. The chase was the main occupation of the Iranian nobles from which he is descended. It is part of the tradition he inherited and the environment in which he was brought up. His grandfather, his father, had hounds, hawks and horses, the swiftest and finest money could buy or they could breed. On the death of his father only twenty or thirty of the ninety race horses he had possessed were kept and they, through the Aga Khan's minority, were raced under his colors all over Western India. Racing is in his blood. But first and foremost he is the spiritual head of a sect of Islam which counts its adherents by the million. He has a secure belief in the faith which was the faith of his great ancestors and he is ever mindful of the sacred charge, with the great responsibilities it entails, which is his by right of birth. We are none of us all of a piece. The Aga Khan says somewhere that we are all composed of diverse and conflicting elements: of few men could this be more truly said than of himself. But he is fortunate in that the elements in him only superficially conflict; they are resolved by the strength and consistency of his character.

ACKNOWLEDGMENTS

I MUST RECORD my deep and warm gratitude to my old friend, Mr. Somerset Maugham, for the foreword which he has been kind enough to write for this book, and for the agreeable and gracious observations that he has made. To Miss Merioneth Whitaker go my thanks for her invaluable skill and patience in the preparation of the manuscript, without which it would have been a far more arduous labor.

A recent portrait of His Highness the Aga Khan.

A recent portrait of Her Highness the Begum Aga Khan.

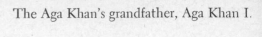
The Aga Khan's grandfather, Aga Khan I.

[BELOW LEFT] Aly Shah, the Aga Khan's father.

[BELOW RIGHT] Her Highness Lady Aly Shah, mother of the Aga Khan.

The Aga Khan as a young boy.

[BELOW] At his installation as Imam, the Aga Khan ascends the Gadi (the seat of office) in Bombay in 1885.

The Aga Khan as a young man.

[RIGHT] A portrait of the Aga Khan
taken during the reign of George V.
Created G.C.I.E. in 1902, he is shown
wearing the Badge of the Order of
the Indian Empire.

The Aga Khan with his younger son, Prince Sadruddin, and his two grandsons, Prince Karim Aga and Prince Amyn Mahomed.

The Aga Khan leads in Blenheim, winner of the 1930 Derby (*Associated Press*).

With Mahatma Gandhi and Mrs. Sarojani Naidu in London during the Round Table Conference of 1931 *(Planet News)*.

[OPPOSITE] The Aga Khan being weighed against diamonds at his Diamond Jubilee celebration in Bombay, 1946. The diamonds are in plastic boxes on the scale *(Associated Press)*.

With the Begum Aga Khan and Prince Sadruddin at the Diamond
Jubilee celebration.

Part One

❦

CHILDHOOD AND YOUTH

A Bridge Across the Years

THE TRUTH about a man as much as about a country or an institution is better than legend, myth and falsehood. I am someone about whom a whole fabric of legend has been woven in my own lifetime. Of recent years I have often been urged by editors and publishers to write my memoirs, my own account of my life and experiences, of my beliefs and opinions, and the way in which they have been molded. Friends have advised me that it is my duty to my own reputation, now and in the future, to tell the truth about myself as I see it, and to refute the falsehoods that have gained credence. Flattering this persuasion may have been, kind in intention certainly.

There are certain obvious and gross fictions which need to be corrected—the grandiose estimates, for example, of my own and my family's wealth. I have seen estimates both of my capital and my income so inaccurate that not one but two noughts at the end should have been knocked off. Not long ago an alleged biography was published; in the matter of dates the margin of error in it was anything from one to ten years. If there is this amount of misinformation on simple, easily discoverable fact, what sort of veracity is likely in wider, more profound and more intangible matters?

My life in many ways has been a bridge across vastly differing epochs. Looking at it for the moment simply from the Western point of view—I had a full life in the Victorian era, and I am leading now an equally full life in this new Elizabethan era. When I was a young man I sat next to Queen Victoria at a dinner party and

3

talked to her throughout it; the other day I sat next to Queen Elizabeth II at a tea party and talked to her throughout it. In my youth the internal combustion engine was in its early, experimental phase, and the first motorcars were objects of ridicule; now we all take supersonic jet propulsion for granted, and interplanetary travel is far more seriously discussed today than was even the smallest flying venture at a time when I was quite grown up and had already lived a full and active life. I had the great honor of knowing Lord Kelvin, in his time the greatest physicist in the world; he assured me solemnly and deliberately that flying was a physical impossibility for human beings and quite unattainable. Even H. G. Wells in his early book, *Anticipations*, put off the conquest of the air and the discovery of atomic power for two or three centuries. Yet these and much more have come to pass in a brief half century.

During this period I have been not only an onlooker but by the accident of birth an active participant in affairs. The extent of the revolution which I have witnessed is not yet to be measured, but we can see manifestations of it at many levels of human experience. Throughout the Western world the whole way of life has undergone fundamental and far-reaching changes, perhaps the greatest of which is that the expectation of life has been increased by nearly twenty years. Old age begins for men and women in the West at anything from ten to twenty years later than it did in my youth, and in India and in the East generally a similar, though at present smaller, extension of the span can be noted. In Europe and America it is most marked. There are far, far more old men and women alive and active. Walking along a busy street like Piccadilly or any of the Paris boulevards, a man of my age sees the difference. In Europe there has been a widespread restriction of families among the upper and middle classes; the family of the nineties, with seven or eight children, has almost completely disappeared. In no European country is divorce looked upon as anything unusual; when I was young, men of the stature of Charles Dilke and Charles Stewart Parnell were driven out of public life—Dilke not indeed because he was a "guilty party," nor even as a principal, but solely on the grounds of association with a divorce case. Today all over Europe men to whom the strictly legal term "guilty party" is applicable are to be found in the highest, most responsible positions in the state. Indeed the only penalty to which they are subject seems to be nonadmission to the Royal Enclosure at Ascot—a privilege which, I daresay, few of them care about anyway.

The changes in the status of women, economic and social, have been enormous; fifty or sixty years ago almost the only career open to them was marriage or indirect dependence on man's protection, but today they possess the avenues of countless honorable and profitable callings, and they carry themselves with self-confidence and self-assurance. Homosexuality was looked upon very much like leprosy. Today in most European countries either there is Freudian pity or there are excuses, and by men like André Gide and others, open justification if not glorification.

I was a grown-up man in that old world. I feel that it is therefore my duty to give an account in some detail of my experience over this long, momentous epoch, and to record my personal acquaintance— often indeed my real and deep friendship—with some of those who have had their share in bringing about its vast political, social and economic changes.

England—we still talked naturally of England when I was young— dwelt then in "splendid isolation," a state of affairs which stimulated a far deeper, stronger pride than did the more extreme American isolationism of the twenties and the early thirties. To that England, France was the traditional enemy and Germany the only potential friend in Europe. Only a handful of men whose thoughts converged from very different origins—Sir Charles Dilke, imperialists like Admiral Maxse, and a few radical "Little Englanders"—championed friendship with France and distrust of Germany.

In vast regions of the East, England's hegemony was virtually undisputed, and her Indian Empire seemed among the most solidly based and most durable of contemporary political organizations. A man like Lord Curzon—and indeed I should say ninety-nine per cent of the British ruling class—would have been horror-struck at the thought of the formation of an Indian Republic, or its inevitable corollary, and even more appalled by the prospect of the partition of the enormous Indian Empire and the emergence of two healthy national states each with its own historic personality. Even as late as the 1930's, when the promise of eventual Dominion status had been made, this same British ruling class permitted itself to be obsessed with the childish delusion that the Indian Empire, which their predecessors had built up, could be handed on—like an estate after the owner's death—to successors who would preserve the artificial unity of the structure as if it were a true unity rooted in spiritual and intellectual foundations. Even in the 1940's men like Lord Wavell and others hoped and believed that even after the British quitted India, it would be possible to maintain a united Indian Army. Other European colonial powers nourished delusions no less futile. Less than a decade ago it was seriously held in France that the three Indo-Chinese states would join, humbly and as junior partners, in a French Union of which Paris must be the head and heart.

I have seen the long revolution of Asia against European rule. In the nineties it was a cloud no bigger than a man's hand. What did it seem to amount to then? The mild little hope of a few jobs, and a few honorific titles. Today in Asia the revolution is accomplished, everywhere east of the Middle East there has been an end of European rule in fact and in name; and I have lived long enough to see the same process begin in Africa. But fortunately the western European governing classes have learned the lesson of Asia. The British in West Africa, the Belgians in the Congo and the French in their African Equatorial possessions are preparing and planning that transfer of power for which in Asia they were never prepared.

I have had my share in these changes. However, I must stress that whatever part I may have played in public affairs and in political developments in India and elsewhere, none of it has been my main task or duty. Since my childhood my chief concern, my chief responsibility, throughout the whole of my life, has been the great charge which I have inherited as Imam of the Ismaili branch of the Shia sect of Muslims. Elsewhere in this book I shall give a detailed account of what I mean by this statement. Here, however, I must only affirm that my duties in this task have always been my prime concern; in all aspects—in a vast and varied correspondence, in the maintenance of countless links of personal and religious loyalty and affection—they have occupied a large part of every day of my life.

As I look back, there is one memory, one piece of self-knowledge, which gives me the utmost satisfaction. I was myself personally responsible for the conversion to Islam of some thirty thousand to forty thousand caste Hindus, many of them of the upper and professional classes. They had been people without a faith, and they found a faith. Neither my father nor my grandfather had attempted a religious task of this magnitude. Its fulfillment has had one important and interesting effect: the great majority of these converts lived in what is now Pakistan; had they remained Hindu they would in all probability have been involved in and suffered by the mass displacement and all the other terrible and horrible happenings that accompanied Partition in 1947.

Everything else that I have done or striven to do, enjoyed or suffered, has been of necessity secondary. With this important reservation clearly stated, I think I can give an account of many of the other events and experiences of my life. I have tried all the years I spent in public life to do my best so far as I could. It is not possible for me to assess the success or failure of what I have tried to do; final judgment lies elsewhere.

But since I have witnessed this rapid and all-developing process of change in every domain of human interest and experience—the technical and mechanical revolution of our time, man's developing mastery of natural forces, the recognition of the importance of the subconscious, the vast increase in longevity, the rise of new moral standards and the corresponding profound changes in outlook, and great political changes undreamed of in my youth—I hope in these coming chapters to give some picture of each epoch as it unfolded before the eyes and in the mind and heart of one who was usually an onlooker but sometimes and actively a participant.

II

Islam, the Religion of My Ancestors

THE ORIGINS of man's religious aspirations are to be found in what we nowadays call science. Those who have studied mythology and primitive psychology know that magic in various forms started various trains of thought in primitive man by which he achieved what seemed to him to be rational accounts of the natural phenomena around him. It seemed to him rational that these phenomena, these events like the rising and the setting of the sun, the passage of the seasons, the flowering of the bud and the ripening of the fruit, the wind and the rain, were caused and controlled by deities or superior beings. Primitive religious experience and primitive scientific reasoning were linked together in magic, in wizardry. Thus, at one and the same time mankind's experiences in the realm of sensation and his strivings to explain and co-ordinate those experiences in terms of his mind led to the birth of both science and religion. The two remained linked throughout prehistoric and ancient times, and in the life of the early empires of which we have knowledge. It was difficult to separate what I may call proto-religion from proto-science; they made their journey like two streams, sometimes mingling, sometimes separating, but running side by side.

Such is the background to Greek and Roman thought and culture as well as to ancient Iranian and Hindu philosophy before the beginning of the Christian era. Aristotle, however, gave a more scientific turn to this mingling, introducing categories and concepts which were purely reasonable, and shedding those vestiges of religious awe and mystery which are visible even in Plato.

With the decline of the Roman Empire and the break-up of the great and elaborate system of civilization which Roman law and administration had sustained for so many centuries, the Dark Ages enfolded Europe. In the seventh century of the Christian era there was a rapid and brilliant new flowering of humanity's capacity and desire for adventure and discovery in the realms of both spirit and intellect. That flowering began in Arabia; its origin and impetus were given to it by my Holy ancestor, the Prophet Mohammed, and we know it by the name of Islam. From Arabia the tide of its influence flowed swiftly and strongly to North Africa and thence to Spain.

Ibn-Rushd, the great Muslim philosopher, known to Europe as Averroes, established clearly the great distinction between two kinds of apprehensible human experience: on the one hand, our experience of nature as we recognize it through our senses, whence comes our capacity to measure and to count (and with that capacity all that it brought in the way of new events and new explanations); and on the other hand, our immediate and immanent experience of something more real, less dependent on thought or on the processes of the mind, but directly given to us, which I believe to be *religious experience*. Naturally, since our brain is material, and its processes and all the consequences of its processes are material, the moment that we put either thought or spiritual experience into words, this material basis of the brain must give a material presentation to even the highest, most transcendent spiritual experience. But men can study objectively the direct and subjective experiences of those who have had spiritual enlightenment without material intervention.

It is said that we live, move and have our being in God. We find this concept expressed often in the Koran, not in those words of course, but just as beautifully and more tersely. But when we realize the meaning of this saying, we are already preparing ourselves for the gift of the power of direct experience. Roumi and Hafiz, the great Persian poets, have told us, each in his different way, that some men are born with such natural spiritual capacities and possibilities of development that they have direct experience of that great love, that all-embracing, all-consuming love, which direct contact with reality gives to the human soul. Hafiz indeed has said that men like Jesus

Christ and Muslim mystics like Mansour and Bayezid and others
have possessed that spiritual power of the greater love; that any of us,
if the Holy Spirit* ever present grants us that enlightenment, can,
being thus blessed, have the power which Christ had, but that to the
overwhelming majority of men this greater love is not a practical
possibility. We can, however, make up for its absence from our lives
by worldly, human love for individual human beings; and this will
give us a measure of enlightenment attainable without the intervention of the Holy Spirit. Those who have had the good fortune to
know and feel this worldly, human love should respond to it only
with gratitude and regard it as a blessing and as, in its own way, a
source of pride. I firmly believe that the higher experience can to a
certain extent be prepared for by absolute devotion in the material
world to another human being. Thus from the most worldly point
of view and with no comprehension of the higher life of the spirit,
the lower, more terrestrial spirit makes us aware that all the treasures
of this life, all that fame, wealth and health can bring are nothing
beside the happiness which is created and sustained by the love of
one human being for another. This great grace we can see in ordinary
life as we look about us, among our acquaintances and friends.

But as the joys of human love surpass all that riches and power
may bring a man, so does that greater spiritual love and enlightenment, the fruit of that sublime experience of the direct vision of
reality which is God's gift and grace, surpass all that the finest, truest
human love can offer. For that gift we must ever pray.

Now I am convinced that through Islam, through the ideal of
Allah, as presented by Muslims, man can attain this direct experience which no words can explain but which for him are absolute
certainties. I have not discussed experience of this order with non-
Muslims, but I have been told that Buddhists, Brahmins, Zoroastrians
and Christians—I have often heard it of Jews, except perhaps Spinoza
—have also attained this direct, mystical vision. I am certain that
many Muslims, and I am convinced that I myself, have had moments
of enlightenment and of knowledge of a kind which we cannot com-

* It must be realized that the Muslim concept of the Holy Spirit differs profoundly
from the Christian idea of the Third Person of the Trinity.

municate because it is something given and not something acquired.

To a certain extent I have found that the following verse of the Koran, so long as it is understood in a purely nonphysical sense, has given assistance and understanding to myself and other Muslims. However, I must warn all who read it not to allow their material critical outlook to break in with literal, verbal explanations of something that is symbolic and allegorical. I appeal to every reader, whether Muslim or not, to accept the spirit of this verse in its entirety:

> Allah is the light of the heavens and the earth; His light is as a niche in which is a lamp, and the lamp is in a glass, the glass is as though it were a glittering star; it is lit from a blessed tree, an Olive neither of east nor of the west, the oil of which would well-nigh give light though no fire touched it,—light upon light;—Allah guides to His light whom He pleases; and Allah strikes our parables for men; and Allah all things doth know.

(CHAPTER XXIV "Light," 35)

From that brief statement of my own personal beliefs, I move on to as concise and as uncontroversial an exposition as I can give of Islam as it is understood and practiced today. The present condition of mankind offers surely, with all its dangers and all its challenges, a chance too—a chance of establishing not just material peace among nations but that better peace of God on earth. In that endeavor Islam can play its valuable constructive part, and the Islamic world can be a strong and stabilizing factor provided it is really understood and its spiritual and moral power recognized and respected.

I shall try to give in a small compass a clear survey of the fundamentals of Islam, by which I mean those principles, those articles of faith, and that way of life, all of which are universally accepted among all Muslim sects. First therefore, I shall propound those Islamic tenets which are held in common by the larger community of Sunnis, and by Shias as well. Having thus made as clear as I can the faith which binds us all as Muslims, I shall then give a brief sketch of Shia doctrine and of those special tenets held by that subdivision of the Shias known as the Ismailis, the sect of which I am the Imam.

First it must be understood that, though these fundamental ideals are universally accepted by Muslims, there does not exist in Islam and there has never existed any source of absolute authority; we have no Papal Encyclical to propound and sanction a dogma, such as Roman Catholics possess, and no Thirty-nine Articles like those which state the doctrinal position of the Church of England. The Prophet Mohammed had two sources of authority, one religious which was the essential one of his life, and the other secular which, by the circumstances and accidents of his career, became joined to his essential and Divinely inspired authority in religion.

According to the Sunni school—the majority of Muslims—the Prophet's religious authority came to an end at his death, and he appointed no successor to his secular authority. According to Sunni teaching, the faithful, the companions of the Prophet, the believers, elected Abu Bakr as his successor and his Khalif; but Abu Bakr assumed only the civil and secular power. No one had the authority to succeed to the religious supremacy, which depended on direct Divine inspiration, because the Prophet Mohammed and the Koran declared definitely that he was the final messenger of God, the Absolute. Thus, say the Sunnis, it was impossible to constitute an authority similar to that of the Papacy; it remained for the Faithful to interpret the Koran, the example and the sayings of the Prophet, not only in order to understand Islam but to ensure its development throughout the centuries. Fortunately the Koran has itself made this task easy, for it contains a number of verses which declare that Allah speaks to man in allegory and parable. Thus the Koran leaves the door open for all kinds of possibilities of interpretation so that no one interpreter can accuse another of being non-Muslim. A felicitous effect of this fundamental principle of Islam that the Koran is constantly open to allegorical interpretation has been that our Holy Book has been able to guide and illuminate the thought of believers, century after century, in accordance with the conditions and limitations of intellectual apperception imposed by external influences in the world. It leads also to a greater charity among Muslims, for since there can be no cut-and-dried interpretation, all schools of thought can unite in the prayer that the Almighty in His infinite mercy may forgive any mistaken interpretation of the Faith whose cause is ignorance or misunderstanding.

I am trying to put before my Western readers, not the doctrine of the Ismaili sect to which I belong, not Shia doctrine, nor the teachings of the Sufi school of Islamic mysticism, of men such as Jalaleddin Roumi or Bayazid Bostami, nor even the views of certain modern Sunni interpreters who, not unlike certain Christian sects, look for literal guidance in the Koran as Christians of these sects find it in the Old and New Testaments; but the main and central Sunni stream of thought, whose source is in the ideas of the school founded by al-Ghazali and whose influence and teaching have flowed on from century to century.

First, however, we must ask ourselves why this final and consummate appearance of the Divine Will was granted to mankind, and what were its causes. All Islamic schools of thought accept it as a fundamental principle that for centuries, for thousands of years before the advent of Mohammed, there arose from time to time messengers, illumined by Divine Grace, for and among those races of the earth which had sufficiently advanced intellectually to comprehend such a message. Thus Abraham, Moses, Jesus and all the Prophets of Israel are universally accepted by Islam. Muslims indeed know no limitation merely to the Prophets of Israel; they are ready to admit that there were similar Divinely inspired messengers in other countries—Gautama Buddha, Shri Krishna and Shri Ram in India, Socrates in Greece, the wise men of China, and many other sages and saints among peoples and civilizations, trace of which we have lost. Thus man's soul has never been left without a specially inspired messenger from the soul that sustains, embraces and is the universe. Then what need was there for a Divine revelation to Mohammed? The answer of Islam is precise and clear. In spite of its great spiritual strength, Jewish monotheism has retained two characteristics which render it essentially different from Islamic monotheism: God has remained, in spite of all, a national and racial God for the children of Israel, and His personality is entirely separate from its supreme manifestation, the Universe. In far-distant countries such as India and China, the purity of the Faith in the one God had been so vitiated by polytheism, by idolatry and even by a pantheism which was hardly distinguishable from atheism that these popular and folklore religions bore little resemblance to that which emanated from the true and pure Godhead. Christianity lost its strength and meaning for Muslims in that it saw its great and glorious founder not as a man but as God incarnate in man, as God made Flesh. Thus there was an absolute need for the Divine Word's revelation, to Mohammed himself, a man like the others, of God's person and of his relations to the Universe which he had created. Once man has thus comprehended the essence of existence, there remains for him the duty, since he knows the absolute value of his own soul, of making for himself a direct path which will constantly lead his individual soul to and bind it with the universal Soul of which the Universe—as much of it as we perceive with our limited vision—is one of the infinite manifestations. Thus Islam's basic principle can only be defined as mono-realism and not as monotheism. Consider, for example, the opening declaration of every Islamic prayer: "Allah-o-Akbar." What does that mean? There can be no doubt that the second word of the declaration likens the character of Allah to a matrix which contains all and gives existence to the infinite, to space, to time, to the Universe, to all active and passive forces imaginable, to life and to the soul. Imam Hassan has explained the Islamic doctrine of God and the Universe by analogy with the sun and its reflection in the pool of a fountain; there is certainly a reflection or image of the sun, but with what poverty and with what little reality; how small and pale is the likeness between this impalpable image and the immense, blazing, white-hot glory of the celestial sphere itself. Allah is the sun; and the Universe, as we know it in all its magnitude, and time, with its power, are nothing more than the reflection of the Absolute in the mirror of the fountain.

There is a fundamental difference between the Jewish idea of creation and that of Islam. The creation according to Islam is not a unique act in a given time but a perpetual and constant event; and God supports and sustains all existence at every moment by His will and His thought. Outside His will, outside His thought, all is nothing, even the things which seem to us absolutely self-evident such as space and time. Allah alone wishes: the Universe exists; and all manifestations are as a witness of the Divine will. I think that I have sufficiently explained the difference between the Islamic doctrine of the unity of God and, on one side, the theistic ideas, founded upon the Old Testament, and on the other, the pantheistic and dualistic ideas of the Indian religion and that of Zoroaster. But having known the real, the Absolute, having understood the Universe as an infinite succession of events, intended by God, we need an ethic, a code of conduct in order to be able to elevate ourselves toward the ideal demanded by God.

Let us then study the duties of man, as the great majority interpret them, according to the verses of the Koran and the Traditions of the Prophet. First of all, the relations of man to God: there are no priests and no monks. There is no confession of sins, except directly to God.

A man who does not marry, who refuses to shoulder the responsibilities of fatherhood, of building up a home and raising a family through marriage, is severely condemned. In Islam there are no extreme renunciations, no asceticism, no maceration, above all no flagellations to subjugate the body. The healthy human body is the temple in which the flame of the Holy Spirit burns, and thus it deserves the respect of scrupulous cleanliness and personal hygiene. Prayer is a daily necessity, a direct communication of the spark with the universal flame. Reasonable fasting for a month in every year, provided a man's health is not impaired thereby, is an essential part of the body's discipline through which the body learns to renounce all impure desires. Adultery, alcoholism, slander and thinking evil of one's neighbor are specifically and severely condemned. All men, rich and poor, must aid one another materially and personally. The rules vary in detail, but they all maintain the principle of universal mutual aid in the Muslim fraternity. This fraternity is absolute, and it comprises men of all colors and all races: black, white, yellow, tawny; all are the sons of Adam in the flesh and all carry in them a spark of the Divine Light. Everyone should strive his best to see that this spark be not extinguished but rather developed to that full

"Companionship-on-High" which was the vision expressed in the last words of the Prophet on his deathbed, the vision of that blessed state which he saw clearly awaiting him. In Islam the Faithful believe in Divine justice and are convinced that the solution of the great problem of predestination and free will is to be found in the compromise that God knows what man is going to do, but that man is free to do it or not.

Wars are condemned. Peace ought to be universal. Islam means peace, God's peace with man and the peace of men one to another. Usury is condemned, but free and honest trade and agriculture—in all its forms—are encouraged, since they manifest a Divine service, and the welfare of mankind depends upon the continuation and the intensification of these legitimate labors. Politically a republican form of government seems to be the most rightful; for in Islamic countries, which have witnessed the development of absolute monarchies with a great concentration of power within them, the election of the monarch has always remained a lifeless formula which has simply legitimized the usurpation of power.

After death Divine justice will take into consideration the faith, the prayers and the deeds of man. For the chosen there is eternal life and the spiritual felicity of the Divine vision. For the condemned there is hell, where they will be consumed with regret for not having known how to merit the grace and the blessing of Divine mercy.

Islamic doctrine goes further than the other great religions, for it proclaims the presence of the soul, perhaps minute but nevertheless existing in an embryonic state, in all existence—in matter, in animals, trees, and space itself. Every individual, every molecule, every atom has its own spiritual relationship with the All-Powerful Soul of God. But men and women, being more highly developed, are immensely more advanced than the infinite number of other beings known to us. Islam acknowledges the existence of angels, of great souls who have developed themselves to the highest possible planes of the human soul and higher, and who are centers of the forces which are scattered throughout the Universe. Without going as far as Christianity Islam recognizes the existence of evil spirits which seek by means of their secret suggestions to us to turn us from good, from that straight way traced by God's finger for the eternal happiness of the humblest as of the greatest—Abraham, Jesus, Mohammed.

Thus far I have described those tenets of Islam which are professed and held in common by all Muslims of any and every sect or subsect. I now come to the divergence of the streams of thought. The Sunnis are the people of the *Sonna* or tradition. Their *Kalama* or profession of faith is "There is no God but God and Mohammed is the Apostle of God." To this the Shias add: "And Ali, the companion of Mohammed, is the Vicar of God." Etymologically the word "Shia" means either a stream or a section.

The Prophet died without appointing a Khalif or successor. The Shia school of thought maintains that although direct Divine inspiration ceased at the Prophet's death, the need of Divine guidance continued and this could not be left merely to millions of mortal men, subject to the whims and gusts of passion and material necessity, capable of being momentarily but tragically misled by greed, by oratory, or by the sudden desire for material advantage. These dangers were manifest in the period immediately following our Holy Prophet's death. Mohammed had been, as I have shown, both a temporal and a spiritual sovereign. The Khalif or successor of the Prophet was to succeed him in both these capacities; he was to be both *Emir-al-Momenin* or "commander of the true believers" and *Imam-al-Muslimin* or "spiritual chief of the devout." Perhaps an analogy from the Latin, Western world will make this clearer: he would be Supreme Pontiff as well as Imperator or temporal ruler.

Ali, the Prophet's cousin and son-in-law, the husband of his beloved and only surviving child, Fatima, his first convert, his bold champion in many a war, who the Prophet in his lifetime said would be to him as Aaron was to Moses, his brother and right-hand man, in the veins of whose descendants the Prophet's own blood would flow, appeared destined to be that true successor; and such had been the general expectation of Islam. The Shias have therefore always held that after the Prophet's death, Divine power, guidance and leadership manifested themselves in Hazrat Ali as the first Imam or spiritual chief of the devout. The Sunnis, however, consider him the fourth in the succession of Khalifs to temporal power.

The Imam is thus the successor of the Prophet in his religious capacity; he is the man who must be obeyed and who dwells among those from whom he commands spiritual obedience. The Sunnis have always held that this authority is merely temporal and secular, and is exerted only in the political sphere; they believe therefore that it appertains to any lawfully constituted political head of a state, to a governor or to the president of a republic. The Shias say that this authority is all-pervading and is concerned with spiritual matters also, that it is transferred by inherited right to the Prophet's successors of his blood.

How this came about is best described in the words of Mr. Justice Arnold in his judgment delivered in the High Court of Bombay on November 12, 1866, in the great lawsuit brought against my grandfather, to which I later refer.

"The influence of Ayesha, the young and favorite wife of Mohammed, a rancorous enemy of Fatima and of Ali, procured the election of her own father Abu Bakr; to Abu Bakr succeeded Omar, and to him Osman, upon whose death, in the year 655 of the Christian era, Ali was at last raised to the Khalifat. He was not even then unopposed; aided by Ayesha, Moawiyah of the family of the Ummayads, contested the Khalifat with him, and while the strife was still doubtful, in the year A.D. 660, Ali was slain by a Kharegite, or Muslim fanatic, in the mosque of Cufa, at that time the principal Muslim city on the right or west bank of the Euphrates—itself long since a ruin, at no great distance from the ruins of Babylon."

Mr. Justice Arnold's judgment gives a lucid and moving account of the effect on Muslim life and thought of this assassination and of the subsequent murders—nine years and twenty years after their father—of Ali's two sons, Hassan and Hussein, the Prophet's beloved grandchildren whom he himself had publicly hailed as "the foremost among the youths of Paradise"; of the tragic and embittered hostility and misunderstanding that developed between the two main Muslim sects, and all the sorrow and the strife that afflicted succeeding generations.

Of the Shias there are many subdivisions; some of them believe that this spiritual headship, this Imamat which was Hazrat Ali's, descended through him in the sixth generation to Ismail from whom I myself claim my descent and my Imamat. Others believe that the Imamat is to be traced from Zeid, the grandson of Imam Hussein, the Prophet's grandson martyred at Kerbela. Still others, including the vast majority of the people of Persia, and Indian Shias, believe that the Imamat is now held by a living Imam, the twelfth from Ali, who has never died, who is alive and has lived thirteen hundred years among us, unseen but seeing; those who profess this doctrine are known as the Asna Asharis. The Ismailis themselves are divided into two parties, a division which stems from the period when my ancestors held the Fatimite Khalifat of Egypt. One party accepts my ancestor, Nozar, as the rightful successor of the Khalif of Egypt Mustansir; whereas the other claims as Imam his other son the Khalif Mustalli.

Thenceforward the story of the Ismailis, of my ancestors and their followers, moves through all the complexities, the ebb and flow, of Islamic history through many centuries. Gibbon, it has been said, abandoned as hopeless the task of clearing up the obscurities of an Asiatic pedigree; there is, however, endless fascination in the study of the web of characters and of events, woven across the ages, which unites us in this present time with all these far-distant glories, tragedies and mysteries. Often persecuted and oppressed, the faith of my ancestors was never destroyed; at times it flourished as in the epoch of the Fatimite Khalifs, at times it was obscure and little understood.

After the loss of the Fatimite Khalifat in Egypt my ancestors moved first to the highlands of Syria and the Lebanon; thence they journeyed eastward to the mountains of Iran. They established a stronghold on the craggy peak of Alamut in the Elburz Mountains, the range which separates from the rest of Persia the provinces lying immediately to the south of the Caspian. Legend and history intertwine here in the strange tale of the Old Man of the Mountains, and of those hereditary Grand Masters of the Order of the Assassins who held Alamut for nearly two hundred years. In this period the Ismaili faith was well known in Syria, in Iraq, in Arabia itself, and far up into Central Asia. Cities such as Samarkand and Bokhara were then great centers of Muslim learning and thought. A little later in the thirteenth century of the Christian era, Ismaili religious propaganda penetrated into what is Sinkiang and Chinese Turkestan. There was a time in the thirteenth and fourteenth centuries when the Ismaili doctrine was the chief and most influential Shi'ite school of thought; but later with the triumph of the Saffevi Dynasty in Iran (particularly in its northwest province, Azerbaijan) the Asna Ashari, or Twelfth Imam, sect established its predominance. Remnants of the Ismaili faith remained firm and are still to be found in many parts of Asia, North Africa and Iran. The historical centers of Ismailism indeed are scattered widely over all the Islamic world. In the mountainous regions of Syria, for example, are to be found the Druzes, in their fastness in the Jebel Druze. They are really Ismailis who did not originally follow my family in their migration out of Egypt but remained with the memory of my ancestor, Al Hakem, the Fatimite Khalif of Egypt, but they established their doctrines on lines very similar to those of the Syrian Ismailis, who, in present times, are my followers. Similar Ismaili "islands" exist in southern Egypt, in the Yemen and of course in Iraq. In Iran the centers are around Mahalat, westward toward Hamadan and to the south of Tehran; others are in Khorassan to the north and east around about Yezd, around Kerman and southward along the coast of the Persian Gulf from Bandar Abbas to the borders of Pakistan and Sind, and into Baluchistan. Others are in Afghanistan, in Kabul itself; there are many in Russia and Central Asia, around Yarkand, Kashgar and in many villages and settlements in Sinkiang. In India certain Hindu tribes were converted by missionaries sent to them by my ancestor, Shah Islam Shah, and took the name of Khojas; a similar process of conversion occurred in Burma as recently as the nineteenth century.

Now that I have brought this brief record of Ismaili origin, vicissitudes and wanderings within sight of the contemporary world, it may be timely to give an account in some detail of the life and deeds of my grandfather, the first to be known as the Aga Khan, who emerged into the light of history early in the nineteenth century of the Christian era. His life was (as Mr. Justice Arnold observed) "adventurous and romantic." He was the hereditary chieftain of the important city of Kerman and the son-in-law of the powerful and able Persian monarch, Fateh Ali Shah, holding considerable territorial possessions in addition to his inherited Imamat of the Ismailis.

In 1838 he was involved in conflict with the then ruling Emperor Mohammed Shah, for reasons of which Mr. Justice Arnold gave the following account: "Hadji Mirza Ahasi, who had been the tutor of Mohammed Shah, was during the whole reign of his royal pupil (from 1834 to 1848) the Prime Minister of Persia. A Persian of very low origin formerly in the service of the Aga Khan, had become the chief favorite and minion of the all-powerful minister. This person, though his patron, had the impudence to demand in marriage for his son one of the daughters of the Aga Khan, a granddaughter of the late Shah-in-Shah! This, says the Persian historian, was felt by the Aga Khan to be a great insult; and the request, though strongly pressed by the Prime Minister, was indignantly refused. Having thus made the most powerful man in Persia his deadly enemy, the Aga Khan probably felt that his best chance of safety was to assert himself in arms—a course not uncommon with the great feudatories of disorganized Persia. Making Kerman his headquarters, he appears to have kept up the fight with varying fortunes through the years 1838-1839 and part of 1840. In the latter year, overpowered by numbers, he was forced to flight and with difficulty made his escape, attended by a few horsemen, through the deserts of Baluchistan to Sind."

In his wanderings of the next few years my grandfather encountered and rendered stout assistance to the British in their process of military and imperial expansion northward and westward from the Punjab. In Sind he raised and maintained a troop of light horse (the descendants of whose survivors were so grave an anxiety to me many years later) and during the latter stages of the first Afghan War, in 1841 and 1842, he and his cavalry were of service to General Nott in Kardahar and to General England when he advanced out of Sind to join Nott. For these services and for others which he rendered to Sir Charles Napier in his conquest of Sind in 1843-1844, my grandfather received a pension from the British Government.

In 1845 my grandfather reached Bombay where—as Mr. Justice Arnold expressed it—"he was received by the cordial homage of the whole Khoja population of this city and its neighborhood." For a year or two from 1846 he was in Calcutta as a political prisoner because Mohammed Shah had remonstrated to the British Government about his presence in a port of such ready access to Persia as Bombay. However, in 1848 Mohammed Shah's reign came to an end, and my grandfather settled peaceably in Bombay and there established his *durkhana* or headquarters. Not only was this a wise and happy personal decision, but it had an admirable effect on the religious and communal life of the whole Ismaili world. It was as if the heavy load of persecution and fanatical hostility, which they had had to bear for so long, was lifted. Deputations came to Bombay from places as remote as Kashgar, Bokhara, all parts of Iran, Syria, the Yemen, the African coast and the then narrowly settled hinterland behind it.

Since then there has been no fundamental or violent change in the Ismaili way of life or in the conditions in which my followers can pursue their own religion. At present no deputations come from Russia, but Ismailis in Russia and in Central Asia are not persecuted and are quite free in their religious life; they cannot of course send the tribute, which is merely a token tribute and never has been the sort of mulcting which a few fanatical enemies of the Ismailis have alleged it to be.

With Sinkiang, Kashgar and Yarkand we have no communication at present, since the frontier is closed—no more firmly against Ismailis than against anyone else—but we know that they are free to follow their religion and that they are firm and devoted Ismailis with a great deal of self-confidence and the feeling that they constitute by far the most important Ismaili community in the whole world. From Iran representatives and commissions come and go; from Syria they used to come to India regularly, but now from time to time members of my family go to Syria, or my Syrian followers come and visit me in Egypt. Not long ago I went to Damascus where a great number of my followers came to pay their respects. In nearly all those countries the greater part of the tribute to the Imam is spent on schools, or prayer houses, and on the administration of various religious and social institutions. A considerable measure of local responsibility prevails; questions of marriage and divorce, for example, are entirely the concern of the local representative of the Imam. At times prosperous communities among the Ismailis help less prosperous ones in respect to similar institutions. I issue general instructions and orders; but the actual day-to-day administrative work of each local community is done by the Imam's representative and local chief. Many of these local headships throughout Central Asia, for example, are hereditary. But we have no general, regular system. Sometimes a son succeeds, sometimes a grandson. Sometimes he is known as Vizir, or Kamdar (a title which by constant use has degenerated into Kamria). Sometimes he is Rais or Rai. In Syria the Imam's representatives are known as Amirs; in some parts of Central Asia such as Hunza, the word "Amir" has been colloquialized and shortened to Mir.

The headship of a religious community spread over a considerable part of the world surface—from Cape Town to Kashgar, from Syria to Singapore—cannot be sustained in accordance with any cut-and-dried system. Moral conditions, material facilities, national aspirations and outlook and profoundly differing historical backgrounds have to be borne in mind, and the necessary mental adjustments made.

There is therefore great variety and great flexibility of administration. In the British, Portuguese and French colonies of East Africa, in Uganda, Portuguese East Africa, Madagascar, Natal and Cape Colony there is a highly developed and civilized administrative system of councils. Educational administrators, property agents, executive and judicial councils all perform an immense amount of day-to-day administrative work, and under my general orders vast financial administration as well.

In India and Pakistan there is a similar technique of administration but in a less developed and looser form. In Burma and Malaya the organization closely resembles that of the Ismailis in Africa. Syria, Iran and the Northwest Frontier Province of Pakistan are all countries with their strongly marked individuality, historical background and traditions. These historical variations over centuries, the accessibility, or lack of it, for many of the more isolated communities, and the development of communications between my family and my followers have all had their effect.

In Central Asia the leadership of the Ismailis is by inheritance in the hands of certain families and has been handed down in continuous line through centuries. This is true of my followers in Afghanistan, and in Russia and Chinese Turkestan, where certain families have been since their conversion to Islam administrators and representatives of the Imam. The local leadership passes down in a close connection of kinship from one generation to another. Sometimes it is the hereditary chieftain and occasionally—as in the case of Hunza—the secular king, himself an Ismaili, who is the administrator of the religious brotherhood.

The correspondence which I maintain with all these far-scattered communities is affected by local circumstances. In Baghdad I have special representatives who deal with Arabian matters; in Iran I have special representatives in every province who deal with Ismaili affairs, who are also generally members of families that have as a matter of inheritance supplied local Ismaili leaders for probably as long as these people have been linked with my family. In Syria, one such family of representatives has retained an unbroken connection with my family for more than a thousand years.

Ismailism has survived because it has always been fluid. Rigidity is contrary to our whole way of life and outlook. There have really been no cut-and-dried rules; even the set of regulations known as the Holy Laws are directions as to method and procedure and not detailed orders about results to be obtained. In some countries— India and Africa for example—the Ismailis have a council system, under which their local councilors are charged with all internal administrative responsibility, and report to me what they have done. In Syria, Central Asia and Iran, leadership, as I have said, is vested in hereditary recommended leaders and chiefs, who are the Imam's representatives and who looks after the administration of the various Jamats, or congregations.

From all parts of the Ismaili world with which regular contact is politically possible a constant flow of communications and reports comes to me. Attending to these, answering them, giving my solutions of specific problems presented to me, discharging my duties as hereditary Imam of this far-scattered religious community and association—such is my working life, and so it has been since I was a boy.

Much of the work of the Ismaili councils and of the Imam's representatives nowadays is purely social, and is concerned with the proper contractual arrangement of matters such as marriage and divorce. On this subject I should perhaps say that nowhere in the world where Ismailis are now settled is there any persecution of them or interference with their faith and customs except if and when the general laws of the country are contrary to institutions, such as plurality of wives. It is generally overlooked that among Ismailis no one can take a second wife or divorce his first wife for a whim or—as is sometimes falsely imagined in the West—some frivolous or erratic pretext. There are usually, to our way of thinking, some very good reasons for either action. To beget children is a very proper need and desire in every marriage; if after many years of married life there is still no issue, often a wife herself longs to see her home brightened by the presence of children with all the laughter, hope, joy and deep contentment that they bring with them. In other instances there is so profound a difference of character that a divorce is found to be the best solution for the happiness of both parties. But in every case—whether a second wife is taken or a divorce is granted—the various councils or (where there are no councils) the representatives of the Imam have an absolute duty to safeguard the interests of the wife; if a second wife is taken, it is a matter of seeing that full financial protection is assured to the first wife, or if there is a divorce, of seeing that there is a generous, adequate and seemly monetary settlement. It is important that it should be realized among non-Muslims that the Islamic view of the institution of marriage—and of all that relates to it, divorce, plurality of wives and so on—is a question solely of contract, of consent and of definite and mutually accepted responsibilities. The sacramental concept of marriage is not Islam's; therefore except indirectly there is no question of its religious significance, and there is no religious ceremony to invest it with the solemnity and the symbolism which appertain to marriage in other religions, like Christianity and Hinduism. It is exactly analogous to—in the West—an entirely civil and secular marriage in a registry office or before a judge. Prayers of course can be offered—prayers for happiness, prosperity and good health—but there can be no religious ritual beyond these, and they indeed are solely a matter of personal choice. There is therefore no kind of marriage in Islam, or among the Ismailis, except the marriage of mutual consent and mutual understanding. And as I have indicated, much of the work of the Ismaili councils and of the Imam's representatives in all our Ismaili communities is to see that marriages are properly registered and to ensure that divorce, though not a sin, is so executed that the interests of neither party suffer from it, that as much protection as possible is given to women, and most of all that the maintenance of young children is safeguarded.

The past seventy years have witnessed steady, stable progress on the part of the Ismailis wherever they have settled. Under the Ottoman Empire, in the reign of Abdul Hamid, there was a considerable degree of persecution. A minority, like several other minorities in his empire, they suffered hardship, and many of their leaders endured imprisonment in the latter years of his despotic rule. With the Young Turk revolution, however, the period of persecution ended. And now, in spite of all the vast political shifts and changes which the world has undergone, I think it may reasonably be claimed that the lot of the Ismailis in general throughout the world is a fairly satisfactory one; wherever they are settled their communities compose a happy, self-respecting, law-abiding and industrious element in society.

What has been my own policy with my followers? Our religion is our religion, you either believe in it or you do not. You can leave a faith but you cannot, if you do not accept its tenets, remain within it and claim to "reform" it. You can abandon those tenets, but you cannot try to change them and still protest that you belong to the particular sect that holds them. Many people have left the Ismaili faith, just as others have joined it throughout the ages. About a score of people out of many millions—a small group in Karachi and in India—pretended to be Ismailis but called themselves "reformers." The true Ismailis immediately excommunicated them. There has never been any question of changing the Ismaili faith; that faith has remained the same and must remain the same. Those who have not believed in it have rightly left it; we bear them no ill-will and respect them for their sincerity.

What about political guidance? It has been the practice of my ancestors, to which I have strictly adhered, always to advise Ismailis to be absolutely loyal and devoted subjects of the State—whatever its constitution, monarchical or republican—of which they are citizens. Neither my ancestors nor I have ever tried to influence our followers one way or another, but we have told them that the constituted legal authority of any country in which they abide must have their full and absolute loyalty. Similarly if any government approaches me and asks me for my help and my advice to its subjects, this advice is invariably—as was my father's and my grandfather's—that they must be loyal and law-abiding, and if they have any political grievances they must approach their government as legally constituted, and in loyalty and fidelity to it. All my teaching and my guidance for my followers has been in fulfillment of this principle: render unto God the things which are God's and to Caesar those which are Caesar's.

In matters of social reform I have tried to exert my influence and authority sensibly and progressively. I have always sought to encourage the emancipation and education of women. In my grandfather's and my father's time the Ismailis were far ahead of any other Muslim sect in the matter of the abolition of the strict veil, even in extremely conservative countries. I have absolutely abolished it; nowadays you will never find an Ismaili woman wearing the veil. Everywhere I have always encouraged girls' schools, even in regions where otherwise they were completely unknown. I lay with pride that my Ismaili followers are, in this matter of social welfare, far in advance of any other Muslim sect. No doubt it is possible to find individuals equally advanced, but I am convinced that our social conditions as a body—education for both boys and girls, marriage and domestic outlook and customs, the control over divorce, the provision for children in the event of divorce, and so forth—are far ahead. We were pioneers in the introduction of midwifery, and long before any other Muslim community in the Middle East, we had trained nurses for childbirth. With the support and help of Lady Dufferin's nursing association in India, I was able—at a time when normal conditions in these matters were terribly unsanitary—to introduce a modern outlook on childbirth, with trained midwives, not only in India and Burma but in Africa and (so far as general conditions permitted) in Syria and Iraq.

In Africa, where I have been able to give active help as well as advice, we have put the finances of individuals and of the various communities on a thoroughly safe basis. We established an insurance company—the Jubilee Insurance—whose shares have greatly increased in value. We also set up what we called an investment trust, which is really a vast association for receiving money and then putting it out on loan, at a low rate of interest, to Ismaili traders and to people who want to buy or build their own houses.

About my own personal wealth a great deal of nonsense has been written. There must be hundreds of people in the United States with a larger capital wealth than mine; and the same is true of Europe. Perhaps not many people, in view of the incidence of taxation, even in the United States, have the control over an income that I exercise; but this control carries with it—as an unwritten law—the upkeep of all the various communal, social and religious institutions of my Ismaili following, and in the end only a small fraction of it—if any—is left for members of my family and myself.

When I read about the "millions of pounds a year" I am supposed possess, I know only that if I had an income of that size I should be ashamed of myself. There is a great deal of truth in Andrew Carnegie's remark: "The man who dies rich, dies disgraced." I should add: The man who lives rich, lives disgraced. By "lives rich" I mean the man who lives and spends for his own pleasure at a rate and on a scale of living in excess of that customary among those called nowadays "the upper income group" in the country of which he is a citizen. I am not a communist, nor do I believe that a high standard of private life is a sin and an affront to society. I feel no flicker of shame at owning three or four cars; in India, where a great many people from outside come and go, I always have more cars for their use.

Nor am I ashamed of being the owner of a big racing stable, about which I propose to say something in a later chapter. My family, as I have indicated, have had a long, honorable and affectionate association with horsemanship in all its forms. Had I to contemplate either giving up a considerable number of horses in training or turning the stable into a paying concern, I have no doubt that by selling a considerable proportion of my stock I could turn it into a paying business any day of the week. Neither my grandfather, my father nor I have ever looked on our racing as simply a money-making matter, but as a sport which, by careful attention and thoughtful administration, could become self-supporting and a permanent source of pleasure not only for ourselves, as owners, but for thousands—indeed for millions—who follow our colors on the turf; and we have considered our studs and our training stables as sources of wealth for the countries in which they are maintained and of practical usefulness from the point of view of preserving and raising the standard of bloodstock.

A specific charge of extravagance against our family related to the period in which some two thousand people a day were living and feeding at our expense. These two thousand were, after all, descendants and dependents of people who had exiled themselves from Iran with my grandfather and had given up their homes and estates, and in the conditions of the time we, as heads of the Ismaili community, were responsible for their welfare and maintenance. As soon as I could, and as thoroughly as I could, I dealt with that problem, so that now their descendants are far happier and far more self-reliant than they were, and I have nothing on my conscience about the way in which I dealt with it.

I would have been a profoundly unhappy man if I had possessed one tenth of the fabulous amount of wealth which people say that I have at my disposal, for then indeed I should have felt all my life that I was carrying a dead weight—useless alike to my family and my friends or, for that matter, to my followers. Beyond a certain point wealth and the material advantages which it brings do more harm than good, to societies as to individuals.

So far as their way of life is concerned, I have tried to vary the advice which I have given to my followers in accordance with the country or state in which they live. Thus in the British colony of East Africa I strongly urge them to make English their first language, to found their family and domestic lives along English lines and in general to adopt British and European customs—except in the matter of alcohol and slavery to tobacco. I am convinced that living as they must in a multiracial society, the kind of social life and its organization which gives them the greatest opportunities to develop their personalities and is the most practically useful is the one which they ought to follow. On the other hand, to those who live in Burma I have given the same sort of advice—but that they should follow a Burman way of life rather than any other. In Muslim countries like Syria, Egypt, Iraq and Iran of course there are no difficulties at all. My own family's home and social life has always followed an Iranian-Muslim pattern; this has involved no violent or radical readjustment wherever I have lived, so that the European ladies whom I have married, one after the other, have in fact easily and happily acquired an Iranian-Muslim outlook and rhythm of life.

In Africa, however, my followers faced a much more acute problem. They arrived there with Asiatic habits and an Asiatic pattern of existence, but they encountered a society in process of development which is, if anything, European-African. To have retained an Asiatic outlook in matters of language, habits and clothing would have been for them a complication and socially a dead weight of archaism in the Africa of the future. In Pakistan and modern Bharat the Ismailis are likely in the future to assume two totally different patterns of culture. In West Pakistan they will probably speak Urdu or what used to be called Hindustani, and their social habits and customs will be molded accordingly. In East Pakistan Bengali dress and language will play a major part in Ismaili life. In Bharat the languages which they will speak will probably be Gujerati and Marathi, and their outlook and way of life similarly will take on a Gujerati-Marathi shape. Yet I am certain that so long as they retain their faith the brotherhood of Islam will unite all these people of varying social outlook and patterns of behavior and will keep them together in spirit.

III

Boyhood in India

M Y FIRST CONSCIOUS MEMORY is of something that happened
when I was a child of three and a half. I have a clear recollection of an old man, almost blind, seated on a gray Arab horse,
peering to watch a line of horses galloping in training. The time
was February or March, 1881; the old man was my grandfather, the
Aga Khan, whose name, title, privileges and responsibilities I was to
inherit. I too was on a pony, standing near my grandfather, and I
was held up in the saddle by a man on either side of me. The scene
was Bombay, where my grandfather, after the years of wandering
and various vicissitudes described earlier, had settled with most of
his family and a considerable retinue.

I was born in Karachi on November 2, 1877, but I spent the
whole of my boyhood and youth in Bombay and Poona. That was
a Bombay in countless respects inconceivably different from the
huge, glittering, commercial and industrial city that is present-day
Bombay. It is true that it was a large and prosperous port, the
capital of the Bombay Presidency, one of the leading provinces of
British India, the seat of a Governor and his Administration, and
of an impressive judicature, and the headquarters of a not incon-
siderable army. The outstanding difference between that Bombay
and Bombay today lies, of course, in the two words "British India."
If the capital and focus of the British Raj in India lay, in those
days, many hundreds of miles to the northeast in Calcutta (and in
the summers in the hill town of Simla), there was in Bombay a
long and close tradition of association with Britain. Had not indeed
Bombay first been joined to the possessions of the British Crown as
part of the dowry of Catherine of Braganza, the wife of Charles II?

The Bombay of the mid-nineteenth century in which my grandfather settled was a much smaller, more compact city than its present-day descendant. The home—or homes—of my family covered a great deal of some of the more densely populous and prosperous parts; even in my childhood in the eighties it was a huge rambling place, taking in most of two divisions of the present city, Mazagaon and Byculla, stretching from Nesbit Road to Hassanarbad, my grandfather's tomb. This would be comparable to a large part of the West End of London or downtown Manhattan being a single enclosed estate; or to put it in terms of Paris, an enclosure in length from, say, the Madeleine to well beyond the Opéra, and in breadth from the Madeleine to the Pont d'Iena. Within this great area there were several big palaces and innumerable smaller houses and outbuildings; there were gardens and fountains and also a small zoo. There were many stables, since the equine population of the estate—evidence of my grandfather's inherited and persistent interest in and love for horse racing and horse breeding—never numbered less than a hundred.

The human population, of course, was far more numerous, and with endless ramifications, divisions and subdivisions. It was the household of a political pretender (in the proper sense of that word) of accepted standing. My grandfather in his migration from Persia had brought with him more than a thousand relatives, dependents, clients, associates, personal and political supporters, ranging from the humblest groom or servant to a man of princely stature, a direct near-descendant of Nadirshah of Delhi fame, who had taken my grandfather's side in the disputes and troubles in Persia and with him had gone into exile.

With the passage of years, however, it had become no longer exile. My grandfather had been confirmed in his rights and titles by a judgment of the Bombay High Court in 1886.* He was an accepted and honored leader of the community, accorded princely status by the British Raj and its representatives in India. Aga Hall, our Bom-

---

* The judgment delivered on November 12, 1866 by Mr. Justice Arnold, contains a classic, fully detailed account of the origins of Ismailism and of the beginnings of my family.

bay home, was his chief seat, but he had another palace, or group of palaces, in Poona, whither we all made seasonal migrations. His life and his world, the life and world into which I was born, were feudal in a fashion far removed from, and indeed not understood by, people of the present day. He was the head and center of a loose but clearly comprehended system of allegiance and adherence; wherever he went, his home, even if only temporary, was a focus of loyalty and homage—in the Ismaili word, a *durkhana*, a place of pilgrimage to be visited from time to time by as many of his associates and supporters as possible. This necessitated the maintenance of an impressive establishment—a need reinforced by the circumstances of my grandfather's departure from Persia and by the number of dependents whom he brought with him.

His family and his dependents, his sons and their wives, his officials, servants and followers, were disposed in a series of houses and palaces around him, both in Bombay and in Poona. In course of time many of his Persian followers married Indian wives, many of them of Ismaili families. They and their children remained under my grandfather's protection and, after his death, under my father's and then under mine. When my grandfather died, there was a rough-and-ready and unofficial division of property, though not of leadership and responsibility, between my father—his sole rightful heir as Imam—and my various uncles and aunts. I was my father's sole and unique heir in accordance with Muslim law—unlike my father in relation to his grandfather.

From my earliest childhood I was trained to be conscious of my inheritance, and of the magnitude of its responsibilities. My early years were in many ways difficult, even harsh. I was the only surviving heir, for my two full brothers both died in infancy and my two half-brothers in their young manhood. I was known to be delicate— a succession of English doctors had prophesied, with somber unanimity, that I would not live to be twenty-five. I was therefore watched over by my mother with extreme vigilance and trepidation. I was petted and spoiled by nurses and foster-mothers and by a group of my mother's ladies in waiting, many of whom were already elderly, in whose eyes I was the "*petit prince chéri.*"

My childhood was saddened—and complicated—by my father's sudden death from pneumonia, only a little over four years after my grandfather's. My father had inherited to the full my grandfather's sporting interests, not only in horse breeding and racing but as a shot and hunter of big game. In this latter pastime he was extremely skilled and utterly fearless, for his bag over years consisted not only of thousands of deer of every kind and every sort of game bird but of a great many tigers. In tiger shooting his courage was as great as his skill. When the Prince of Wales (later King Edward VII) paid his state visit to India, he was entertained at Aga Hall by my grandfather, and commented with interest on the number of tiger skins displayed. How, he asked, did my father get them?

Perhaps I should explain that ordinarily a tiger-shoot in India is conducted either (in the north) from the back of a specially trained elephant or (elsewhere) from a platform constructed in a tree overlooking a tiger's known or suspected haunt or lay.

"Do you go up trees?" asked the Prince of Wales, who—being stout—had doubtless recent and rueful memories of being pushed and pulled up trees in this most exciting and aristocratic of all varieties of big-game shooting.

"No," said my father, whose girth, though considerable, was not as great as his guest's, "I am too fat for tree work. I can't climb up. I stand and shoot."

My father's death was occasioned not by any mishap when he was out after tiger, but by a long day's water-fowling near Poona in August, 1885. There were several hours' heavy rain, the going under foot was heavy and wet and my father was soaked to the skin. He caught a severe chill which turned swiftly and fatally to pneumonia. He was dead eight days later.

This was, I can see now, the first big emotional and spiritual crisis of my life. It ended the only carefree period I had ever known. There was at once a forlorn and kindly attempt to prevent me from missing my father or being allowed to feel unhappy. But the prevalent sense of deep mourning and sadness enveloped the eight-year-old boy that I was. As his heir I was in a sense the immediate focus of a great new and pressing sense of responsibility. Our family, our *émigré* dependents, our Ismaili supporters all over the Islamic world deeply mourned my father's death, but they also turned to me, child as I was, now and for the rest of my life henceforth entrusted with the sacred charge to which I had been born. The change in my circumstances came home to me early and insistently. My father's body was embalmed and brought from Poona to Bombay and thence sent to be buried at Nejaf on the west bank of the Euphrates, near Cufa and the tomb of our ancestor the Imam Ali—one of the holiest places on earth for the Shias. No sooner were these rites accomplished than a new regime was immediately instituted for me.

It was, of course, a direct consequence of my new station, but to this day I cannot understand why I did not die or turn into an utter dunce under the treatment which I was given. My education for the responsibilities and tasks which I had inherited was serious and strenuous, and it had to be fitted into a regular system of seasonal family migration. From November to April during the cold weather of each year we were in Bombay; in April and May we were at Mahabaleshwar; from June to October we were in Poona and in October we went for a short spell to one of the smaller hill stations, thence back to Bombay. For ten years—from 1885 to 1895—this system continued unchanged; there was no room for a holiday for me, a month, a fortnight, even a week off the chain—at the most a rare day. And relentlessly was I held on the chain.

This was the typical and unchanging pattern of my days: I was called between six and half past and had my breakfast—a weak tea, bread, butter, jam and a Persian sweet. At seven, whether I wanted to or not, I had an hour's riding—a canter or sometimes a gallop on one of the Poona rides or on the racecourse or, at Bombay, along the sands. From eight to half-past eleven I had lessons with my English and French teachers. Then I had luncheon, and I was free until two o'clock. Thereafter I had three hours' instruction in Arabic. A drive or some tennis in the garden or some sort of relaxation was then permitted until dinner at seven o'clock. After dinner came the horror of horrors. I was set down to two hours of calligraphy of the dreariest and most soul-destroying kind. My mother had been impressed by the advice—the foolish advice as it turned out—of Arabic and Persian scholars and pedants, who had assured her that calligraphy in the classical Persian and Arabic scripts was of the highest importance, and they pointed out to her that my two half-brothers who had died had both had beautiful handwriting. My mother, my uncles and everyone else in our household united in compelling me to this horrible calligraphy. It was in fact a very real martyrdom for me because no one had realized that I was from birth so shortsighted that to read or write I had to hold a book or paper an inch or two from my nose, and in my vision of the world further than those few inches from my nose there was no definition and no delight, for everything I saw—gardens, hills, sea or jungle—was a haze. The simplicity and the sadness of my affliction were for years unnoticed, and how in the end it came to be rectified I shall describe a little later.

The discipline to which I was subjected was rigid, and even the little free time that I was allowed was subject to invasion. For it was my duty, young as I was, to receive those of my followers who came to our home to offer their loyal respect. Saturdays and feast days were the usual occasions of the receptions, and my guests would sit in the garden, bowing and paying compliments, bringing gifts and receiving thanks, blessings and benedictions. My part in these ceremonies was august and ordained by tradition—but a child resented the fact that they came in the small amount of free time allowed by the curriculum and never, never in lesson time.

Such was the regime to which, at eight, I was subjected. Perhaps it might be appropriate to give a brief account of my way of life in later years. However, I must stress that although I have not changed my basic principles in outlook, there have obviously been certain marked modifications in my pattern of existence. The Aga Khan who dined with Queen Victoria in 1898 was not quite the same person as the Aga Khan who had tea with Queen Elizabeth in 1953. But throughout this long period I snatched hours out of my daily routine as even now I snatch them for reading poetry, fiction, newspapers and literary and critical periodicals. This has been a persistent trait in my character for sixty years. In the same way I have daily given a certain amount of time to physical exercise. Until I was about fifty, the time that I gave to physical exercise was devoted to boxing, Sandow's exercises, Indian clubs, long walks, and, in the early years of the century, long cycling tours through France, Italy, Germany, and other European countries. After I was fifty I had to substitute tennis and golf for these more violent forms of exercise. And since I became sixty I have had to confine myself to golf and walking.

My social life also has naturally varied—not only because I myself have grown older but because the economic conditions of the world before 1914 were totally different from those of today. In the spheres in which I lived forty years ago and more, social activity was intense. If not daily, certainly four or five days a week there were either dinner parties or luncheon parties wherever I happened to find myself, and there was the same round of theater and opera parties. Between the two wars this part of life very much decreased, and I might say that social engagements dropped in the ratio of twenty to one hundred. After the Second World War these social engagements have withered away—except when my wife and I ask a few friends wherever I may be to lunch or opera or theater parties. The great social epoch was between 1898 and the opening of the 1914 war. I knew most of the members of the royal families of Europe whom I met over and over again, with the aristocracy and plutocracy that were like satellites revolving about major planets whether in London or Paris, Rome, Berlin, Monte Carlo or Cannes, Nice or Saint-Moritz. That social life is a thing of the past for me. Really it came to an end with the outbreak of the 1914 war because the society I met between the two wars was fundamentally a different one. To give an idea of the social change I might say that between 1898 and 1914 I was a guest ninety-nine times out of one hundred and only one per cent a host—between the two wars it became about fifty-fifty and gradually it came down to be less and less; and since the last war I find that it is I who am the host nine times out of ten.

Now with the changes in my own life and the society in which I move thus briefly assessed against the background of nearly sixty years, how do I live now, when I am at home in my villa at Cannes, when we are in our house in Bombay, or when we are in hotels in London or Paris, in Venice, Geneva or Evian—some eight months in every year?

The day begins for me—as it has begun since my early youth—at 4 A.M. I wake up automatically about that time and spend the first hour—between four and five—at intense prayer. There are no statues in my bedroom but a special prayer carpet is always prepared and my *tasbee*, my rosary, is always with me. At five I go back again to sleep and wake up some time between eight and nine when I have immediately a breakfast of toast, tea, and honey—but no butter. By ten I have looked at the newspapers, had a wash, am dressed and then usually go out for a walk of anything between one and two miles, or I play nine holes of golf. If there is rain I do not go out. Until about one o'clock I am at work with my secretaries, dealing with my correspondence, writings and various business matters. I rarely leave anything undone from one day to another and usually have very little leftovers. At one or one thirty I lunch at Cannes in our own house, but everywhere else at some restaurant or other— rarely in the hotel restaurant. Lunch is my main meal of the day and consists of fish, eggs or meat, but only one of the three, and never a combination of the three—rice regularly, two vegetables and cooked fruit, ice cream or sometimes pudding.

When in Paris or London, sometimes in the afternoon I may go to a race meeting, or I may catch up with activities such as my correspondence, or my reading. About five or six a cup of tea and then until seven or eight I usually try to read again, poetry, works of fiction, magazines of literary criticism, and I read thoroughly the morning and evening newspapers. Dinner consists only of fresh fruit. I never take anything cooked or salty at night. If the fruit is not good, then a salad. When on rare occasions I am asked to dinner, I usually ask the host to give me salad and fruit or such raw vegetables as celery, tomatoes, etc.

Both my wife and I are devoted to the theater, the opera, and the ballet. In towns like London and Paris we go to one or the other four or five times a week and usually take a few friends with us. In

places like Cannes we occasionally go to the local theater during
the season—sometimes to the Nice opera or to Monte Carlo or similar places. I usually go to bed quickly after the theater. My lifelong
experience has taught me that sleep is like walking—you can derive
from four or five hours of sleep as much benefit as you can from
eight or nine hours, just as in twenty minutes' brisk walk you can
get as much benefit as from two hours of loitering about the
streets and looking in shop windows. In a word, you can either sleep
slow or sleep fast. I am a firm believer in brisk sleeping. I am happy
to say that while I sleep I sleep; when I go to bed I have no time
to lose—even if they wake me up for anything, I immediately fall
back; and practically all my life I have never had dreams. I think
that is owing to the fact that I have rationalized my sleep as I have
rationalized my exercise. Those who suffer from dreams may find a
measure of peace and may overcome physical and moral strain if
they can so arrange their habits as to concentrate on the business at
hand.

To return to earlier days and disciplines: I had three English tutors—a Mr. Gallagher, who was Irish, a Mr. Lawrence and another
Irishman, Mr. Kenny. All three were found for me by the Jesuits
in Bombay. It may seem strange that my family turned to the Jesuits for my education in Western matters, but both in Bombay
and in Poona there are big and important Jesuit schools, and both
quite near where we lived—St. Mary's in Bombay and St. Vincent's
in Poona. All the children of our considerable household—the ever-
multiplying descendants of my grandfather's hangers-on, pensioners,
relatives and old soldiers—went to these Jesuit schools. The whole
household knew the Jesuit fathers well, and nothing was easier than
to get their advice and help.

Incidentally, there was never a hint of their attempting to convert any of our Muslim children to their own creed. They respected
Islam, and never by open argument, by suggestion or insinuation
did they seek to weaken a Muslim's faith. This is one of the clearest
recollections of my childhood, and I have seen the same phenomenon repeated in contemporary Egypt and Pakistan. One day a few

years ago I discussed it with an eminent Jesuit, a Spaniard, and cross-examined him about it.

"What the devil do you want to come and waste your time for?" I said. "You're a missionary, and you've got all these opportunities to do your missionary work, but you never try to convert a single boy! What are you here for? What do you get out of all these huge sums you're spending on teachers and building? What's it all about?"

The Jesuit, who was an old friend of mine, smiled his sidelong smile and said: "Don't you see what we're getting out of it?"

"No."

"You are paying us. To every Muslim and non-Christian boy we give the best education we can. But we make them pay through the nose for it. For those who pay, our school fees are enormous, but our poor Catholic children get their education free. So indirectly you're paying for it, and our poor get a first-class education at your expense."

So far as I was concerned, the three teachers the Jesuits found for me were all excellent men. The schooling which they gave me was not in the least narrow or restricted. They lifted my mind to wide horizons, they opened my eyes to the outside world. They were wise, broad-minded men, with a stimulating zest for knowledge and the ability to impart it—whether in science, history or politics. Most important of all perhaps they encouraged me to read for myself, and from the time I was ten or thereabouts, I burrowed freely into our vast library of books in English, French, Persian and Arabic. My three tutors gave me the key to knowledge, and for that I have always been profoundly grateful to Mr. Gallagher, Mr. Lawrence and Mr. Kenny.

Of them I can say nothing but good. But, alas, of the man responsible for my education in Arabic and Persian and in all matters Islamic I have nothing but bad to say. He was extremely learned, a profound scholar, with a deep and extensive knowledge of Arabic literature and of Islamic history, but all his learning had not widened his mind nor warmed his heart. He was a bigoted sectarian, and in spite of his vast reading his mind was one of the darkest and narrowest that I have ever encountered. If Islam had indeed been the thing he taught, then surely God had sent Mohammed not to be a blessing for all mankind but a curse.

It was saddening and in a sense frightening to listen to him talk. He gave one the feeling that God had created men solely to send them to hell and eternal damnation. However deep and precise his knowledge—and I admit that in both these respects it was almost unique—it had withered into bitterness and hate. In later years he returned to Tehran, where he became a great and renowned teacher of Islamic lore and acquired the reputation of being one of the most learned scholars in all Iran; yet to the end, I think, he must have remained the bigoted mullah whom I knew.

Perhaps it was this early experience which for the rest of my life has given me a certain prejudice against professional men of religion—be they mullahs or maulvis, curates, vicars or bishops. Many of them I admit are exemplary people. The simple religious—village curés in France, the humbler priesthood in rural Italy, humble, pious and gentle sisters in hospitals all over the world—I have known, admired and revered. In England I have had many friends all my life among the Quakers, and I am aware of a tranquil sense of mental and spiritual communion with them, for our mutual respect for each other's beliefs—mine for their Quakerism, theirs for my Islamic faith—is absolute. The vast majority of Muslim believers all over the world are charitable and gently disposed to those who hold other faiths, and they pray for divine forgiveness and compassion for all. There developed however in Iran and Iraq a school of doctors of religious law whose outlook and temper—intolerance, bigotry and spiritual aggressiveness—resembled my old teacher's, and in my travels about the world I have met too many of their kind—Christian, Muslim and Jew—who ardently and ostentatiously sing the praises of the Lord, and yet are eager to send to hell and eternal damnation all except those who hold precisely their own set of opinions. For many years, I must confess, I have sought to avoid this sort of person.

It was strange and it was out of place that a boy, whose home and upbringing were such as mine in India, should have been submitted in adolescence to a course of this narrow and formalist Islamic indoctrination. For my early environment was one of the widest tolerance; there was in our home never any prejudice against Hindus or Hinduism, and a great many of our attendants and servants—our gardeners, messengers, sepoys and guards, and many of those whose work was connected with buying and selling, marketing and rent collection—were Hindus.

In addition, my mother was herself a genuine mystic in the Muslim tradition (as were most of her closest companions); and she habitually spent a great deal of time in prayer for spiritual enlightenment and for union with God. In such a spirit there was no room for bigotry. Like many other mystics my mother had a profound poetic understanding. I have, in something near ecstasy, heard her read perhaps some verses by Roumi or Hafiz, with their exquisite analogies between man's beatific vision of the Divine and the temporal beauty and colors of flowers, the music and magic of the night, and the transient splendors of the Persian dawn. Then I would have to go back to my gloomy treadmill and hear my tutor cursing and railing as was his habit. Since he was a Shia of the narrowest outlook, he concentrated his most ferocious hatred not on non-Muslims, not even on those who persecuted the Prophet, but on the caliphs and companions of the Prophet, his daughter and two grandchildren, his son-in-law Ali and about four or five of the closest companions of Hazrat Ali; all others were enemies of God and of His Prophet, who had striven to encompass the Prophet's death and after his death had brutally murdered Ali—his adopted son and natural successor—and Ali's sons, his beloved grandchildren. This form of Shiaism attains its climax during the month of Muharram with its lamentations and its dreadful cursings. Reaction against its hatred, intolerance and bigotry has, I know, colored my whole life, and I have found my answer in the simple prayer that God in His Infinite mercy will forgive the sins of all Muslims, the slayer and the slain, and that all may be reconciled in Heaven in a final total absolution. And I further pray that all who truly and sincerely believe in God, be they Christian, Jew, Buddhist or Brahmin, who strive to do good and avoid evil, who are gentle and kind, will be joined in Heaven and be granted final pardon and peace. I could wish that all other creeds would have this same charity toward Muslims; but—with those honorable, humble exceptions whom I have mentioned—this is not an attitude that I have encountered among Christian divines. It is a sad and harsh thing to say, but I believe it to be true that, in general, the higher a man's position in any of the various churches, the more severe and the less charitable is his attitude to Muslims and to Islam.

The home in which I was brought up was, as you can see, a literary one. I have referred to my mother's poetic sense. She was deeply versed in Persian and Arabic literature, as were several of her ladies in waiting and closest women friends. My mother knew a great deal of poetry by heart and she had a flair for the appropriate classical quotation—a flair which, I may say, she never lost throughout her long life. Even when she was nearly ninety she was never at a loss for the right and apt quotation, not merely from one of the great poets such as Hafiz and Firdausi or Roumi but from many a minor or little-known writer.

One little anecdote may explain it. Shortly before she died a cousin of mine quoted one night at dinner a verse of Persian poetry which is rarely heard. In order not to bother my mother or worry her, I attributed it to Hafiz. Not at all, said my mother, that is not by Hafiz, and she gave the name of the poem and the name of the rather obscure poet who had written it.

A consequence of this characteristic was that mealtimes at my mother's table were no occasions of idle gossip or tittle-tattle. Our conversation was of literature, or poetry; or perhaps one of the elderly ladies who traveled to and from Tehran a great deal would talk about her experiences at the Court of the Shah.

A clear light shines on this phase of my boyhood. Was I happy or unhappy? I was solitary, in the sense that I had no companions of my own age, except my beloved cousin Aga Shamsuddin and his brother Abbas who were of the same age and the same outlook and were the closest and dearest friends of my youth, but I had so few holidays and so little free time, what could I have done with a host of friends? One fact stands out extremely clearly—I worked hard, a great deal harder than most young schoolboys. By the time I was thirteen I could read and write English, tolerable French, perfect Persian and fair Arabic; I had a sound knowledge of Roman history as well as of Islamic history. I was well grounded in at least the elements of science—chemistry and physics, botany, biology and zoology. Nor was my scientific education merely theoretical; in each of our houses I had a small laboratory and I had a set period of practical, experimental laboratory work every day.

As I have remarked, I early acquired an insatiable taste for reading. It developed rapidly from the time that I was ten or so, and when I had temporarily, at any rate, plumbed the resources of our library, I looked elsewhere. I wanted to buy books for myself. But there was one small impediment: my mother allowed me no pocket money. My cousin and I organized ourselves a brilliant way around this difficulty. Each of us put on an abba (a wide, all-enveloping cloak which is, or used to be, a universal piece of clothing in Persia and the Arab countries). Thus garbed we made our way to a well-known Bombay bookshop. One of us engaged the shopkeeper in eager conversation, and the other slid some books into the folds of his abba. Our little device was pretty soon spotted, and the proprietor of the shop told my uncle and my mother. Naturally our bill was promptly settled, but the family decided that we should be taught a lesson. Nothing was said to us and we continued our naughty little game. We were at it one day when into the shop walked my uncle.

"Take off your abbas!" he ordered sternly.

As we did so, the books which we had stolen tumbled to the floor. Our shame and our mortification were immediate and complete, and from that day to this I don't think I have ever so much as picked a flower in anyone else's garden without telling him.

I continued my reading—but not with stolen books. And a year or two later my reading and indeed my whole outlook on life were profoundly and permanently transformed by a small, wise decision; much that had hitherto been pain and hardship became pleasure and delight, my health was immediately improved, and I am sure I was saved much trouble and misfortune in later life. Mr.

Kenny, the third and last of my European tutors, had at one time been employed by a firm of opticians. As soon as he saw me settle down to work he realized how terrible—and how dangerous—was the torture to which, through my congenital short sightedness and the ignorance on these matters of those by whom I was surrounded, I was being daily and hourly submitted.

It is strange and sad to recall that already, more than once before Mr. Kenny's arrival, I had in fun picked up and put on a pair of glasses left lying about by one of our family or friends. The moment I put them on I discovered the joy of a new and exciting world: a world of human beings of definite and different shapes, a world of green trees and brightly colored flowers, and of sharp, strong light instead of the perpetual haze and fog, the world blurred at the edges, which was all that an extremely myopic little boy could see. But those minutes of joy were of short duration, and were indeed forbidden, for the servants had orders to take the glasses away from me, since my family could not believe that a child could be short-sighted and thought that I was being self-indulgent and silly. Mr. Kenny immediately recognized my present plight and its implications for my future. He insisted on taking me to the firm of opticians whose employee he had been; he had my eyes tested and had me fitted with proper glasses both for reading and for distance. My uncles strove to interfere, but Mr. Kenny was adamant; he carried with him the prestige of the West, and he won the day. This sensible and kindly action saved me infinite pain and worry, and gave me a new world in which to live.

What sort of world was it to which my boyish eyes were thus opened? What sort of life was it to which I was being educated? First and most important, I was by inheritance the spiritual head and leader of a far-flung, extremely diverse community of far from negligible significance in the Islamic world. As soon as I was capable of doing so, I had to assume responsibility and take decisions. I was installed on the Gadi of Imams in 1885, when I was eight years old, and there is a photograph in existence of this ceremony, which vividly recalls a vanished epoch. A few years later I found myself exercising my influence and authority in a matter of considerable importance in the life of Bombay—a security matter as we should say nowadays. In the early nineties there was an outburst of savage communal rioting in Bombay. I issued strict orders to all my followers that they were to avoid participation in the disturbance. The effect of my order was not merely negative; it helped to abate anger and re-establish peace in Bombay between Muslims and Hindus. This—my first independent political action—earned the thanks of the Governor and the Commissioner of Police in Bombay, and boy though I still was, it did much to win for me the regard of political leaders of all communities.

For by this time my household, followers, supporters, relatives and hangers-on made up an important element in the population of Bombay, and (as I shall have to relate shortly) they ultimately created a security problem of their own. My grandfather, conscious that he was an exile from Persia, and conscious perhaps that the greater part of his adventurous and exciting career was over when he settled in Bombay, took no part in Indian politics. My father, during the Governorship of Sir James Fergusson, accepted a seat on the Bombay Legislative Council. In my maturity my political interests and ideals were to take me far afield, but the domain to which in the late eighties and early nineties I was growing up was not without its own political, administrative, social and economic problems and perplexities.

My grandfather, both in Poona and Bombay, had been able to lead a largely insulated life of his own, almost medieval in its style and pattern, the like of which has long since passed away. He brought with him from Persia the pastimes of Persian noblemen of that era, and the splendid and feudal manner of organizing those pastimes. Field sports were a major passion in the society in which he grew up; lavish racing stables were maintained; packs of hounds were bred, and there was continual searching for the best hawks to be found in Iran and Iraq. All these interests he brought with him into exile—and a great retinue of followers who were identified with them. As soon as he settled in Bombay he bought and raced horses —Arab, English, Australian, even Turkoman; he collected hawks and hounds anew; and the pattern of his life was arranged round these diversions. His day began at six in the morning either with a deer hunt or after birds, or—in the racing season—a visit to the training grounds to watch his horses being put through their paces. By nine o'clock he would be home. He would have a substantial breakfast, and then go to bed. In the middle of the afternoon he would get up, go to a race meeting or more hunting until dusk. Then he would come home and spend the night on his tasks as the leader of his community—receiving his followers, conducting his correspondence, looking into matters of finance and the like. He would break for a fairly big meal about nine o'clock, and then work on until five in the morning, when he would have a light meal before beginning the day's round again. These were habits familiar to him and many others of the ruling class of his time in Iran and Afghanistan, and he saw no reason not to maintain them in the surroundings of his later life.

I may say, incidentally, that my grandfather had a run of success as an owner on the Indian turf, in the fifties, sixties and seventies of the last century, very similar to my own in England and France from the twenties to the fifties of this century.

My father, during his brief reign, continued much the same manner of living, widening and increasing the stud and organizing his hawks and his hounds in a fashion and on a scale that evoked the admiration of everyone who understood these matters, travelers from Europe, for example, and members of the British ruling class who held high official positions in India. It was to fall to me to adapt and modify this outlook and way of life to changing times.

It was inevitable that during my minority the British Raj and its representatives in Bombay should take a close interest in my welfare and my upbringing. My boyhood coincided with what was no doubt the heyday of British paternalism in India. The Raj seemed effortlessly secure and unshakable; its representatives and officials—most of whom were enlightened and liberal men whose minds were in tune with the temper of the high Victorian age in which they had matured—were serenely self-confident. Their actions and their decisions found their source in a mental and spiritual strength which their successors were to lose. The mutiny was a far-off memory, and indeed its effect had seemed to be almost totally confined to Northern India. Nationalism was only just beginning to stir in the womb of time. Congress existed, having been brought into being in the early eighties by the energy and effort of a British member of the Indian Civil Service, a Mr. Hume. A similar Muslim organization was established a little later, and my eldest half-brother was one of its founders. But few would have believed that these were the first portents of all the stress and upheaval of later years.

Relations between British and Indians were in general easy, amiable and without strain. The then Governor of Bombay, Lord Reay, was a Gladstonian Liberal, high principled, benevolent and affable, and sustained in his duty by a charming and talented wife. And the Bombay Army Commander was no other than H.R.H. the Duke of Connaught, Queen Victoria's youngest son, who made soldiering his career, as befitted a godson and namesake of Arthur, first Duke of Wellington. From the first it was my particular good fortune that the Duke and Duchess of Connaught took in me a close, affectionate and continuing interest. They would come to tea at our house several times a year, and I, as a child, was more frequently asked to their home and there agreeably spoiled and given perhaps more toffee and chocolate than was altogether good for me. These visits back and forth were red-letter days for me. At Poona and at Mahabaleshwar the Duke was a very near neighbor; every day, and often several times a day, we would encounter him out riding, and we would stop and the Duke would have a talk with me. Thus in a fashion I was brought up close to the British Royal Family and in later years, when I met Queen Victoria, she said at once, I remember, that she had heard all about me and my home from her son.

Similar frequent and informal visits were exchanged between my family and the Governor; and as a boy in the Reays' time I was often taken to tea at Government House. There was in these relationships at this period no sense of tension, no standoffishness and no condescension; they were cordial and confident—very different relationships from those that developed in later years. The narrow, intolerant "imperialistic" outlook associated with Kipling's name, and with some of his more unfortunate observations (of the order of "East is East and West is West and never the twain shall meet," for example), had not then emerged. Had social life and relations between British and Indians continued to be as they were in the eighties, I greatly doubt whether political bitterness would have developed to the extent it did, and possibly something far less total than the severance of the Republic of India from the Imperial connection would have been feasible.

Queen Victoria herself was of course sharply conscious of the responsibilities, not only political but personal and social, which she had assumed with the splendid title of Empress of India. She insisted that Indian Princes and Indian gentlefolk should receive the respect and the dignified status accorded in those days to European princes and gentlefolk. The Duke of Connaught faithfully practiced her principles during his time in India. The Viceroy and Vicereine, Lord and Lady Dufferin, were, like Lord and Lady Reay, people of kind and gentle sensibility, warm hearts and graceful manners. A tone thus set could not be ignored, and Indo-British relationships in general were in this pattern. There was agreeable and unstrained social mixing at receptions, on the racecourse, or on the polo ground.

There is an outstanding example that I recall: Sir Jamsetjee Jeejeebhoy, a notable figure in the Parsee community in Bombay, gave a reception for the Viceroy and Vicereine, Lord and Lady Dufferin, for the Governor of Bombay and his wife, Lord and Lady Reay, and for the Duke and Duchess of Connaught. All the leading representatives of all the communities in Bombay were present, and just as would have happened in England or any other country, Sir Jeejeebhoy, as host, offered his arm to Lady Dufferin and went into the supper room, and the Viceroy followed with his hostess, Lady Jeejeebhoy, and everyone else went after in turn. A few years later— and thereafter, until the end of the Indian Empire—it would have been inconceivable that the Viceroy, a Prince of the British Royal House and the Governor of the great province of British India, would have gone to a reception at the house of a Parsee gentleman, however distinguished, and allowed him to lead the Vicereine in first and then have followed with his hostess. Rigid protocol replaced easy good manners—to the grave detriment not only of social life but of something, in the end, much more important. But in those happy days Empire did not mean "imperialism"—social vulgarity, and worse, social aggressiveness and highhandedness. It is true that the clubs were closed to Indians but that fact had none of the neurotic significance which it took on subsequently; nobody minded Europeans having a small enclave of their own, and social relations outside were on a basis of free equality.

A curious fact not without a tinge of irony is that in the eighties many Indian ladies on their own initiative were coming out of purdah and were receiving Europeans in their homes with cordial hospitality. It was the result of a spontaneous feeling among Indian ladies that they could not keep back in the general atmosphere of good will and the removal of restraint. Had this atmosphere been maintained it is possible that, in Western India at any rate, purdah would have broken down gradually among the upper classes decades before it did.

This was a happy period whose temper and outlook I have sought to evoke in some detail, for in the harsh and strained years which followed, it was forgotten. The change, it seems to me, set in sharply in 1890. The Duke of Connaught went home and his great influence for good in all social matters was lost. He was followed as Army Commander by General Sir George Greaves (reputedly the original of General Bangs in Kipling's "A Code of Morals").* Lord Reay too retired and was succeeded by Lord Harris, a famous and enthusiastic cricketer, but a Conservative of the rising new imperialist school of thought. Our relations with Government House, though perfectly friendly, became more formal and less familiar. The whole tone of relationships stiffened. No longer were the easy, frequent receptions and entertainments attended by people of all communities. At Government House there were merely a

---

* Years later, long after he had retired, I encountered General Greaves on the Dover-Calais steamer. He was alone, and I put the conventional question that courtesy prompted: "Is Lady Greaves going with you to Paris?" To which the warrior replied, "I don't take a ham sandwich when I go to a banquet."

few rigidly formal garden parties at which social mingling began to be discouraged. Less and less did Europeans invite Indians to their houses, and soon it became rare for the races to meet around a luncheon or dinner table. Even on occasions where rigid separation was obviously impossible, as at race meetings, color differences began to show themselves. Sets were formed, not on the natural basis of personal sympathy and antipathy, but on the artificial and unwholesome basis of race and color. This is an outlook against which I, who had spent my most impressionable years in a totally different atmosphere, was to react strongly.

In Bombay in the nineties perhaps the first sufferers were the Parsees. Energetic, efficient, socially as well as commercially gifted and adapted, they played an important role in easing and smoothing relations between British and Indians. They now suffered the fate of the go-between who is no longer wanted. They were looked down on by both sides, and were more and more isolated to their own company and that of a few advanced Hindu and Muslim families. Europeans would no longer associate with them because they were Asiatics; Hindus and Muslims considered that they had thrown in their lot with the Europeans and then had been cast aside. It was a disagreeable and unjust plight.

An even unhappier change—and much more far-reaching in its effects—came over the official British view of nascent political feeling. Congress, benevolently encouraged in its beginnings in the eighties and regarded (probably rightly) as a sign of maturity in one or more members of the great Imperial family, was now thought to be a hostile political organization whose ultimate aim could only be to weaken and destroy the British connection. The alienation of the British ruling classes (or at any rate, the greater number of those they sent to India) from India's educated classes, who were growing in numbers and capacity, was both mental and spiritual. There was frigidity where there had been warmth; and in this process there were sown almost all the seeds of future bitterness.

What happened to the Englishman has been to me all my life a source of wonder and astonishment. Suddenly it seemed that he felt his prestige as a member of an imperial, governing race would be lost if he accepted those of a different color as fundamentally his equals. The color bar was no longer thought of as a physical difference, but far more dangerously—in the end disastrously—as an intellectual and spiritual difference. As long as Indians who adopted and imitated the European way of life were few, it was possible for a servant and upholder of the Raj to feel that there was little danger that his unique position would be undermined by familiarity and overthrown by numbers. But now racialism—on both sides— marched on with giant's strides. It was soon not merely a matter of the relationship between British rulers and the Indian ruled. The pernicious theory spread that all Asiatics were a second-class race and "white men" possessed some intrinsic and unchallengeable superiority.

The infection had, I will admit, its ridiculous aspects. The Turkish Consul General in Bombay happened—like many of the ruling and official classes in Ottoman Turkey—to be a Bosnian, a Slav, of one hundred per cent European stock, but because he was a Muslim ignorant prejudice set him down as an "Asiatic"! Some English acquaintances took him into one of their clubs. Other members made such a row about it that the Consul General said flatly that, as a Muslim and the representative of a semi-Asiatic Empire, he had been treated with discourtesy and contempt on racial grounds, and while he would do his duties as Consul General, his contacts with the British in Bombay would henceforth be severely official and he would have no personal relations with them. The Persian Consul shared his experience and his sentiments. The Japanese, who were emerging from their long seclusion from outside contact, moved cannily; they established their own commercial undertakings first, so that when their Consul came he found Japanese clubs and social gatherings already organized and did not feel isolated or dependent on the good graces of the Anglo-Indian community—in the old-fashioned sense of that word, Anglo-Indian.

A root cause of the new attitude was fear and lack of inner self-confidence. A contributory factor was the presence, in increasing numbers, of British wives, with no knowledge of or interest in the customs and outlook of Indians. Fear afflicted people in trade and commerce just as much as—perhaps even more than—officials. The rift deepened and widened as time went on. The color bar had to be kept rigid and absolute, or (so fear nagged at those in its grip) some mysterious process of contamination would set in, and their faith in their own superiority and in their right—their moral, intellectual and biological right—to rule others would be sapped.

It was a neurotic attitude, very different from that of earlier times when men like Sir John Malcolm, Sir Mountstuart Elphinstone and, later, Lord Ripon and Lord Reay, took it sublimely for granted that England's duty—once she had brought peace, unity and prosperity to India and had taught its peoples the secrets of liberal government—would be in the fullness of time to depart. There was no talk then of Dominion status, but the precedents of Canada and of the rapidly growing colonies of Australia and New Zealand were clear to see. But by the nineties all ideas of this sort had been thrown overboard as inimical to the security of the Raj, disloyal and seditious.

I recall a breakfast party which I gave in Bombay for some senior British officials. Another guest was a cousin of mine—a devoted and loyal subject of the Queen and profoundly pro-British. But he was a student of history. He discoursed on the fact that an Asiatic race, the Arabs, had ruled Spain for five hundred years and, after their departure, had left indelible and splendid marks of their civilization all over southern Spain; and on the fact that another Asiatic race, the Turks, had established a major empire in the Balkans and around the Eastern Mediterranean and were still ruling it after several centuries. My British guests took this as an affront.

"We will not have such comparisons made," they said. "Our rule is permanent, not something that lasts a few centuries and then disappears. Even to think as you think is disloyal."

Ideas like these seem strange indeed now in the 1950's, when we have seen British rule in India dissolve and pass away like early morning mist before strong sunlight. But this was the atmosphere in which my later boyhood was spent, with its unhappy, brooding awareness of deepening difference and of growing misunderstanding and hostility.

I Visit the Western World

WITH APPROACHING MANHOOD my life shaped itself into new channels of its own. More and more the duties and decisions implicit in my inherited position devolved on me. I was never indeed subject to any Regency, in the accepted sense, and as my capacity to make decisions increased, so my mother and my uncles encouraged me to accept responsibility. My mother, who had insisted on the educational discipline of my early boyhood, was as shrewd and watchful as she was loving. She and I remained, throughout her long life, in the closest, most affectionate intimacy. Every night in those years I would go to her apartments and join with her in prayer—that prayer for unity, for companionship on high, which is the core of Muslim faith. This shared experience gave us both, I think, the strength to bear our load of fatigue and anxiety, mental and spiritual, which was by no means light during these difficult years. But my mother's religion was resolutely practical as well; she saw no virtue in faith without works, and from the outset of my public career I accepted and sought to practice the same standards.

My education continued until I was eighteen. Mr. Kenny, my English tutor, once more exerted his beneficent influence and persuaded my mentors that I could give up my hated calligraphy. My mind was opening rapidly to new horizons; in my reading I began to range widely, in English and French as well as in Persian and Arabic; I discovered the intellectual delight—the precision and clarity—of Mill's system of logic. I read voraciously in history and biography, and with my cousin Shamsuddin I became an insatiable reader of novels—a diversion, I may say, whose pleasures have never faded.

On my father's death his racing stables, of course, became my property; and although I was a minor my horses raced under my name year after year, and long before I was out of my teens His Highness the Aga Khan's horses were well known—and not without their successes—on the turf of Western India. There my inherited and environmental influences made themselves obvious from the first. All my family—my mother not excluded—were keen followers of racing form, English as well as Indian. We were knowledgeable about the English turf; Ormone's glorious triumphs, for example, meant almost as much to us as they did to his backers on English racecourses. I well remember that when I was quite small the victor in any pony races between myself and my cousins was hailed for the rest of the day as "Fred Archer." Archer's death in tragic circumstances plunged us all in gloom, almost as if a close friend had committed suicide.

My successes as an owner were not insignificant. I may claim that for a time I—and my cousin Aga Shamsuddin, who was part owner with me of a number of excellent horses—dominated the turf in Western India. Four times in succession I won the Nizam's Gold Cup—the most important and valuable race in Western India. With a horse called Yildiz I won the Governor's Cup in Poona during these years, and again somewhat later.

I took up hunting, not of course fox hunting as in England, but jackal hunting both in Poona and Bombay. It happens that I have never hunted the fox in England, but frankly I know no more exhilarating sport than jackal hunting over the rice fields in Bombay on an early, cold winter morning when the scent is good and the hounds get a good long run after the wily jackal.

I was a pioneer of another sport in India—hockey, which nowadays is one of the main national games of both India and Pakistan. I began to play it with my cousin and other companions of my own age in the early nineties. I encouraged interest in the game; I gave the cups; I got the Indian Army to play. Teams were built up among the various communities in Bombay, and competitions extended steadily all over India. Hockey and cricket developed at much the same time in India, cricket fostered and encouraged by the then Governor of Bombay, Lord Harris; young Indians who had been to England for some part of their education continued the game when they came home, and it exerted an appeal which it has never lost and which has extended to wider and wider circles in India and Pakistan, both of which now produce teams of Test Match caliber and quality.

In my late teens I took up boxing, and made a serious study and use of Eugene Sandow's System of Physical Culture. All my life I have been a keen advocate and practitioner of simple, forthright principles of physical fitness. I have always been a believer in steady exercise. I was a great walker, I took up golf after I was fifty, and one of the catchphrases which journalists used about me was that my two great ambitions were "to win the Derby and the Open Golf Championship." Well, I have won the Derby—and more than once; the other ambition (if it was ever more than a journalist's invention!) is unfulfilled, but my handicap for years was twelve. I have never believed, as many Englishmen do, in cramming a great deal of exercise into a few hours over the week end, and taking little or none during the rest of the week; a certain amount of steady exercise every day has been my habit—exercise to be fitted into the program of a busy day.

A memorable experience of my later boyhood was meeting Mark Twain. I spent a whole afternoon in his company and finished by having dinner with him at Watson's Hotel in Bombay, where he was staying. He had a pleasant, utterly unassuming charm and a friendliness of manner which captivated the serious-minded lad that I was.

He had amassed a considerable fortune, I believe, and had lost it in bad speculation. Now in old age he had to begin to earn his living all over again; therefore he was traveling around the world and interviewing people on the way.* He showed absolutely no sign of bitter-

* Incidentally, he refers to our encounter in his subsequent book, *Following the Equator*.

ness or resentment against his misfortune. He seemed to me dear, gentle and saintly, sad and immensely modest for so great and famous a genius.

More and more as my teens advanced, my days were busy. I was keenly aware that I possessed a dual responsibility, perhaps a dual opportunity: first, in India, as the leader of an influential group within the wide Muslim community at an epoch when political aspirations were stirring and second, as the head of a far-ranging international community, a spiritual chief whose authority extended, in a tenuous yet sensitive network, into the heart of many lands and many peoples. I could never be solely an Indian nationalist, although from 1892, under the influence of wise and good men such as Sir Pherozeshah Mehta and Mr. Badruddin Tyebjee, I took the standpoint of moderate Indian nationalism of that time. My unique task, in a world in which the first hints and rumbles of impending conflict were to be discerned, was surely international. My followers were to be found in Burma and Southeast Asia, in greater and greater numbers along the East African seaboard from Mombasa to East London and inland in South Africa; in Syria, Persia, Afghanistan, in Chinese Turkestan, in Russian territories in the heart of Central Asia, and the Mesopotamian provinces of Turkey which were later to be known as Iraq. My home inevitably was a sounding board of ideas and beliefs, hopes, fears and aspirations from all over the Islamic world. My primary advice, indeed my mandate, to my followers who were citizens of many countries had to be then—and always has been—that the loyalty which they owe to my house and person is a spiritual and nontemporal loyalty, that their temporal allegiance is fully engaged to the State of which they are citizens, and that it is an absolute part of their duty to be good citizens. All my work, in politics and diplomacy all my life, is comprehensible in terms of this dual responsibility with which from my earliest days I have been charged.

At the end of 1895 and the beginning of 1896 I was on the verge of manhood. The reins of my life's task were now fully in my hands. My tutors took their farewell and bowed their way out of my life.

I, like many youths of my age in the East, thought of marriage; and naturally enough I looked around me in the small, confined family circle in which I had grown up. One of my earliest playmates in my childhood had been my cousin, Shahzadi Begum, whose father, Aga Jungishah, was my uncle and one of my early mentors and exemplars. In our adolescence, as was usual in our time and society, we saw little or nothing of each other, but as I approached manhood I became sharply aware of my cousin's beauty and charm, and I fell in love with her. It has been alleged, unkindly and unjustly, that my first marriage was a "state marriage," arranged for my cousin and myself by our parents for dynastic reasons. Nothing could be further from the truth. I was a youth in love, groping toward that experience, that mingling of joy and pain, which turns a boy into a man. Mine and mine only was the initiative in the matter of marriage. I told my mother of my feelings and begged her to approach my uncle and his wife on my behalf, and ask their permission for me to marry Shahzadi. The overtures were made, my formal proposal was accepted. We were to be married within the year. Meanwhile my uncle and aunt, with their daughter and her brother, Shah Abbas, set forth on a pilgrimage to Mecca. The party, having made the Haj, set out for home, and on their way stayed for a time, as was customary, in Jeddah, the port on the Red Sea through which the vast majority of pilgrims to Mecca come and go. My uncle and cousin were assassinated in brutal and violent circumstances; and my aunt and her daughter were in the house when the murders were committed. Police investigation in the Western sense did not exist in Jeddah in those days; communications were scanty and unreliable. The Bombay police closely questioned returning Indian pilgrims and though much about the affray was, and has always remained, obscure, and although the assailants were said either to have immediately poisoned themselves or to have been beaten to death by the horror-struck attendants and bystanders, it is at least clear that my uncle and his son were the victims of dastardly religious fanaticism.

This ghastly tragedy had a profound effect on me, both physically and emotionally. All through that summer I was seriously ill, a prey to a succession of fevers, with painful rheumatic symptoms. In October, when the great heat of the summer was over and the monsoon rains had passed, I made my first journey to Northern India. Hitherto my traveling outside Western and Southern India, except for visits to Baghdad and to Bushire and Muscat, had been extremely restricted. I now, however, acquired a taste for travel which I have certainly never abandoned. On this first trip I visited the great shrines and centers of Muslim India at Agra, Delhi and Lahore: that magnificent group of monuments to Islamic civilization and culture—the Taj Mahal, the Red Fort in Delhi, and the Friday Mosque, and those exquisite gems, the Pearl Mosques at Delhi and Agra. My way led me, too, to the Anglo-Muslim College (as it then was) at Aligarh, where I met Sir Syed Ahmed and Nawab Mohsen-ul-Molk. This was the origin of what was for many years one of the crucial concerns of my life—my interest in the extension and improvement of Muslim higher education, and specially the college and university at Aligarh.

I took up its cause then with a youthful fervor which I have never regretted. Aligarh in the 1890's was an admirable institution, but it was hampered and restricted by lack of funds and lack of facilities. Did I realize then, young as I was, that it had in it to become a great powerhouse of Muslim thought and culture and learning, in full accord with Islamic tradition and teaching, yet adapted to the outlook and the techniques of our present age? No one could have foretold all that did in fact happen; but I do know that I was on fire to see Aligarh's scope widened and its usefulness extended, and to find the money for it, by any short-cut means if necessary. Why not, said I in my youthful rashness, go to some great American philanthropist—Mr. Rockefeller or Mr. Carnegie—and ask for a substantial grant?

My new friends were older and sager. It was our responsibility, they said, within our own sixty or seventy million-strong Muslim community in India; if we sought for outside help, even from the richest and most philanthropically inclined of American multimillionaires, we should be dishonored for all time. They were right, of course. For this was an age which had not experienced two world wars and had never heard of Point Four. But that decision, and my own zeal in the cause which I had taken up, led (as such decisions are apt to lead) to years of arduous and all-demanding toil, the journeyings, the speechmaking, the sitting on committees, the fight against apathy and the long, long discussions with those in high places, which are the lot of those who commit themselves to such an endeavor.

Often in civilized history a university has supplied the springboard for a nation's intellectual and spiritual renascence. In our time it has been said that the American Robert Missionary College in Constantinople led to the re-emergence of Bulgaria as an independent, sovereign nation. Who can assess the effect on Arab nationalism of the existence of the American University of Beirut? Aligarh is no exception to this rule. But we may claim with pride that Aligarh was the product of our own efforts and of no outside benevolence; and surely it may also be claimed that the independent, sovereign nation of Pakistan was born in the Muslim University of Aligarh.

Reinvigorated and restored to health by my travels I went home at the end of the year to our wedding ceremonies and celebrations. It was a double wedding. For at the same time Shahzadi's brother, my trusted friend Aga Shamsuddin, was married to another of our cousins. Our nuptials were celebrated with all the appropriate ritual and rejoicing; and then sorrow beset myself and my bride.

It is a long-ago story of young unhappiness, and it can be briefly and sadly told. We were both ignorant and innocent; our ignorance and innocence set a gulf between us which knowledge, wisely and salutarily applied, could have bridged. We were too shy to acquire that knowledge, too innocent even to know how to set about getting it. Tenderness and diffused affection—and my wife had all that I could give—were no use for our forlorn plight. Ours was no less a tragedy because, under the iron conventions of the time, it was both commonplace and concealed. Mine, I thought, was the blame for the grief and misunderstanding that embroiled us; and this deepened my affection for my wife; but for her, baffled and bewildered as she was, the affection I offered was no substitute nor atonement.

Inevitably we drifted apart, she to a private purgatory of resentment and reproach, and I to the activities and interests of the outside world.

For me relief was legitimately much easier, for my official and political life rapidly became full and vigorous, and there was a great deal of sheer hard work to be done. If my marriage was a sour sham, my duties and responsibilities were real and earnest in this year of 1897.

During the previous year there had been sinister rumors that an epidemic of bubonic plague was sedulously and remorselessly spreading westward across Asia. There had been a bad outbreak in Hong Kong; sporadically it appeared in towns and cities farther and farther west. When in the late summer of 1897 it hit Bombay there was a natural and general tendency to discredit its seriousness; but within a brief time we were all compelled to face the fact that it was indeed an epidemic of disastrous proportions. Understanding of the ecology of plague was still extremely incomplete in the nineties. The medical authorities in Bombay were overwhelmed by the magnitude, and (as it seemed) the complexity, of the catastrophe that had descended on the city. Their reactions were cautious and conservative. Cure they had none, and the only preventative that they could offer was along lines of timid general hygiene, vaguely admirable but unsuited to the precise problem with which they had to deal. Open up, they said; let fresh air and light into the little huts, the hovels and the shanties in which hundreds of thousands of the industrial and agricultural proletariat in Bombay Presidency lived; and when you have let in fresh air, sprinkle as much strong and strong-smelling disinfectant as you can. These precautions were not only ineffective; they ran directly counter to deep-rooted habits in the Indian masses. Had they obviously worked, they might have been forgiven, but as they obviously did not, and the death roll mounted day by day, it was inevitable that there was a growing feeling of resentment.

It was a grim period. The plague had its ugly, traditional effect on public morals. Respect for law and order slipped ominously.

There were outbreaks of looting and violence. Drunkenness and immorality increased; and there was a great deal of bitter feeling against the Government for the haphazard and inefficient way in which it was tackling the crisis. The climax was reached with the assassination (on his way home from a Government House function) of one of the senior British officials responsible for such preventative measures as had been undertaken.

Now it happened that the Government of Bombay had at its disposal a brilliant scientist and research worker, Professor Haffkine, a Russian Jew, who had come to work on problems connected with cholera; he had induced the authorities to tackle cholera by mass inoculation and had had in this sphere considerable success. He was a determined and energetic man. He was convinced that inoculation offered a method of combating bubonic plague. He pressed his views on official quarters in Bombay—without a great deal of success. Controversy seethed around him, but he had little chance to put his views into practice. Meanwhile people were dying like flies—among them many of my own followers.

I knew that something must be done, and I knew that I must take the initiative. I was not, as I have already recounted, entirely without scientific knowledge; I knew something of Pasteur's work in France. I was convinced that the Surgeon General's Department was working along the wrong lines. I by-passed it and addressed myself directly to Professor Haffkine. He and I formed an immediate alliance and a friendship that was not restricted solely to the grim business that confronted us. This, by now, was urgent enough. I could at least and at once give him facilities for his research and laboratory work. I put freely at his disposal one of my biggest houses, a vast, rambling palace not far from Aga Hall (it is now a part of St. Mary's College, Mazagaon); here he established himself, and here he remained about two years until the Government of India, convinced of the success of his methods, took over the whole research project and put it on a proper, adequate and official footing.

Meanwhile I had to act swiftly and drastically. The impact of the plague among my own people was alarming. It was in my power to set an example. I had myself publicly inoculated, and I took care to see that the news of what I had done was spread as far as possible and as quickly as possible.

My followers could see for themselves that I, their Imam, had in full view of many witnesses submitted myself to this mysterious and dreaded process; hence there was no danger in following my example. The immunity, of which my continued health and my activities were obvious evidence, impressed itself on their consciousness and conquered their fear.

I was twenty years old. I ranged myself (with Haffkine, of course) against orthodox medical opinion of the time—among Europeans no less than among Asiatics. And if the doctors were opposed to the idea of inoculation, what of the views of ordinary people, in my own household and entourage, in the public at large? Ordinary people were extremely frightened. Looking back across more than half a century, may I not be justified in feeling that the young man that I was showed a certain amount of courage and resolution?

At any rate it worked. Among my own followers the news circulated swiftly, as I had intended it to do, that their Imam had been inoculated and that they were to follow my example. Deliberately I put my leadership to the test. It survived and vindicated itself in a new and perhaps dramatic fashion. My followers allowed themselves to be inoculated, not in a few isolated instances, but as a group. Within a short time statistics were firmly on my side; the death rate from plague was demonstrably far, far lower among Ismailis than in any other section of the community; the number of new cases, caused by contamination, was sharply reduced; and finally the incidence of recovery was far higher.

A man's first battle in life is always important. Mine had taught me much, about myself and about other people. I had fought official apathy and conservatism, fear and ignorance—my past foretold my future, for they were foes that were to confront me again and again throughout my life.

By the time the crisis was passed I may have seemed solemn beyond my years, but I possessed an inner self-confidence and strength that temporary and transient twists of fortune henceforth could not easily shake. A by-product of the influence and the authority which I had exerted was that others than my own Ismaili followers looked to me for leadership. The year 1897 was Queen Victoria's Diamond Jubilee. It was natural enough that I should go to Simla to present to the Viceroy, Lord Elgin, an address of loyalty and congratulations to Her Majesty as hereditary Imam of my own Ismaili sect; but, in fact, I went in a triple capacity. I presented three addresses, one from my own community, another as leader and representative of the Muslims of Western India, and a third on behalf of a representative assemblage of the citizens of Bombay and Poona.

Lord Elgin received me graciously and hospitably. I was invited to luncheon by Field Marshal Sir George White, then Commander in Chief in India. The Field Marshal's nickname was Sir George the Dragon Killer, and no man could have better looked the part than this gauntly handsome, old warrior—immensely tall, strong and stern of visage. Sitting there beside him at luncheon I had a sudden vision of the old man kilted, claymore in hand, fiercely challenging all comers, human and animal, a dragon or two, a squadron of cavalry or a herd of rhinoceros. There was still, you see, a vein of romanticism in the young man who had with gravity and propriety presented his three official addresses to His Excellency, the Viceroy.

I returned to Bombay to prepare for my biggest and most important journey hitherto.

I set out to discover the Europe of which I had read and heard so much, which beckoned with so insistent and imperious an attraction.

In our distracted and war-battered epoch there is a deep, nostalgic sadness in recalling the splendors and the security—both seemingly unshakable—which Western European civilization had attained in the last decade of the nineteenth century. As a young man I saw that old world at its zenith. I have lived to watch all the vicissitudes of its strange and swift decline. When I first set foot on the soil of Europe, just half a century had elapsed since the convulsions of

1848. Peace, prosperity and progress seemed universal and all-enveloping. True enough the Franco-Prussian War of 1870-1871 had flashed grim warnings for those prescient enough to see them, but to many that conflict seemed a temporary and regrettable divagation from the general and steady trend toward human betterment. Britain, whose world hegemony, founded on absolute naval supremacy, seemed unchallengeable, was powerful and prosperous as never before under the rule of her august Queen; not since 1815 had she been compelled to intervene in any major Continental conflict, and generations of her statesmen and diplomats were trained in the essential art and duty of retaining the balance of power in Europe. In spite of a few minatory signs of military, social and economic danger or discontent, the dominant notes in the Europe of 1898 were those of serenity and affluence.

Thither I set out from Bombay early in February. I was a little more than twenty years of age. Two members of my household accompanied me as personal attendants. We traveled to Marseilles in a brand-new liner of the Messageries Maritime fleet. In passing I may say that—at any rate so far as the routes to India, Africa and the Far East are concerned—the crack ships of the late nineties were really much better to travel in than their alleged "luxury" twentieth-century successors. Their cabins were more spacious and comfortable and all their amenities were on a far more civilized scale. A great deal of show and chromium plate does not, to my mind, compensate for a decrease in solid comfort.

From Marseilles I went straight to Nice. It was the height of the Riviera winter season; in those days the south of France had no summer season. Every hotel in every resort along the Côte d'Azur was packed, and I had the greatest difficulty in finding accommodation. After all, a considerable proportion of the royalty, nobility and gentry of Europe was concentrated along this strip of coast line. Queen Victoria was at Cimiez; and at length I found myself a room in the hotel in which the Queen was staying. Of pretty small account I was in the vast, glittering, aristocratic and opulent company gathered for the Riviera season: the Emperor Franz Joseph at Cap Martin, a score or so of Russian grand dukes and Austrian archdukes in their villas and palaces, half the English peerage with a generous sprinkling of millionaires from industry and finance; and most of the *Almanach de Gotha* from Germany, the Austro-Hungarian Empire, the Balkan countries lately "emancipated" from Ottoman rule, and Czarist Russia. The young man from Bombay was dazzled and awed.

I knew nobody. I think the only people, other than my own personal attendants, to whom I spoke half a dozen words were the hotel staff and the officials at the Casino in Monte Carlo. But I enjoyed myself enormously—looking and listening. I went out for long drives from Cimiez along the coast to Monte Carlo and Menton. I stared at the shop windows—and what shop windows, those of jewelers especially! After more than fifty years I have a vivid recollection of the solid wealth on display for the eyes of the wealthiest people in Europe, whether they were financiers or landowners from England or Moscow millowners. There were none of your present-day bits and pieces of gold and silver and worthless stones made up into trumpery trinkets; no—this was real jewelry, great sparkling diamonds, pearls, rubies, emeralds and sapphires winking and gleaming in the bright winter sun.

At Cannes, at Nice, at Monte Carlo the streets were packed in the fashionable hours with the carriages of the great and the wealthy, handsome landaus and victorias with fine, high-stepping horses and coachmen and footmen in dashing liveries. I remember that there were one or two automobiles on show as curiosities in front of the Hôtel de Paris at Monte Carlo. How elegant was the disdain with which the fashionable crowd regarded these noisy, smelly toys! Few then had the foresight to see in them the predecessors not only of today's Concours d'Élégance but of the great, silver-winged, jet-propelled aircraft which shoot across the sky.

Though prosperity was to some extent diffused through all the towns and villages along the Côte d'Azur and though there was no hunger and there were no rags, and the poorest had at least one solid meat meal a day, it cannot be said that living was cheap on the Riviera in the nineties. For accommodations and service at the best hotel for myself and two valets, my daily bill—with no extravagance and no entertainment of any kind—was about two hundred gold francs. That translated into present-day terms would be nearly forty thousand francs a day. But were it possible to live at the same rate and on the same scale as I did on that first trip of mine, I daresay my bill— in contemporary terms—would work out at about six thousand to seven thousand francs a day. So in relation to the gold standard of the nineties, the cost of living—my sort of living in those days—was five or six times as high as it is now.

Since I was staying in the same hotel as Queen Victoria, I had frequent opportunities of watching her go out to and return from her daily drives in her landau. She was helped in and out of her carriage by Indian servants from her personal household. I and my own attendants reached the same, rather strange conclusion, and, I may say, it was reinforced later when I saw her servants at closer quarters at Windsor: they were distinctly second-class servants, of the kind that you find around hotels and restaurants, the kind that the newly arrived or transient European is apt to acquire in the first hotel in which he stays—very different from and very inferior to the admirable, trustworthy and very high-grade men whom, throughout the years of British rule in India, one would encounter at Viceregal Lodge or at Government House in any of the provinces. It seemed highly odd, and frankly it still does. Was the explanation possibly that the pay offered was not good enough to attract the first-rate man overseas? Of course after Queen Victoria's death there was a change; successive King-Emperors had no Indian menial servants, but there were several posts of honor in the Royal Household for Indian aides-de-camp and orderly officers.

I had ten memorable days on the Riviera, and then off I set for Paris. I have praised the comfort of the liners of those days, but no, not the sleeping cars—anyone who knows the modern *wagon-lits* or Pullman car, and the glories perhaps of the Blue Train, can have no idea of the cramped, primitive, alleged sleeping car of the nineties and the early 1900's. However, it took me to Paris. I repeat: I was twenty years old, I had steeped myself in French literature and French history of the whole nineteenth century and earlier. I knew the names of the streets, I knew the way Parisians lived, acted and thought. Mine in dreams and in reading was the Paris of the two Napoleons, the Paris of Balzac and of Barrès, of the boulevards and the barricades. Where did I stay but at the famous Hôtel Bristol? What did I do on my first morning in Paris but pay my call at the British Embassy?

I have hinted that I was a solemn young man, very serious about my cultural and scientific interests. In the absence of the Ambassador, the Minister gave me the introductions that I wanted and supplemented those that I had brought with me. To the Carnavalet Museum I went, to the Louvre, to the Bibliothèque Nationale. There I was shown around by the curator of Oriental books and manuscripts, accompanied by M. Solomon Reinach, an eminent archaeologist. He was astonished, he said, that a young man who spoke English and French so fluently could read with ease ancient classical Persian and Arabic manuscripts. I was astonished in my turn (though I did not say so) that so distinguished a *savant* should forget that Persian and Arabic were, after all, my native languages, the languages which my forebears had spoken for hundreds of years.

My friend Professor Haffkine in Bombay had given me a letter of introduction to Dr. Roux of the Pasteur Institute. In the evenings I sallied forth to the theater and the opera. It was not the season in Paris, and therefore there was not the display and the elegance that I had seen at the Riviera. Still I saw Madam Bartet at the *Comédie Française* and thought her the most enchanting and accomplished actress I had ever seen—and now with a lifetime in between, that is a verdict which I see no reason to alter. I saw Sarah Bernhardt, but frankly she disappointed me. I never thought she came up to Bartet. I went several times to the opera and except for *Faust*, every opera that I saw was by Meyerbeer. Who ever hears an opera by Meyerbeer nowadays? His reputation suddenly dropped like a plummet, and yet I think he has been unfairly treated, with a fierce contempt which he does not merit. I know that he is no Wagner; I know that he cannot compare with the best of Mozart or Verdi, but I have a hankering belief that a Meyerbeer revival might prove quite a success.

Not all my time in Paris was spent on culture. I did have letters of introduction to members of the Jockey Club; I did go to the races. And after a fortnight I headed for London.

The private, incognito status in which I had hitherto traveled was no longer possible. I had reached the capital and center of the Empire. At the station to meet me when I arrived was an equerry from Buckingham Palace, representing Her Majesty; and from the India Office, representing the Secretary of State, there was the Political Aide-de-Camp, Sir Gerald Fitzgerald. I went to the Albemarle Hotel in Piccadilly, which was my headquarters and base throughout that spring and summer.

Soon after I reached the hotel the Duke of Connaught, who had known me in my childhood and boyhood at home, paid a call and stayed for a long time. The British Royal Family's watchful and friendly interest in me had not abated.

London in the nineties has been written about *ad nauseam*, yet it is difficult to exaggerate the magnetic effect and the splendor of London in that sunlit heyday of the Victorian age—the ease, the security, the affluence, the self-confidence. The City was the financial center of the civilized world, immensely rich, immensely powerful. From Westminster a great Empire was governed with benevolent assurance. If the Foreign Office were dowdy and inconvenient, if the India Office's methods of administering a subcontinent were tortuous and archaic, who could deny the irresistible sense of power and authority concentrated in those few small acres? The outward show of that power and that authority was magnificently impressive. The pound sterling was a gold sovereign, and purchased about eight times what its paper equivalent does today. The gradations from rich to poor were steep; yet throughout much of society there was diffused a general sense of prosperity. There was no welfare state, but there was a robust, genial feeling that Britain was top dog, and there was gaiety, vigor and adventurousness about life for the mass of the people.

Real power, political and economic, was in the hands of a few. The rulers of England and the Empire consisted of a small closed circle of the aristocracy and those members of the rising plutocracy who had attached themselves to, and got themselves accepted by, the aristocracy. To that circle my own rank and the august connections which I possessed gave me a direct and immediate entry. I who have lived to see the demagogue and the dictator in power in a large part of what was once civilized Europe saw in my young manhood, at very close quarters, the oligarchy which controlled Victorian England and the Empire.

The London season was just beginning when I arrived. I was immediately swept into the middle of it all. All doors in society were open to me. I took my place in a glittering, superbly organized round and ritual: Epsom, Ascot, Newmarket; a dinner at Lansdowne House, at Lord Ripon's or Lord Reay's; the opera and a ball at a great ducal mansion; garden parties, country-house week ends. Formal clothes were *de rigueur* in London, a frock coat or a morning coat, a stiff collar and a silk hat and gloves, however hot the weather. Church parade on a Sunday morning in Hyde Park was a stately occasion, with its own elaborate ceremony. There was the detailed ritual of calling. From royalty downward the whole of society was organized with a care and a rigidity inconceivable today. To recall it all now is indeed to evoke a vanished world.

In due course I was summoned to an audience with Her Majesty at Windsor Castle. She received me with the utmost courtesy and affability. The only other person in the room during this first audience was my old patron, the Duke of Connaught, in whose presence I did not feel shy or overawed. The Queen, enfolded in voluminous black wraps and shawls, was seated on a big sofa. Was she tall or short, was she stout or not? I could not tell; her posture and her wraps made assessments of that kind quite impossible. I kissed the hand which she held out to me. She remarked that the Duke of Connaught was a close friend of my family and myself. She had an odd accent, a mixture of Scotch and German—the German was perfectly explicable by the fact that she was brought up in the company of her mother, a German princess, and a German governess, Baroness Lehzen. She also had the German conversational trick of interjecting "so"—pronounced "tzo"—frequently into her remarks. She observed that since I was a prince myself and the descendant of many kings, she would not ask me to kneel, or to receive the accolade and the touch of the sword upon my shoulder, but she would simply hand the order to me. I was greatly touched by her consideration and courtesy. This, the K.C.I.E. was the first British Order which I received.

A little later I was bidden to stay the night at the castle and dine with Her Majesty. This too was a memorable experience. I sat at dinner between the Queen and her daughter Princess Beatrice—Princess Henry of Battenberg, mother of Queen Ena of Spain. The Queen was wearing her customary black—that mourning which, from the day after her husband died, she never put off. On her wrist she wore a large diamond bracelet set in the center of which was a beautiful miniature of the Prince Consort, about three inches long and two inches wide. The Queen was then seventy-nine; the vigor of her bearing and the facility and clarity of her conversation were astonishing.

There were several high officers of State present, including the Lord Chancellor, the Earl of Halsbury, a small, squat, unimpressive-looking man. I was both surprised and amused when the Queen murmured to me that Lord Halsbury, though not much to look at, was a formidable lawyer and statesman. The Queen talked to me especially about India. Were British senior officials and representatives, she asked, civil or were they wanting in manners toward Indian Princes and gentry? I replied truthfully that so far as I and my family were concerned, we had always been treated with impeccable kindness and courtesy by British officials with whom we came in contact. Throughout dinner the Queen and the two guests to right and left of her—myself and the Lord Chancellor—were served by her Indian attendants, who were the same kind of rather second-rate servants whom I had noticed in her entourage at Nice.

The dinner was long and elaborate—course after course, three or four choices of meat, a hot pudding and an iced pudding, a savory and all kinds of hothouse fruit—slow and stately in its serving. We sat down at a quarter past nine, and it must have been a quarter of eleven before it was all over. The Queen, in spite of her age, ate and drank heartily—every kind of wine that was offered and every course, including both the hot and the iced pudding. After dinner, in the state drawing room each guest was presented to Her Majesty and had a few moments' conversation with her. She gave me a jeweled portrait of herself, decorated with the rose of England, the thistle of Scotland and the harp of Ireland—and the harp was in emeralds. Next morning her *munshi*, her Indian secretary, came to me and gave me something which the Queen had herself written in Urdu and Arabic characters.

To be Queen-Empress was for Queen Victoria to possess no formal and remote title. She was keenly alert and sensitive to the views and needs of her Indian subjects, and her liking and sympathy for them were warm and genuine. I particularly remember that at dinner she said to me with great earnestness she hoped that when British people in India visited mosques and temples, they conducted themselves with respect and reverence as they would in cathedrals in their own land.

During this visit to England I first made the acquaintance of various other members of the British Royal Family—first among them, of course, the Prince of Wales, later to become King Edward VII. From the first the Prince was extremely kind to me. He had me at once made an honorary member of his own club, the Marlborough, and some months later, early in 1899, he himself nominated me for full membership. In those days membership in the Marlborough, thus conferred, had a special social and personal significance; one was stamped, as it were, as a personal friend of the Prince of Wales. I may mention in passing that I am still, after more than fifty years, a member of the Marlborough-Windham; and when I am in London, I still drop in there to look at the newspapers. The head hall-porter and I are by now quite the oldest inhabitants; he entered the service of the Club in, I think, 1896 or 1897. Together he and I recall old times, and our conversation evokes many, many ghosts whose living presence, as we knew them in our youth, are very real to us.

For the last decade of his life I was honored with the warm, personal friendship of King Edward VII. My association with him was far from formal. He was elderly and I was young, and at the outset a stranger, but he treated me always with the greatest kindness and benevolence. Indeed if I search for a word in which to sum up King Edward's character, the answer is to be found in "benevolent." He wished everybody well. It is perfectly true that he had a great taste for the good things in life, that he enjoyed having a good time; but sincerely and steadily he wanted everyone else—the humblest as well as the highest of his subjects—to have a good time too.

He cared a great deal about the alleviation of pain and suffering. His patronage of hospitals was something which he undertook not as a mere Royal duty, nor for that matter as a fad or personal fancy; it was one expression of a deeply felt attitude toward life, a spontaneous and generous sympathy with suffering in all its forms.

Two of his remarks on this subject have been often quoted. I who knew him so well know that they came from the bottom of his heart. "The man who discovers a cure for cancer ought to have a statue to his memory in every capital of Europe." I can hear the very inflexion in his voice as he said that; and the other, about certain diseases which doctors describe as preventable, "If preventable, why not prevented?"

In 1904, when a state visit to India by the then Prince of Wales—later King George V—was being discussed, I happened to be in England, and the King sent for me in private audience at Buckingham Palace. He questioned me closely and at length about hospital conditions in India, and disclosed considerable knowledge as well as great concern. He was especially worried about the terrible state of hospitals in the big cities, particularly Calcutta, and he told me that he proposed to brief his son thoroughly on this subject and make him insist on a close, personal report on several city hospitals. He said too that he advocated the establishment of homes in the mountains, and in healthier areas of the country, for the prevention and early treatment of tuberculosis.

Nearly two years later, in the summer of 1906, the King, in another long private conversation, reverted in great detail to this subject. He commended the Prince of Wales' work along the lines he had himself indicated, and it was a commendation which I could support from my own knowledge. The King had also had a series of independent reports, and he knew that I, with a group of friends, had established a sanatorium in a hill station for the treatment of tuberculosis in its earlier stages.

King Edward's close interest in pain and sickness and their alleviation (had it something to do perhaps with his own attack of typhoid, which so nearly proved fatal?) was not prompted by his sense of kingly duty, but sprang—I am convinced—from his real humanity. It is significant, I think, that it was enhanced and deepened after his own other grave illness, just before his Coronation. He himself was dignified and brave in face of physical pain; but he disliked it exceedingly and sought to diminish its assaults—for others more than for himself.

It has been widely held that King Edward was anti-German, and that he had a prejudice against Germany as a nation because he did not get on well with his nephew, the Kaiser William II. The evidence to the contrary is strong, both from the King's own lips and from witnesses as reliable as Baron von Eckardstein and Count Wolf Metternich—both of whom held positions of influence and authority in their respective periods in the Embassy in London—who went out of their way to tell me that the King was completely sincere in his desire for friendship between Britain and Germany, and that he strove, to the utmost of his ability, to remain on good terms with his nephew. That there were deep and subtle personal differences and difficulties between them cannot be denied. The relationship was almost bound to be strained. The Kaiser acceded to his throne as a very young man, and for a decade or more he was in full control of all the affairs of state in his own country; whereas his uncle, a middle-aged man, chafed at not being allowed any sort of responsibility and indeed not being allowed even to read the Foreign Office papers. The Kaiser was never the most tactful or self-effacing of men; in twentieth-century terms he suffered from an enormous inferiority complex. He never forgot to assert himself. His uncle strove valiantly to repress his natural irritation; it was rarely indeed that he blew up, or behaved toward his nephew other than with courtesy and consideration, albeit tinged with the irony which a sage and experienced man of the world could command.

King Edward had a stern sense of decorum; he knew what was

fitting in a King and what was fitting in behavior toward a King. He strongly disliked anybody's taking liberties or taking advantage of his own urbanity and kindness. But I do know of several examples of lapses which earned his peremptory disapproval; yet when the delinquent either wrote directly to His Majesty and apologized or asked for pardon through one of the officials of the palace, and demonstrated that he sincerely regretted his offense, the King not only forgave but forgot, and the offender was never shown the slightest hostility or coldness. King Edward was genuinely magnanimous.

He also possessed a great fund of considerate tact in matters great and small. One winter a wealthy and well-known American resident in Paris, a Mrs. Moore, who was the King's friend and mine (the King was often her guest at dinner at Biarritz), was visiting London. The King called on her one bleak afternoon, when there had been a hard frost all day. Mrs. Moore received the King in her warm drawing room upstairs, and he stayed to tea by her fireside. A few minutes after he had taken his leave there was a knock on the drawing-room door. A Royal footman came in and gave her a note. It was a habit of the King always to have paper, pencils and small envelopes close at hand so that he might jot down any ideas that occurred to him. The King's note to Mrs. Moore that winter afternoon warned her that when she went out she must be very careful because the pavement was slippery and she might easily fall and hurt herself. The King sat waiting in his car until the footman came back from delivering the message.

I recall one occasion when he showed the same tact toward me, and after forty-four years I can still give the precise time and place. It was the Friday of Ascot Week in 1909. The King had asked me to luncheon in the Royal Box. I was sitting at His Majesty's table. When the main dish was served, the waiters by-passed me, a little to my surprise, and then a couple of cutlets were put in front of me.

The King called to me across the table in his strong, deep voice. "I thought you wouldn't like the thing on the menu," he said, "so I ordered those cutlets for you."

I glanced at my neighbor's plate and saw a piece of ham on it.

The King had realized that I, as a Muslim, would not want to eat the ham, nor would I like to refuse what was put before me at his table, so carefully he had made his own arrangements.

Digressing for a moment, may I say this sort of tact is essential for people in high places. During Lord Curzon's viceroyalty the eldest son of the then Amir of Afghanistan paid a state visit to Calcutta. On the night of his arrival a special state banquet was given in his honor. I was one of the guests; I sat opposite the Afghan Prince and had a front-row view of a lamentable affair. To my dismay I realized that the soup was well laced with sherry; before the Prince had time to lift his first spoonful to his lips, the political agent who was sitting beside him said in officious and self-important tones: "Your Highness, there is sherry in this soup."

In supposed strict conformity with Muslim canons, the Prince put aside his soup untouched. His fish course had nothing obnoxious about it and he tucked into it happily enough. The first entree had some slices of ham in it, and sadly the Prince watched that go past him. Then there was a vegetable dish, and it was clearly, blatantly decorated with bits of bacon fat. All the main part of the dinner was thus an unprofitable blank for the poor Prince. At last came the ice cream. Eagerly the Prince prepared to attack it.

"Your Highness," said the officious politico, "it's got chartreuse in it."

Resignedly the Prince put his spoon down again—and compensated himself, in the end, with a cheese savory and some dessert. It was curious that Lord Curzon never had the slightest awareness that his chief guest left the table hungry. It was all the more odd in that Lord Curzon in his own house—I was more than once his guest at Hackwood—was the most considerate and thoughtful host imaginable. The explanation was, I suppose, that as Viceroy he left the day-to-day running of his house to his staff, and someone blundered—in a fashion which Lord Curzon would never have permitted in his own home.

I will confess that I myself have been embroiled in a similar disaster—in Bombay, and at the Willington Club of all places, whose head steward was a Parsee. I gave a big dinner party at which a number of Hindu Maharajahs were my guests. I went to the Club beforehand and told the steward who my guests were to be; I said that they were very strict about their food and that of course on no account should beef be served.

"I understand, Your Highness," said he. "I shall be very careful. Nothing wrong will happen, I assure you."

We sat down to dinner, quite an assemblage of Hindu Maharajahs, some of them Rajputs of the most orthodox religious outlook. Everything went along agreeably until the main course was served. Then to my horror I saw plate after big plate of ox-tongue. My guests could well construe this miserable *faux-pas* as a direct and studied insult; I apologized abjectly. As soon as dinner was over, I found the steward and rated him soundly.

"What on earth were you up to? I warned you not to serve beef!"

"But, Your Highness," he expostulated, "they were ox-tongues."

He was a Parsee, he had lived in India all his life, and incredible as it may seem, he still thought that ox-tongue would not count as beef.

The effect of this kind of prohibition or instruction about diet, imposed in one's childhood, with the sanction of religion to support it and the tradition probably of many centuries, is strong and long enduring. I remember that I was once dining in Europe with an Indian friend, a Hindu, a man of profound learning and wide culture, whose reaction when a calf's head was put on the table was one of obvious shock and deep distress. He seemed to be almost on the edge of a nervous collapse. A few days later when I asked him why—apart from a quite understandable religious disapproval— he had been so upset, he said that for him to see a calf's head thus displayed on a table was as immediately horrifying as if a human baby's head had been offered.

"How would you feel," he said, "if the chef cooked you a baby's head and served it in aspic, tastefully garnished?"

There is no ready answer. I once asked another friend, a wise and highly educated Brahmin, a Cambridge scholar, whether he— who had never had any animal food in his life, except milk products, and whose ancestors for two thousand years or so had never touched eggs, fish or meat—had any instinctive feeling of repulsion to this kind of food.

He hesitated for a long time and at length answered, "You know, if you had been brought up as I have been, I doubt if you would ever, all your life, get over the instinctive horror of the stink of meat or fish or eggs."

Well, I have wandered some distance from London in that far-off summer of 1898, a long way from my first introduction to London society. I have spoken of its gaieties, its splendors, its race meetings, its garden parties, its great dinners, its nights at the opera, perhaps after the opera a final, late-night call at the Marlborough, and a chat with the Prince of Wales—he had a way of dropping in at the club on his way home for a last drink (hot water, lemon and gin it always was)—but I must not give the impression that I spent all my time frivolously.

My friend Professor Haffkine in Bombay had given me more than one introduction to distinguished scientists in England, including Lord Lister, the great surgeon, who was most hospitable. I also met Lord Kelvin, then the doyen of English scientists, who (as I have remarked elsewhere) assured me that flying in heavier-than-air machines was a physical impossibility. I was often the guest of the Baroness Burdett-Coutts, at whose house I met several of the leading spiritualists of the period.

I called too on Miss Florence Nightingale. She and the Baroness, next to Queen Victoria herself, were the most eminent women of the time. Though by now advanced in years and a complete invalid, confined to a sofa in her drawing room in her Park Lane home, Miss Nightingale retained a formidable interest in affairs. One of the topics on which she kept herself most closely and fully informed was the British administration of India—especially so far as it concerned matters of health and hygiene. Over the years she had constituted herself an august unofficial adviser to the Raj, although she had never been to India. Both the India Office and the War Office knew the strength and urgency of Miss Nightingale's memoranda. No newly appointed Viceroy would have dared, before he left

England to take up his appointment, to omit a call on Miss Nightingale, and for all of them a profitable and helpful experience it proved to be. She laid out the plans for the system of military cantonments established for British garrisons all over India; she devised a medical administrative system, and systems of pay and allowances which subsisted almost without change in detail, certainly without change in principle, until the end of British rule in India.

It was perfectly natural that I should call on her. Lytton Strachey, that entertaining but far from reliable historian, chose in his essay on Miss Nightingale in *Eminent Victorians* to give an account of my first visit to her which is a ludicrous caricature. What he omits to mention is that we became fast friends and that I went back to see her again and again. Naturally enough she talked at length, eloquently and earnestly, about what could and could not be done for the betterment of health in India, particularly among women and children.

I ventured, however, on more general topics. I was, as I have indicated, a serious young man, and I asked Miss Nightingale whether she thought that there had been any real improvement in human affairs since her youth, whether faith in God had extended and deepened. Lytton Strachey waxed sarcastic about my question, but I still think it was very much to the point. Miss Nightingale, anyway, saw it as such, and discussed it with the gravity with which I had propounded it. After all, there had occurred in Miss Nightingale's lifetime (and in mine it has been redoubled) a vast and rapid increase in man's power to exploit his natural resources—from steam propulsion to the internal combustion engine and thence to atomic fission—whose relation to or divorce from faith in God and all that such faith means in action, is a topic of some importance. Miss Nightingale did not see fit, like Mr. Lytton Strachey, to dismiss it with a snigger; she gave me her views on it and she honored me henceforth with her friendship.

That same summer I met another great figure in the history of the British Army, Field Marshal Lord Wolseley. Sir Alfred Lyall gave a breakfast party at which the guests were Leonard Courtney, the Liberal writer and politician (later Lord Courtney), Mr. Paul, historian and editor, Lord Wolseley and myself. Somebody mentioned Mr. Gladstone, and the Field Marshal immediately launched into a passionate denunciation of Gladstone and all his works; there was no word too bad for him, none of us could get a sentence in, and we sat listening to an unbridled tirade. Gladstone was the most evil and destructive influence of his time, responsible for a catastrophic decline in Britain's prestige and authority in Europe and throughout the world, responsible for the disaster in the Sudan, personally accountable for the death of General Gordon— in short and despite the fact that at least half the population of England idolized him (irrespective of what the other half thought), a malefactor who ought not to be at large in civilized society.

Although Lord Wolseley's depth of feeling and degree of outspokenness surprised me greatly at Sir Alfred Lyall's breakfast table, I subsequently came to recognize this attitude and manner, in regard to Gladstone, as not unusual. I remember that when Gladstone died, although the tone of public comment was respectful, society's private remarks as I heard them at dinner parties or in great country houses (and the most influential sections of society were Conservative and Unionist) were fiercely critical and unforgiving. In latter years too I recall how the same people talked about Lloyd George (of whom I shall have a good deal to say). Even now, so I believe, a certain member of the Labor party, of Welsh origin like Lloyd George, is a ferocious bogey to his Tory opponents.

Of course in purely liberal circles one heard very different opinions. I was the guest that summer of Lord Spencer, who had been a close colleague of Gladstone's and a member of his Cabinet. He took a small house near Birmingham for the agricultural show. On the last night of my stay, when all the other guests had gone, Lord Spencer talked freely if somberly about that perennially critical issue in British politics in the Victorian Age, the Irish Question. This was 1898; Gladstone's attempt to introduce Home Rule had long been shipwrecked; Lord Salisbury's Unionist Government was securely in power, and its Irish policy consisted of "firm government"—associated with Arthur Balfour's name—and attempts to tackle the thorny problem of land tenure. Lord Spencer insisted that there was no way of settling Ireland's problems except by giving her full political freedom, that twenty years—or two hundred years—of police rule would not make the Irish "loyal" or submissive; that a great chance had been missed in 1886 and that it would not occur again; the inevitable consequences, soon or late, would be an armed rebellion, with all its accompanying bloodshed and murder, and at the end the loss of Ireland to the Empire. Within a quarter of a century every detail of the prophecy to which I listened that summer night in 1898 was to be meticulously fulfilled. And in India there were those who watched the working out of Ireland's destiny and were fully cognizant of the lessons it taught, the message it signaled across the world.

Back in London I saw the season through to the end; and then in August when English society began its stately annual exodus to Cowes and to Scotland, I set forth on my European travels again, to Paris once more and thence to Geneva and Lausanne, to Italy and to Vienna, still then the capital city of a great, historic Empire.

During this otherwise pleasant summer I was greatly shocked and saddened by a grievous piece of news from India. A near kinsman, Hashim Shah, whose father was my elder half-brother, was murdered by a steward in my house in Poona. Mercifully this was not, as the assassinations in Jeddah in 1896 had been, prompted by motives of religious fanaticism, but the outcome of personal resentment and some personal grudge. However, its warning could not be discounted; there was an element of lawlessness and violence in my own close surroundings which would, sooner or later, have to be dealt with firmly if it were not to become a running sore in the life of Bombay and Poona.

Part Two

❦

YOUNG MANHOOD

❧ V ❧

Monarchs, Diplomats and Politicians

M Y EXPERIENCES IN LONDON and during my Continental tour widened my horizons and stimulated my growing interest in— and desire to play my part in—the world of politics and diplomacy. Not long after my arrival in England I was in touch with and was soon fully in the confidence of Sir William Lee Warner, the head of the Political Department of the India Office, the department which handled all the secret and confidential aspects of foreign relations. Through my friendship with a leading race horse owner, Sir J. B. Maple (founder and head of the big furniture store which bears his name), I made the acquaintance of his son-in-law, Baron von Eckardstein, who, since the Ambassador was a sick man, was in virtual charge of the German Embassy.

In the close and frequent company of these friends of mine I was able to observe at first hand the working out of a series of diplomatic moves of considerable importance. There was a growing awareness in certain circles in Britain that that "splendid isolation," which had seemed so natural and desirable only a short time before, had its grave disadvantages. The South African crisis was soon to reveal sharply how truly isolated Britain was; the depth and bitterness of anti-British feeling throughout Europe were far too pronounced to ignore. The leading spirit in Lord Salisbury's Cabinet in these years was Mr. Joseph Chamberlain, the Colonial Secretary, a realist, despite the sometimes visionary nature of his imperialist ideals, who was acutely cognizant of the dangers of Britain's situation. Surveying the trends of world power at that time he believed that it might be possible to reach an understanding with Germany, and he saw clearly the perils ahead if that understanding were not reached. His official biography* has lately revealed the extent and the pertinacity of Chamberlain's efforts to secure an Anglo-German entente.

My own recollections confirm this to the hilt. It was a sincere and strenuous effort on Britain's part to achieve an understanding; and it failed solely because of the German attitude, which was the result of the outlook and prejudices of the chief German negotiators, Prince von Bülow and Herr von Holstein. Not only did I watch the British approaches; I was fully cognizant of the German reactions to them, through my friendship with von Eckardstein. I could see how sad Eckardstein became at the constant rejection of Britain's sincere hand of friendship—a rejection always based on new and artificial pretexts and evasions. It is sad indeed to reflect on the long-term results of the breakdown of these negotiations. Might not the course of history in the twentieth century have been profoundly different had Chamberlain succeeded in averting the steady, implacable growth of Anglo-German antagonism? Would we not quite possibly have avoided two world wars? Had the Germans played the game, this would certainly have happened; but the great question mark for European peace lay always in Germany's attitude.

The temperament of the two Germans involved in these negotiations prevented them from rising to the greatness of the chance they were given. They had grown up in the shadow of the great Bismarck, but they were not of his quality of statesmanship. They were essentially small bureaucrats with all of Bismarck's arrogance, and they were ineradicably suspicious of what they thought of as British cunning and perfidy.

Long, long afterward Lord Rennell—formerly Sir Rennell Rodd, and for many years British Ambassador in Rome—told me that after the First World War, when Prince von Bülow was living in retirement in Rome, they discussed this whole episode. Von Bülow

* The Life of Joseph Chamberlain, Vol. III, by J. L. Garvin; Vol. IV, by Julian Amery (London, Macmillan & Co. Ltd.).

admitted with great hesitation and ruefully that he had been wrong to reject the hand of friendship which had been offered by Britain in sincerity and earnestness of purpose.

When my first European tour ended, I set off for East Africa. This, however, was no pleasure jaunt. One or two delicate and important tasks demanding the exertion of a certain amount of diplomatic skill and finesse awaited me there. There were several Ismaili settlements down the coast, which were rapidly increasing in numbers and in wealth; and more than one of these communities was involved in disputes—by no means of a trifling character—with the local authorities.

East Africa was at the beginning of its rapid, even sensational, opening up and development, but at the turn of the century it presented a very different picture from that which it presents today. Several European powers with colonial aspirations were embroiled, down the thousands of miles from the Red Sea to the Cape, in what proved to be a late but dramatic phase of the scramble for Africa. Abyssinia, the only native African state with expansionist ambitions, had lately collided, bloodily but victoriously, with the Italians. At the Battle of Aduwa in 1896 Ras Makonen, the able lieutenant and ultimate successor of the Emperor Menelik, had heavily defeated an Italian army and put an end, for over thirty years, to Italy's efforts to extend her somewhat precarious coastal foothold. The British, having entered into a treaty with the Sultan of Zanzibar, established what was then known as the East African Protectorate (today the flourishing colony of Kenya with its complex multiracial community), with its base at Mombasa, under the supervision of the Foreign Office; and shortly afterward there were projects of settlement being put forward by Lord Delamere and others, in what came to be called "the white highlands" in the hinterland of the Protectorate.

Southward the Germans had staked their claims inland from Dar es Salaam in the territories now known as Tanganyika. Farther south the Portuguese, who were the first Europeans to venture into these regions in the great age of exploration, had an old-established colony. And inland from this, Jameson and his pioneers were carv-

ing out of the empty veld and savannahs the lands which were to
become Northern and Southern Rhodesia. And to the south again
the British and the Boers were already committed to the long, grim
struggle of the South African War.

If the beginnings of future economic prosperity and greatness
were already visible in the Africa which I visited for the first time
in 1899, no less noticeable were the seeds of future political and social difficulties and problems.

Zanzibar, which I visited first, was an ancient seat of Arab culture. The Sultan no longer exercised absolute powers but was a
constitutional sovereign, acting on the advice of his British Resident and officials. Between these officials and my Ismaili followers
there had arisen a complicated dispute concerning the ownership
and tenure of a tract of land on the seashore, the value of which
had rapidly increased but which was an Ismaili burial ground.
The dispute had been stubborn and protracted. I was able, however, to arrange a settlement which was admittedly a compromise.
I confess that I have worked all my life on the principle that a
compromise is better than rigid and unyielding disagreement. The
compromise which we reached in Zanzibar was workable to this extent that there has never been any other major dispute in the years
since then between the Ismailis and the British authorities.

In Dar es Salaam I was faced with a similar sort of conflict, in
this case between the German authorities and my followers over
land trading rights. This dispute had smoldered and flickered
throughout the nineties; the Germans were suspicious of my Ismaili followers, and there were accusations that they were smug-
gling in arms and had had a hand in the Arab rebellion of some
ten years before. There was a certain stiffness on the part of the
German Governor and his officials when I first arrived. However I
persevered, and before I left I was able to see the dispute settled
and the suspicions (which were probably one cause of the stubbornness of the dispute) thoroughly dissipated. When I left, it
was in the knowledge that there was a clean slate, so far as differences between my followers and the German administration were
concerned.

From East Africa I went back to Europe for a short time. Then, as winter set in, I turned south and east. On my way home to India I visited Egypt for the first time. Those who have not experienced it, who have not been lucky enough to fall under Egypt's spell, will find it difficult, I suppose, to realize the sheer magic of the first sight of Egypt. Add that my first sight was on a perfect early winter day, and need I say that all my life since then I have had a special corner in my heart for Egypt and that I have returned there as often as I could.

There is a unique quality about Egypt's charm; the wide, tranquil skies, the extraordinary clarity of its light and atmosphere, the glories of its sunsets and its starlit nights, and its tremendous monuments of a majestic past. But I had other objects than mere sightseeing. I wanted to make personal contact with the large Ismaili community of Syria and the remnant of Egyptian Ismailis who had not yet come to see me in India. I also visited the great seat of Muslim learning, the Al Azhar University.

It was a time of momentous and stirring events. Lord Kitchener's great victory at Omdurman in the Sudan was still fresh in everyone's mind. General Wingate had just returned from the south. The Khalifeh had been killed, and the last of his dervish following exterminated.

I called on Lord Cromer, the British Resident in Egypt, whose power and authority in Egypt at that time were paramount. He said that Egypt badly needed a man like Sir Syed Ahmed, to do for its Muslim population the sort of educative and regenerative work which he had done in Aligarh. There was in Egypt at that time a deep rift between, on the one hand, the old-fashioned conservative, pious Muslim, who was contemptuous of modern science and techniques and who spoke and read Arabic and, on the other hand, the Frenchified upper classes, whose reading matter was mainly French yellow-back novels, whose meeting place was the club, whose diversions were cards and nocturnal gambling, who detested the British, yearned to see them out and longed for a return to the regime of the Khedive Ismaili. There was nothing like Aligarh to show the vast Muslim population the way toward a compromise with and understanding of modern, Western science, and to raise an elite capable of co-operating with British administrators and technicians in that process of economic and social uplift of which the country was in such desperate need.

Unfortunately the Khedive Abbas Hilmi was ill at the time—it was suspected that he had some form of paratyphoid—and I was therefore unable to see him. In later years we became great and intimate friends and I admired the brilliance of his intellect and his wide and deep knowledge of politics and history. I will have occasion to refer to him later. The Egyptian Ministers whom I met were merely nominees of the British—of Lord Cromer, in fact.

People who know only the Cairo of today can have no idea of the social conditions of the early 1900's. The hotels were full of rich foreigners, who were "wintering in Egypt," then a highly fashionable pastime. They would make trips up the Nile in hired dahabiyehs or in one of Messrs. Thomas Cook's steamers. They spent money profusely and had a high old time, surrounded by magnificent-looking Egyptian guides and alleged interpreters, who were apt to speak the most grotesque pidgin variety of every European language.

The contents of the Cairo Museum were as fascinating as they have always been, and always will be; although of course Lord Carnarvon's magnificent Tutankhamen discoveries had not yet been made, there was more then enough to see, but the arrangement of it all was less convenient than it is today. A disagreeable and irreverent custom prevailed of exposing in full view, for anyone who wanted to see them, the actual mummies—not merely the sarcophagi—of all the great Pharaohs. You could see Rameses II, with his noble hawklike features, lying in his coffin—looking almost as he had in life all those centuries ago—and other former mighty kings and conquerors, at the feet of any chance passer-by.

To me, however, more concerned with the present than the past, possibly the most remarkable fact about Cairo in those days was that it was for all practical purposes another Poona or Simla. It was even more of a citadel of British supremacy than India. The British were not merely in political control of the country; they assumed a social superiority which the Egyptians appeared humbly to accept. What little political agitation that existed was attributed to the "machinations of the Palace." The general attitude of all classes toward the British Occupying Power—its agents and officials, the British Army officers and the growing number of employees of British firms—was one of outward submissiveness and obedience. Unhappily, just as in India in the late nineties and early nineteen hundreds, there was scarcely a link between the British community, political, military and commercial, and either the Egyptian aristocracy or the well-to-do *bourgeoisie* of Cairo and Alexandria. When rich Egyptians came to Europe, they went to Paris, to Switzerland, to Austria or Germany or Italy; they carefully kept clear of England. Few of the winter tourists, except for some individuals from the Continent, bothered to get to know Egypt's upper and middle classes. Even the Gezira Sporting Club, in the heart of the metropolitan Cairo, barred Egyptians from its membership other than in very exceptional cases. The only non-British whom the British encountered—except for their office subordinates and their servants—were the members of a few wealthy Levantine families who sought to identify themselves completely with the ruling power and were thus accepted. The depth and virulence of this social division can be seen in the fact that I myself, who naturally in my European travels met Egyptians—largely of the aristocracy and members of the ruling dynasty—seldom met one of them when I was in Cairo except in their own homes. There was really no common ground of social intercourse. Inevitably, therefore, behind the façade of humility there developed a sullen and brooding, almost personal, resentment which later on needlessly, bitterly poisoned the clash of Egyptian nationalism with Britain's interests as the Occupying Power. After three weeks or so in Cairo I went home to India, where the work I had done had not passed unnoticed by those concerned. The Sultan of Zanzibar bestowed on me the highest order in his gift, the Brilliant Star of Zanzibar, and later the German Emperor awarded me the Royal Prussian Order of the Crown (First Class).

From India I made a brief tour of Burma and met my followers there for the first time. I recall one somewhat daunting experience. A Muslim of my acquaintance—not one of my followers—had been very kind to me and had helped me in a variety of ways. I called on him to thank him, and as we exchanged courtesies he sent for a glass of sherbet for me. It was brought. The tall tumbler was held out toward me by a servant, and I saw that the hands that held it were the hands of a leper. Time seemed suspended as I stared horror-struck. I found every excuse I could, said that I was not thirsty, tried to get out of accepting the tumbler still held out toward me. But my host earnestly pressed me and went on pressing me. At last I shut my eyes, took the tumbler and gulped the sherbet down; but the horror of those hands remained.

I was back in Europe in 1900, and in Paris in that year—the year of the Great Exhibition—met the Shah Musafaradin of Persia. No other Shah, in my view, did more to harm Persia than he did. He was sickly, he was weak and he was grossly ignorant. He was capricious and extravagant, squandering gifts on his favorites, and incapable of any awareness of his duties and obligations as Shah. All the treasure which his father, Nasruddin, had amassed in fifty years of prudent and capable rule, he dissipated in folly and waste. He had a childish, pitiable passion for the silliest, most costly gadgets—musical boxes, for example, adorned with jewels and gold and silver, and on these and similar trumpery objects he spent a fortune. It was no wonder that making a pun on his name, Musafaradin, the Persian intelligentsia nicknamed him *"mauvaise affaire,"* and their gibe was taken up by foreigners in Tehran.

He was indeed a *"mauvaise affaire"* for his country. Since I was his relative, connected with him on my father's and my mother's sides of the family, he received me with eager affection, gave me one of his highest decorations and made me presents of diamond ornaments. But he was a sad nincompoop. Talking to him was like talking to a child—and not a very intelligent child at that. His infantile outlook and behavior were sustained and exploited, for his own purposes, by his Prime Minister, the all-powerful Atabeg, who in his morning audiences with his sovereign did not give him serious reports but told him the sort of fantastic fairy tales a grown-up man will tell a small child to keep him entertained.

When I saw the poor man I happened to mention that I had just been to Burma.

"Oh!" said he, "haven't the Burmans heads far bigger than other human beings?"

When he was in Paris he heard about Monsieur and Madame Curie and their discovery of radium. He asked to be shown radium at work. The two distinguished scientists said that they would come to his hotel and give him a demonstration of the properties of radium; but they explained that absolute darkness would be necessary for the demonstration. One of the hotel cellars was turned into a dark room; black curtains were put up and all light was completely shut out. The Shah and some of his courtiers went down to the cellar. Monsieur and Madame Curie arrived and produced a piece of radium whose vivid glow lit up the whole room. Suddenly the Shah took fright. He began to scream and shout and run round the room. He raved and ranted and accused the Curies of trying to murder him.

The Curies were not used to this kind of treatment and, much affronted, they took their leave. The Shah was at last made to understand that he had gravely hurt their feelings. As a recompense he awarded each of them one of his highest decorations, and for good measure he ordered each star to be set in diamonds. Off went the baubles to the Curies, who stiffly returned them with formal thanks, pointing out that they had been exposed to far too gross an insult to be able to accept anything of this kind.

Naturally the Shah had to go up the Eiffel Tower, and, naturally, about halfway up he panicked; the lift had to be stopped and he had to be brought down again.

His behavior in public and in private was deplorable. Since I am myself of Iranian descent and a member of the then ruling dynasty, the Kajar family, I was acutely aware of the shame and humiliation of it. So too were Iranian statesmen and diplomats, who were scandalized at what he was doing to his own and his country's reputation. We all tried to cloak it as much as we could and made excuses about his ill health, which had a certain basis of truth because he was a chronic sufferer from kidney trouble.

His folly, of course, had different, deeper roots. He exhibited, in an especially lurid light, all the dangers of the old-fashioned autocratic Oriental monarchy. However incompetent, silly or criminal such a despot was, not one of the able and intelligent statesmen of the world around him ever stood up to him and told him the truth about himself. The mysterious prestige surrounding kingship and the blood of kings induced a kind of mental paralysis even in good and sincere men, so that they were quite unable—in the interests of their king and their country, even in their own interests—to give true advice and guidance. From what I have been told by distinguished Russian friends, this sort of atmosphere prevailed in Czarist Russia. Did it disappear, I wonder, even in Stalinist Russia? You could not call the men who were thus paralyzed cowards; they were not time-servers, they were not utterly lacking in courage or scruples. It was simply that for them such divinity hedged their king that it was not a matter merely of pardoning his follies and weaknesses—for them those follies and weaknesses simply did not exist. Again and again history teaches this lesson: a tough, self-made man founds a dynasty, his frailer descendants bolster themselves with this atmosphere of semidivinity, and then the dynasty collapses and the process starts anew, unless, as happened in Japan for centuries, the semidivine monarch is shut up in his palace, unapproachable, invisible, and all power is exercised on his behalf by mayors of the palace. Poor Musafaradin was a glaring example of the more pitiable defects of this kind of despotism.

From Paris I went on to Berlin. There I met von Holstein at luncheon—one of the two men responsible for frustrating the attempts to achieve an Anglo-German understanding. He was a gray, withdrawn, taciturn man who ate heartily and said little. I also had an audience with the Kaiser at Potsdam. William II was then, I suppose, at the summit of his strange and ill-starred career. To me he was gracious and cordial. I had been warned that he was acutely sensitive about his physical deformity and disliked having his withered left arm looked at. But members of his court and others who knew him said that the curiosity of human beings is such that everybody, meeting the Kaiser for the first time, found his gaze drawn automatically and irresistibly to the left side of his uniform. While I awaited my audience I said to myself over and over again, "You won't look at his arm, you *won't* look at his arm."

He strode into the room; my eyes became a law unto themselves, and there I was staring at his left arm. Fortunately for me, I suppose, he must have been so accustomed to this that he did not let it diminish the warmth and courtesy of his greeting.

He held out his right hand and shook hands with me. This was literally a crushing experience. As a compensation for his deformity the Kaiser had, from childhood, determined that his right hand and arm should be so strong that they would do the work of two. He took constant, vigorous exercise; every day he had at least twenty minutes' fencing; he played lawn tennis often for two hours at a time, and undertook all manner of other remedial exercises. The result was an immense development of strength in his right hand and arm; one of its effects was this appallingly powerful handshake. I am told that mine was no unusual experience. The Duchess of Teck (later the Marchioness of Cambridge) told me that she—like most other women with whom His Imperial Majesty shook hands—had the greatest difficulty in not letting out a cry of pain as he took her hand in his.

I am sure that he was quite unconscious of what he was doing. He was far too great a gentleman to do it on purpose; but just as our eyes went to his withered arm, so his subconscious made him exert this violent physical strength.

Looking back, I realize that I was having a good many audiences with monarchs at this time. Later in this same year I went to Constantinople. The Sultan, Abdul Hamid, made me his guest at the Pera Palace Hotel, and I had a long audience with him at the Yildiz Palace. This encounter was the subject of a good deal of rather wild political speculation—most of it arrant guesswork—at the time and subsequently. The Sultan was also Caliph and therefore the recognized head of the whole Sunni branch of the Islamic world, and I was the head of the Ismaili section of the Shias. The grounds for speculation were obvious.

Our meeting had for me, I must say, its own rather curious flavor of drama. Abdul Hamid lived then in neurotic fear of assassination.* He was a chain smoker, and I have all my life been, as they say, allergic to cigarettes. When I was ushered into his room, the doors were immediately locked, and the Sultan and I were alone except for an interpreter. I do not speak Turkish and Abdul Hamid, though I believe he could read both Arabic and Persian, refused to speak either of these languages. The room was warm and cigarette smoke hung stale and heavy in the air. The Sultan sat huddled in an enormous greatcoat, with field marshal's epaulettes heavy on its shoulders. Slowly I realized that this bulky and cumbrous garment was armored, and about as bulletproof as was possible in those days. Did he think, I wondered, that I had come there to murder him?

Over the lapels of the overcoat a strange and somewhat sinister countenance confronted me. For Abdul Hamid wore heavy make-up—his beard dyed black, his lips carmined, his cheeks rouged and his eyebrows made up to an extent that was comic. He might have been a clown in a circus, but his eyes glowed in this preposterous make-up. Yet this *maquillage* was no expression of the effeminacy of perversion; he was most virile, the sire of many children and the affectionate husband and protector of a large harem.

Our conversation was amiable and courteous. I recall that he was interested and impressed by the fact that I, by way of Kashgar and Sinkiang, had up-to-date and reliable information about the Muslims of western China.

It was said that as an aspect of his neurosis about assassination, every particle of food sent up to him had to be tasted by several

* It is interesting and not without irony to realize that the word "assassin," which has its special contemporary meaning, was first applied many centuries ago to my ancestors and their Ismaili followers. From time immemorial, small and oppressed minorities have had to be given a bad name—after all, you cannot kill a dog unless you give it a bad name—and in the Middle Ages the Ismailis were such a minority, fighting for their lives and their rights. Their oppressors had to give them a bad name, they associated the Ismailis with the manufacture and use of the drug hashish, and it was alleged that they were addicts. The bad name, thus invented, stuck.

people on the way, including the cook. As I had no meal with him I cannot vouch fully for the truth of this story, but I do know that he had an idea that the food at my hotel was not particularly good, so twice every day a landau drove up from the palace with a cargo of china wash basins filled with excellent dishes, both Turkish and Persian, prepared for me in the palace and sent to me by Abdul Hamid's express command.

From Constantinople I made my way home to India to tackle a task in my household and entourage—a cleaning-up job of nightmare complexity which was to demand a great deal of energy, patience and endurance for many months to come.

VI

The Edwardian Era Begins

THE MURDER of my kinsman at Poona in the summer of 1898 had emphasized, in the most sensational and unpleasant fashion, the disruptive qualities latent in the huge, ramshackle, feudally extravagant household and entourage which I had inherited, and which I have in previous chapters described at some length.

I was responsible by now for a dependent population of about two thousand people in my households in Bombay and Poona. I actually supported them—most of them in idleness. They were housed and fed at my expense. The financial burden, considerable as it was, was not as worrying as certain other thoroughly undesirable aspects of their manner of life.

When my grandfather left Persia, he took with him—as seemed to him natural and proper—the train of a medieval prince. But in Bombay in the last years of the nineteenth century we were not living in the Middle Ages.

There was not only the immediate family, which was large enough. During the earlier part of his wanderings my grandfather was accompanied by a troop of cavalry, who fought under his command in Persia and in Afghanistan, and later rendered redoubtable assistance to Sir Charles Napier in his conquest of Sind. At the beginning these numbered probably some two hundred, some of princely birth, some knights and peasants, but all devoted in their allegiance to my grandfather. When he settled in Bombay they settled around him—were they not his liegemen who had endured and fought in his company?—and long before I was born and throughout my childhood, there they were, aging warriors whose battles were done, in houses or rooms dotted about the rambling estate, with their families growing up around them. Some of them, after they had settled down, sent for their wives from Iran, but most of them married Indian wives.

These ex-soldiers and their families were not all. During the fifties followers came in fair numbers from Central Asia, from Turkestan and Sinkiang, from Bokhara and Afghanistan, to offer their loyalty and bring their tribute to my grandfather. Some returned to their own distant homes, but some stayed, and those who stayed took Indian wives or married the daughters of those who had settled earlier. Some Ismailis came from Africa and they brought Negro slaves, but when they went home some of their slaves refused to go and stayed in Bombay. Intermarrying and multiplying, all these diverse elements had grown, by 1898 or thereabouts, into a vast assembly of two thousand people, men, women and children, with little or nothing to do and nothing to occupy them, with no background and no roots. In my grandfather's time and in my father's time (though they were not of course as numerous), their dependent status was taken for granted, and throughout my long minority my mother really had no choice but to go on housing and feeding them. As one generation aged and another grew up (after all, half a century and more had gone by since my grandfather exiled himself from Persia), the whole affair took on, in the view of those who accepted our bounty, the air of a custom established in right.

The old soldiers, of course, took pensions from my grandfather. As they died off, the pensions continued to be paid, first by my father and then by my mother during my minority; but the original sum had to be divided among its first recipient's descendants. These were often so numerous that by the late nineties the actual incomes received by all these beneficiaries were small. Most of them augmented their incomes in one way or another—as race-course tipsters or as stable-hands, for example. Long years of this rather raffish, irresponsible life, in and around the rapidly growing city and port of Bombay, had not tended to make particularly worthy or useful citizens of them. But they came of high-spirited, proud stock, and their natural energies and abilities were now being dissipated in intrigues and feuds. Quick to take offense, they were apt to be quick, too, in drawing the knife.

Dangerous as the potentialities were, the situation had not been too bad until the murder of my kinsman in Poona. This, as it were, touched off a fuse. From then on any attempt to control this nest of hornets, internally by the household or from the outside by the police, met with fierce threats. While I was on my travels I was warned that if I tried to clear up a clutter of ne'er-do-wells, who had become a scandal and a menace, my life too would be in danger.

I was determined however to put an end to this situation. The police in Bombay were extremely anxious for me to do nothing too summary or too rash, such as stopping all pensions and turning the lot out into the street. Idle, well-fed, unruly, two thousand of them from half-a-dozen races in Africa, Central Asia, Persia and Afghanistan, suddenly loose among the population of Bombay as vagrants, would be a real public danger. And it was a danger which the Government—as I was given firmly to understand—was not prepared to allow.

It was essential, therefore, that if I were to deal with my problem, I must act all the time with the full support of the Government and in close co-operation with the police. It was particularly fortunate that I was on terms of warm friendship and understanding with Sir William Lee Warner at the India Office. He was a tower of strength in the background. In Bombay itself a new Governor, Lord Northcote, had succeeded Lord Sandhurst; he too sustained me with his constant friendship and helped me through an extremely difficult task. Without allies of this stature and authority it would have been immeasurably more difficult.

As it was, I went at it gradually and persistently. Some of the rowdiest and unruliest of all were technically not British subjects; these were deported to the Persian Gulf and turned loose in regions where their propensities were less dangerous than in populous, urban Bombay. To a number I gave lump-sum gratuities, on condition that they too took themselves off. One group I got sent off, with the help of the police, to remote hill stations, whence they were forbidden to make their way back to Bombay. With the removal of the worst among the older malcontents, we were able to get down to the more agreeable task of reclaiming and educating their children. We set up schools for them and some went to the Jesuit schools nearby; some who were conspicuously bright went on to a higher university education. They all went out to work, and the majority of them are now, I am glad to say, and have long since been, worthy and law-abiding citizens. Among them may be counted barristers, engineers, senior officers of the I.M.S. and prosperous members of other professions.

But the clean-up was not an easy job, and it was not completed in a day. It was a long struggle that was with me for many months.

Meanwhile, engrossed as I was in this arduous and unpleasant job, I had not lost touch with the wider world. Queen Victoria's death in January, 1901, seemed the end of an age to those of us who had been born and had grown up under the ample and glorious shade of her long reign. We were conscious that Finis had been written to a mighty chapter.

My friend and patron, the Prince of Wales, was now upon the throne, with the title of Edward VII. He graciously honored me with a personal invitation to be present at his Coronation in 1902. Therefore, to London I returned that summer, to a London which I knew well, to a society in which I had many friends and where I was made warmly and happily welcome. Already it was possible to recognize that the Edwardian Age was opening. There was a new tone noticeable in society, a shift of standards, a recognition of the meaning and challenge of the new century.

At first it was a gay and eventful summer. There was a whole round of shows and entertainments, and a great deal of hospitality was shown to me and the other Indian Princes and Maharajahs who had been invited. Suddenly on the eve of the Coronation the King, who was no longer a young man, was taken ill. Few, I think, at the time were really aware of the gravity of the King's illness, and the narrowness of his escape. Appendicitis was not in those days the almost routine affair it is considered today, and an appendectomy was a serious and danger-fraught operation. The Coronation had to be postponed; the ceremonies and rejoicings were held in suspense; many of the distinguished foreign Royal guests, unable to wait as long as was obviously necessary, took their leave and went home. The King made a wonderful, rapid recovery from his operation, and by August was willing, nay eager, to face the strain and fatigue of the elaborate and beautiful Coronation ceremony. It was not generally realized at the time that during much of the service the King, who bore himself with great dignity throughout, was in considerable pain.

For myself there was one particularly gratifying circumstance connected with the Coronation. The King advanced me from the rank of K.C.I.E. to G.C.I.E. in his Coronation Honors.

In accordance with custom there was a great Coronation naval review at Spithead, which I had the privilege of attending as the King's guest aboard his own yacht. Among the other guests there was, I remember, the thin, slight but formidable figure of Ras Makonen, the Abyssinian feudal chieftain who was the victorious general, right-hand man and Viceroy of the Emperor Menelik, whom he subsequently succeeded. He possessed the quality of inscrutability. I recall that the British Minister in Addis Ababa told me that he could always read Menelik's mind and divine his intentions, but never Ras Makonen's. The mutability of human affairs is aptly illustrated by the vicissitudes endured by his son, Ras Tafari, who became the Emperor Haile Selassie, resisted the Italian invasion of his country in 1935, was defeated and driven into exile, pleaded his cause before the League of Nations in Geneva, then bided his time in exile and in 1941, when the Italians were crushingly defeated in East Africa (by a small, valiant army to which India contributed magnificently), returned in triumph to his throne. Surely this is one of the most extraordinary romances of our time, in danger of being forgotten because there have been so many other romantic and strange stories.

I returned to India in November of that year, 1902. I was surprised to find waiting for me a letter from the Viceroy, Lord Curzon, asking me to become a member of his Legislative Council. This was a considerable honor to a young man still in his twenties (I was by far the youngest member), for the Viceroy's Legislative Council in those days was a small, select body of influential people, wielding real authority. My acceptance necessitated my moving, for the time being, to Calcutta, which was then the seat of British power in India.

The two years in which I was a member of the Legislative Council (I was asked if I would accept nomination a second time, but I refused) had a profound and permanent effect on my life and character, in their private and personal as well as their public aspects. For the first time in my life I had a real, normal home of my own, with the ordinary complement of servants and the ordinary social and domestic life of a man in my station, free of the extraordinary accretion of hangers-on and ne'er-do-wells (remnants of whom never entirely disappeared from Bombay and Poona) whose disruptive and menacing activities I have described earlier in this chapter.

The effect on my public and political life was hardly less marked. I found myself working alongside men of the caliber and quality of Lord Curzon himself and of the Commander in Chief, the redoubtable Field Marshal Lord Kitchener of Khartoum. Among my Indian colleagues there was the brilliant Mr. G. K. Gokhale, the outstanding Indian nationalist statesman until the rise of Mahatma Gandhi and the Nehrus, father and son. Gokhale and I struck up a friendship which ended only with his death. He was a caste Hindu and I was a Muslim, but our friendship crossed the barriers of creed and race. He was a man of vision, courage and generosity. His influence on my thought and outlook was probably considerable. Not of course that he was the first political thinker of a different background from my own with whom I had come in contact, or with whom I found the exchange of ideas stimulating. Some years previously in Bombay I had come to know and like Mr.

Navroji Dumasia, a talented Parsee in the service of *The Times of India* and Mr. (later Sir) Frank Brown, a British journalist and publicist who was on the staff of *The Bombay Gazette* and subsequently of *The Times*; to these friends I owe a great deal, both in what I have done and what I have tried to do in my political work.

In Gokhale I encountered a powerful as well as a lovable personality. I realized how deep and strong were the forces in India of which he was the spokesman. I also saw that the Government had become remote from the people of India, not the masses only, but the increasing and ever more articulate and active intelligentsia. I saw at close quarters how foreign the Government was in spirit and in atmosphere. On the other side, I saw that India's political leaders, dissatisfied at not having succeeded in obtaining their earlier moderate demands, had begun to seek not merely administrative reforms but the full control of their own political destiny.

For myself, I continued to pin a great deal of faith on educational advancement. Illiteracy I saw as a menace to people and Government alike. Poverty and disease were its sinister consequences and accompaniments. More than once my speeches in the Legislative Council turned into strong pleas for generous and judicious expenditures on education. I urged the adoption of a system of universal primary education such as almost every civilized country possessed, and pointed out as often as I could that in my view the fundamental cause of India's extreme poverty was India's extreme ignorance.

At the same time I began to realize, during these two crucial years, that the Congress party, the only active and responsible political organization in the country, would prove itself incapable— was already proving itself incapable—of representing India's Muslims, or of dealing adequately or justly with the needs and aspirations of the Muslim community. The pressure of Hindu extremism was too strong. Already that artificial unity which the British Raj had imposed from without was cracking. Deep-seated and ineradicable differences expressed themselves, once political activity and aspirations had advanced beyond the most elementary stage. The breach was there—in Hindu intransigence and lack of perception of basic Muslim ideals and hopes. I did all I could to prevent the breach's being widened. I maintained a campaign of remonstrance with Sir Pherozeshah Mehta, who was high in the counsels of the Congress party, who was a friend of my family and who had known me since childhood. I begged him to use his influence and to make Congress realize how important it was to win Muslim confidence, but all to no avail.

Whatever the reason for their attitude, the Congress leaders persisted in ignoring the realities of the communal situation. There were provinces in which the Muslims were in a clear majority: in Bengal, for example, and in the Punjab, out of which the Northwest Frontier Province had not then been carved. And about Delhi, Agra and Aligarh there had been built up a spiritual home, sanctified by some of the most valuable of Muslim traditions and adorned with imperishable treasures of Islamic art and culture. Some comprehension of what this meant in Muslim minds was all we asked. And the time was propitious—as never again—for an understanding; earlier grave differences of opinion with Congress had dwindled into comparative insignificance, and even the memory of them that remained could have been wiped out—as I argued as forcibly as I could—if certain of our proposals for equitable representation and a fair ratio of Government employment for Muslims had been accepted and acted upon.

The primary step was that Congress should choose as its representative on the Viceroy's Legislative Council a Muslim from Bengal or the Punjab. We drew a blank there. For Congress obstinately continued to send third-rate Muslims from preponderantly Hindu provinces like Madras and Bombay. Gokhale, I am convinced, was sincerely anxious to do all he could to change his party's attitude. He could never publicly admit it, but privately he was deeply distressed to watch his political friends and associates thus deliberately sowing the seeds of permanent disunity between Hindu and Muslim. I made frequent, urgent representations of practical, feasible steps by which we could have integrated Muslim political feeling into the Congress party and presented a united front to the British Government. Yet even the private support which Gokhale gave to my representations brought no change of mind or heart.

I turned to my friends at Aligarh, and in particular to Nawab Mohsen-ul-Molk, who had succeeded Sir Syed Ahmed as Muslim leader. Mohsen-ul-Molk was not hidebound; he was moderate and realistic and not at all antagonistic either to Congress or to Hindus in general. If there had been give-and-take in what were then quite minor matters, he would have been willing to join forces with Congress. In such an atmosphere—assisted by the existence of a joint electorate and joint representation—a political alliance between the two communities was possible. Our hopes were dashed again and again. Conditions deteriorated at the next elections; and by 1906 Mohsen-ul-Molk and I, in common with other Muslim leaders, had come to the conclusion that our only hope lay along the lines of independent organization and action, and that we must secure independent political recognition from the British Government as a nation within a nation.

While I lived in Calcutta, I came to know the Right Honorable Syed Amir Ali, later a Privy Councilor, then a Judge of the High Court in Calcutta. I had of course read his famous books on Islam; my admiration for his learning, and for his capacity to expound and interpret our Muslim religion, was unstinted. Although he was excluded from any participation in politics, I had no hesitation in going to him for advice and help in my own political endeavors— above all, to secure equitable representations of Muslims and to open the eyes of the Congress High Command to the perils of the course on which they seemed set. But when our hopes were frustrated, it was encouraging that Syed Amir Ali, with all his personal prestige, and his great knowledge of Hindu-Muslim political relations (especially in Bengal), urged us on in our efforts for the establishment of a separate Muslim organization and gave us quiet, constant support when Nawab Mohsen-ul-Molk and I argued that our only hope of getting a fair deal from the British was to convince them of the width of the gulf—historical, cultural and religious— between us and our neighbors.

The Congress party, by its blindness to legitimate claims and aspirations, and by its persistence in its ridiculous habit of choosing

Muslim yes-men from Madras and Bombay as its representatives on the Viceroy's Legislative Council, lost a great opportunity which was not to occur again. These then were critical years, not merely in my own political development but in that vast and complex process which brought about, in little more than forty years, the partition of the Indian subcontinent· into the separate states of Bharat and Pakistan.

A notable event during my period of service on the Viceroy's Legislative Council was the Coronation Durbar in Delhi, the climax of which was a magnificent parade of some forty thousand troops who, headed by the Commander in Chief, Lord Kitchener, marched past the representative of the King-Emperor. That representative was the King's brother, my watchful and kind friend since my childhood, the Duke of Connaught. Immediately after the Durbar we held a Muslim Educational Conference in Delhi, at which I spoke at some length on several of the educational projects in whose furtherance I was active—most important of all, Aligarh.

I ventured to make a direct plea to my friends and colleagues: "I beg of you that the cause of a Central University—a university which, please Heaven, may rank some day with Oxford and Leipzig and Paris as a home of great ideas and noble ideals—a university where our youth may receive the highest instruction in the sciences of the West, a university where the teaching of the history and literature of the East may not be scamped over for a mere parrot-like knowledge of Western thought, a university where our youth may also enjoy, in addition to such advantages, a Muslim atmosphere. I earnestly beg of you that the cause of such a university should not be forgotten in the shouts of the market place that daily rise among us."

Those sentences of mine, spoken fifty years ago, sum up the aspirations which I cherished from the outset on behalf of Aligarh and which I have been happy to live to see fulfilled.

I had had two arduous and formative years on the Viceroy's Legislative Council. In the summer of 1904 I returned to Europe and picked up the threads of my social and personal life there. In the political sphere there were big changes impending. Arthur Balfour had succeeded his uncle, Lord Salisbury, as Prime Minister and leader of the Conservative party, but it was obvious that the long epoch of Conservative dominance in British politics was drawing to a close. The dynamic Joseph Chamberlain had flung the issue of Protectionism into the ring, and in so doing had gravely split the Conservative party. The Liberals were steadily gathering their forces; the Irish Question, after some years of deceptive calm, was simmering again; and the emergence of the Labor party— still very small in numbers—was a portent well worth noting.

I had as yet formed no intention of racing or breeding horses in Europe, and was not to do so until many years had elapsed, but my interest in these matters was unabated. I went regularly to race meetings while I was in England, and it was during this summer, as I recall, that I first made the acquaintance of Colonel Hall Walker (later Lord Wavertree), who was one of the outstanding personalities of the British turf, immensely knowledgeable about everything to do with horses, independent in his judgment, outspoken and didactic. Some people considered his views and his methods so eccentric that he was nicknamed "Whimsical Walker," but I would be the last to impugn his wisdom, his sagacity and experience. He was then the owner of the famous Tully Stud in Ireland, which later became the Irish National Stud, and with which in after-years I had much to do.

I returned to Bombay that winter and set out in the following year, 1905, on my second visit to East Africa. I urged on my Ismaili followers there some of the ideas, in intellectual and physical education, which I was practicing and preaching in India. I was especially distressed by the low standards of physique noticeable in Zanzibar; the incidence of tuberculosis was high. If it was argued that the fierce tropical climate enervated those who lived in it and induced listlessness and apathy, I could point out that the same could be said of India, and there we were beginning to take energetic steps to combat it. In Zanzibar I had consultations with the *mukhis*, the leaders of the local communities. I had a palace turned into a sports club and center for physical training, with a running track and football and cricket pitches. I gave prizes in all sorts of competitions, from billiards to cycling. I am glad to say that my innovations proved a marked success.

While I was in Africa a suit was brought against me in the Bombay High Court by certain discontented members of my family, collateral descendants of my grandfather. A series of claims, financial and otherwise, were made against me. This case, which dragged on for many months, was not so much a sequel of the earlier case brought against my grandfather in the sixties, by dissident elements among the Khojas (to which I have referred in a previous chapter), as a consequence of the generous, feudal manner in which my grandfather's establishment in Bombay had been set up and maintained. During the protracted proceedings a great deal of the history and background of my family and the Ismaili sect were gone into again, commissions of inquiry were sent into distant regions of Asia and Africa to collect evidence about my ancestors' property and affairs. My mother gave evidence on my behalf and was complimented by the judge, who said that she had "displayed an extraordinary memory." I was fortunate in my counsel, Mr. Inverarity, a keen and able lawyer. When at length the hearings ended and the presiding judge, Mr. Justice Russell, summed up, his judgment proved to be a classic example of its kind—a masterly, lucid, wide-ranging survey of Islamic history, religion, custom and law. At the conclusion of the long and costly business, I was fully and finally confirmed in my rights and status, and have never thereafter been subjected to a similar challenge.

I returned to India for the cold weather of 1905-1906, in time to pay my respects to the Prince of Wales (later King George V) in Calcutta. He was there, of course, in the middle of that state visit to India which had been under discussion when I was in England in 1904. This was not my first meeting with His Royal Highness (as he then was). My friendship with him and with his beloved consort, Queen Mary, was of long standing. I first met Queen Mary in 1898 when she was Duchess of York; she was at home in England with her three young children (King Edward VIII, later the Duke of Windsor, the late King George VI, and the Princess Royal) while her husband was out of the country on his first tour of duty as a naval officer.

All my memories of this good and gracious pair are warmly affectionate. I have always been proud that I won King George V's friendship and maintained it to the end of his life. He gave me his confidence to the same degree as his father had done. He talked to me always with utter frankness on all sorts of subjects, personal, political, sporting and social. I often had the honor of being his guest at luncheon, first at Marlborough House when he was Prince of Wales, and after his accession at Buckingham Palace. Luncheon was an informal, quiet family affair, with Queen Mary and one or two of their children and myself the only guest. Usually these luncheons were noted in the Court Circular; but from time to time, for special reasons, public reference was not made to them. King George carried all his life the stamp of his early training as a professional officer in the Royal Navy, with his trim and elegant figure, his strong, fresh complexion, his nautical beard, and the tone and accent of his admirably clear voice—an especially vivid reminder that he had exercised command at sea for many years before the death of his elder brother had placed him directly in the succession to the Throne. He had a short temper and was apt to show it when small things went wrong, but he quickly got over his anger. He had a very kind heart that was easily stirred to sympathy by the suffering of others.

I know of one example of the spontaneity and generosity of his sympathy. During the King-Emperor's Coronation Durbar in Delhi, the Maharajah of Baroda resented the fact that he had to go and make a public bow to the King. He demonstrated his resentment by performing his homage in a haphazard and casual fashion. This shocked everyone who saw it, British and Indian alike, because there was no justification for his showing open discourtesy to the King-Emperor. He apologized in writing to the Viceroy, and, although the apology was accepted, the King naturally felt sore about the episode and went on feeling sore for some years. But later misfortune descended upon the Maharajah of Baroda; more than one of his sons died in their young manhood, and then another fell grievously ill. When the King learned of these sorrows, he forgave the Maharajah wholeheartedly, blotted out the memory of the insult, and more than once I heard him refer to the Maharajah of Baroda as "that poor, unfortunate man" in tones of sincere commiseration.

King George V, like his father, was extremely meticulous about the way in which orders and decorations were worn, and, again like his father, had an extraordinarily keen eye for the slightest mistake in their arrangement on anyone's chest.

He once remarked to me: "Some people are surprised that my father and I are so particular about these things. But wouldn't it be peculiar if in ordinary society people turned up with their shirts outside their trousers, their collars or their neckties on back to front, and the buttons of their coats and waistcoats all wrong? Just as ordinary society has its rules for the proper wearing of clothes, so a King and his Court must have their rules for the proper wearing of unifoms, decorations and orders."

Once at some big Court function the late Maharajah of Rajpipla appeared in the King's presence not wearing—as he should have worn—the collar of one of his decorations because it caused him discomfort. The King was angry and showed that he was angry, but Queen Mary made a quick, conciliatory gesture toward the unhappy young man, as if to say, "Don't worry, it'll blow over." It did, and the King soon forgave him.

In connection with this same Maharajah of Rajpipla, I can give an example of King George V's pertinacious and all-round interest in all sorts of matters. The Maharajah won the Derby in 1934 with a horse called Windsor Lad. He had somehow delayed giving to his trainer the present which it is customary for a winning owner to give to his trainer after the Derby. His trainer was Mr. Marcus Marsh, the son of King George's former trainer. Weeks passed and the Maharajah still gave no present. One afternoon I was at a solemn and imposing state ceremony, where Ambassadors, Cabinet Ministers and exalted Court functionaries abounded. The King caught sight of me in the august throng, took me quietly into a corner and told me that he knew Marsh had not had his present.

"You were a great friend of his father's, weren't you?" he said earnestly, "and you know the young man himself. Do please tackle him and make him see that this present is a normal affair, and he's got to give it."

Naturally I did as the King asked, and the Maharajah belatedly sent Marsh his present. Nearly twenty years afterward I told Marsh my side of the episode. Now, although Marsh was the son of the King's trainer and quite often saw the King, he had never mentioned it to the King but had told a friend of his about the Maharajah's curious absence of mind. The friend was a general on the King's staff; he told the King and the King decided to use me as a go-between.

During the thirty-four years that I knew him I saw a great deal of King George V, at his home, at race meetings at Ascot and Epsom and elsewhere, and on his two visits to India as Prince of Wales and as King.

On the former visit in 1905, which has set me off on this train of reminiscences, there was a state ball in the Viceroy's House in Calcutta. The Prince of Wales took me into his room and told me that he was fully in favor of the appointment of Indians to the Viceroy's Executive Council and that he considered it most unfortunate that there were no Indians on it at the moment. He said, "I have strongly urged both Lord Morley and Lord Minto that an Indian be appointed."

He went on to talk to me at length about the Calcutta hospitals, to which his father had referred a year before; he was not at all happy about them.

The Morley-Minto reforms (of which I shall have much to say a little later) were promulgated in the following year. In private the Prince of Wales made no secret of the fact that he regarded these reforms as necessary and right. Like Queen Victoria, he had a quick and real sympathy for his Indian subjects, and he understood the real needs of India, above all, for a vigorous, united drive against ignorance and poverty and the appallingly low standard of living. During the Round Table Conferences he sent me more than one message urging me on and encouraging me in my efforts to bring about a settlement of Hindu-Muslim differences in order that we might then get on with the practical, economic and social reforms which were so long overdue. One day after I had the honor of lunching with him at Ascot, he spoke to me warmly along the same lines.

I remember that when the news leaked out from Berlin during the First World War that Indian anarchists were being trained in Germany, the King was shocked and grieved at the thought that the Kaiser could demean himself to countenance such underhanded and savage tactics. In the same way his grief was profound but private at the dreadful murder of the whole Russian Royal Family, his cousins, the Czar and Czarina and all their children, at Ekaterinburg in 1918. He never made any public reference to it, but more than once in our private talks he had no hesitation in opening his heart to me and telling me of his sorrow.

Sir Harold Nicolson, in his recently published biography of King George V, lays stress on the fact that the King was always fully aware of the constitutional proprieties, and of his inability to intervene in politics, however strong his private wishes or feelings might be. Sir Harold gives a vivid account of the way in which, after he had aired his views—vigorously, doubtless, and with singular pungency of phrase—he would make a gentle gesture, his right hand passing across his body, and say with a resigned smile, "It's not for me to have opinions, or to interfere." I so well remember that gesture and that smile. I have seen them so often, in many an after-luncheon talk. The most industrious, diligent and hard-worked of men, King George yet possessed the delightful faculty of collecting and remembering small personal details about his friends' private lives. Some years before the First World War the Maharajah of Gwalior was affianced to the Maharajah of Baroda's daughter (now the Maharani of Cooch Behar). During the Delhi Durbar of 1912 she broke off the engagement. Outwardly the Maharajah of Gwalior took his disappointment bravely, but inwardly he was greatly distressed. The King heard about it. He knew that Gwalior and I were close friends. At one of the state functions he sent for me, told me how grieved he was for Gwalior, and asked me to do all I could to ease matters.

As I have said, I knew Queen Mary even before I met her husband. For well over fifty years I was proud and glad to be counted among her friends. In 1952—less than a year before she died—I had two affectionate personal messages from her; the first, a telegram of congratulations after my horse Tulyar won the Derby, and with it a solicitous inquiry about my health, for she knew that I had been gravely ill and was glad to hear that I was on the mend; and the other (the last message I ever had from her) was when the same horse, Tulyar, won the King George and Queen Elizabeth Cup at Ascot, and she got an equerry to convey her congratulations and her regards to me.

She was a staunch, invaluable support to King George; a truly great English lady, she seemed to me to mingle in herself all the best qualities of royalty in the constitutional pattern, of wifely, maternal, domestic excellence, and of sturdy middle-class realism.

One of the most touching—in a way, one of the most painful—experiences of my life was a conversation which I had with Queen Mary shortly before King Edward VIII's abdication. I had just had a long audience with King Edward VIII, having returned to London from Geneva after one of the interminable conferences of the League of Nations, and in this audience I made my report to the King. I spoke fervently and sincerely to Queen Mary of my great admiration for King Edward, for his clarity of view, for his realism, and, above all, for his full appreciation of the dangers of the coming war. I could see that she was immensely proud of her son, yet I could see too that she was holding back tears—tears which were an indication of her awareness of the sorrow that impended for the Royal Family. No open hint did she give of it, and no reference could I make, or would I have made, to it. Having come from abroad I had had no sense of how near and how great was King Edward's danger. Realization in that sad silence was all the more shocking. In all that we did not say, in the quiet of her drawing room, there was a profound and tragic apprehension, a sense of the clouds massing for the terrible storm that was to burst around her and around those she dearly loved.

In the summer of 1906 I was again in England. There had been a General Election since my last visit, the Conservatives had been heavily defeated, and the Liberals were in power with a record majority and a Government under the Premiership of Sir Henry Campbell-Bannerman. Assembled in the Cabinet room and on the Front Bench was a galaxy of brilliant and able men, unequaled in recent British history: Asquith, Grey, Haldane, Lloyd George, John Morley, Herbert Samuel, and Winston Churchill, to name only a few of that memorable Administration. Morley—Gladstone's intimate friend, Cabinet colleague and biographer, the possessor of one of the most powerful, constructive intellects of his day—held what was to me and my political associates the supremely important post of Secretary of State for India. Soon his name was to be associated with that of the Viceroy, the Earl of Minto, a Scottish nobleman of Liberal outlook, sagacity and equability, in the Morley-Minto reforms, which marked so momentous an advance in India's journey to political emancipation. Asquith was Chancellor of the Exchequer, Lloyd George was president of the Board of Trade; and Winston Churchill, then just turned thirty, and a recent recruit from the other side of the House, held at first a minor ministerial post but was soon to rocket into prominence.

I have had the privilege and pleasure of Sir Winston Churchill's friendship for over half a century. As I recall, it was at Poona in the late summer of 1896 that our paths first crossed. A group of officers of a British cavalry regiment, the Fourth Hussars, then stationed at Bangalore, called on me. I was ill at the time and did not meet them, but my cousin Shamsuddin entertained them and showed them my race horses. When he later told me of their visit he said that among the officers none had a keener, more discriminating eye, none was a better judge of a horse, than a young subaltern by the name of Winston Spencer Churchill. My cousin described him as perhaps a little over twenty, boyish-looking, eager, irrepressible, and already an enthusiastic, courageous and promising polo player.

It is impossible to think of the young Winston Churchill without recalling his mother, the brilliant and much-loved Lady Randolph

Churchill. Her beauty, her grace and her wit have now a legendary quality. The wife of one famous man, the mother of another, she herself was a woman of the utmost distinction.

From many recollections of Lady Randolph, on many occasions and in many places, I choose one saying of hers that seems to me especially typical of the felicity and the pointedness of her wit. One day at Aix-les-Bains, Sir Rufus Isaacs (later the first Marquis of Reading) observed, about some particular action of which he disapproved, "No man would respect a woman who would do that."

"No woman," said Lady Randolph gently, "wants to be respected."

In later life our paths were destined to cross again and again. We met in the summer of 1902, King Edward VII's Coronation Year, at Warwick Castle as guests of Lord and Lady Warwick over a long week end. In six years the ebullient cavalry subaltern had traveled far and achieved much; wherever there had been fighting he had contrived to be, regardless of the views of senior officers— Malakand, about which he wrote the first of his many books, Kitchener's "River War" along the upper reaches of the Nile, the cavalry charge at Omdurman; as a war correspondent in South Africa he had been taken prisoner, escaped and had had a price put on his head by Kruger; and by 1902 he was Conservative member of Parliament for Oldman. At Warwick that week end he was in a holiday mood. He and I involved ourselves in a vigorous argument about the comparative merits, in sheer sporting quality, of polo and hunting. He was firmly for polo; I who had followed hounds from boyhood was as stubbornly for hunting. But I recall another conversation that same summer week end which was less lighthearted. He, with his imperialist traditions and outlook, reverted—as so many politically minded Englishman had to in those days—to the question of Ireland; he echoed something that Lord Spencer had said to me some years earlier: "Twenty years of firm government is no solution of the Irish problem.

"So long as the people of Ireland are dissatisfied," continued the young Tory M.P, the nominal supporter of Arthur Balfour, "there can be no solution. Only when the Irish people are politically satisfied will we be able to solve the Irish problem."

As young men will, we talked a great deal about a great many subjects. Churchill, whose verbal memory is one of his many remarkable characteristics, quoted freely from Fitzgerald's translation of *Omar Khayyám*. He assured me that he knew virtually the whole poem by heart. I remember being genuinely surprised by the enthusiasm which he displayed, for to those of us whose mother tongue is Persian, Omar Khayyám seems a minor poet with a very limited outlook. I tackled Churchill along those lines, and he countered me by saying that what he admired in Omar Khayyám was not his philosophy but his poetic power. Then suddenly he made a dialectical *volte-face* and said: "You know, there's a great deal in his philosophy. After all, it doesn't greatly matter what we do now—it'll be all the same in a hundred years."

I took strong exception to this flippant observation.

"What you do now," I said, "may be of little account a thousand years from now. But certainly events a hundred years hence will very much be the direct results of our present deeds and misdeeds."

As I remember, he came round into agreement with me. Now a good deal older, and with a good deal more experience behind me, I think that I would argue that events a thousand years hence can be strongly affected by what we do now—or leave undone.

Think of my own august ancestor, Mohammed the Prophet of Islam. If Mohammed had been killed in his first encounter with his enemies, Islam would never have arisen; Arabia might have been the home of a number of minor Christian sects; the Middle East would have been Christian instead of predominantly Muslim; and that part of the Indian subcontinent which became Muslim might have been converted to some version of Christianity. I go further: if after our Holy Prophet's Ascension into Heaven the succession had gone to the Ansar of Medina—a kindly, steadfast clan of yeomen, content to live on and work by the land—instead of to the Prophet's own tribe, the Quraish of Mecca—internationally minded, virile, reckless folk with a lust for travel and adventure, who journeyed to

Constantinople and Alexandria, to Rome even, to Iran and by sea to India in search of trade—then Islam would have taken a totally different turn. Under the leadership of the Ansar of Medina it would have been today—if indeed it still survived—one of many minor, little-known Eastern sects.

It needed the imagination, the international experience of the trade-conscious Quraish, the citizens of Mecca, to have made Islam a world religion whose call was spread abroad to all mankind.

In our own time too, there are many examples of decisions—political and otherwise—whose influence stretches far beyond the immediate present into a distant future. If in 1871 Bismarck had left Alsace and Lorraine out of the peace terms which he imposed on France in his hour of victory, would there ever have been the cry of *"Revanche, revanche!"* which echoed fiercely down the years afterward? The Franco-Prussian War might have slipped into oblivion with the other vainglorious follies of the Second Empire; and that United Europe, which is the eager hope and desire of us all today, would have come to pass without the bitter experience of two world wars. Even after the First World War had the Western Powers hearkened to the advice of men like Lord D'Abernon during the early, critical years of the Weimar Republic, we might never have heard of Adolf Hitler; the old League of Nations which had many good points—not least of which was its rapid acceptance of Stresemann's Germany into full membership—would have gone a long way to heal the wounds of the First World War. But there were other less enlightened counselors to whom the peoples of Western Europe listened, and in the succeeding years nothing was left undone to show the German people that there was one way in which they could get what they wanted, and that was by power politics.

Ah, well, the two young men who sat talking so ardently at Warwick Castle long ago had much to learn; and, if I may say so, one of Sir Winston Churchill's outstanding characteristics—perhaps the most valuable of all to him in his career as a statesman—has been his capacity to learn by experience and, having learned, to wipe the slate clean.

In 1906, four years after our memorable encounter at Warwick

Castle, he was a junior Minister in Campbell-Bannerman's Liberal Government, and I remember that John Morley, his senior Cabinet colleague, said to me, "The young Churchill, like the young Joseph Chamberlain that I knew, possesses the greatest natural political sense. There is in Churchill the same innate and natural readiness to tackle and solve problems as they arise that there was in Joe."

Sir Winston Churchill unites and blends in his strong personality two usually conflicting strands: the romantic, the deeply emotional and poetic interpreter of history and the common sense, practical, down-to-earth realist, the hardheaded and coolly calculating strategist. It is an irresistible, at times a majestic, combination.

And he accepted the fact that India was to remain in the Commonwealth on her own terms and as a republic. As he himself has said to me, "Half a loaf is better than none."

His whole relationship with the problem of India is a manifestation on the highest political plane of these two interlinked facets of Churchill's character. Part of his being responds with instantaneous romanticism to a highly colored conception of Empire, to the Union Jack unfurled to the breeze in some distant outpost, to the vigilant picket-keeping guard in the desolate Khyber, to all the trumpet calls of more than a century of British Imperial history. But in another part of his being he is capable of resolute practicality and common sense, solid and realistic yet magnanimous. It is this latter facet which has predominated since 1947; he has cheerfully accepted a political fact for what it is, and has striven—with a good deal of success—to make the best of a quite new situation.

I would have wished, though, that his connection with India (after his brief period of soldiering there was over) had been closer, and his responsibility for decisions on Indian matters more immediate, at some time or another in his career.

I saw a good deal of him during the First World War, and we often discussed politics. Not long after the end of the war, when Lord Chelmsford's term as Viceroy was ending and before the appointment of Lord Reading, Lloyd George asked two of us, myself and an intimate friend of mine, Mr. Bassou, a member of the Council of India, to come and see him on the matter of a successor. I suggested to Mr. Lloyd George, on behalf of the pair of us, two candidates for this great post: Lord Derby and Winston Churchill. He did not turn down either of them outright. He then turned to Mr. Bassou. Mr. Bassou's suggestions of course coincided with mine. To me Lloyd George had made no comment on either name. With Mr. Bassou, as with me, he passed over Lord Derby's name in silence. Then he turned round sharply and said to Mr. Bassou, "Do you know Churchill?"

Mr. Bassou admitted that he had not the pleasure of Mr. Churchill's personal acquaintance.

"I know Churchill," said Lloyd George with finality.

Looking back, and with the knowledge of all the great positions under the Crown which Sir Winston Churchill has occupied with such luster, I still think that it was a pity Lloyd George did not accede to our joint suggestion. If Churchill had had direct and recent Indian experience, his whole outlook at the time of the Indian Round Table Conference from 1930 on, and his speeches in the Parliamentary debates leading up to the passing of the Government of India Act in 1935, would, I am certain, have been different. And the effect of that changed outlook would have been felt throughout the whole later history of Anglo-Indian relations. I go further; I believe that with the direct knowledge of India which he would have acquired as Viceroy, he might have found other and far less terrible means of bringing about the downfall of Hitler and the saving of Germany for Western civilization.

Every time that I have discussed political matters with Sir Winston, I have been impressed anew by the extraordinarily practical realism of his outlook. He is never the slave of his past ideas, his desires or his dreams; he is their master.

During the First World War, when so many British statesmen were anxious to save Turkey from the doom which seemed bound to engulf her, I remember Churchill's telling me brusquely that Turkey would be the victor's prize. Turkey, he said, was the sick man of Europe, dying and degenerate, whom it was no use trying to save.

Who in the Second World War and since has been a warmer admirer, a more staunch supporter and friend of modern Turkey than

Winston Churchill? He has come round to a firm belief in the vitality and stubborn strength of the contemporary Turkish character, nurtured in the Anatolian Highlands, and to a genuine admiration for the vigor of Turkey's revival under Kemal Ataturk—a revival like that of the phoenix out of the ashes of the Ottoman Empire, whose disasters were the result of the blind and foolish policy of her leaders.

So far as India is concerned, the evolution in Churchill's outlook is even more startling. I remember his attitude at the time of the Round Table Conference, the whole tone in which he addressed us, and his determined opposition to the very idea of Dominion status. Yet this was the Churchill who in 1942 sent Sir Stafford Cripps to India with a directive which could only lead in the end to complete independence and to the emergence of the Indian Republic. And when the severance was finally accomplished, when the highest jewel in the British Crown was no more, when the last British soldier and the last British administrator had left Indian soil, Churchill's acceptance of the fact of Indian independence was made sincerely and with good grace.

Churchill, as leader of the Conservative party, faced with equanimity the momentous sequence of events which brought about Indian independence, the partition of the subcontinent into the two new and sovereign states of Bharat and Pakistan, and the division of the Indian Army.

As I look back down the long vista of the years that I have known Sir Winston, I am sure that the greatest blessing God has given him has been his health. He has a constitution of iron, and all his life he has taxed it to the uttermost. He has disregarded all the do's and don't's which doctors impose. He has worked unceasingly; he has played hard, he has excelled in countless activities from polo to painting, and have I ever seen him refuse any good dish put in front of him, or a liqueur glass of brandy, or a cigar? This gusto and this vitality have been sustained by his magnificent constitution. The young subaltern who came to look at my horses had it, and the veteran statesman, honored and revered by the whole civilized world, has it.

The electoral change in England in that crucial year 1906 had its effect on India. While I was in England that summer my friends in India wrote and told me that at last the Government was beginning to realize that there was something called a Muslim problem in India and that they could no longer dismiss it as an idle fabrication.

Since 1857 and the transference of authority in India from the East India Company to the Crown, the Muslims had, in a political sense, been more or less ignored by the British. Perhaps not unnaturally the new rulers of India turned away from those who, by religion and by language, were connected with the rulers who had been ousted. Muslims were not brought into the administration or into politics; few studied or read English. If the end of the Moghul emperors was pitiable, its effects lingered on for two generations in the sense of isolation and powerlessness which enveloped the Muslims of India in their own land. The Hindu majority were in an advantageous position under their new rulers; and they made full use of it. The Muslims had been for long what the French call *"quantité negligeable,"* but at long last we were going to be heard. The Viceroy, Lord Minto, had agreed to receive a deputation from us and I was to lead that deputation.

We were acutely aware that we had long been neglected, that to the Hindu majority—as represented by its leaders in the Congress party—we seemed a tiresome splinter in the flesh of the body politic, and that though there was great talk of nationalism, we were not ever considered in the aspirations that were being fostered, the plans that were being laid. They continued to send to the Viceroy's Legislative Council third-rate yes-men instead of truly representative Muslims, with the result that our separate identity as a community and the status that would have appertained to it had been forgotten by the British.

Now we decided that the time had come to make a stand for a change in attitude. If constitutional advancements were to be mooted, we must have our say in their disposition. Reform was in the air, but it must be understood—in the utterly different political atmosphere of more than forty years later—that it was reform within extremely limited terms of reference. British supremacy in

India, administrative and legislative, was to remain uninfringed, unaltered. In the Morley-Minto reforms, as they came to be known, and in the Indian Councils Act of 1907 in which they were embodied, there was no hint of a process of evolution toward ultimate Indian self-government, no hint of transference of power from British to Indian hands. John Morley himself said, "A fur coat may be all very well in Canada, but no use at all in India"—the political and constitutional evolution which had been Canada's experience was thus by implication rejected for India (though not, of course, *by* India). All that the Morley-Minto proposals were intended to achieve, and did achieve, was a modest devolution in communal and local matters and the admittance of Indians, on a rigidly restricted basis, to consultation—though not to decision—about their own affairs.

Within these limits, however, they were an advance, and from the Muslim point of view they were especially significant. Our experience from the time of the Cross-Lansdowne reforms in 1892 had pointed the way; there was no hope of a fair deal for us within the fold of the Congress party or in alliance with it. Now in 1906 we boldly asked the Viceroy to look facts in the face; we asked that the Muslims of India should be regarded not as a mere minority, but as a nation within a nation whose rights and obligations should be guaranteed by statute. History has amply demonstrated since then, after the First World War and again and again later, that the existence of minorities—of one nationally conscious community within another, numerically weaker perhaps but not less firmly aware of itself as a nation than the majority—is one of the major issues of our time. Ireland, Poland, Czechoslovakia, Jugoslavia—the world's maps are plentifully dotted with these minority problems, with all their complexity and difficulty.

For ourselves in 1906 we asked for the establishment of a principle, a principle which would have to be embodied in any legislation as a consequence of these proposals for reform. We asked for adequate and separate representation for Muslims both on local bodies and on the legislative councils, we asked that this representation be secured by a separate communal franchise and electoral roll. In

short, we Muslims should have the right of electing our own representatives on it. We conceded that in areas where we were in the
majority, like the Punjab and what was then the Province of Eastern
Bengal, we would give a certain number of extra seats to the
Hindus, in order to safeguard their interests, but in return we asked
that in areas in which there was a big Hindu majority we likewise
should be conceded a certain number of extra seats.

Lord Minto listened with sympathy to the statement of our case.
He assured us that the political rights and interests of the Muslim
community would be safeguarded in any change in administration
that might occur. Our principle was accepted. Most of our demands
in detail were conceded, though not all. It would, in my view, have
been better had there been provision for two Indian members of
the Viceroy's Executive Council—one Muslim and one Hindu—instead of the one finally provided for. But after all, it was John
Morley himself who said to me when I raised this point, "You
mustn't get too much power, you know."

It is perhaps unnecessary to stress the irony of history's comment
on that observation. But within their own time, the Morley-Minto
reforms were a genuine step forward. We had had established a major political principle; its application was henceforward to be a
permanent feature of all constitutional developments in India. It
was not conceded however without opposition. And if in retrospect
there is an element of irony about Lord Morley's remark which I
have just quoted, there is a much more freakishly ironic flavor about
the name and personality of the chief Muslim opponent of the stand
which we took. For Lord Minto's acceptance of our demands was
the foundation of all future constitutional proposals made for India
by successive British Governments, and its final, inevitable consequence was the partition of India and the emergence of Pakistan.

Who then was our doughtiest opponent in 1906? A distinguished
Muslim barrister in Bombay, with a large and prosperous practice,
Mr. Mohammed Ali Jinnah. We first became acquainted when he,
having been called to the English Bar, settled in Bombay and—entirely without private fortune and without influence—rapidly built
up his successful practice there. We had always been on friendly

terms, but at this juncture he came out in bitter hostility toward all that I and my friends had done and were trying to do. He was the only well-known Muslim to take this attitude, but his opposition had nothing mealy-mouthed about it; he said that our principle of separate electorates was dividing the nation against itself, and for nearly a quarter of a century he remained our most inflexible critic and opponent. In a later chapter I shall discuss more fully the circumstances—most of all the stubborn folly and intransigence of the Hindu majority in Congress—which converted this stoutest champion of Indian unity into its most determined opponent; and I shall trace in detail the paths of destiny which brought him, as the unchallenged leader of eighty million Muslims, that victory—the creation of the separate and independent State of Pakistan—for which we at the beginning were working unconsciously and indirectly, and he at the end consciously and directly and with all the force of his will and intellect. For the moment I merely reflect upon the irony implicit in it all.

Our achievement in 1906 seemed important enough; and it was obvious to those of us most closely associated with it—especially Nawab Mohsen-ul-Molk and myself—that since we had obtained separate electoral recognition, we must have the political organization to make that separate representation effective. The All-India Muslim League was therefore founded at a meeting at Dacca later that year at which, as it happened, I was unable to be present. I was, however, elected its first President, and as such I remained until 1912.

All these events—our deputation to the Viceroy, his acceptance of our demands, the subsequent foundation of the All-India Muslim League and my election as its President—marked for me the culmination of a period of concentrated political effort. The strain had shown itself physically and during our visit to Simla to see the Viceroy, I fainted. I needed physical recuperation and I thought that I would combine this with widening my experience and knowledge. I set out on a world tour in the company of a French friend of mine, Monsieur René Talomon, who subsequently became a professor of French literature in the United States, and who died recently. We headed east, going first to Malaya and Singapore and then on to China.

China's condition at that time was saddening. In Peking the aged Dowager-Empress dwelt in seclusion within the vast confines of the summer palace; beyond its walls her Empire was crumbling in confusion and decay. In towns along the seaboard and far up the great navigable rivers that were the arteries of China's lifeblood, foreign —European—trading communities had established an elaborate system of treaty ports and concessions. Here on the territory of a country which was in no sense a colony of any of the European nations involved, it was astonishing, and disquieting, to see that the most arrogant and hidebound kind of colonialism prevailed. The foreign concessions in towns like Shanghai, Hankow and others were alien cities and strongholds of power, political and financial. It was indeed merely a matter of extraterritorial foreign administration within the various concessions and settlements; the power and prestige of the foreigner was so great, and the authority of the Manchu Government so feeble, that the real rulers of China in those days were the consuls of the European Powers, chief among them the British Consul General in Shanghai. In the disintegration from which China's administration was suffering, wealthy Chinese brought their money and their investments into the foreign settlements for safety and protection—just as today many Europeans send their capital to the United States and Canada.

The atmosphere of colonialism was as nauseating as it was all-pervasive. In the P & O ship in which I traveled from Hong Kong to Shanghai, one of my fellow passengers was the Imperial Viceroy of the Province of Yunnan—a personage, one would have supposed, of some consequence in his own country. When we reached Shanghai I was genuinely astonished, and a good deal shocked, to see the way in which the officials of the so-called Chinese Imperial Maritime Customs—after all, they were nominally the servants of the Chinese Government—treated this dignitary, compared with their attitude toward the British passengers, myself and even my Indian servants.

For us there was every mark of consideration and courtesy. He was dealt with brusquely and rudely, all his baggage was opened, and the customs officials ruffled busily through his robes and his mandarin orders. It was a nastily enlightening comparison which I have never forgotten.

Within the foreign settlements the general attitude toward the Chinese was little short of outrageous. All the better hotels refused entry to Chinese, except in wings specially set aside for them. It was the same in restaurants. From European clubs they were totally excluded. Even in shops a Chinese customer would have to stand aside and wait to be served when a European or an American came in after him and demanded attention. We hear a great deal about the color bar in South Africa today. In the early years of this century in China the color bar was rigidly imposed—not least offensively in discrimination against officials of the very government whose guests, under international law, all foreigners were supposed to be. Is it any wonder that the Chinese intelligentsia long retained bitter memories of this attitude?

The old mandarin class, of course, did not travel and knew little of the world outside China, but already, even in 1906, there were a number of Chinese students attending universities in the United States and then returning home. Their bitterness was probably sharper and deeper than the cool, self-isolating disdain which was the natural reaction of the mandarin class.

In Shanghai Talomon and I were entertained at dinner—Chinese style—by some wealthy Chinese merchants to whom we had letters of introduction from a Chinese friend in Singapore.

We had the usual chicken dishes and something which they called tartar grilled meat, which was really a kebab similar to that which is eaten in Persia, Turkey, Egypt and all the Middle Eastern countries, and even in the Caucasus. When we remarked that it was a well-known dish in a large part of the world and a part with which I particularly was familiar, our hosts said, "Yes, it has been prepared for us by a Chinese Muslim cook." There followed the classical Chinese dishes, such as bamboo shoots and buried eggs. And then we were offered a dish which at first we thought was eel.

Luckily—oh, how luckily!—Talomon said, "We know this very well."

Our host laughed in courteous deprecation of Talomon's little mistake. "Oh, no," he said, "this is snake."

There is a limit, and for us this went beyond it. Under the cover of our napkins, and with what we hoped was the greatest care so that we should not be seen, we got rid of it. I remember, long years later, reading a newspaper account of the effect of a similar dish on some foreigners at a Chinese official dinner. All were very ill and some died.

Students of sociology may be interested in the existence in those days, both in Shanghai and Hong Kong, of what were called "welcome houses," maintained by small groups of American women. There was not a hint of coarseness or vulgarity about these establishments; they were enveloped in an almost oppressive atmosphere of decorum. The first impression on any novice who walked into one of them for the first time was that he had entered an agreeable but fairly strait-laced social gathering. Only Europeans and Americans of impeccable social background were admitted. The women who ran them—many of whom were known to be well-to-do, several indeed owning race horses in Shanghai—were regarded with a proper degree of respect. They resembled, shall I say, the Greek hetaera rather than the fashionable lady of the European demimonde of that time. Most of the women were of Scandinavian origin and had come, I believe, from the vicinity of Minnesota where there is a considerable degree of Scandinavian settlement. The current theory in the Far East was that they came thither with one set purpose: to accumulate a dowry which their families could not afford to give them and that having in a few years piled up quite sizable fortunes, home they went to be absorbed into a respectable and blameless family life.

Talomon and I went on to Japan. Since the world picture has changed so irrevocably in the years since then, it may perhaps be necessary to recall two important facts in connection with Japan in 1906: first, that Britain and Japan were allies, under the terms of an agreement signed early in the century and, second, that Japan had just emerged victorious from the Russo-Japanese War, the first in modern times in which an Asiatic Power had taken on and soundly defeated a European Great Power in a combat on modern terms and with modern arms and equipment. The Foreign Minister, Count Hayashi, who had been Ambassador in London at the time of the signature of the Treaty of Anglo-Japanese alliance, gave a big luncheon in my honor. During the course of the meal he and I discussed the Anglo-Japanese alliance; and Count Hayashi, whom I had known quite well in London, assured me that influential military circles in Japan had been opposed to the idea of an alliance with Britain and had advocated an alliance with Russia. Simultaneous negotiations had in fact been conducted, and the Russian plan failed only because Russia's acceptance of the terms proposed arrived after the treaty with Britain had been initialed. It is interesting and a little awe-inspiring to speculate on how different the history of our century would have been had the Czar's Government moved more speedily. There would have been no Russo-Japanese War to weaken—as it in fact did irreparably—the Czarist regime; might not Lenin have remained an obscure agitator in permanent exile?

Among Japanese leaders whom I met was Field Marshal Oyama. I remember being struck by his modesty of demeanor, absence of self-satisfaction and lack of any display of power, and I remember thinking—for, after all, he was one of the men who had just led their country to victory in the war against Russia—that his bearing was very different from that which a European or American military leader would have adopted in a like situation. Friends told me that the bearing of Admiral Togo, the victorious commander in the great naval battle of Tsushima, was very similar to that of the Field Marshal.

I was fortunate enough to be granted an audience with the old Emperor, the great Mikado of Japan's revolution, the Emperor during whose reign Japan had stepped at one bound from a medieval way of life to a modern industrial and military power able to challenge the West in its own terms. As a boy before the Revolution, although he was the Mikado, he had been kept in Kyoto by the

Shogun in obscurity and something near poverty, rationed daily to a small issue of rice by those who were supposed to be his servants. He threw off this overweening tyranny—with tremendous results. What surprised me was that he was a tall, powerful, robust man; he would have been thought a big man anywhere, but in Tokyo his size seemed much more conspicuous. My audience with him was a noisy affair. He talked at the top of his powerful voice, shouting questions at me and shouting back his answering comments. When he wasn't shouting he was uttering loud, explosive exclamations. The courtier who acted as interpreter told me afterward that these exclamations indicated that the Emperor approved of my answers to his questions.

We took a Japanese boat across the Pacific and called at Honolulu. People who know Honolulu nowadays can have no idea of what it was like then—its charm and its quiet air of absolute peace and happiness. There were no trans-Pacific clippers bringing holiday-makers overnight from the United States. It had not been discovered and exploited by the cinema; its romance was genuine. There was no tourist industry, and there were no vast naval and air bases.

All the young women of the island went about garlanded, and whenever we were introduced to any of them they took off their garlands—so gay and beautiful were their smiles, so graceful and delicate the movements and touch of their hands—and put them round our necks. Talomon and I were still young and impressionable; we were both pleased and gratified by this courteous custom.

On we went toward the United States and reached San Francisco in December, 1906, in the aftermath of the earthquake. The whole city was one vast ruin. People talk of the material havoc of war in France and in Germany, and I myself have seen, at the conclusion of two world wars, many cities and towns in ruins, but San Francisco in 1906 exceeded anything I have ever seen. It was difficult to find a shop open, but we chanced on a drugstore; it was a curious experience—amid all this devastation—to be served with ice cream and cold drinks in what elsewhere in the world we call a chemist's shop. One or two hotels and restaurants were open, but in general life and work were only just beginning again in that terrible and pitiable havoc.

From California we crossed the continent by train, stopping off from time to time and staying a day or two in various cities on the way. In Chicago we were taken on a conducted tour of the stock-yards and slaughter houses. Not long before this, Upton Sinclair's propagandist novel about the slaughter houses had been published and caused a considerable sensation. I must say the conditions in the slaughter houses which I was shown bore no similarity to the lurid horrors described in the novel.

Perhaps I ought to point out that such knowledge of America as I then possessed was not derived from novels. I had read Lord Bryce's classic work on the American Constitution, I knew the writings of authors as diverse as Walt Whitman, Hawthorne, Thoreau, Henry and William James and Mark Twain (whom, as I have recorded, I had met in Bombay). I had many American friends and acquaintances in Europe. Like all visitors to the United States I suppose I had my preconceived notions, but they were founded on some real, if academic, knowledge of the structure of American social, economic and political life.

Just after the New Year of 1907 we reached New York. It was the height of the city's winter season. Talomon and I went to stay at the St. Regis; forty years later it was the habit of my younger son, Sadruddin, when he was a Harvard undergraduate, to stay there whenever he was in New York.

From all that my friends tell me, there is no comparison between the social life of New York as it was in those days and the swift, swirling existence of the city today. Of course I had many introductions, largely from my American friends in Europe, and I was immediately and generously entertained. Americans are the most hospitable people in the world, and they receive foreigners with so much kindness, their welcome is so open and so goodhearted, that anyone who has once been to the United States never forgets his time there. I seemed to be invited out to luncheon and dinner every day, and night after night I was someone's guest at the opera. The

Metropolitan Opera House in those days was like a superb exhibition of jewelry and fashion. I knew the Opera in Paris and London, but for elegance and opulence among the audience neither was comparable with New York's Metropolitan in the early years of this century.

One New Yorker of some consequence to whom I had an introduction was the then District Attorney, Mr. Jerome, Lady Randolph Churchill's cousin. He was kind enough to arrange for me a special pass which enabled me to watch one of the most interesting and sensational *causes célèbres* of the time. This was the trial of Harry K. Thaw, accused of the murder of Stanford White, the architect and designer of skyscrapers.

At his trial Thaw was found guilty but insane and thus escaped execution. It seemed that Mrs. Thaw had confessed to her husband that before her marriage she had been taken by Stanford White to his apartment, given drugged champagne, and seduced. This confession aroused Thaw to maniacal jealousy, all the more ferocious because he suspected (groundlessly) that White was still pursuing his wife. In the ballroom of Madison Square Roof Garden White was waltzing with a girl friend when Harry Thaw strode across the floor and fired six shots into his body.

I was especially interested in this melodramatic and colorful affair, for two years before I had met Thaw and the former Evelyn Nesbit together in Paris. Thaw, whose fortune was derived from railroads, cut something of a figure in international society at that time. He had, however, an uncontrollable temper and was an extremely jealous and possessive individual. I met them once at dinner and later on that evening I was talking pleasantly and light-heartedly with the young woman, who was extremely beautiful and attractive. Thaw in the background looked grim and preoccupied, and a friend who was in the party quietly warned me that there was a dangerous streak in Thaw.

There was a grim but bewildering fascination about the trial. I had grown up accustomed to British methods in a court of justice; the whole system of questioning and cross-examination and all the rules of evidence in an American court were startlingly different. It took me a little time to realize that, although the basis of the criminal law is the same in the United States as in England, it has developed along different lines since the eighteenth century and the American legal profession has evolved its own technique and traditions.

By 1907 the motorcar was coming into its own and was no longer the despised and smelly toy it had been a decade earlier, New York was still a city of fine carriages and glossy and well-groomed horses, and the taxi had not yet replaced the elegant hansom cab. How affable and good-tempered American people of all classes were in those days. The clerks and the assistants in the shops and stores seemed friendly and alert, never giving one those sour, disapproving looks that one got in shops in Europe. The policemen on the beat, the New York cops, were genial and talkative when you asked them the way, not curt like the Paris gendarme or aloof and majestic like the old-fashioned London bobby.

I realize that I was extremely fortunate both in the time of this my single visit to New York and in the social world—now almost entirely vanished—to which I had the entree. I met the great hostesses and leaders of society of those days: Mrs. Cornelius Vanderbilt, Mrs. John Jacob Astor, Mrs. Whitelaw Reid, Mrs. Phipps, Mrs. Ogden Mills and others. How kind and hospitable they were, how stately were the parties and the dances they gave—more than one, I may add, in my honor.

I spent a good deal of time in the museums, as I always do in any city that I visit for the first time. Many of the wealthier private houses, of course, were museums and art galleries in their own right. It was curious, I remember remarking, that although in Europe the heyday of the French impressionists had dawned and connoisseurs were already beginning to collect their work, American taste remained still classical and traditional, and the walls of many of the big houses that I visited were hung with examples of English, Italian, German, Flemish and Dutch painting of many epochs.

I was made an honorary member of the Union Club. I discovered the joys of native American cooking; surely canvasback duck and terrapin are two of the best dishes in the world. I went to the theater a great deal, and here "modernism"—as it was then understood—had certainly hit New York. Ibsen was the rage, and several of his plays were being performed at theaters around the town. But it was also, of course, the day of the musical comedy, before it had been displaced by other noisier, more synthetic forms of amusement.

It was a time of great expansion and prosperity for New York and for America generally, an outward and visible sign of which was the rising skyline of New York. We talked about skyscrapers then, but they were modest little affairs of twenty or thirty floors—still, they seemed to us gigantic.

Altogether I had a wonderful time in New York. I have never forgotten it. I only wish that I had been able to go back again. That this has never proved possible has been my misfortune and, I may say, a cause of great and lasting regret.

My tour had set me up in health and in spirits. The year 1907 saw the Morley-Minto constitutional reforms in India turned from tentative proposals, whose shape and pattern we had been able effectively to influence, into law. John Morley, with his liberal background and outlook of the purest theoretical and academic kind, was extremely reluctant to accept the principle of separate electoral representation for the Muslims. It went against the grain of his character. However, the Viceroy, Lord Minto, had given his assent to the undertaking, and Morley—however scrupulous his theoretical objections—could not be permitted to go back on it. For Syed Amir Ali and myself, 1907 was a period of what I can best describe as guerrilla warfare, whose aim was to keep up to the mark. We won in the end, but it was hard going.

In my personal life I was able to effect radical and permanent adjustments. Any hope of reconciliation with my wife, Shahzadi Begum, had unhappily but finally receded; we agreed to a deed of separation and, not long afterward, to a divorce under Muslim law. While of course I remained responsible for her maintenance until her death, she passed completely out of my life and we never met again.

From 1907 I visited Europe every year. My life moved in an agreeable and spacious round. As a shy, raw young man on my first visit to Europe in 1898, I had lost my heart to the French Riviera. Now in my maturity my affection for it had deepened and ripened, and I found myself returning to it again and again. In 1908 this affection found a personal focus. I made the acquaintance of Mlle. Theresa Magliano, one of the most promising young dancers of the Ballet Opéra of Monte Carlo, a ballerina who—in the opinion of the teachers of both the Paris Opéra and of La Scala in Milan—was assured of a brilliant future in her profession. She was then just nineteen. We fell deeply in love. In the spring of that year she accompanied me to Egypt and we were married in Cairo in accordance with Muslim law.

My new marriage brought me spiritual and mental satisfaction and enrichment. It also opened for me a path into a new and absorbing world. My young wife's nature was intensely aesthetic. She was a truly creative artist. Although inevitably she gave up the stage after our marriage, she turned to a serious study first of painting and later of sculpture. It was here that her talents flowered. She took the professional name of Yla. Her work was exhibited on the Continent and in England.

Before she died in 1926, at the tragically early age of thirty-seven, my wife had attained recognition as a sculptor of merit and high artistic capacity. She had been asked to design a number of war memorials in England and France and also a number of those monuments to Unknown Soldiers which so poignantly expressed the emotions of the interwar years. The last commission which she was offered gave her especial satisfaction; it was from the city of Vienna, obtained in open competition with a strong candidature of more than a hundred, to design a fountain in which statuary was an important part of the decorative scheme.

My wife's aesthetic interests and tastes encouraged me to explore the world of art for myself.

My own first loves in the world of aesthetic experience were always music and the ballet. My reactions to music and to dancing have been emotional and sensuous. I have a vivid recollection of the first time I ever heard a waltz played and watched it danced. I was a boy of thirteen or fourteen at the time. The scene was a ball at Government House in Poona. I daresay the orchestra was worse than mediocre; I doubt if the dancers were particularly expert. I had no standards to judge by. My taste was utterly unformed. But there in the brightly lit ballroom the dancers swirled before me; it was as if the figures on some beautifully carved frieze had come suddenly to warm and glowing life; the lilt and sway of the music swept into my heart like a flooding tide of joy. The lights that shone in that ballroom have been extinguished sixty years and more, and the dancers are all gone, but the memory of the music and movement has never faded.

I had discovered a source of happiness which I was never to lose. As life has gone on I have become more and more interested and I have found more and more refreshment and solace in music, in the ballet, the opera and the theater. These for me have ranked first among the arts. Pictures I have liked, but in a comparatively restricted field. Like many others of my generation I was brought up on the work of the great masters of the Italian and, to a lesser extent, the Dutch and British schools; but dutifully though I went around the art galleries, they never stirred me. It was when I first saw Turner's work that I saw what painting really could mean. Then about 1904 I saw my first French impressionists; here for me was an extension and development of the same satisfaction that Turner gave me—their early landscapes, not their portraits. Turner, Monet, Renoir, Pissarro, those are my painters. In sculpture and in furniture my taste is sheerly Egyptian—the great statuaries of ancient Egypt, the simple, pure, formal yet flowing lines of the ordinary, day-to-day furniture that you see exhibited in the Cairo Museum, those are enough for me. English and French furniture, even of the "great" periods, leaves me cold. I care little for jewelry or work in precious metals, except silver; beautiful silver has always held a considerable attraction for me.

But in those realms of aesthetic experience that I do care about, much have I traveled and much have I profoundly enjoyed. I am proud to recall that I have counted among my personal friends many of the great artists of this century. I know Stravinsky well, and my knowledge of much of his early work was close and intimate. In his association with Diaghilev he wrote, as everyone knows, the music for some of the finest ballets ever created by that master impresario; I heard much of that music before it was orchestrated.

I knew Puccini quite well. I think I must have been one of the first of his friends to notice a troublesome and increasing hoarseness in Puccini's voice, a hoarseness which was the first indication of the malady which ultimately killed him—as tactfully as I could, I suggested to him that instead of perpetually sucking cough lozenges, he ought to go to see a doctor. Massenet was another friend of mine, and we often dined together at the Hôtel de Paris in Monte Carlo. Once when he was, as I had been given to understand, laid low with bronchitis, I drove over from Cannes to see him at the Hôtel de Paris. I was shown up immediately to his sitting room. He was stark naked in the room next door in a marble bathtub before a blazing fire. He was busily dictating music to a woman secretary. Neither he nor she seemed at all discomposed; I was, I must confess, somewhat taken aback. Massenet, however, was voluble in his explanation. He had had a rush of creative ideas which had to be put down on paper. Since I had come all the way from Cannes to call on him, would it not have been discourteous to refuse to see me?

"Please sit down," he said. "I must just finish this piece of work."

For nearly an hour he sat on in the bath, turning the hot tap on from time to time, repeating and trying out bars and single notes of music, and making his secretary sing them back to him, so that it began to sound as if he were giving her a singing lesson. At last the flow of inspiration ceased, the young woman shut her notebook and hurried away, and only then did the old gentleman—he was, after all, about seventy—realize that he was sitting there naked and that the water had grown chilly. He jumped out of the bath, ran into his bedroom, put on a bathrobe, and came back to bid me a friendly and courteous good-by.

I have known many actors and singers: Madame Bartet of the *Comédie Française*; Jean de Reszke, the great tenor and teacher of a new generation of singers; Caruso, whose magnificent voice seemed literally to shake Covent Garden to its foundations when he soared to his highest notes. Though perhaps not as pure an artist as Tomagno, I think that he was, without doubt, the greatest tenor of my time. I remember Melba in her magnificent prime; it was told of her that when she first presented herself at the Opéra in Paris the director, though he recognized the potentialities of her voice, said that her Australian accent was so formidable that he would be able to do nothing with her. Like many other great singers Melba was a hearty eater; she liked a good, rich supper after the opera, and to top it off she had a habit of ordering ice cream, a fresh peach, strawberries, and cream and consuming the lot together. Escoffier, the famous restaurateur, heard about this habit, made an established dish of it and named it in her honor. So was born the now universally known Pèche Melba.

In England I knew well many of the most famous figures of the stage, from Sir Henry Irving (whom I often visited in his dressing room at the Lyceum Theater) to the George Alexanders, the Trees, Sir Seymour Hicks and his wife Ellaline Terriss, and many, many others.

I made the acquaintance of Sir Johnston Forbes-Robertson through a friend of mine, a fellow member of the Marlborough, Douglas Ainsley. Ainsley himself was a man of originality of character and some talent; formerly a member of the diplomatic service, he established in his own person a kind of unofficial liaison between the world of society and the world of the stage. Forbes-Robertson suggested that I should write an Oriental tragedy for him on an historical theme, leaving it to me to choose my subject out of the great mass of Islamic lore and legend. I chose the sad and stirring story of the murder of the Prophet's grandson, my ancestor, Hussein, at Kerbela, and made a beginning with it. One day in the summer of 1904 at Douglas Ainsley's house I read Forbes-Robertson what I had written; I don't think he liked it very much. Thenceforward I abandoned any idea of writing dramatic poetry.

To return to composers—when I first arrived in Europe the great controversy about Wagner was still in full swing. But it was of course, as all musical appreciation was in those days in every Western European country except Italy, restricted to a comparatively few. One of the great changes that I have seen in my lifetime has been the vast extension of musical understanding, taste and appreciation through all sections of society. The old, snobbish glamour may have departed; but the breakdown of class distinction not only in England but in France and Switzerland too has, in my opinion, done a great deal of good. It is especially noticeable over the ballet; and here I may claim that I have watched, from very close quarters, an immense revolution in taste from its beginnings.

Diaghilev was the creator and inspirer of this revolution. As Caesar in Britain, so was the Russian, Diaghilev, in prewar Western Europe—he came, he saw, he conquered. He himself maintained that he would never have had a chance to demonstrate his originality or exert his influence as he did in Western Europe had he remained in Russia, where—although it was the home of the ballet in a certain sense—the classical mold was firmly fixed, and there was no opportunity for that creative fire which, once he was abroad, Diaghilev set burning so furiously.

From the first I was one of Diaghilev's enthusiastic and unwavering supporters, and so I remained till his untimely death. I doubt if the magnitude of Diaghilev's achievement is generally realized today. A new generation takes it all for granted. Ballet, as it was understood and practiced in Western Europe, before he came on the scene, was a sterile and virtually static minor art form from which real vitality and excitement—as distinct from mere repetitive prettiness—seemed to have ebbed away. Then in 1909 and 1910 Diaghilev burst like a bomb on the aesthetic consciousness of Europe. His dynamic influence was not confined to the ballet; it spilled over into all the allied arts and revolutionized their fundamental ideas, creative and critical. On the concepts of uniting music and motion and the representation of abstract ideas and ideals through movement as much as through music, Diaghilev's influence was tremendous and lasting. This obviously was the core of his unique achievement; but what would stage *décor*, costume design, feminine fashion, furnishings and interior decorations have been in the first half of this century without Diaghilev? His impact on the major plastic arts of sculpture and painting was no less revolutionary. Yet his wonderful, unique quality was one of indirect creativeness. It is possible to argue that he himself in fact never created anything, but the truth is that the creative work of everyone who collaborated with him was, profoundly and really, his creation too. How many artists did what the world now recognizes to be their best work for him and with him? Not only dancers like Karsavina, Nijinsky, Lifar and Massine, but a painter like Bakst, a musician like Stravinsky. He was an impresario of genius, and he was something more. He so infused and inspired others that, working for him, they were better and bigger than they ever could have been without him and the result of the association has been that some of them have become today the most famous and wonderful choreographers in the world. Nijinsky was the supreme and tragic example of this mysterious power which he exerted, of genius evoking genius. But his influence was no less important on many others, over whom his hold was not so obviously hypnotic. Imposing his strong, original taste on a band of talented artists and extracting from them their best and most original work, he imposed that taste on Europe—with unforgettable, immeasurable effect.

I often used to be present at his conferences with all of his leading associates—"heads of departments" as he called them: Stravinsky, Bakst, Nijinsky, Karsavina, his ballet master, his choreographer in chief, a young poet perhaps, a venerable and venerated artist like Rodin. A conference was like a council of war. Each would pour out his ideas into a common pool, but Diaghilev—have no doubt of it— was the supreme commander; he imposed a unity of form and aesthetic conception, he turned a mass of brilliant projects into an ordered and coherent work of art. The clash of ideas was subdued and hammered into shape, and the final result, far more often than not, was a masterpiece.

The practical foundation, on which this exuberance of talent was based, seemed at first sight fragile in the extreme. Diaghilev was always in debt; he never—apparently—had a penny in hand. His creative imagination—and his own faith in it—outsoared these (as it seemed to him) minor considerations. He knew that he was creating a masterpiece, a series of masterpieces; he trusted implicitly that his audiences would recognize the value of his work. He possessed that faith which moves mountains—and mountains of difficulty dissolved as he went along. Whenever the financial situation looked most desperate, some new wealthy patron, some Maecenas would turn up; the most immediate and pressing difficulties would be smoothed away; and he would sweep in confidence to his next triumph. On the stage, too, his capacity for improvisation and his total reliance on it were all-pervasive. Until the last minute every new production bore the appearance of total chaos, but somehow by some magic of his own, between the final rehearsal and the first night, when everyone else around him was despairing and on the edge of nervous collapse, Diaghilev would induce order out of the hurly-burly; and another thunderously acclaimed success would be added to the lengthening roll. Night after night the HOUSE FULL board would go out in front of the theater. The whole season would be triumphant. At its close, off Diaghilev and the company would go to London and to other capitals and provincial centers, to the same acclamation, with the same story of success, until the money ran out.

He was indeed unique, but the revolution in art which his genius precipitated has continued to run its course since his death. The revitalized and flourishing art of the ballet all over the world—in Paris, London and the United States—is the beautiful and fruitful tree whose seeds this strange, turbulent and brilliant man so lavishly sowed. It is a profound cause of satisfaction to those who, like myself, saw his work at close quarters and almost from its inception to know that this great aesthetic revolution, as fundamental and as far-reaching as that which Wagner brought about in the world of music, was the work of a genius whom we were privileged to know as a friend.

Diaghilev and the ballet were the center of that fascinating world of highly sophisticated, highly cultivated creative work and critical appreciation in which, during those years immediately before the First World War, I lived so full and so zestful a life. Time, chance, war, economic and social change have wreaked havoc with the rich fabric and pattern of a civilization and a way of life which then seemed indestructible. However, if much is lost, much has been gained in those magnificent and widespread effects of the revolution in all artistic matters achieved by Diaghilev. While the classes have lost, the masses have gained. The diffusion of culture is not just a textbook phrase nowadays; it is a reality. When I think of the theaters and opera houses, the concert halls and art galleries of Western Europe today, and of the people of all social classes (and not just a wealthy and leisured few) who throng them, whose pleasure and mental and spiritual enrichment are so obvious; when I think of how real and eager understanding and appreciation of the arts have extended in recent decades to every level of society—then I see far more reason to rejoice than to lament. There are some, however, who cannot share my optimism. The sadness of one facet of the years of transition is for me summed up and symbolized in an encounter which I had in the theater in Zurich, in the middle of the Second World War, with Richard Strauss. I had known him well at the height of his international fame. Around us there was a continent, a world, locked in relentless conflict, a nightmare projection into grim reality of all Wagner's most terrible imaginings and forebodings. Strauss was an old, heartbroken man. He saw me, flung up both his arms in a sad, despairing gesture, rolled his eyes upward and muttered some incoherent phrase in which I could just catch the word "God," and stumbled forlornly away.

From 1907 until the outbreak of war I was in Europe for some part of every year. Movement from country to country, from continent to continent, though more leisurely than it is today, was also a great deal easier and freer. Civilization had not learned all the tortuous refinements of passports and visas, of exchange control and security regulations. The number of Americans who were coming to Europe was increasing year by year; many of them were affluent; many were people of cultivated and sophisticated tastes; some stayed permanently, some came back and forth, some maintained large-scale establishments on the Riviera or elsewhere. Many of them were "characters" in their own right—the remarkable James Gordon Bennett, for example, the famous proprietor of the New York

Herald who had a villa at Beaulieu-sur-Mer. He was then an old man, and he looked his age. He was apt to be short-tempered and peppery, but he had a warm, kind heart. The hospitality which he and his delightful wife most liked to dispense was breakfast, big and elaborate meal with every kind of characteristic American dish. I recall that during the First World War he developed the strongest antipathy to bad news of any kind. If his attention were drawn to any tactical or strategic reverse suffered by the Western Allies, his temper became terrible, the unhappy bringer of bad tidings was so abused and berated that it was difficult not to believe that he was not actually responsible for the reverse which he had been so rash as to mention.

Others whose acquaintance and friendship I made at this time included Mr. Harjes, of Morgan's Bank, a staunch supporter of the Allied cause from the day war broke out, and his wife—one of the world's most beautiful women, a queenly, glorious, magnificent woman; Mr. Ralph Curtis—a lively amusing conversationalist— and his wife; Mr. and Mrs. James H. Hyde; Mr. and Mrs. Bernard Berenson; and Walter Berry, who had been a judge of the mixed courts in Cairo, and who was a lifelong friend of Edith Wharton, the novelist-historian of New York.

Bernard Berenson took considerable pride in the care and precision with which he pronounced the English language. His verbal armor, however, had one curious chink in it; he pronounced the simple word "corkscrew" as if it had a third syllable in it—"corkerscrew." Some of his friends who knew of this little vagary, having got him off his guard, mischievously put him to the test one April Fool's Day. To everyone's delight out popped "corkerscrew"; and for years afterward if he dared to take up a stand on correct pronunciation, he would be vociferously reminded of that intrusive syllable.

Ralph Curtis had an addiction to puns; years before I knew him he happened to be in Bombay when Mr. W. K. Vanderbilt (the father of Consuelo, Duchess of Marlborough, later Madame Balsan) arrived in his yacht. Lord Harris, then Governor, held the erroneous opinion, frequently held by Englishmen, that American society was built on money. Aware that the Vanderbilts were very rich, he condescendingly asked Ralph Curtis if he knew Mr. Vanderbilt, clearly implying that it would be quite an honor if he did.

"I never knew the Vanderbilts," said Ralph Curtis, demurely, "for when I lived in New York they were still Vanderbuilding."

At James Hyde's house I met several times Monsieur Hanotaux, the famous historian, member of the *Académie Française,* and statesman, who had been France's Foreign Minister from 1894 to 1898. He took a fancy to me and often we found ourselves discussing politics. I remember that he affirmed with great earnestness that if the Méline Cabinet of 1898, of which he had been a member, had not fallen, and if the coalition of parties that had put Méline in office had maintained their support of him instead of backing Delcassé, it might have proved possible to achieve a fair and friendly solution of the problem of Alsace-Lorraine which would have been honorable and satisfying to both France and Germany. If Hanotaux's assertion was right, here was another of those missed chances in diplomacy, another wrong turning, where if the right decision had been taken, the First World War need never have happened.

Walter Berry brought me into acquaintanceship with Mrs. Edith Wharton and with Marcel Proust. Walter Berry, a bachelor and an agreeable and charming conversationalist, had somehow or another achieved among the women members of the little circle in which he and I then moved the reputation of being the greatest marital submarine torpedo that had ever existed. The ladies averred that he had told each of them separately that she was far too good for her husband; he was a distinguished man, a famous lawyer—what could they do but believe him? And every time there was another marriage torpedoed. It was the kind of joke which a small, sophisticated society can get hold of, work almost to death and never let go. But Walter Berry had one remarkable claim to fame. He was one of the few people in the world who could at any time ask Proust to dinner and always be sure of an acceptance. Oddly enough, I never met Proust at the Ritz, where he used to go a great deal, but I did meet him several times at dinner at Walter Berry's. What I remember most about Proust was his silences; I recall only one remark of his. A Mademoiselle Atoucha, an Argentine lady who was affianced to a French Marquis, was Berry's fourth guest. Proust surveyed her, observed that she looked like Cleopatra, and said nothing else for the rest of the dinner. On this, as on other occasions, Berry and I did our best to sustain the conversation, and the great novelist sat silently watching and listening to us; it was a slightly disconcerting experience.

This was the society, these were some of the friends of my leisure in these happy and agreeable years. Work, of course, continued unabated. I spent a considerable part of each year in India, concerned not only with my duties toward my followers but with the interests and the responsibilities which I had acquired in Indian politics. These were the years in which the Morley-Minto reforms were being put into practice. It was proved that the principle of separate electoral representation for Muslims, which we had fought so hard to have established, was sound and workable as well as theoretically just. Muslim political consciousness, under the leadership of men like Nawab Ali Chowdry and the Nawab of Dacca in Bengal, and of Sir Mohammed Shaffi and Sir Sulfiqar Ali Khan in the Punjab, matured and strengthened steadily.

I myself was devoting a good deal of time, energy and interest to the affairs of Aligarh. I suppose that I was a sort of one-man "ginger group" on behalf of the project of converting Aligarh into a great Muslim university. Steadily during these years we aroused interest in and extended support for our project. Of course it provoked opposition from that powerful British element whose argument was that a Muslim university would be undesirable and that its tendencies and teachings would be narrowly sectarian and particularist. I strove hard to counter these criticisms, making it a cardinal point of all my appeals for help, all my speeches and articles, that the sons of Aligarh University would go forth "through the length and breadth of the land to preach the gospel of free inquiry, of large-hearted toleration and of pure morality."

I was not without support in high places. Lord Minto was succeeded by Viceroy Lord Hardinge of Penshurst, a statesman and diplomat with a wide and long experience of life with and among Muslim people in Iran and throughout the Near East. As the member of the Viceroy's Executive Council responsible for education there was a brilliant and devoted administrator, Sir Harcourt Butler, uncle of Mr. R. A. Butler, Chancellor of the Exchequer in Sir Winston Churchill's Government of 1951 onward, and the minister responsible for Britain's great Education Act of 1944. Interest in education is a tradition in the Butler family. Both Lord Hardinge and Sir Harcourt understood our Muslim position and were aware of the fundamental differences in the social, cultural and spiritual background of Muslim and Hindu. For myself, I tried again and again to make it clear that I regarded Muslim educational advancement not as an end in itself, but as a means to an end. If we were to advance down the road toward independence and self-government—however distant that goal might seem—we must, as a community, possess the knowledge and the intellectual equipment to cope with the political responsibilities to which we were beginning to aspire. I had no narrow sectarian purpose in view. I urged from the outset that Sanskrit should be taught, and with it the history and evolution of Hindu civilization, religion and philosophy, in order that our people should be able better to understand their neighbors. A university of our own was essential because it was the best and most enduring means of developing the spiritual unity of Islam.

The work of converting others to this belief which I held so ardently, of building up support for it and of raising funds was extremely strenuous. I traveled all over India. I went to great Muslim leaders, to the poor and to the rich, to princes and to peasants. My own monetary contribution was one hundred thousand rupees, which was quite a sum in those days; in all I collected more than three million rupees. These were years of unremitting hard work. For days and weeks at a time, it seemed, I lived in railway trains. In every town at which the train stopped I would address Muslim gatherings on the platform of the railway station. At every opportunity I preached the cause of Aligarh. My honorary private secretary, and my right-hand man throughout the campaign, was the late Maulana Shakak Ali; without his steadfast, unwearying help

I doubt if I should ever have been able to make a success of it.

We reached a climax in the long campaign with the Muslim Educational Conference at Nagpur in 1910 at which the Aligarh project was the principal item on the agenda, and indeed dominated the proceedings. Our aims were well expressed by the chairman of the conference, Mr. Yusuf Ali, who defined the scope of the university which we hoped to establish in these words: "It will have no tests; freedom and originality of thought will be encouraged. It will be a Muslim university in the sense that it will promote the ideals which the Muslims of India have evolved out of the educational experience of two generations."

Now when all is said and done, when I look back on all that the Muslim University of Aligarh has stood for and achieved in the past forty years, this is without doubt one of the facets of my life which I can record and contemplate with real and abiding satisfaction. I do not want to stress only its political consequences, momentous as those have been. Where else than in a Muslim university would it have been possible to establish and maintain, alongside and fully integrated with the libraries, the laboratories and all the facilities essential for a full understanding of our world and our time, a true center of Islamic faith and culture, in which can be expounded and practiced the principles of our religion, its universality and its real modernity, its essential reasonableness, its profound spirit of tolerance and charity and respect for other faiths? That I played my part in establishing such a center is for me one of the happiest, most consoling and most fortifying thoughts to take into old age.

VII

In Czarist Russia

THE YEARS 1910 to 1914 were eventful, busy and active. Joy and sorrow, work and travel, disappointment and fulfillment, sport and friendship—I had my ample share of them all during these years. My wife lived largely in France. In 1909 my first son was born to her, to whom I gave the name Mehdi. His brief little life ended in February, 1911, and my second son, Aly, was born in the following June. His birth was a profound solace and joy to my wife and me, but for her the happiness of his babyhood was tinged with a solemn sense of responsibility. Long years had passed since there had been a son in our family. The grief we felt at the loss of our first-born gave an especial sharpness and watchfulness to the care which we exercised over his brother's upbringing. When he was quite little he was pronounced to be delicate; one of the leading child specialists of the time had a great belief in the health-giving and health-maintaining properties of the Normandy coast in summertime, especially the sea air and bathing. From the time that he was two or three, therefore, my wife took him each summer to Deauville, and their winters they spent in the south of France. For some years my wife lived in Monte Carlo and then she moved to Cimiez.

In May, 1910, my great and good friend, King Edward VII, died in London. As loyal duty and friendship bade, I hastened to attend his funeral; and I had an audience with his successor, King George V.

The King was buried in St. George's Chapel at Windsor; my

place in the procession and my seat in the chapel were near the Royal Family and the Royal guests from foreign countries. In the procession the German Emperor walked beside King George V. This placing provoked a minor but significant diplomatic incident. When a number of sovereigns are assembled together in one place, the protocol is that they take precedence, not according to the size or importance of their countries nor alphabetically (as do delegates at an international conference), but according to seniority of accession to the throne. Thus if the King of Bulgaria (in the days when there was a reigning King of Bulgaria) had been longest on the throne, he would take the head of any procession, and if the sovereign of the United Kingdom or the Emperor of Japan had only just acceded, he would go last. But on this occasion the German Emperor was put next to King George V, the principal mourner, and all the other monarchs followed him. The storm arose indirectly because the King of Greece, who was senior in the matter of accession, walked ahead of the King of Spain. Now the King of Spain had acceded to his throne in babyhood, before the German Emperor had come into his inheritance; and King Alfonso considered himself every whit as good as the Kaiser, if not his superior. As soon as the various sovereigns had taken leave and were on their way home, the Spanish Ambassador made a formal protest on behalf of his Royal Master and his Government against the affront offered by the placing of the German Emperor ahead of His Most Catholic Majesty, and added that since the King of Greece had been put ahead of the King of Spain on the grounds of seniority of accession, then both the King of Greece and the King of Spain should have preceded the German Emperor if protocol were to be properly observed. This put the Foreign Office and the Court in a quandary. An apology would have been worse than useless because high officials of Court and State are not expected to make mistakes of this sort. Finally the problem reached the King. He solved it diplomatically and ingeniously: the Kaiser, he said, was King Edward's nephew and his own first cousin, and for these reasons alone he had been given precedence, not as a reigning sovereign, but as a family mourner.

This rather pitiable little complication aside, the whole ceremony was deeply affecting.

Later there was trouble too about the precedence accorded to the former President of the United States, Mr. Theodore Roosevelt, who was his country's official representative. Since he was not a Royal personage, his place in the funeral procession and at other solemn functions was a lowly one. The United States and France both protested at this procedure which, although it was in full accord with international custom in those days, seemed even then both undignified and anachronistic. From that time on, the representatives of republics were deemed to rank with royalty and a new and more fitting order of precedence was established.

There were many wet eyes that day—mine, I am not ashamed to admit, among them. Shortly afterward King George V issued instructions to the India Office that I was to be invited to the Coronation as a special and honored guest of his own, and the invitation was to cover not merely the ceremony but all the functions, banquets, state receptions and so forth. I sat in his box at the special gala performances at the Royal Opera House.

The Coronation of King George V was held in June, 1911. It was one of great pomp and splendor, a stately showing forth of all Britain's grandeur, wealth and power. The year 1911, however, was a year of increasing international tension; and the internal political conflict in Britain over Mr. Lloyd George's budgetary measures, over Ireland and over the constitutional position of the House of Lords had become extremely embittered. Against the dark clouds of the approaching storm, the Coronation Season shone with a special brightness of its own. I have two vivid recollections of this time. The first is of the ballet that was given at the gala performance at Covent Garden; it was *Pavilion d'Armide*—surely the most appropriate ballet possible for such an occasion—and the principal dancers included Nijinsky and Karsavina. It was of unforgettable beauty and grace; it stands out in my memory as one of the most exquisite theatrical experiences that I have ever seen.

My other lasting impression is of the presence of the Crown Prince of Germany, of the attention that was paid to him, of the real and sincere effort made by everyone, from the King and Queen down, to convince him of Britain's good will and peaceful intentions toward his country. I recall that at Covent Garden he sat on Queen Mary's right, and I saw that she engaged him in earnest conversation and that her courtesy to him was not formal or chilly.

A few months later the King and Queen set out on their journey to India—the first and only reigning Sovereign and his Consort to visit India during the period of British rule. Early in 1912 the magnificent Coronation Durbar was held in Delhi; it was announced that the capital and seat of government were to be transferred to Delhi from Calcutta, and a new city built commensurate with the dignity, authority and (as it seemed then) permanence of the Indian Empire. The partition of Bengal was annulled, and— as a climax and crown to my work in past years, and the work of those who had co-operated with me zealously and so steadfastly— Aligarh was given the status of a university. The King-Emperor personally bestowed on me the highest decoration which it was possible for any Indian subject of the Crown to receive, a Knight Grand Commander of the Star of India.

Splendid as were the Durbar ceremonies, they were marred by two curious contretemps. At the great state banquet, to which most of the notables of India had been invited, some disaster occurred in the kitchen, and the food that emerged was just enough to give the King and a handful of people sitting near him a full meal. For almost all of the guests it was the only chance in their lives that they would ever have of dining in the King's company, but most of them had no dinner.

The other had far more alarming implications. The investiture, at which I received my decoration of the G.C.S.I., was held at night in an enormous and brilliantly lighted tent. It was a full state ceremony: the King-Emperor and his Consort sat enthroned; the Viceroy, the Provincial Governors, the Commander in Chief and the senior military commanders, a superb assemblage of Ruling Princes, all the leading officials, Indian and British, from every corner of India, were gathered in honor of a stately and memorable occasion. Suddenly one of the electric light bulbs, high up near the canvas canopy of the roof, began to play pranks. All eyes went to its flickerings. Suppose it were to explode—in that instant the same silent, horrifying thought occurred to almost everyone present. Whistles were blowing, we could hear fire engines clanking up; behind their Majesties' thrones officers had already drawn their swords and were hacking at the hangings and the canvas to make a way out for the King and Queen. But the rest of us were trapped. Had the tent caught fire it would have blazed up like a celluloid ping-pong ball put near the hearth, and scarcely one of us inside would have survived. The humanitarian aspect of the disaster which we contemplated was appalling enough. Even more fearful to most of us was the thought of the political, administrative and social chaos all over India that would have followed. The country would have been left without a single leading figure. Next day both the King and the Viceroy told me that instant orders had gone forth that no ceremony of this sort was ever to be held again by night in a tent.

A great military parade was a central feature of the Durbar celebrations. Many of us, Indian and British alike, were becoming more acutely aware of the importance of the Indian Army in Britain's world-wide imperial strategy, with her vast commitments and the growing sense of international tension. Britain's own Regular Army, a considerable portion of which was habitually stationed in India, was—though well trained and of admirable morale—small in comparison with those of any of her possible challengers. Haldane, as Secretary of State for War, had thoroughly reorganized the military machine and had brought into being the volunteer and part-time Territorial Army; but Britain had refused to heed the urgent pleas of the veteran Field Marshal, Lord Roberts, for a Continental system of universal national service. I was able to link the developing recognition of Britain's military needs and of India's position in relation to those needs with my own passion for Indian education.

In an article which I contributed to Leo Maxse's *National Review* in July, 1911 (it was not a journal whose imperialist politics I shared, but it was widely read by people whom I was eager to reach with my views), I put my arguments as forcefully as I could.

Educate, educate, educate. Look for a passing moment at the question of manpower. India could put troops into South Africa as quickly as they could be sent from England; she could land soldiers in Australia long before England could so do; and forces from India could reach western Canada almost as soon as from England. If by education the myriads of India can be taught that they are guardians and supporters of the Crown, just as are the white citizens of the Empire, then the realization that India and the self-governing dominions stand and fall together, bound by a community of interests and a common cause to maintain, will have come. It is imperative to give Indians the education to fit them for their future role in the British Empire.

In two world wars, one of which was to break out only three years after these words were written, my arguments were justified to the hilt.

The autumn of 1912 found me on my travels again—this time to Russia. The Czar Nicholas II, in appearance almost the double of his cousin, King George V, had visited India when he was Czarevitch; however, that was a good many years earlier, and I had never met him since. Many of his relatives habitually visited the south of France—the Grand Dukes Boris and Nicholas among them, and the Czar's own brother, the Grand Duke Michael—and with several I was on terms of warm friendship; they had often asked me to visit them at home.

Patrician and aristocratic life in England and in many other European countries had its own magnificence and stateliness; but they were as nothing compared with the luxury and opulence of the elaborate and gilded existence that was led by the Russian aristocracy in Saint Petersburg, as I saw it that winter.

More than thirty years have passed since the Revolution shattered their world; many were murdered, many went into exile, in towns like Harbin and Shanghai, in Constantinople, in Berlin, Paris and the south of France. Among those who had to refashion life from its foundations was a distinguished soldier, formerly Military Attaché in London, General Polovtsoff, who for many years has been a well-known and much-liked figure in Monte Carlo. Like many of his companions in exile, he has borne his vicissitudes with courage, dignity and a fine, high spirit. It happened that in 1912 I was the guest of General Polovtsoff and his brother in the house —the palace—which they had inherited from their father who had been a minister of the Czar.

The splendor of that house was beyond description. The banquet hall, in which my hosts gave a luncheon party in my honor, was, I am sure, fully three times the size of the great salon of any eighteenth-century Italian *palazzo*. Its walls were hung with magnificent pictures and tapestry; there were great, many-colored, strongly scented banks of hothouse flowers, and the luncheon itself was on a prodigious scale. And this was only one of many similar functions at which I was entertained in similar houses of almost fairy tale magnificence that I visited.

Life was adjusted to a curious and, at first, somewhat unsettling timetable, for which—accustomed as I was to social life in London and Paris—I was not immediately prepared. The first of my many invitations to supper showed me what I had to learn. I had been asked to what I knew was to be a big supper party at a famous general's house, to be attended by several of the grand dukes and a number of leading ladies of the theater. With my notions of this kind of entertainment in London or in Paris, I arrived at the house a little after midnight. To my surprise there was no one else there; even the servants looked as if they had just awakened, as they scurried around turning on the lights. For an hour or thereabouts I waited in some embarrassment until at last my host and hostess came downstairs. Between half past one and two the other guests began to arrive and the vast salon began to look a little less empty. It was well after two o'clock when we went in to supper. After supper there was some music, and it was nearing half past four when the party broke up and we went home. This, I quickly learned, was the normal convention.

Saint Petersburg was a winter capital. Its season was a winter season. I arrived there near its beginning, in late November. The cold was already intense. The days were dark and short, the nights long and bitter, and the city itself snowbound. Here are—to me—the reasons for the unusual tempo and rhythm of life there. The day ordinarily began about noon; shops, banks and offices remained open until late in the evening. Work was done and business transacted from midday on; and the nights were given up to the varied and elegant pursuits and distractions of a gay, cultivated and sophisticated society. The theaters were excellent, so were the opera and the ballet. There were innumerable parties; there were moonlight drives in *troikas* across the icebound Neva to some of the islands that were not too far distant from the capital. In the few hours of daylight there were often shooting parties in the surrounding countryside; enthusiastic sportsmen hunted not only game birds and deer but also bears.

All the houses were, to my way of thinking, grossly overheated and thoroughly underventilated. In cities like London and Paris I had grown accustomed to houses in which, even in cold weather, the windows and the doors were constantly open, and I was shocked and not a little disgusted by Russian habits in this matter. All houses were built with double glass windows. Some time in early November, when winter was setting in, workmen would nail down all these windows so that they could not be opened again until the end of April. One small pane was left free at the top of each window; every morning this would be opened for an hour or so and then shut again. This was all the fresh air that any room got. On my very first night at the British Embassy I said to my hostess, the Ambassador's wife, Lady Buchanan, that I thought this a most unhygienic and most unpleasant custom. She answered me that when she and her husband first went to Saint Petersburg, they tried to live as they would in England with the windows hardly ever fully shut, either by day or by night. However, the whole family fell ill. They had had to adopt the custom of the country, and since then there had been no illness. She told me too that in all the big houses, at which parties were given and large numbers of people gathered together, the rooms were scented and the air specially sweetened and purified.

The corollary of this permanent overheating of the houses was that Russians of all classes had comparatively light indoor clothing. But when they went out of doors everyone piled on heavy furs.

The well-to-do would be thickly wrapped in sables, the poorer classes in sheepskin. Everyone had sheepskin caps, thick warm gloves and snow boots. I had been accustomed to being told that one ought not to go suddenly from warm rooms into bitter cold outside, and at first I thought the whole Russian way of life—similar to some extent, I suppose, to that in Canada in the winter and in many of the northerly states of the United States—"unhealthy"; but a few weeks in Saint Petersburg and Moscow rid me of this prejudice.

I soon came to the conclusion that the Hermitage Museum was the finest I had ever seen, far superior to the Louvre, the National Gallery or New York's Metropolitan Museum. Its superiority lay in its rigid selectivity. There was nothing indifferent or third-rate on view; everything shown was of supreme merit. There was no need, as in every other big museum or art gallery that I have ever been to, to trudge mile after mile past inferior works, questionable attributions, copies and studies by the pupils of great masters. At the Hermitage, under the direction of Count Tolstoy, a relative of the great novelist, all this had been sternly relegated to the vaults. He had instituted, so I was given to understand, a regime whereby everything was taken off the walls which, whether by a great artist or merely alleged to be by him, did not possess its own intrinsic beauty and merit. The effect therefore was of a small, pure collection of masterpieces, and it was extraordinarily refreshing.

One of the treasures of the Hermitage was a wonderful collection of old English silver of the period of Charles II, when the art of the silversmith in England was at its height. The collection, so I believe, was made by Peter the Great, who visited England as a young man and worked in the shipyards at Deptford. Half savage, half genius, he had a strong and genuine aesthetic streak in him, excellent taste—witness the pictures which he chose while he was in Holland—and sure, clear judgment.

I remember being transported with delight by the choral singing in the Cathedral of St. Isaac in Saint Petersburg. I have often listened to fine singing in both Catholic and Anglican cathedrals in Western Europe, but never have I heard a choir whose singing was as pure and as majestic as that. Boys were recruited, I was told, from all over Russia, trained from an early age and given sound professional or technical schooling at the same time.

Despite the full social life that I led with the Czar's brother, the Grand Duke Michael, his cousins, and the officers of his crack regiments, I never met or had an audience with the Czar. He lived a strangely secluded existence; and in the last years of his sad and troubled reign his seclusion deepened and his circle narrowed. He was of a nervous, shy and naturally melancholy disposition; his Empress was superstitiously pious, courageous and dignified but utterly out of touch with reality; his son and heir was delicate and ailing. All the circumstances of his life combined to encourage him in a somber remoteness. I was told that if I wanted to see him, an official approach and a request for an audience would have to be made through diplomatic channels and that it would have to have the character of an official visit. I did not, therefore, even make the attempt. One of the Czar's few sociable characteristics, so I was informed, was his love and enjoyment of the theater, especially ballet and the opera. He had a habit of coming into a theater after the performance had started, accompanied only by one or two officer friends, and would slip unobserved into a small stage box. The only indication of his presence would be the loud and enthusiastic applause, the hurrahs and bravos, which were heard behind the curtain of his box. Perhaps only there, a few feet from the make-believe world beyond the footlights, could this shy, sad, solitary man forget his sorrows and shed his inhibitions.

From Saint Petersburg I went on to Moscow. Moscow's prosperity in those days was founded on commerce and industry. The court and the aristocracy made Saint Petersburg their headquarters; rich industrialists were the chief citizens of Moscow. Their wealth was derived from various sources: sugar, the rapidly developing oil industry of the Caspian Sea region, and piece goods from the cotton factories of Moscow. They bore a considerable similarity to the same powerful capitalist class in the United States. They lived in magnificent style; their houses were virtually palaces and museums, for, like the nobles of Saint Petersburg, many of these merchant princes were connoisseurs of the arts. I noticed, incidentally, that Moscow's tastes seemed more catholic than Saint Petersburg's; my favorite French impressionists had to some extent taken their fancy, whereas in Saint Petersburg all the paintings that I saw were of the classical schools.

The gulf between rich and poor was truly appalling. I took some trouble to study labor conditions in the mills and textile factories; they resembled in many ways Bombay's cotton mills, but conditions in them were infinitely worse. I have no hesitation in saying that, poor, miserable and ill-fed as were the Bombay mill hands of those days, they looked happier and livelier than the Moscow workers of the same sort. In Bombay you could at least see smiles; every Moscow mill hand looked drawn, haggard and tired to death. Yet I doubt if either in the matter of wages or diet the Moscow worker was worse off than his Bombay counterpart. The reason for the difference lay, I think in one simple fact—the climate. In his hours off work, for at least eight months of the year, the Bombay mill hand, however poor and downtrodden, could walk in the fresh air, could see the sun and the moon and the stars. For eight months of the year life for the Moscow worker, on the other hand, was only possible indoors—in the hot, steamy atmosphere of the mill or in an overheated, overcrowded little room in one of the great, grim barracklike buildings that served so many of them as homes.

An odd custom prevailed in those days in the public baths of Russia's great cities—I visited one in Moscow, so I am not talking from hearsay—in the administration of what were known as Russian steam baths, really very like our Turkish baths. The attendants who looked after you, who gave you your soap and your towels, massaged you, looked after all your wants, were women—but elderly and of so plain and sour a visage that it would have been utterly impossible to imagine even the slightest misbehavior with them. Nor, I was assured, did misbehavior occur. This was simply regarded as useful employment for women past middle age; and no one—except the raw foreign visitor like myself—thought it in the slightest degree unusual.

While I was still in Russia the first match was set to the conflagration that soon was to engulf the whole world. The Balkan Wars—

first the attack by a combination of small Balkan countries on the Ottoman Empire, and then their ferocious quarrels with each other —were not then merely localized conflicts, which many tried to convince themselves that they were; in fact they were unmistakable indications of what was to come. Turkey, whose internal difficulties and troubles had accumulated and deepened in recent years, reeled under successive blows from her enemies. Day after day news of fresh disasters reached the outside world. By the time I returned to Paris and before I left for India the extent of Turkey's plight was obvious; it seemed to be only a matter of time before her foes had her completely at their mercy. The feelings of Muslim India, indeed of the whole Islamic world, were deeply stirred. I made as much haste as I could to get back to Bombay. My closest political friends and associates were active on behalf of the Turks. An organization had been set up, representing all branches of Muslim opinion in India and including many of those most closely concerned with Aligarh, the purpose of which was to render all possible assistance to Turkey and to bring maximum pressure to bear on the British Government in order that Britain's influence should be exerted in the Concert of Europe to make defeat tolerable and honorable for the Turks. A practical gesture of help had been made in the equipment and dispatch to the war area of a Red Crescent medical mission, led by Dr. Ansari—one of India's outstanding medical practitioners. This was the kind of worthwhile, humane work which I was happy to support. I contributed too to Turkey's war loans; but I found myself involved in a distressing difference of opinion with the majority of my Muslim brethren in India over our attitude toward this conflict—a difference of opinion which, I am sorry to say, disrupted for some time the hitherto close and intimate associations, in thought and action, which had subsisted between myself and other Muslim leaders in India.

We were giving as much aid as we could to Turkey, but how much, in fact, did it amount to? The honest answer was—very little. We were not, of course, our own masters; and our real influence on British policy toward the whole Turco-Balkan issue was negligible. The Government lent a courteous if distant ear to our earnest supplications, but they could well afford to pay no practical attention to us. British opinion in general about the Ottoman Empire—"the Sick Man of Europe," as portrayed by the political cartoonists of *Punch* and other papers—was at best lukewarm. The European political situation was tense and precarious. Britain's friends in the Concert of Europe—France, Russia and to a lesser extent Italy—were anything but pro-Turkish, and the main concern of all of them was to avoid an open breach with Germany and Austria. A delicate but chilly policy of nonintervention was the furthest that Britain was willing to go. But the general run of Muslim opinion in India was far more fiery; the honor and integrity of Islam were at stake; and we should urge the Turks to hold on, to face every risk and accept every sacrifice and to carry the war on to the utmost end.

Fine sentiments, but I demurred from them. I pointed out that it was not really in our power to help the Turks; great and generous as our emotions doubtless were, we were quite incapable at that time of turning our feelings into action. To call on the Turks to stand, fight and die for the cause of Islam, to the last piastre and the last Turk, while we survived was unfair and unjust to the Turks. Far from helping them, it was actually worsening their plight.

I did not mince my words. I gave an interview along these lines to *The Times of India*, the most widely read and most responsible newspaper in the subcontinent. I observed that it was all very well to send heartening telegrams to the Turks: GO ON, FIGHT ON! DO NOT ACCEPT DEFEAT, WHATEVER THE SACRIFICE! But we who had sent the telegram could then go home and sleep soundly in our peaceful beds. These were not popular comments, and they evoked a storm of protest from Muslims all over India. However, as such storms will, it passed, and soon enough this controversy was forgotten in the whirlwind of perils and problems of the First World War.

VIII

The First World War

THE EARLY MONTHS of 1914 found me on another visit to Burma.
I then took a step of some importance in respect to my Ismaili
followers. I advised them to undertake a considerable measure of
social and cultural assimilation. Burma, although annexed to the
British Empire and at this time under the control of the India
Office, was a country in which national, patriotic sentiment was
strong, and nationalism a spontaneous, natural and continuous
growth. I was convinced that the only prudent and proper policy
for my followers was to identify themselves as closely as possible
with the life of Burma socially and politically, to give up their
Indo-Saracen names, habits and customs and to adopt, permanently
and naturally, those of the people alongside whom they lived, and
whose destiny they shared.

From Burma I made a brief trip to Europe in that last spring
and early summer of the old epoch; and thence I went to East Africa. Somewhat to my surprise and greatly to the distress and in-
dignation of my followers there, the authorities in German East
Africa requested me not to visit their territory. While I was on my
way to Africa, the Archduke Francis Ferdinand and his wife were
assassinated in the little Bosnian border town of Sarajevo; and the
casus belli had been provided. By the time I reached Zanzibar
the situation had become critical; in the last days of July and the
first days of August there was an exchange of ever graver and
more grave telegrams. Russia and Germany were at war; the Germans invaded Belgium; and on August fourth Britain declared war
on Germany.

I had no hesitations, no irresolution. Ambitions, aspirations, hopes and interests narrowed down to one or two intensely personal, solitary decisions. I had one overruling emotion—to go to England as fast as I could and offer my services in whatever capacity they could best be used. I was in good health; I was still young and strong; my place was with the British. I returned immediately and without comment the insignia of the Prussian Order of the Crown (First Class), which the Kaiser had conferred on me. I telegraphed instructions to my followers in and on the borders of all British territories that they were to render all possible help and support to the British authorities in their area. I offered my personal services to the British Resident in Zanzibar, and I took the first steps in organizing, from among members of the Indian community, a transport corps to assist in maintaining communications from the coast to the interior. Then I made haste to get to England. There were rumors—well-founded as it proved—of a German sea-raider at large in the Indian Ocean, and the authorities in Zanzibar asked me not to go to Mombasa as I had intended and thence to England by the first available ship, but to proceed by way of South Africa. From the Union I got passage to England, and I was in London by mid-September. I had had no practical military experience, so it seemed to me that my immediate contribution to the war effort was likely to be humble. I volunteered for service in the ranks in any unit in the British or Indian Army. I called on Lord Kitchener, the Secretary of State for War, whom I had known well in India and with whom I had served on the Viceroy's Legislative Council more than a decade earlier; I urged that I should be enlisted as a private in the Indian contingent then on its way to the Western Front.

Kitchener, however, whose knowledge and experience of the East were massive and profound, had other views as to the sort of service I could render. He was fully cognizant of both the perils and the possibilities latent in the involvement of Eastern, predominantly Islamic, peoples in a conflict of these dimensions. Germany's intrigues and influence in Constantinople had greatly increased in recent years; the great dream of a German hegemony extending from Berlin to Baghdad was one of the many fantasies on which German imperialist thinkers and teachers had dwelt eagerly and lovingly. The Turkish Government seemed deeply disrupted and drained of the capacity to take independent and effective decisions of its own. For Britain it was essential to retain control over the then vital artery of Empire: the seaway through the Mediterranean, the Suez Canal, the Red Sea and the Indian Ocean, which led not only to India but to Australia and New Zealand and to the Colonial territories of Southeast Asia. In all this complex of political and strategic needs and obligations, it seemed to the British Government that I held a position of considerable importance. Soldiering in the ranks was not, Kitchener gave me firmly to understand, for me.

Most significant of all, it had not passed unnoticed by the British Government that I had won and held the respect and trust of many important Turks. Lord Kitchener requested me to use all my influence with the Turks to persuade them not to join the Central Powers, and to preserve their neutrality. I discovered that Kitchener was by no means alone in his idea of the sort of employment to which I could best be put. His opinion was shared and supported by the Secretary of State for India, by the Foreign Secretary, Sir Edward Grey, and by the Prime Minister, Mr. Asquith. Indeed even the King, when I had the honor of lunching with him, referred to it.

Therefore while overtly I busied myself with rallying young Indians in England—of whom there were considerable numbers—to volunteer for the Indian Field Ambulance Corps, and in raising a comforts fund for them, discreetly and urgently I got in touch with the Turkish Ambassador, Tawfiq Pasha. At my request he sent an invitation to the Young Turks, who had assumed power in Turkey's revolution of 1908, to send a ministerial delegation to London to enter into direct negotiations with His Majesty's Government. Britain was prepared, on her own behalf and on behalf of Russia and her other allies, to give Turkey full guarantees and assurances for the future.

We had high hopes of bringing off what would have been, from every point of view, a diplomatic victory of first-rate importance. I was quite aware that my own emotions were deeply involved. As a Muslim I was most anxious that Turkey should be spared the trials and the horrors of renewed war, not against a ramshackle alliance of small Balkan states, but against the mighty combination of some of the greatest industrial and military nations in the world. The Turks had but lately emerged from their earlier ordeal; they were in desperate need of a breathing space; it seemed impossible that they could enter a new struggle and not face almost illimitable catastrophe. It had to be admitted that the Turks were justifiably suspicious of "guarantees," however specific, offered by the Western Powers; they had had too recent and too rueful an experience of similar guarantees which seemed to them promises made only to be broken. Yet even allowing for the most cynically realistic appreciation of the situation, as it existed in the last months of 1914, neutrality (which was all the Western Powers asked of Turkey) would have given the Young Turks the time they needed in which to carry out their program of social, economic and military reform.

Tawfiq Pasha was a key figure in our approaches. He had been for many years the Sultan Abdul Hamid's Foreign Minister. The Young Turk Revolution had displaced him from that office; nevertheless the new regime maintained their trust in a most experienced and capable statesman. In London and other Western capitals he was held in the highest esteem. Venerable, sage and shrewd, he was a good friend of mine; he and I trusted each other implicitly. What was even more important, he was in full agreement with my attitude in this business.

He took occasion immediately, however, to warn me that our negotiations would have had a much greater chance of success if the Allies had asked Turkey to come in on their side rather than proposed mere neutrality, for which at the end of the conflict nobody would thank her. He went on to say that he was convinced also that Russia would never agree to Turkey's joining the Allies, as such a step would put an end to all Russia's hopes of expansion at Turkey's expense, either in the northeast, around Erzerum, or southward from the Black Sea. In confidence I communicated these observations to Lord Kitchener. Within a few hours he told me that the Allies had no desire to bring Turkey into the war on their side. In view of this preliminary exchange, we entered negotiations under a considerable handicap. Nevertheless I was an optimist for several days, and my optimism seemed far from groundless.

Suddenly it became known that two German warships, the *Goeben* and the *Breslau*, had evaded Allied naval vigilance and were lying at anchor off Constantinople. Their presence drastically altered the whole situation. The Turks accorded them hospitality and protection. They were a visible sign of German naval vigor and capacity. Combined with the remarkable moral ascendancy which had been established in Constantinople by the German Military Mission, under its extremely able and resolute commander, General Liman von Sanders, the ships presented the gravest possible menace to our hopes—lately so high—of maintaining Turkish neutrality. By the close of 1914 the Central Powers were confident of a quick victory on their own terms; an elderly Prussian general named von Hindenburg had inflicted a crushing defeat on the immensely gallant but incompetently led Russian armies in the marshes of Tannenberg in East Prussia; in the west the German armies, held almost within the sight of Paris, had stabilized themselves along that six hundred-mile front which, with pitiably little variation and at appalling cost of life on both sides, was to be maintained until August, 1918; a solitary cruiser, the *Emden*, at large in the Indian Ocean, had inflicted spectacular shipping losses on the Allies, and turned up impudently in Madras Roads. Tragically misled by all these signs and portents dangled before their eyes by the exultant Germans, the Turkish Government took the irrevocable step of declaring war on Russia. This automatically involved the Ottoman Empire in war with Great Britain and France.

To a strategist like Churchill this decision offered an opportunity (which was never fully seized) of ending the slaughterous deadlock on the Western Front and of striking at Germany and Austria from the southeast. To me at that moment it was a shattering blow. Its sharpness and severity were mortifying in the extreme; and when the Turkish Government, striving to put a respectable and popular façade on what was in fact unprovoked, inexcusable aggression, proclaimed this a *jehad,* a holy war against Christendom, my distress and disappointment crystallized into bitter resentment against the irreligious folly of Turkey's rulers. My resentment was given a razor edge by my knowledge of how near we had been to success in our negotiations. The fruit was just about to be plucked from the tree when not merely the tree but the whole garden was blown to pieces.

I reacted strongly. I joined with other Muslim leaders in an earnest appeal to the whole Islamic world to disregard the socalled *jehad,* to do their duty and stand loyally with and beside the Western Allies—especially Britain and France in whose overseas possessions the Muslim population could be counted in many millions. On my own responsibility I published a manifesto setting out my view of the grievous error committed by Turkey. I pointed out that the Ottoman Government and such forces as it would dispose of were bound to be regarded as pawns in Germany's aggressive, imperialist strategy; that in declaring war on Britain and the Allies the Turks were acting under the orders of their German masters; and that the Sultan and his advisers had been compelled by German officers and other non-Muslims to take this step. I stressed the fact that neither Turkey in particular nor Islam in general need have any apprehension about the purely defensive actions of the Western Powers.

"The British and Russian Empires and the French Republic," I said, "have offered to guarantee Turkey all her territories in complete independence on the sole condition that she remain neutral. Turkey is the trustee of Islam, and the whole world is content to let her hold the holy cities in her keeping. All men must see that Turkey's position was not imperiled in any way and that she has not gone to war for the cause of Islam or in defense of her independence. Thus our only duty as Muslims is to remain loyal, faithful and obedient to our temporal and secular allegiance."

It is not, I think, an unjustifiable claim that these words of mine, coming when they did and whence they did, had a genuine and steadying effect when it was needed. The vast majority of Muslim subjects of the Western Powers faithfully preserved their allegiance; Muslim soldiers fought and died alongside their Christian comrades on battlefields all over the world. The whole ugly idea of a *jehad,* manufactured and exploited by the Kaiser and his advisers for their own purposes, collapsed and little more was heard of it after the early months of 1915.

However, I do still regard the failure of our attempt to open my negotiations with the Sublime Porte in the last months of 1914 as a tragic turning point in modern history. Had Turkey remained neutral, the history of the Near East and of the whole Islamic world, in the past forty years, might have been profoundly different. What had been Islam's natural center and rallying point for hundreds of years, the Sultanate in Constantinople, was destroyed. Turkey, as we shall see later, emerged from her tribulations under the inspiring leadership of Mustafa Kemal, restored and purified in spirit, but shorn of her Empire. Millions of Arabs, who had lived for centuries under the tolerant suzerainty of the Turks, discovered, not only on the high plateau of central Arabia but in the lands of the fertile crescent, the joys and sorrows, the difficulties and the ardors of nationalism. And the British Empire, in the years from 1918 on, fell heir—by accident rather than by intention—to that Near and Middle Eastern hegemony so long exercised by the Ottoman Empire; and to *vilayet* and *pashalik* succeeded mandatory government. French involvement in Syria, the Greek adventures and disasters in Asia Minor, the clash of Zionism and Arab aspirations, Ibn Saud's carving of a new kingdom in Arabia, the emergence of the Sharifi family from a local chieftainship in Mecca to the foundation of ruling dynasties in two kingdoms—all these complex consequences and many more were to flow from the Young Turks' rejection, under German pressure, of the advances made to them at the end of 1914.

Kitchener, whatever doubts may have begun to make themselves felt in early 1915 as to his capacity to organize and conduct Britain's war effort in the West, was certainly alert to every contingency in the East. It was not long before he sent for me with another proposal, for a diplomatic or quasi-diplomatic task, which had Cabinet backing, and indeed the personal approval and interest of King George V. This concerned Egypt, where the political situation was confused and delicate. Kitchener himself had been peremptorily recalled to take up his duties at the War Office, when he was about to board the cross-Channel steamer on his way back to his post as British Representative in Cairo. Egypt was nominally part of the domain of the Ottoman Emperor, the Khedive was nominally his viceroy. This status had been preserved—in name, though in nothing else—after the British Occupation in 1882. As every Egyptian statesman and politician for many years past has had occasion to point out times without number, the British Occupation of Egypt was always said—by the British—to be purely temporary. Yet somehow in defiance of logic and in defiance of promises and undertakings, it continued; until in the early years of this century, as I have recorded in an earlier chapter, Egypt looked to all intents and purposes like a British colony.

In the First World War, as in the Second World War, Egypt was a military base of the highest strategic and logistical importance for Britain and her allies. By the beginning of 1915 the number of British, Indian and Dominion troops stationed in Egypt was large and growing steadily. Alexandria was a great naval harbor and dockyard. The Suez Canal was a vital strategic waterway. On its Sinai banks, however, although Sinai was theoretically part of Egypt, were units of the Turkish Army, whose role at this time was purely static and defensive. But British strategic thinking had not cast Egypt for any quiescent, nonactive role. It was to be the base whence every offensive against Turkey was to be launched. Already thousands of transports were bringing to Alexandria, Port Said, Kantara and Ismailia the men from Britain, from Australia and New Zealand and from India, who were to fight and die, with unforgettable heroism and to no avail, on a barren, rocky little peninsula that guarded the European shore of the Dardanelles Straits leading to Constantinople. As great a degree of certainty and stability as possible in Egypt's internal political situation was, from the military point of view, a prerequisite if this huge operational base was to be preserved in good order.

The confusion began at the top. There was no Egyptian political leader of any caliber, and the Khedive himself, Abbas Hilmi, was in, of all places, Constantinople. Since he had not returned to Egypt when called, it was perhaps inevitable that Allied opinion should believe him to be pro-German and that Allied propaganda should portray him as such in the crudest terms. However, I came to know Abbas Hilmi well in later years during his long exile in Europe, and I am convinced that he was wronged and misjudged. I developed a real affection for him and a real admiration for the clarity and brilliance of his intellect. He told me what I am convinced was the true story of his "defection." Shortly before the Turkish declaration of war, he was attacked by a would-be assassin and wounded in the face and jaw. For the rest of his life he carried the heavy scar which was the effect of this attack.

From 1920 until his sudden death at the end of the Second World War, I saw a great deal of Abbas Hilmi and we became very firm friends. He had a beautiful yacht called *Nimat Ullah* which was more or less his home on the Riviera during the winter months and the early spring; and he usually spent the late spring and summer in Paris and Switzerland. I often lunched with him aboard the *Nimat Ullah*, and in Switzerland I saw a great deal of him. Of one thing I am convinced; he was never anti-British, and he had the greatest affection for his English friends. Naturally when he was Khedive he greatly resented the fact that, without any legal right or authority and no moral claim to power and prestige, the British occupation authorities were treating his country as a colony and he himself more or less as a glorified maharajah. This brought him constantly into conflict with Lord Cromer, who was in fact though not in name the absolute ruler of Egypt. However, he always told me that Cromer was a great gentleman, that his word was his bond and that however bitter their personal relations because of their political differences, he for his part never lost his respect for Lord Cromer. With Lord Kitchener the personal differences had led to bitterness, and he never forgave Kitchener for the strife between them. He told me that he thought it most unfortunate that Lord Kitchener was never grateful to him for having

helped him to become Sirdar of the Egyptian Army at the beginning. When Kitchener's predecessor retired, there were two or three
candidates for the post; and Abbas Hilmi maintained that he himself sent a telegram to Queen Victoria particularly asking for Kitchener's appointment.

He told me that had he not been wounded, he would certainly
have escaped from Constantinople. He had no wish nor desire to
remain, and as soon as he got better he wanted to go to Egypt; but
the British authorities were by no means keen to have him there.
It was his opinion that while he was shown that he was not wanted,
he was at the same time made the scapegoat. However there was
no bitterness toward the English either as a people or as individuals.
He accepted the whole episode as a game of cricket in which he
had been the loser; and as a good sportsman he said, "The game is
over and done with—now let's have a drink together."

Though he was a good Muslim, a real believer who said his prayers regularly, he also had a great admiration for the Catholic hier-
archy and was in touch with them in Paris; and I believe that his
donations to their charities and good works were on a large scale.
He always told me that the Church of Rome could do far more
for their friends when they were in trouble than any freemasonry.
He was a brilliant financier; he made a large fortune for himself
even after he had lost the greater part of his original capital in
Egypt. He had, however, a curious trait. After his death it became
apparent that he had often put his money on the wrong horse.
Shrewdly suspicious of all respectable bankers, high-class *agents
de change* on the Continent or stockbrokers in England, he was
yet capable of being taken in by a lot of fourth-rate intriguers, and
he would hand over large sums of money to them for all kinds of
wild-goose projects. Apart from this, he had some extremely doubtful characters in his entourage—hangers-on who won his confidence,
goodness knows how. I believe that after his death his heirs found
that he was nothing like as rich as he had been and that a considerable portion of his fortune had disappeared. I think I can explain how this must have happened. Before and during the Second
World War he often told me that in view of the uncertainty of the

future and the possible difficulties of movement or of getting control of his investments in America or Canada or even in South America (though he knew all the tricks of forming holding companies in harmless places such as Cuba or Tangiers and transferring large blocks of stocks and securities to them), he felt that he might be stranded in wartime without getting the benefits of his investments. He dreaded the possibility of years of want and difficulty in which, like Midas, he might be full of gold and yet die of hunger.

In telling me these things he was really advising me to follow his example. I asked him therefore how he got around it. Was it by having a considerable part of his fortune with him in safes and vaults? Naturally I pointed out that bank notes in such amounts in wartime would be a real hindrance, whereas gold in the quantities that he wanted would be too heavy and not practicable except for comparatively small sums. Ah, he said, but the finest type of jewelry—that which is the very best and free from taint—like gold maintains its value. If it is perfect—large or small—jewelry can always find a purchaser; and it has the advantage that its possessor has a large fortune at his disposal wherever he happens to be. I naturally concluded from this argument that he had vast sums invested in jewelry, particularly since he frequently urged me to do likewise.

He died of heart failure suddenly about three o'clock one morning in an apartment in Geneva; and it was not until much later, about mid-morning, that people came and opened his various boxes and vaults. I naturally informed his son and his heir of what he had told me about having large amounts of jewelry with him, but to my surprise and rather to my distress his son told me that they found nothing except small amounts of cash. There are two possible solutions: first, that if he had had the jewelry he had sold it at the end of the Second World War when he thought there was no immediate possibility of a third war, or, second, that it had vanished during the hours between his death and the official opening of his personal effects.

To return to his miscalculations in 1914-1915, in the fog of war the Allies could not be expected to have any accurate knowledge either of Abbas Hilmi's real views or intentions, or of the way in which those intentions were frustrated. The result in Egypt, however, was something near chaos; the confusion was deepest about Muslim opinion, and for the reasons which I have outlined it was essential to maintain the internal security of Egypt.

My mission therefore was to clarify and stabilize opinion. I was asked to take a colleague with me, and I therefore turned to an old and dear friend, Sir Abbas Ali Baig, who was then the Indian member of the permanent Council which advised the Secretary of State for India in London. We set off for Cairo as soon as we could; and we were received there with almost royal honors. We were there as the official guests of the British Commander in Chief; and we addressed ourselves forthwith to a delicate and difficult task, with many ramifications into many levels of Egyptian society.

First there was the palace to be won over, or rather the principal personages in the Egyptian ruling dynasty. There was the Sultan who had been nominated in Abbas Hilmi's absence; there was his brother, Prince Fuad, who later became King Fuad I, who had both German and Italian affiliations; there were several other influential princes, and most important of all the Sultan's son who was married to the Khedive's sister. There were the Ulema, the Muslim divines who were the heads of Al Azhar University, the great, intensely conservative and traditional theological school which is a center of religious life not only in Egypt but in the whole of Islam. And there were the ordinary people of Egypt—the literate who sit in their cafes endlessly and eagerly discussing every edition of every newspaper, and the villages and peasants, the *fellahin* who from time immemorial have been the real source of Egypt's strength.

We conceived of our task as one of explanation and exhortation. We had to convince those to whom we spoke, in private as well as in public, that not only their interest but their duty, as good Muslims, lay in supporting and sustaining the cause of the Allies. I could, of course, speak with authority, from recent and personal knowledge; I pointed out that the Turks had had every possible chance of fair terms from the Allies, that Great Britain and France were willing to exert all their influence on Russia to safeguard Turkey's interests for the future, and most important of all, that neutrality would have given Turkey that breathing space she needed. While Europe was engaged on its grim process of self-destruction, Turkey would have had time to reorganize the whole loose, vast system of provincial administration, to conciliate the increasing discontent of the Arab nationalists, and to carry out all those social, political and economic reforms which would have strengthened and unified the Empire. All these advantages had been lost in a single gambler's throw; gamblers, after all, are not winners, and history shows that political punters have as little chance of success as punters on the racecourse or at the casino.

Our mission produced the effects for which we had hoped. The internal stability of Egypt throughout the First World War and the assistance that this tranquillity gave to the Allies were factors of notable and continuing importance right up to the time of General Allenby's final victorious advance across Palestine and Syria to Aleppo and the foothills of the Anatolian mountains.

From Egypt I made my way to India, having visited the Indian forces—already of considerable strength—who were encamped in the Canal Zone, having encouraged them (many, of course, were Muslims) and having exhorted them to do their duty, to fight loyally for the King-Emperor, the Sovereign to whose service they were bound by oath. In India I realized—by the volume of enthusiastic praise and thanks that greeted me, from the Viceroy downward—that we had done a good job. One particularly agreeable personal consequence of this mission to Egypt was the strengthening of my affection for Sir Abbas Ali Baig, who became and thenceforward remained one of my closest, lifelong friends. In a new generation his sons, incidentally, are no less distinguished public servants than he was; one is now Pakistan's Minister in Moscow and the other, formerly permanent head of the Foreign Office in Karachi, is now High Commissioner in Ottawa.

Later in the year I went back to London, and once more was heartened by the sense of success in our mission in Egypt. The King himself, the Prime Minister and other members of the Cabinet thanked me warmly, and I was genuinely gratified to feel that I had been of real service.

In April 1916, His Majesty accorded me an honor of very special personal significance. He sanctioned the grant to me of a salute of eleven guns and the rank and precedence of a First Class Ruling Prince of the Bombay Presidency. The end of the Indian Empire, and the vast political and social changes consequent on that passing, have deprived this gesture of any contemporary meaning, but in the circumstances and conditions of 1916 it was a high honor and a most generous and thoughtful action on the part of the King. The salute granted to a Ruling Prince, and the number of guns in it, was an important matter of precedence and prestige; there was only one previous instance of such a salute being granted to anyone who was not a territorial Prince, and that was to Sir Salar Jung, the Prime Minister of Hyderabad, who in 1857 was chiefly responsible for keeping Central India and the Deccan loyal to British authority. *The Times*, commenting on this honor in an editorial, observed: "It has fallen to the Aga Khan to serve in vastly wider fields than Sir Salar Jung and to exert much more than local or provincial influence in a crisis of British rule even greater than that of the mutiny."

Inevitably sorrow and loss came, as the result of war, to me and to my family, as to so many other families across the width of the world in those harsh times. My cousin, Aga Farrokh Shah, while engaged at my request on a political mission to the tribes and my own Ismaili followers in Kerman, was assassinated at the instigation of German agents. India's losses on the battlefield in Flanders and in Mesopotamia were grievous. I myself was laid low with a difficult, painful and protracted illness. Early in 1916 I began to be aware of considerable ocular distress and difficulty; my pulse was extremely irregular, and although I was on no diet and was eating well, I began to lose weight rapidly. A physician in Paris diagnosed my malady as Graves' disease, of which the symptoms were protruding eyes and a small goiter. I went to Switzerland to the famous Dr. Kocher at Berne, who was the greatest contemporary authority on all forms of goiter, to see if my case was operable. After I had been under observation in a Swiss sanatorium for several weeks, I was told that it was inoperable. Frankly I seemed to be going downhill fast; for eighteen months and more I stayed in Switzerland, making no progress at all but rather deteriorating steadily.

Suddenly the British Government took urgent and alarmed cognizance of what subsequently became known, in Swiss legal history, as the affair of the Lucerne bomb. The German Secret Service did not believe that I was really ill. They thought, however, that their country's cause would be well served were I put out of the way for good. They arranged to have a bomb thrown at me; and to make the operation certain of success they also arranged, with typical German thoroughness, to have my breakfast coffee poisoned. The bomb did not go off; I did not drink the coffee. For years after the war ended the Swiss painstakingly investigated the whole episode and the inquiry attained a good deal of notoriety at the time. In 1917, however, all that the British Government saw fit to do was to request me to leave Switzerland. So I returned to Paris.

My host of friends there, including those of the American colony to whom I have referred elsewhere, were thoroughly shocked and alarmed; I was (so they told me later) in their view a lost case. For myself, I still kept hope—though it flickered feebly. It seemed to me that many famous doctors had seen me in Switzerland and in France. All kinds of treatments, batteries of drugs, had been tried on me to no avail. Then a Professor Pierremarie examined me and produced a startlingly novel diagnosis. I had not been suffering from goiter at all. He began a fresh line of treatment, and within a year I was thoroughly on the mend. One effect remained, however, in that my eyes never quite resumed their normal position.

However, this long illness meant that I was of necessity withdrawn from all public activity for more than three years, until the summer of 1919.

It was a long seclusion which I ameliorated slightly in its later stages by writing a book, called *India in Transition*, which set forth my views on the future of India and of all Southeast Asia, and to which I shall have occasion to refer later.

Part Three

THE MIDDLE YEARS

IX

The End of the Ottoman Empire

THE WORLD to which I, restored at last to health and eager to get back into harness again, returned in that summer of 1919 had undergone vast and far-reaching changes in the three years of my seclusion: the collapse of the Czarist regime in Russia, and the passage granted by the Germans to Lenin and his fellow conspirators to let them loose in their native land; the Treaty of Brest-Litovsk; the complete defeat of the Central Powers on all fronts in 1918; the abdication of the Kaiser and the end of the Austro-Hungarian Empire; the emergence of the militant Socialist revolutions in sundry European countries; in the Near and Middle East the end of the Ottoman Empire. President Wilson seemed in those months an almost apocalyptic figure of deliverance, with his doctrine of "self-determination" for all peoples. Everywhere the war had unleashed huge tides of political feeling which were not to be smoothed or subdued. The peacemakers assembled in Paris to contemplate, with profoundly mingled and complicated emotions, a world scene bristling with difficulties and dangers, an awe-inspiring chaos which the peoples of many nations looked to them to resolve immediately and tidily into an ordered millennium. Relief at the end of the long, bloodstained nightmare of the war mingled with a naïve but vigorous optimism. Peace was to usher in an epoch of unmarred political, social and economic tranquillity. Even so august a figure as my old friend, Lord Curzon, then Leader of the House of Lords, was affected by the prevailing mood, and in his speech in the House of Lords, in November, 1918, announcing the Armistice he intoned with fervor Shelley's lines which begin: "The world's great age begins anew."

India was far from unaffected by all that had happened. In 1917 when the conflict was at its sternest, there was a general feeling in Britain, official and unofficial, that India's contribution to the Empire's war effort, the valor of her soldiers, the staunchness of her leaders and people, earned more than formal recognition. On the strong recommendation of the Viceroy and of the Secretary of State for India, Edwin Montagu, the Government on August 20, 1917, published a statement of its aims in respect to India.

"The policy of His Majesty's Government," said this statement, "is that of increasing association of Indians in every branch of the administration and the gradual development of self-governing institutions with a view to the progressive realization of responsible government in India as an integral part of the British Empire."

This was a momentous pronouncement. It marked the explicit commitment of the then British Government and its successors to a radical departure from what, in conflict with the principles of the Act of 1833, had grown to be the basic and accepted purposes of British rule in India. In the earlier schemes of administrative reform, the Cross-Lansdowne proposals of the 1890's and the Morley-Minto of the early 1900's, there had been no hint of any intention to transfer fundamental power and responsibility from British to Indian hands; self-government in India had never been mentioned. Now, there it was in words that all could read. I have been told that in the original draft which went to the Cabinet the words "self-government" were used; Lord Curzon—of all people—changed them to "responsible government." He thus made it inevitable that when the constitutional reforms to implement the declaration were introduced, they took the pattern which came to be known as "dyarchy"; for the word "responsible" implies in those who exercise it, responsibility *to* someone—to whom? To Governor or Viceroy, and thus to Britain and British Parliament, or to the Indian electorate and people? Dyarchy, workable compromise though it was sometimes made, was bound to present this dilemma to ministers, both in the provinces and at the center. It was the expression, in terms of practical and day-to-day administration of that almost schizophrenic duality of outlook—that split between ideal intention and workaday application—which henceforth characterized the British attitude toward India. Schizophrenia is not a basis for happy relations; in it, however, is to be found much of the explanation of the estrangement, deepening to embittered hostility which ended only, and then with miraculous swiftness and completeness, with the final and total withdrawal of British rule in India.

In 1919 all this lay in the future, and I for my part was taken up with a wider, bolder vision in which—formulated first in my book, *India in Transition*—I sought to interest everyone who had any responsibility for Indo-British relations, principally, of course, Edwin Montagu, the Secretary of State. Edwin Montagu was a Jew, totally assimilated into the British pattern and way of life, brilliant and lovable, a member of that interlocked Montagu-Samuel-Isaacs Anglo-Jewish group of families which has made so notable a contribution to British life in the past half century.

I was eager in 1919 that under British inspiration and guidance there should be built up a South Asian federation of self-governing states extending from the Malayan Peninsula to the confines of Egypt—a federation on what may loosely be termed Commonwealth lines, and within the framework of the British Empire (Commonwealth, of course, was a word which had not come into use in 1919). It seemed to me—it still seems to me now—that this was *then* a feasible scheme and a better solution to world troubles than that adopted. Had the British Government accepted it, and had it been executed resolutely, I am certain that there would have developed in southern Asia a strong power—an association of powers—in which healthy democratic institutions would have evolved naturally and easily and which would have provided effective support for Britain and (as it turned out) the United States and the Southern Dominions in an hour of grave need and a permanent bulwark against aggression.

In a measure these proposals of mine were a fulfillment and an extension of ideas and hopes which had been implanted in my mind during my years of close association with Gokhale. In the autumn of

1914 when I hastened back to London from Africa to make as effective a contribution as I could to the war effort, I was met by Gokhale, who, though extremely ill at the time with diabetes—and constitutionally averse to London's mild, foggy climate—had prolonged his stay there in order to see me. Amid the pressure of a great deal of other work, we saw much of each other and discussed freely and frankly all our hopes and fears for India. We strove to compose a draft memorandum which we intended to address to the Government embodying the very large measure of agreement which we had hammered out in our conversations.

Early in 1915 Gokhale was dead. But before he died he completed his political testament which he addressed to me, with the request that I should make it public in two years' time, when (as he hoped) the war might be over and India capable of facing the supreme task of working out her own destiny.

In due course I published Gokhale's testament as he bade; and on my own behalf I added a memorandum pleading that after the war East Africa might be reserved for Indian colonization and development in recognition of India's war services.

However these were and are dreams of what might have been. History has taken a different road. The final scheme of reform, as it was promulgated in the Government of India Act of 1919, was very different, on a far smaller scale, and limited only to India. And, alas, it produced not the peaceful, gradual evolution, slow step by step, toward responsible government that had been hoped for, but instead a phase of extreme unrest and violent political turbulence. Moderate, constitutional-minded leaders in Indian politics, such as my friends Sir Pherozeshah Mehta and Gokhale, were dead. A new generation sought for new methods of achieving much more far-reaching aims—and in a hurry.

Even before Parliament considered the Government of India Bill, the situation in India had taken several turns for the worse. A committee set up under the chairmanship of Lord Justice Rowlatt to consider the juridical aspects of political agitation issued its report which recommended the establishment of special courts to deal with acts of sedition. The report had a hostile reception. The ex-

ample of Ireland was not lost on India. Extremism on both sides
took charge. The Rowlatt Committee's recommendations were accepted by Parliament; and as soon as the bill embodying them became law Congress declared a *hartal*, a general strike, in protest.
More than once during these harsh and distressing months, I urged
restraint, not only on the part of my followers but of the Muslim
community in general; less than a fortnight later, however, occurred
the dreadful "Amritsar incident" which set back by many years
any hope of constructive and abiding amity between Britain and
India.

The shock of this episode and the bitter memories it left behind
poisoned relations for years. I suppose that if I had been the sort of
person to despair, I should have despaired then. But I was so actively engaged in seeking from the British Government a clear and
honorable line of conduct on a matter involving the highest political principles that despair was a luxury for which I had neither the
will nor the time.

One effect of dyarchy was that it involved the transference of a
good deal of authority in internal matters in India from the center
to responsible officials in the provinces. The effects of a centralized
bureaucracy were as notable in the India Office in London as they
were in Simla or New Delhi. I was asked to be a member of a committee in London charged with the task of decentralizing and reor-
ganizing the work of the India Office. It was mainly a matter of
clearing some of the channels by which the Secretary of State got his
information and defended his department and himself in the eyes
of those to whom he was ultimately responsible, the elected members of the British House of Commons. It was hard work, but it gave
me a clear picture from the inside of the workings of the great administrative machine by which a modern State is conducted.

It coincided, as I had indicated, with a period of strenuous political activity, in which I directed my efforts mainly to trying to prevent the complete dismemberment of the Ottoman Empire and to
establishing a peace settlement in the Near and Middle East which
would be not only just and equitable but also practical.

I must therefore describe in some detail the background to the swirl of political and diplomatic work in which I was caught up. One of the countless major questions which faced the victorious Powers in the immediate postwar period was, What was to be done about the Ottoman Empire, over vast regions of which the Allies were, by the end of 1918, in military occupation? It was true that the Turks retained control of their own homeland, Anatolia, and of the historic, ancient capital, Constantinople, but from Tripolitania in the west to Kurdistan in the east, from north of Aleppo to Wadi Halfa, in enormous territories whose populations, in a great diversity of races and culture but predominantly Muslim, had once owed allegiance to the Sultan of Turkey, the controlling authority was now an Allied Military Governor.

In the heat of the war many promises of spoils in the hour of victory—spoils to be torn off the vanquished body of Turkey—had been made; by the beginning of 1919 few were capable of fulfillment, nearly all were irreconcilable one with another. The MacMahon letters, addressed by the acting High Commissioner in Egypt in 1915 to the Sharif Husan in Mecca, could not possibly be reconciled with the Balfour Declaration issued in 1917; both conflicted sharply with the Sykes-Picot agreement, by which Britain and France shared out huge areas of the Ottoman Empire as "spheres of influence." The most flagrantly impossible undertaking of all was that Constantinople (since Czarist Russia had retained an historic interest in what had once been the Graeco-Roman city of Byzantium) should be given to Russia. This at least could be ignored, since the Bolshevik leaders had made their own peace arrangements with the Germans in the Treaty of Brest-Litovsk and since the Soviet regime and the Western Allies were in a state of undisguised hostility. But for Turkey as a whole the hopes of a tolerable peace settlement looked slender.

Almost all the British political leaders who were to have any influence over the peace discussions were markedly anti-Turkish. Lloyd George, the Prime Minister, was a friend and admirer of Venizelos, the Greek leader; he saw certain similarities in historical experience and outlook between Greece and his own Wales; he was therefore enthusiastically pro-Greek, and though not actively anti-

Turkish, he was quite indifferent to the fate of the Ottoman Empire. Arthur Balfour, the signatory of the letter to Lord Rothschild announcing that it was Britain's intention to establish a National Home in Palestine for the Jews, was openly and actively pro-Zionist, and he was also extremely prejudiced against the Turks historically and racially.

Now Zionism, I may say in passing, was something of which I had had long and by no means unsympathetic experience. My friend of the early and strenuous days in Bombay, Professor Haffkine, was a Zionist—as were many other brilliant and talented Russian Jews of his generation who escaped into Western Europe from the harsh and cruel conditions imposed upon them by Czarist Russia. Haffkine, like many of the earlier Zionists, hoped that some arrangement could be made with the Turkish Sultan whereby peaceful Jewish settlement could be progressively undertaken in the Holy Land—a settlement of a limited number of Jews from Europe (mainly from the densely populated areas then under Russian rule) in agricultural and peasant holdings; the capital was to be provided by wealthier members of the Jewish community, and the land would be obtained by purchase from the Sultan's subjects. As Haffkine propounded it, I thought this sort of Zionism useful and practical. It contained no hint, of course, of the establishment of a Jewish National State, and it seemed to me worth putting before the Turkish authorities. There were, after all, precedents for population resettlement of this kind within the Ottoman Empire, notably the Circassians—of Muslim faith, but of purely European blood— who were established by Abdul Hamid in villages, in what is today the Kingdom of Jordan, with excellent results. Abdul Hamid could well have done with the friendship and alliance of world Jewry; and on the broader ground of principle, there is every natural reason for the Jews and the Arabs, two Semitic peoples with a great deal in common, to be close friends rather than the bitter enemies which unfortunately for both sides the events of the past thirty years or so have made them. In furtherance of what was then a shared interest in Zionism, Haffkine gave me, when I first went to Paris in 1898, letters of introduction to a number of his Jewish friends including the savant and Rabbi Zadek Kahn,* and through him I met the famous Baron Edmond de Rothschild. Baron Edmond was a princely benefactor of the early Zionist experiments; some of the first settlements in Palestine were financed by him and owed their ultimate prosperity to his generous support and interest. When I called on him I was introduced to his two sons, James, then an undergraduate at Cambridge, and Maurice, a boy in the uniform of a naval cadet. Baron Edmond remained my friend until his death; and for well over fifty years now both James Rothschild and Baron Maurice de Rothschild have been good and close friends of mine.

Rabbi Kahn prepared a statement of his and his friends' ideas on Jewish settlement in Palestine. It was an elaborate plan for colonization on a scale and in a manner which would have helped and strengthened Turkey; and one of its most logical claims to consideration was that the Ottoman Empire was not a national state but multinational and multiracial. With the Rabbi's proposal I made my approaches to Abdul Hamid through Munir Pasha, the Turkish Ambassador in Paris, and through Izzet Bey, the Sultan's confidential secretary. However, the scheme, good or bad as it may have been, was turned down by the Sultan, and I heard no more of it. I must say its rejection has always seemed to me one of Abdul Hamid's greatest blunders.

But just as the defeated Turkey of 1917-1918 was a different country from the Ottoman Empire of the nineties, so the Zionism of 1917-1918 and on was, of course, a very different matter. And the Zionists were only one group among many, anxious to extract all they could from the carve-up of Turkey. Arab nationalism was scarcely less strongly in the ascendant, and it possessed many powerful friends and zealous advocates in and near the British Government. Sir Gilbert Clayton, T. E. Lawrence and many other so-called "political officers" who had served in the Middle East had—I must say, from my own knowledge—encouraged Arab nationalism

---

* There are sometimes complications in nomenclature. Long afterward in London I was introduced to a well-known American society woman, Mrs. Corrigan, by a friend of mine simply as "Aga Khan" with no titles and no further explanation. Brightly smiling Mrs. Corrigan said that she was a great friend of my brother, Otto Kahn, of New York's Metropolitan Opera House!

in and out of season, sometimes openly and sometimes secretly, long before the fall of Turkey. The British had already established a military administration in Palestine. The French advanced the remarkable claim that they had an historic right to protect the Holy Places in Jerusalem. The Greeks, encouraged by another group of romantic, philhellene Englishmen, were in a mood of dangerous expansionism. And at the very heart of real power in the Peace Conference, Clemenceau had no love for the Turks; and President Wilson, in the one interview which I had with him, frankly admitted that he really knew very little about the whole problem.

Almost the only support on the side of the victors that Turkey could muster was Indian. The greater part of Muslim interest in India in the fate of Turkey was natural and spontaneous, and there was a considerable element of sincere non-Muslim agitation, the object of which, apart from the natural revolt of any organized Asiatic body against the idea of European imperialism, was further to consolidate and strengthen Indian nationalism in its struggle against the British.

The reasons for Muslim concern were profound and historic. Turkey stood almost alone in the world as the sole surviving independent Muslim nation, with all its shortcomings; the Imperial regime in Constantinople was a visible and enduring reminder of the temporal greatness of Islam's achievements. In the Khalifate there was too, for all of the Sunni sect or persuasion, a spiritual link of the utmost significance. As the war drew to its close, anxiety had intensified in India in regard to the safety of the Holy Places of Islam and the future of the Khalifate. Gandhi, who had succeeded my old and dear friend, Gokhale, as leader of Congress' political movement and organization, shrewdly seized what he saw to be a chance of maintaining and heightening anti-British sentiment throughout the whole subcontinent. The storm of agitation that swept India on this issue was formidable. The Indian delegates at the Peace Conference, the Maharajah of Bikaner and Lord Sinha, heartily and sincerely supported by Edwin Montagu, the Secretary of State for India, made an emphatic protest against the various proposals for the partition of Turkey and the practical dissolution of the Khalifate that were being eagerly canvassed around and about the conference.

It had been decided to settle the fate of defeated Germany first. This thorny task was accomplished in considerable haste, and the Treaty of Versailles was signed on June 28, 1919. Thereafter protracted discussions continued about the treatment of the other vanquished nations. My friend Syed Amir Ali and I began an energetic campaign to put the real issues, so far as Turkey was concerned, before British and indeed world public opinion. I had private interviews with numerous influential statesmen, together we wrote long letters to *The Times*; on every possible public and private occasion we made our views known.

We drew vigorous attention to certain specific pledges given by the Prime Minister, and in a letter to *The Times* quoted these pledges *verbatim*:

"We are not fighting," Lloyd George had said, "to deprive Turkey of its capital or of the rich and renowned lands of Asia Minor and Thrace. While we do not challenge the maintenance of the Turkish Empire in the homelands of the Turkish race with its capital at Constantinople, the passage between the Mediterranean and the Black Sea being internationalized and neutralized, Arabia, Armenia, Mesopotamia, Syria and Palestine are in our judgment entitled to a recognition of their separate national condition."

We tried to sum up the outlook of those for whom we knew we had a right to speak:

> What do the Muslims want? What do we plead for? Neither they nor we ask for any new status for Turkey. We consider it, however, our duty to urge, for the fair name of England, nay of the British Empire, that the pledge the Prime Minister in the name of England gave to the world, and in particular to the world of Islam, should be maintained; and that the Turkish Sovereign, as the Khalif of the vast Sunni congregation, should be left in absolute possession of Constantinople, Thrace and Asia Minor stretching from the north of Syria proper along the Aegean coast to the Black Sea—a region predominantly Turkish in race. It would, in our opinion, be a cruel act of injustice to wrench any portion of this tract from Turkish sovereignty to satisfy the ambitions of any other people.

Instead of bringing peace to Western Asia, such a settlement will sow the seeds of constant wars, the effect of which cannot be expected to remain confined to the country where they happen to be waged. For the defection of the adventurers who dragged their stricken people, who had already undergone great misery, into the world war, Turkey has been sufficiently punished by the secular expropriation of some of her richest provinces. But we submit that the maintenance of the Ottoman Sovereign's spiritual suzerainty in these countries, whilst maintaining his prestige and thus conciliating Muslim feeling, would be the means of making the position of the Muslim rulers or governors of those countries unimpugnable. But so far as Thrace, Constantinople and the homelands of the Turkish race are concerned, Muslim feeling is absolutely opposed to any interference under any shape with the Sultan's sovereignty.

In India itself, as the months wore on, and as the time came near for signing a treaty with Turkey, the agitation grew to such proportions and was of so unanimous a character as gravely to worry the Viceroy, Lord Chelmsford and the Secretary of State, Edwin Montagu (whose personal sympathies, as I well knew, were warmly engaged on the Turkish or Asiatic side). Most of all they were disturbed at the thought that the Montagu-Chelmsford reforms, on which such high hopes had been pinned, were to be launched in practice into this atmosphere of turbulence and hostility.

In the Viceroy's Legislative Council it was proposed that I should be sent to London as the leader of a deputation to the Prime Minister, representing the views not only of Muslims but of the whole articulate population of India.

The other members of the deputation were the president of the Khilafat movement, Mr. Chatani; one of India's most eminent advocates, Hassan Imam; and Dr. Ansari, a leading member of Congress. Lloyd George saw us, but we realized that our mission was doomed to failure, for meanwhile the Turkish treaty, known to history as the Treaty of Sèvres, was being prepared, with strangely little regard for the realities which, within a few years, were to shape the Near East anew. The unfortunate Sultan was under rigorous supervision, a solitary and helpless prisoner in Constantinople. Turkish, Arab and Greek deputations were hurrying back and forth between the Mediterranean and London. Sometimes their arguments were listened to; often they were not. The Treaty of Sèvres was to be an imposed, not a negotiated, treaty.

Constantinople was at first promised to the Greeks; then this promise was taken back. It was at last decided that Thrace and Adrianople in European Turkey should be Greek, and Smyrna in Asia Minor. Turkey was reduced to a sort of "rump" state in the highlands of Asia Minor, with a strip of coastline along the Black Sea. There was even talk of an independent, sovereign State of Armenia in the far Northeast—if the Russians could be persuaded to stomach it. Some sort of order was hacked out of all these conflicting claims. In August, 1920, the hapless Turkish representatives appended their signatures to the document which embodied them all.

This concluded in a sense the first phase of my own campaign for a just treatment of defeated Turkey. Before I record the events of the second phase which rapidly followed, it may be proper to consider the effect of the decisions which the peacemaking politicians took in 1919-1920, in stubborn and bland disregard of the advice which we proffered them.

Muslim opposition to the break-up of the Turkish Empire had a basis—however much misunderstood it may have been—of true statesmanship and understanding of the absorbing political realities of the Middle East. First we felt that the separation of the Arabs from the Turks (hailed at the time as emancipation from a tyranny, but within a few years all Arab nationalists were singing a very different tune) would not lead to the emergence of a single strong Arab nation extending from Egypt to Persia and from Alexandretta to Aden and the Indian Ocean. We foresaw in large measure what actually happened: the formation of a number of small Arab nations, for many years of little more than colonial status, under British and French overlordship. We predicted that the Arabs would in fact merely be changing masters, and where these masters had been Muslim Turks, they would now be Christians or (as ultimately happened in a large part of Palestine) Jews. Even now after the lapse of thirty years or more, the Arab states that succeeded the

Ottoman Empire—though the ignominious protectorate and man-dated status has been abolished—are nothing but an aggregation of small kingdoms and republics, not one of them capable of standing up alone in the face of any powerful opposition and, despite the Arab League, incapable of maintaining either individually or col-lectively real resistance to the influence of Soviet Russia or the West-ern democracies. Neutrality in any conflict between these two is a forlorn dream.

Consider for a moment how different matters might have been had these emerged after the First World War a federal union of Turkey, the Arab states of the Middle East and Egypt, with a single defense force and a united foreign policy. Our instinctive Muslim faith in the idea of the continuance of Turkey as a great power had wisdom in it, for it would have achieved practical results, in the security and the stability of the Middle East, far transcending any-thing that the makeshift, haphazard policies of the years since the end of the Second World War—piecemeal withdrawal of political suzerainty by Britain, piecemeal financial, economic and military aid by the United States—have been able to effect. Consider the dis-ruption and the political *malaise* which have been the lot of the Middle East in recent years; consider all the unavailing effort that has gone into the attempt to build up a Middle East Defense Or-ganization, in any degree paralleling NATO, and ponder how easily, how honorably all this might have been avoided.

It is, however, no use crying over spilled milk. The victors of the First World War, unlike the victors of the Second World War, were intoxicated with their triumph and the sense of their own victory and believed that they could build a brave new world according to their heart's desire. History was as tragically as categorically to give the lie to that belief.

The Treaty of Sèvres, harsh though it was, was practically still-born. Even by the following spring of 1921 events had overtaken it, and it was obvious that it must be urgently reconsidered. A new con-ference was called in London. At the Viceroy's request I put the Muslim point of view to this gathering. Its sittings however proved abortive. For what everyone in West and East alike had ignored was the emergence from the ruin of Turkey of a soldier and statesman of genius, Mustafa Kemal Ataturk, who in the time of their deepest tribulation had rallied his sorely stricken but indomitable people. Denied access to Constantinople, he had set up a provisional capital at Angora—now Ankara—high on the Anatolian plateau; he had re-built, re-equipped and retrained the shattered Turkish Army. Having obtained a secret understanding with Russia, he could arm his troops, and he was assured of protection in his rear. He was thus prepared to defend his country's cause, not around some distant conference table, but in his homeland and on the field of battle. Few were at first aware of the magnitude of this new development.

The Greeks who, being nearest of all to the scene, should have known most, were blinded by their own lust for military victory and territorial expansion. Taking exception to the establishment of the Turkish provisional government in Angora, they began an ambitious, grandiose, and as it proved, utterly disastrous series of military operations in Asia Minor.

To add to the complications, the British Government became restive over their demands for the release of certain British prisoners held in Turkey. Over this, at least, I was able by direct intervention and a direct appeal to the new Turkish authorities to secure a certain relief in an increasingly critical situation. The Turks released the prisoners, and this crisis blew over.

By the late summer of 1922, however, the prospect looked blacker than ever. Mustafa Kemal's tattered but valiant armies had stood at bay in their own hill country, had stemmed the tide of Greek invasion, and now were in the full flush of victorious advance. They captured Smyrna, the great Graeco-Levantine port on the coast of Asia Minor, put it to the sack, and before the eyes of the crews of Allied warships lying in the harbor, set whole areas of it on fire. It was the Greek army now which was a tattered, defeated remnant in flight. Mustafa Kemal's forces stood at the gates of Constantinople and demanded the right of free, unimpeded passage to reoccupy Thrace and Adrianople.

The whole situation was both ominous and confused. A mixed Allied military force, under the command of a British General, Sir

Charles Harington, held Chanak and the approaches to Constantinople, which the Turks had already renamed Istanbul. A vigilant, cautious but resolute man, Harington awaited orders from London. A single reckless or inconsidered action on his part, even a stray shot developing into a fusillade, might precipitate a general conflict a little less than four years after the cease fire at the end of the First World War. But the character of the military commander on the spot was not the only factor in this grave and delicate crisis. The British Government was in a curiously unrealistic and bellicose mood. A long, trying period of industrial unrest, with a protracted coal strike and a huge roll of unemployed, had been succeeded by the difficult and involved negotiations which ended the worst of the "troubles" in Ireland and which were clinched by the signing of the Irish treaty. But Lloyd George's second Coalition Government, returned to power with a huge majority in the "coupon" election of 1918, had run its course. The Liberals had never really forgiven Lloyd George for his brusque ousting of Asquith in December, 1916, in the central political crisis of the war. The Conservatives supplied the bulk of his Parliamentary support, but they were becoming increasingly restive and suspicious of the Prime Minister's incurable political adventurism. Did he think that in the Chanak crisis, as it was called, he perceived an opportunity to end the dissension and dissolution in the ranks of his supporters, to prevent his own increasing isolation and to rally Parliament and people behind him in a great united effort? Was it a gambler's throw or was it gross miscalculation?

I was in London when the crisis was at its worst, and I exerted every effort to prevent its culminating in what I knew would be a disastrous as well as an unjust war. This time I was not fighting a solitary battle against an overwhelming tide of contrary opinion. Now I had powerful allies and supporters. The columns of *The Times*, as so often in my public career, were open to me. The first Lord Rothermere, who had just assumed personal control of the group of newspapers built up by his brother, Viscount Northcliffe, was my staunch supporter. And Lord Beaverbrook, the man by whose influence and eager advocacy exercised at the right moment

Lloyd George had come to supreme power as Prime Minister in 1916, was now as sincerely convinced that Lloyd George was set on a course that would bring nothing but suffering and hardship. However, the first concern was not to encompass Lloyd George's fall but to prevent—of all unnecessary wars—the most unnecessary that could ever have been waged.

Early in September the British Government issued a statement on Chanak which was both pugnacious and injudicious, and ended with an appeal to the Dominions for their help in the event of another war with Turkey. The tone of this pronouncement thoroughly alarmed British public opinion, which was in no mood to contemplate all the pain and sacrifice involved in another war in support of what could only be described as Greek intransigence and stubbornness. Protests were loud from all sides. The faction that was pro-Government and philhellene had only one strong card to play: Turkish forces were then almost in contact with the Allied—predominantly British—occupying forces in the Straits of Constantinople area. General Harington on his side was quietly determined to avoid any action which might involve his slender forces and commit them to any form of hostilities with the veteran, tough and resolute forces which Mustafa Kemal had already deployed with skill. On the other hand, at the earnest request of my friend, Lord Derby,* I was able to get in touch with the Turkish leaders and point out the grave perils inherent in any attack on the Allied forces; and I assured them that, pending a provisional settlement, their troops' strategic position would not in any way be prejudiced if they abstained from any offensive action. I pressed these considerations on my Turkish friends with all the urgency I could command. I am glad to say that sanity prevailed. An important contributory factor was that France had come to a secret understanding with Kemal and his Government; and French influence exerted by Monsieur Raymond Poincaré was all for a peaceful settlement. The decision for war could only have been a rushed one; once British public

* We met, I remember, at Newmarket, and Lord Derby asked me to use all the influence which I possessed.

opinion had time to ponder the issues, it could crystallize and express itself, and it was firmly for peace. The very real menace of another war in the Middle East was averted.

A vivid account of the handling of this crisis has been given by Lord Beaverbrook.* Throughout it Lord Beaverbrook was as active as he was staunch. Seriously worried by the drift in affairs, he often discussed this matter with me. I was happy to see that we were in full agreement and that in all my endeavors to assist the Turks I had his moral support. He too had reached the eminently sound and practical conclusion that "for Britain to fight Turkey in pursuance of the exploded policy of supporting Greek imperialism was a monstrous error which must be avoided at all costs." Beaverbrook sought the support of his friend and fellow Canadian, Bonar Law, then leader of the Conservative party, which supplied the bulk of the Government's voting strength in the House of Commons.

Beaverbrook's words to Bonar Law were blunt. "These men mean war," he said.

Those four words spelled doom for Lloyd George's Coalition Government. A meeting of the Conservative party was held at the Carlton Club, the party's great sociopolitical stronghold; the speech that swayed the meeting and brought about its decision to withdraw support from Lloyd George was made, not by Bonar Law, who was already an extremely sick man, but by a comparatively unknown back bench M.P., Stanley Baldwin, who less than a year later was to succeed Bonar Law as Prime Minister.

Lord Beaverbrook maintained his onslaught on the pro-Greek, anti-Turkish policy of the Coalition Government. On December 16, 1922, the day after the House of Commons had adjourned for the Christmas recess, *The Daily Express* gave a sensationally detailed account of the happenings of the previous September. It said that within ten days of the fall of Smyrna, when the Greek rout had already begun and it had been recognized by the Greek Government in Athens that their military position in Asia Minor was hopeless, Lloyd George encouraged them to continue fighting. Lloyd George

* In *Politicians and the Press.*

(said *The Daily Express*) took this step after having inquiries made by his principal private secretary, Sir Edward Grigg,* of someone attached to the Greek Legation, who had said that the Greek army could not possibly hold out longer without active British assistance in munitions and in credit. On September second, *The Daily Express* went on, when the Athens Government appealed to Lloyd George to arrange an armistice, another of his private secretaries telephoned the Greek Legation advising them that "their government should be very careful to avoid the mistake made by the Germans in 1918 and not conclude an abject armistice in a moment of panic."

Lloyd George never returned to office. In spite of our difference over Turkey, I am glad to think that he and I, even as late as 1940, when he came and lunched with me at Antibes, remained on terms of firm and sincere friendship until the very end of his life. Lloyd George was a man of infinitely compelling charm. His effective career as a politician was short, from 1905 to 1922. Its brevity may be explicable in terms of his personality, which was like a diamond cut in many facets; every facet had a brilliant light to throw out, but their number and their variety were so great that often contradictions occurred. There was only one phase in his life in which these contradictions and conflicts were resolved, and he appeared—and was—wholly consistent; this of course was during his first two years as Prime Minister, from 1916 to 1918—a period of supreme effort and greatness. Then, in spite of all the efforts of his critics to belittle him, he was as much "the man who won the war" as his great successor Churchill was in the Second World War. With the exception of that one triumphant phase, the brilliant and powerful many-sidedness of Lloyd George's character prevented him from influencing the history of his time to the extent which his talents—his imagination, his practical capabilities and his intellectual superiority —gave his admirers (such as myself) every hope to expect. As one of the Big Four who formulated the Treaty of Versailles, he was convinced—a conviction which I fully shared—that he would have used the power over Germany, which under its terms were given to the

* Now Lord Altrincham.

victorious nations, in a very different manner from that employed by his less imaginative and competent successors.

Of all the statesmen of that time whom I knew, Lloyd George alone, I feel sure, was capable of evoking and sustaining in the Weimar Republic in Germany of the late 1920's and early 1930's that self-respect and that genuine understanding and use of democratic institutions which could have saved it and the world from Adolf Hitler and the Second World War. But, alas, by then the volcano was exhausted not by its internal weakness but by its brilliance. The views which I have expressed here about Lloyd George and Germany were shared, I know, by Lord D'Abernon with all his profound knowledge and experience of Germany.

For myself an eventful period of close association with the politics and diplomacy of the Middle East in general and Turkey in particular drew to a close. The first abortive Lausanne Conference was followed by a second, more fruitful, during which I held what may be described as a watching brief. Britain's new Conservative Government was represented by Lord Curzon, the Foreign Secretary; the Turks sent a strong and capable delegation. Britain's mood was realistic and sensible. It was decided to accept the facts, to give *de jure* as well as *de facto* recognition to the new Turkey, and to let this revived and vigorous uninational State retain not merely its homeland in Anatolia, and the sea coast of Asia Minor, but also Thrace, Adrianople and Istanbul. Along these lines agreement was reached and the Treaty of Lausanne signed. Subsequently the Montreux Convention regularized arrangements for dealing with the passage of international shipping through the Dardanelles.

It might be possible to construe all this as a diplomatic defeat for Britain, but what in fact were its main results? A long period of growing harmony and understanding between Britain and Turkey and a Brito-Turkish relationship in the Second World War which, despite severe strain put upon it, was of great assistance to Britain and her allies. Think too what *might* have happened had Turkey been rebuffed once more: Russia would long since have been installed in Istanbul and, if not in Smyrna itself, along the coast to the north with her ships and aircraft ranging far out into the Mediterranean. The statesmen of the West, heady with the sense of their own political and military power, would have brought about endless complications and misery in an important and sensitive region; destiny and history itself, tugging the other way, gave Asia Minor years of tranquil development and reorganization, social, economic and spiritual. A complement to and a striking contrast with the new Turkey's experience was that of the Arab states in this same epoch— a story of division and weakness, of active nationalist elements in the various countries in constant conflict with Britain and France, and of a relatively submissive minority, installed in office, and therefore loyal to their British or French masters. Such in brief was the history of the Near East from the rise of Ataturk to the outbreak of the Second World War. Of all that happened in those sad and troublous years I was a spectator—occasionally in the columns of *The Times* a critic—but thenceforward I ceased to be, as I had so long been, an active participant.

One other political issue of some complexity and importance to which I devoted a good deal of time and interest in those immediate postwar years was the question of Indians in East Africa, especially in the rapidly developing colony of Kenya. As I have narrated in earlier chapters there had long been Indian settlements along the coastline of East Africa; these settlements contained a considerable and growing number of my own Ismaili followers, who contributed an influential and stabilizing element to the community. In Kenya, where in the 1950's race relations became a political issue of the most crucial significance, there were already clear signs, thirty years ago, of the dangers that were looming ahead. In the so-called "White Highlands" of Kenya there was a rapidly developing area of European—predominantly British—settlement, on the high rolling plateaus which lie between the coastal belt and the Rift Valley and Africa's great lakes and which constitute a temperate region in equatorial latitudes, fertile, climatically agreeable and eminently suitable to intensive agricultural development. The whole of Kenya was administered by the British Colonial Office as a Crown Colony. The British settlers, whose unofficial leader was Lord Delamere, a talented and highly individualistic English peer, had of recent years been demanding an increasing measure of self-government for themselves. They differed from the usual British community in a tropical country in that they were settlers, and they intended to make—and did make—Kenya their permanent home, bringing up their children there, and not merely live there for short tours of duty as did (in general) British officials, traders and planters in India, the Far East and West Africa. But the Indians, rapidly growing in numbers, saw in the settlers' agitation for self-government the imposition of racial, "white" supremacy, and their own permanent political and social exclusion and subjugation. They in their turn demanded complete political and electoral equality. The Colonial Office officials wavered; and they were not themselves competent to take the effective decisions which were made in Whitehall and Downing Street. At no time has it been possible for Kenya to settle its own destiny for itself; all of Kenya's problems have been subject to outside interference, influence and—in the final analysis—external decision.

The end of the First World War had seen in Kenya, as elsewhere, a release of pent-up and sharply conflicting political ambitions and emotions. The British electorate and its representatives in the House of Commons were—although theirs was the final decision in Kenya's affairs—in the great majority massively ignorant of Kenya's problems. From 1920 a series of decisions was made within the Colonial Office in respect to Kenya; each new decision appeared to cancel its predecessor. Matters were not helped by the fact that there were several Governors of Kenya and several Secretaries of State for the Colonies within a very few years. By the end of 1922 and the beginning of 1923 the situation in Kenya was confused and inflammatory. So strong were the sentiments of the British settlers that they had established a militant, secret organization of their own with which—in the event of the British Government's deciding, as they thought, against them—they proposed to take over the administration of the country. Indian opinion, both in Kenya and at home, was greatly agitated. It is fair to say, however, that even in the period of greatest tension no single incident of violence, involving a

European and an Asiatic, was recorded in Kenya; in spite of the deep political gulf between them, the communities remained on good personal terms.

To me the whole situation—had I not in my addendum to my friend Gokhale's political statement suggested that East Africa be set aside for Indian colonization?—was deplorable. I took my customary step of making my views known in a letter to *The Times*. The immediate danger, as I saw it, was that a few hotheads might commit acts that would affect the mind and imagination of Indians not only there and then but all over India and far into the future. In particular I urged that if the settlers really accepted the view that the British Empire of the future (we still had not evolved the concept of the Commonwealth, but we were moving rapidly toward it) was to be a truly co-operative association between men of all races and creeds and customs, then indeed in East Africa more than anywhere else in the Empire they should use their full influence and power to bring about a better general feeling and wholeheartedly accept the fact that, short-term feelings apart, in the long run their own interests made it necessary that the Indian community in Kenya should be as prosperous and as happy as it was large.

The Government of India was fully alive to the dangers of the whole situation. Lord Reading, the Viceroy, Lord Peel, the Secretary of State, and Sir Tej Bahadur Sapru who was one of India's representatives at the Imperial Conference of 1923, urged that there should be a conference—or if necessary a number of conferences— between representatives of India and all concerned with the administration of colonial territories, such as Kenya, Uganda and Figi, where there was any sizable element of Indian settlement, to establish the political rights and responsibilities of Indians in those regions.

Faced with this cogent and powerful request, faced too with the grim possibility of armed rebellion by British settlers in a Crown Colony, the British Government was by now far from unaware of the urgent need for action that would end the dispute. In this somewhat explosive atmosphere I was asked by the Government of India if I would lead the Indian delegation to a committee under the chairmanship of Lord Zetland, charged with the task of finding a solution to the whole delicate and difficult problem.

By the time we were appointed, Lord Zetland had become a member of Mr. Baldwin's short-lived first Government. I was asked to take the chair, but I felt that since I was a party to the dispute and the chief spokesman of the Indian viewpoint, it would be unfortunate for me to be chairman of the committee. We therefore had as our chairman Mr. J. Hope Simpson, M.P.; the other members were Sir Benjamin Robertson, a member of the Viceroy's Executive Council who had paid an official visit to Kenya in 1920, Diwan Bahadur T. Rangachariar and Mr. K. C. Roy. We began our work in April and finished it in July; and by August of that year, 1924, a Labor Government—Britain's first—was in office, and when our report was presented to the House of Commons, the Minister who presented it was Mr. J. H. Thomas, the new Secretary of State for the Colonies.

Jim Thomas and I became fast friends and remained so to the end of his life. I never believed that in the unhappy affair which cut short his political career he acted otherwise than in good faith. His open and genial nature may have landed him in a difficult and distressing situation, from which the only way out—resignation—was the one which he took unhesitatingly. Jim Thomas was a great-hearted man, of fine and generous feelings, whom I always admired and respected.

Though we had spent many weeks of that summer in committee rooms in the India Office and in long discussions with the Colonial Office, our discussions did not receive the seal or hall-mark of any Act of Parliament embodying our suggestions and recommendations. Yet they had, I think, as a compromise, their own genuine value; true, they were only half measures, but they were all that we had either the power or the authority to recommend.

Of one fact my years in public life have convinced me: the value of a compromise is that it can supply a bridge across a difficult period, and later having employed that bridge, it is often possible to bring into effect the full-scale measures of reform which originally would have been rejected out of hand.

On the questions of electoral equality and of unrestricted settlement in the highlands there was no change; Delamere and his friends held their position. But on immigration we secured the abandonment of an offensive ordinance which the Kenya Government had already adopted and which would virtually have put an end to Indian immigration into East Africa; the Secretary of State, however, retained the right to enact any measure at any time should African interests appear to be threatened by the influx of immigrants from abroad. Mr. Thomas announced that certain districts in the coastal lowlands were to be reserved for agricultural immigrants from India. These were to some extent gains. But it was obvious then and it is obvious now that logicality and permanence are impossible of attainment in the whole difficult and complex racial situation which, because of half measures and compromises, has been allowed to develop in East Africa. In some measure, I think, we may claim that we did create a better atmosphere and a wider understanding of the Indian viewpoint, and the fairly practicable *modus vivendi* which subsisted in Kenya for many years, and also in Uganda and Tanganyika, was the result of our committee work and the detailed recommendations which we made.

One fact was apparent then and still deserves emphasis thirty years later: East Africa's problems must not be allowed to become a matter of contention between opposing political parties in Britain. I cannot be disinterested in this issue, for my own followers of purely Indian origin number in East Africa nowadays some fifty thousand—seventeen thousand in Kenya, twenty-seven thousand in Tanganyika and six thousand in Uganda. As recently as July, 1953, I contributed a turnover article to *The Times* in which I set out my views, in principle unchanged by all that had happened in the years between.

"For as long as we can foresee," I said, "the British people are the trustees of the population of East Africa, irrespective of race and color. That trusteeship can never be adequately exercised unless there is a firm bipartisan understanding and interpretation of that duty between the two main political parties and informed public opinion among all classes in Great Britain. There can be no real union in East Africa among the races if any portion of them believes that the trustees are divided or that they have particular favorite wards. The trusteeship of the African colonies is a great responsibility, a touchstone of success or failure for the British race in one of the greatest challenges placed before it by destiny."

Time alone will show how that responsibility is discharged. As a tailpiece to my account of these happenings in East Africa, however, it may be agreeable to mention that Sir Evelyn Baring, the Governor of Kenya, issued a statement on the occasion of the sixtyeighth anniversary of my inheriting the Imamate of the Ismailis, which was of the greatest warmth, kindness and courtesy.

The year 1924 marked the conclusion of a phase of my public life, of five or six years of strenuous and varied activity. Thereafter until 1929 or thereabouts I entered a period devoted almost exclusively to my own personal and private life.

I think, however, that I should make it clear that in public affairs I have always been in a sense an amateur. My public life, as I have shown, has moved in successive, fairly clearly defined phases. But the duties and the responsibilities which are mine by inheritance have never for an instant abated. My normal work as Imam of the Ismailis consists of a constitutional leadership and supervision of the various councils and institutions of all the numerous and far-scattered Ismaili communities, self-administered as they are in each region. In addition, I am in constant communication with thousands of individuals in the community, on all sorts of diverse matters about which they seek guidance, and it is—as I have indicated— a community spread across the globe from the Great Wall of China to South Africa. This is my job, and it has been a regular part of my daily life for nearly seventy years, from childhood into old age.

X

A Respite from Public Life

M Y INTEREST in horses, their breeding, training and racing, has been with me all my life and is of course also part of the tradition which I have inherited, the environment in which I was bred. Persian art, in the various exhibitions which have been held in London and elsewhere, has perhaps helped to make the Western public realize the large and important part which sport played in the lives of that old Iranian ruling class whence I am descended. The chase in its many forms was for them not just a distraction; it was a major occupation all their lives; their hounds, their hawks, their horses were the most beautiful, the swiftest and the finest that they could breed or procure. My grandfather in his young manhood, at the court of Fateh Ali Shah, as the favored son-in-law of that powerful monarch, was as fully absorbed in all the accustomed open-air and athletic sports and pursuits of a sophisticated yet virile society as were any of his contemporaries. After his tribulations and his wanderings ceased and he settled in Bombay, he naturally and happily resumed a way of life not very dissimilar from that which he had known in his youth. And as I have tried to show earlier in this book, such was the atmosphere in which, from the dawning of conscious experience, I spent my childhood and boyhood.

When my father died he left a large and imposing sporting establishment in being—hawks, hounds, and between eighty and ninety race horses. A good deal of this establishment my mother naturally pared down, but she kept twenty or thirty of the horses; and throughout my minority these were raced at meetings all over West-

ern India in my name and under my colors. I have earlier given a
brief account of some of the successes which I—and with my cousin
and racing partner, Aga Shamsuddin—enjoyed during those years.

One effect of this early and sustained prominence on the Indian
turf was that by the time I was in my late teens I had a number of
friends who were important and influential in racing circles, two of
whom were the brothers Lord William and Lord Marcus Beresford.
They were younger sons of the Marquis of Waterford; and Lord
William in particular was a powerful and original personality in
his own right; he was military secretary to three Viceroys of India
in succession, Lord Ripon, Lord Dufferin and Lord Lansdowne.
His long tenure of this key post, in which he had won and maintained the confidence of each of his chiefs, gave him unchallenged
influence and authority over a diverse and far-ranging field of affairs,
military, social, political and diplomatic, in relations with foreign
dignitaries and potentates who visited India, and of course with
the Ruling Princes. He was an utterly fearless horseman of whom
it was said that he had broken every bone in his body in falls sustained while hunting, playing polo or steeplechasing. During his
fourteen years as military secretary he became one of India's leading
race horse owners, on his own and in association with two princes,
with the Maharajah Darbhanga, an immensely wealthy landlord,
and with the Maharajah of Patiala, the leading Sikh prince. The
bookmakers, it was always said, lived in fear and trembling of
Lord William, for he was a past master in the difficult art of bringing off big betting coups. He was a friend of my family's and of
mine from an early age; and whenever he came to Bombay we saw
a great deal of him.

When I first went to England in 1898 I discovered therefore—
and I was young enough to be agreeably surprised by my discovery—
that a good deal was known about my hereditary and personal interest in the breeding of horses and in the turf generally, not merely
in exclusively racing circles but in the India Office, at Court and in
the personal entourage of the Prince of Wales. Either Lord William
Beresford or his brother Lord Marcus—and I have never been able
to find out which of them—had taken steps to have my colors as

an owner registered in England. They both knew that in India my
family's racing colors had always been green and red; they are also
the colors of the Ismaili flag, and when my ancestors were temporal
sovereigns—both in Egypt and in Iran—green and red were the
colors of their standards. Some years later I discovered that
my colors in England were registered as green and chocolate; I
made inquiries from Messrs. Wetherby, who told me that when
the registration occurred, green and red were not available; but they
could never tell me whether it was Lord William or Lord Marcus
—or indeed someone else—who had chosen green and chocolate.
Many years later my elder son was able to get a combination of
green and red; no doubt by that time I too could have changed, but
by then my green and chocolate had become so lucky and so well
known that it would have been neither politic nor practicable to
change them. In France, I may say, and in Europe generally, my
racing colors are and have always been green and red.

I was at once made an honorary member of the Grand Stand at
Epsom. My first serious racing, I well remember, was the Epsom
Spring Meeting of 1898, when I saw the great Ray Ronald win the
City and Suburban. I am proud to think that I told my friends that
this was a fine horse who was sure to make his mark in the history
of bloodstock breeding—especially proud because this particular win,
considering his age and weight, was nothing very wonderful. A few
weeks later I went to the Derby; I had a small bet of a sovereign
at sixty-six to one on a horse called Jeddah. Though my own bet was
at sixty-six to one, the horse actually started at one hundred to one,
and then to everybody's astonishment won the Derby. My friend
the Prince of Wales happened to spot me in the enclosure and
called across to me with a laugh that a horse called Jeddah ought
certainly to have belonged to me.

At Ascot I have had a Royal Household badge for well over fifty
years; I was first given my badge by Queen Victoria, and it has
successively been re-bestowed on me by King Edward VII, King
George V, King George VI and Queen Elizabeth II.

From the beginning, however, my interest in racing has never
been merely idle or transient. From 1898 I went to race meetings

in England or on the continent of Europe and I followed the form of the horses very carefully. In India, at Bombay, Poona or Calcutta, I never, if I could possibly avoid it, missed a meeting.

In France in 1905 I made the acquaintance of Mr. W. K. Vanderbilt, then the leading owner in the country. Although he was a great deal older than I was, he took a special interest in letting me into all the secrets of the administration of his great racing stables. He introduced me to his trainer, William Duke, to whom he gave strict instructions that I was to be allowed to visit his stables for the trials and training of his horses whenever I wished. Mr. Vanderbilt said to me, "I think you'll get more pleasure out of a free run of my stables than out of a free run of my house."

Whenever I was in Paris William Duke would send me word if he had any important trials on hand, and often in the early morning I would go out to the stables and watch these trials. During these sixteen years from 1898 to the outbreak of the First World War, while I watched European racing, breeding and training but took no active part myself, my imagination was stirred by, and I have retained vivid impressions of, a few great horses; there were, of course, many others just as good, great and successful, but they and their performances have not stayed in my memory in the same way. I say without hesitation that of all the horses which I saw in England, Tetrarch and Spearmint were the two that impressed me most. I saw mares like Sceptre and Pretty Polly and horses like Ardpatrick and Sunstar in England and Sardanapale in France. Sceptre and Pretty Polly are the only two mares I have ever known that, in quality and character, were comparable with the great horses I have named. They both possessed speed, strength and soundness of wind and limb on a scale equal to any male horse; so good were they that they were raced until they were five years old, and their descendants have left their mark on bloodstock in England. In general, however, there can be no doubt that the male thoroughbred is greatly superior to the mare. Not one of these mares left on me the durable impression of power that I derived from Spearmint and Tetrarch in England, and one outstanding French horse, Prestige. I am not at all sure that Prestige was not the most impressive race.

horse that I ever saw. Mr. Vanderbilt owned another horse called Maintenon at the same time as Prestige and they were often tried out in gallops together. Maintenon was a good horse and he won the French Derby, but in a hard gallop he could never get within twenty lengths of Prestige. William Duke, who trained both of them, told me again and again that no weight, not even three stone, could have brought the two horses together. Unfortunately Prestige was never entered in a single important race; if he had been he would have won in a canter. He was never defeated and he was never out of a gentle gallop, because nobody seemed to realize the reserve power which he had and could have shown if he had ever been called on to do so. It was the same story with his morning gallops. The jockeys who rode him told Duke that they were actually afraid of pushing him, even to a fraction of his best, lest he run away with them. He was a beautiful-tempered horse; and to this day I have never been able to understand why Mr. Vanderbilt sold him very cheaply and kept far less impressive horses as stallions. True, Prestige never got good mares, but still he sired Sardanapale. When Sardanapale was at the height of his power and his glory, having just won the Grand Prix de Paris and the French Derby, the First World War came. I was then, as I have recorded, in Africa. When I returned to Europe I found that racing for all practical purposes was dead; I myself was busy and intensely preoccupied with the events and doings which I have described. I did not go to a racecourse or follow racing form again until 1919, when the first postwar Derby was run at Epsom. From then until 1921 I got back into the habit of going to any important race meeting, wherever I happened to be, England, France, Belgium, Italy, India or Egypt. I had long ago made up my mind, back in the nineties, to have a few horses in Europe, but the death of my dearly beloved cousin, Aga Shamsuddin, with whom I had intended to open a stable in Europe in 1910, had put an end to all my hopes and ideas on this matter.

Then one day in the spring of 1921 at dinner at Mrs. Edwin Montagu's house, I found myself sitting next to Mrs. Asquith, a daughter-in-law of the former Prime Minister and a sister of Mrs.

George Lambton. We talked horses and she urged me as vigorously as she could to take up breeding bloodstock and racing in England.

"Why don't you," she said, "send for my brother-in-law, George, and ask him to buy a few mares and yearlings for you?"

Back in my room at the Ritz I sat down and wrote a note to George Lambton asking him to call on me. Our conversation bore fruit. He introduced me to Richard Dawson, a well-known Irish sportsman, and recommended him to take up my training for me, while he himself agreed to buy me a few yearlings. When I went back to Paris I sent for William Duke, whose patron, Mr. Vanderbilt, was dead, and who therefore was free to work for someone else. He began to train and buy yearlings for me in France; in England Mr. Lambton did the buying and Mr. Dawson the training. Then I myself began to study the breeding of the yearlings that came up for sale at Deauville and Doncaster. Among the Doncaster yearlings I chose one in particular that became one of the mares on which I founded my stud, the filly to which I gave the name Teresina. At the same time I picked out another yearling by the same sire Tracery; I wired Lambton and I wrote posthaste to Dawson urging the purchase of this colt. The colt was none other than Papyrus, the Derby winner of 1923—my first. Mr. Lambton did not like him, finding him too small and on the stocky side.

That shows how little we ought to go by the make and the shape of a yearling, so long as his legs are sound and he is neither a giant nor a lilliputian. Apart from the all-important factor of his breeding, I have one rule by which to judge a yearling: is he going to be very tall and heavy or will he never be more than a pony? Do his legs look strong enough to stand the hard leg exercises, gallops and so forth of training?

The general public take a great interest in racing; they have their favorites, their likes and their dislikes, but very few people really understand the foundation of the art of training a race horse. The object is precisely the same as that of training a boxer. Your boxer, your wrestler, your weightlifter, by various muscular exercises and movements undertaken daily, in a carefully thought-out and planned program, gets his whole body, his nerves, his muscles, his capacity to give and take punishment all brought to their fullest, most perfect pitch of development—for the day of his crucial contest.

With a horse, of course, there is no question of putting him down on his back to do all the scientifically planned and disciplined exercises that a human athlete can be put through. There is only one way of building up a horse's muscles—and the nervous energy that must take charge of those muscles—and that is by walking, running and, if necessary, a certain amount of jumping. The great trainer is the one who knows how to adjust the pattern of these exercises so that his horses will attain the height of their physical power, fresh and vigorous and with their nervous energy at its peak, on the most important day of their racing careers, just as the prize fighter who wins is the one who is at the top of his form when he steps into the ring in Madison Square Garden.

My recollections of thirty years of European racing, from 1922, when my colors were first seen on English and French racecourses, to 1952, are countless in their variation, both in respect of men and of horses.

Across memory's screen so many great sportsmen come and go —English, American, French, with all their individual characteristics, their quirks of outlook and temperament. I recall immediately, for example, Mr. Joseph Widener, of Philadelphia, one of my closest and kindest friends, among American owners. He had strong opinions about breeding, particularly on the subject of the importance of the dam, as against the sire, in bloodstock. I once said to him that since he was convinced that the maternal was much more important than the paternal, if he applied his theories to human beings, a family would rapidly degenerate unless its young men married Widener girls. Was my joke in good taste? At any rate he was good enough to laugh at it.

My friend the late Lord Wavertree was another who attached little importance to the sire and great importance to the dam. Lord Wavertree indeed went further than anyone else I have known, holding that if your mares are good, it really does not matter what sort of sire you mate them with. My own view is that you must try to secure the best and most suitable breeding through both sire and dam, bring it by both inbreeding and outcrossing as nearly perfect in the abstract as you can. Success will depend on whether any particular foal takes after his dam and the majority of her maternal ascendants or after his sire and the majority of his paternal ascendants. Thus with two horses which are full brothers, unless they are identical twins, it is not possible to say with certainty whether they will possess similar or dissimilar characteristics. One may display the paternal ascendant qualities of the sire and be a very great horse; the other may have the maternal ascendants of the dam and be a poor horse. On the other hand, both or either may possess the maternal ascendants of sire or dam and be a failure. Thus after a great deal of study and careful thought and weighing-up of much experience, I have come to the conclusion that I still must leave it to chance, for it is quite impossible to say in advance that a horse, possessing the best blood in the world, will turn out any good, and this despite anything his own brother or sister may have done.

I advised Mr. Lambton to buy some excellent mares, and he himself picked out some fine ones, like Mumtaz Mahal and Cos; and he picked up a couple of very good colts, Diophon and Salmon Trout. My immediate success, I am convinced, was owing to the fact that I began my European racing career with two of the greatest trainers of all time to look after my horses, William Duke and Richard Dawson.

Trainers as capable as Richard Dawson no doubt exist today, but I do not think there is anyone who has his supreme courage—unless it be Madame Tesio of Italy. Dawson's great quality was that he would risk everything in order that his horse should be at his very best, muscled up to perfection, for the most important event of his life. From all I hear today, the methods that are fashionable both in England and with the majority of French trainers are far more tender. In general, trainers now spare their horses a great deal more than did men like Dawson and Duke, or, for that matter, the man whom I consider the greatest trainer of all, Frank Butters. There is far too much coddling at present, far too much cotton wool. Since nearly all trainers subscribe to the current fashionable views, it does not matter greatly, but I think if any of them came up against one of the hard men of the past or Madame Tesio, they would show up badly. The reason given is doubtless that in the old days many horses were broken down in the process of training. I have been told that Gilpin, one of the greatest of old-time trainers, only a few days before the Derby broke down the filly with which he had expected to win it. Gilpin was not in the slightest bit ruffled; he did not even apologize to the owner. He said, quite rightly, that if he had spared her the gallop in which she broke down, she would never have won the Derby, and that it was his job to take every chance for a win rather than by insufficient preparation ensure defeat.

From 1931 I had the great good fortune of having my very dear friend, Mr. Frank Butters, for whom my family have the greatest affection, train for me. Mr. Butters, one of the most delightful human beings one could ever hope to meet, with a nature as clean and clear as a diamond but without its harshness, was one of the greatest and most successful trainers in the world. He began his career in Austria and Hungary and rose immediately to the top of his profession. He moved on to Italy and there too in no time he was at the top again. Later he took Lord Derby's stable in hand, and with horses like Fairway and others he was the leading trainer in Britain for several years and made his patron the leading owner. When he left Lord Derby and came to me, the tables were quickly turned and I took the front again as leading owner and breeder. For me he trained a succession of magnificent horses like Bahram, Mahmoud, Tehran and Firdaussi, and a great many splendid two-year-olds. Even more wonderful than his success with great horses was his way with quite moderate ones. He had a wonderful knack of getting out of any horse the very best that horse could do.

In some ways Butters and Duke were alike, particularly in that neither of them attached the importance that most other trainers attach to the detailed appearance of the yearlings which came to them. Mr. Duke used to go out of his way to pooh-pooh people who chose yearlings on appearance and make and shape; he held that one yearling was as good as another if it were properly trained and had in it the natural qualities of health and nervous energy and—most important of all—the capacity to rest and to sleep. When he bought yearlings for me he never bothered to make any elaborate inspection of them; in fact I doubt if he ever gave them a second thought. If while an auction was in progress he failed to buy one yearling for which he had been bidding, he was never disappointed but would laugh it off and say that the next would probably be better still. To him it was almost like putting numbers in a hat and pulling them out—plus, of course, absolute confidence in his own methods of training. He believed in himself, not in his year-lings. Long before they were in general use he employed vitamins and other natural methods of sustaining a horse's health and nerv-ous energies. Duke was a man who had a number of enemies, the source of whose hostility was jealousy. Those whose expensive year-lings had been beaten by the ones that Duke had picked up cheaply were apt to hint that he doped his horses. Nothing could be further from the truth. He would laugh and tell me that his dope was first-class food, a great deal of fresh lucerne grass, fresh vitamins, lots of fresh air in the loose-boxes and hard work for every horse.

French training grounds were very bad in those days, though I am told that they have much improved of late. Duke therefore had more or less to train his horses on the racecourse. He had one very honorable rule: that in countries in which the training grounds were impossible, the public had no business judging a horse until he had shown his true form at least once; thereafter any marked inequalities of form were against the public interest, and a good trainer ought not to keep a horse that ran thus but should turn him out of the stable. A horse should be consistent in his form once he had shown it, but the public had no right to expect a trainer or an owner to break his horse on impossible training grounds.

Frank Butters, on the other hand, never needed races as prep-aration for his horses. If his two-year-olds were ever capable of winning, they won the first time they were out. The great Bahram, for example, before his Derby had one race—the Two Thousand Guineas—and he cantered away with that as he did with the Derby. No nonsense about his needing two or three eye-openers.

I have often been asked which I considered to be the greatest horse I ever bred. Until Tulyar came on the scene I would unhesitatingly have said Bahram. But Tulyar has shown a certain capacity for always doing just enough, which makes it difficult to assess his limits as compared with Bahram's. Bahram was probably the most dominating horse I ever saw. From the first, he looked and acted the champion. Tulyar running is a greyhound. In my youth I saw the great Flying Fox as a two- and three-year-old— curiously like Tulyar, he ran with his head in line with his body or perhaps even lower; practically every horse runs with his neck carried higher than his body, and some with their heads up. Tulyar and Flying Fox have been the only two exceptions to this rule that I have ever seen. But the present Lord Rosebery, that great figure in English racing—and how widespread is the regret that he does not take a more leading and active part in its administration— has told me that the famous Eclipse, the ancestor of almost all the good horses in the world, used to gallop with his head down, almost as if he were smelling the ground. When Tulyar gallops, he is straight as an arrow. We must however face the fact that Tulyar— unlike Bahram—is on the small side for a great race horse. Bahram was the tallest Derby winner of modern times, and Tulyar is prob- ably one of the shortest. And there is no getting away from the old, old saying: "A big good 'un is better than a little good 'un."

I am not sure, however, that there is not another side to this question. Many sound judges—like Mr. Frank Butters and the late Captain Greer—have told me that English breeders have gone too much for size and bone and that we need a smaller run of stallions to achieve that concentration of vitality which is so often found in small men and animals. I think that there is a great deal in this, and I am therefore glad to think that Tulyar will remain in Ireland to influence new generations and to check this overemphasis on size and bone. Many of us had hoped that the Derby winner, Manna— also a small horse—would help to bring down size, but Manna unfortunately was a comparative failure. The great Hyperion of course was a small horse, and one of the greatest stallions of all time. But we need more than one Hyperion if we are to prevail against the present tendency to sacrifice vitality and nervous energy to muscle and bone.

Looking back in this fashion over my memories of owning, breeding and racing horses, I do not propose to give a detailed account of my wins, my prizes, my bloodstock sales and so forth. For those who want that sort of record it is admirably supplied by *Ruff's Guide to the Turf*. My own recollections stretch back well over fifty years, to the late nineties, to a generation of jockeys, owners and trainers long since departed, and to methods of riding entirely forgotten except in old prints and pictures. There was the first Duke of Westminster, for example, gentle and kind in appearance, yet with a strain of irascibility in him. When Mr. Gladstone, who had many years before given him his dukedom, announced his support of Irish Home Rule, the Duke unceremoniously bundled Mr. Gladstone's portrait out of his house and into a public auction. He was small and lightly built and—so I was told—actually rode some of his own best horses at trials. He had one odd sartorial whim: always, whatever the occasion, he wore, either with a morning coat or a frock coat, a blue shirt, a blue collar and a blue necktie.

One day the Duke of Westminster went into his stables, and a mare, Vampire, attacked him. He at once ordered Vampire to be destroyed. He was begged to reprieve her and finally agreed. Two or three years later she got him The Bat and later Flying Fox.

There was the Duke of Portland, whom in later years I came to know very well; after the Derby of 1935 he listed for me the points of resemblance between his great St. Simon and my great Bahram. There was Sir J. B.—"Blundell"—Maple, the father-in-law of my friend Baron von Eckardstein, big of build, loud of voice, self-confident, even perhaps self-satisfied, certainly self-made, but withal a truly kindhearted and generous person. However, as founder and owner of his furniture store in Tottenham Court Road, he was not popular with the supremely aristocratic little clique which in those days ruled the Jockey Club; time and again they blackballed him. One day it became known that he was dying; there was remorse all round, and he was elected to the Jockey Club posthaste. There were the brothers Reuben and Arthur Sassoon, two of the kindliest old men I ever met, generous and gentle. They had no hint of snobbishness in them, but they were extremely well liked in society at its highest levels, and were both close personal friends of King Edward. I have always understood that they did his modest betting for him at race meetings; his stakes ranged from twenty-five to fifty pounds, but the Sassoons placed them with as much care and trouble and anxious inquiry as if they had been for thousands of pounds.

The great event in racing in the late nineties, of course, was the revolution in riding that came from America. Lord William Beresford brought over Tod Sloan with his American mount. All the leading owners, like the Dukes of Westminster and Portland, pooh-poohed it at first. But it upset every applecart. Race after race was won by Sloan and his American imitators, who invaded both England and France. The old-fashioned champions, if they were too old or too stubborn to move with the times and change, had to give up and retire altogether. Not long after this, doping was introduced—also from across the Atlantic. This also upset everybody, and it took several years to get it finally barred in England and in France and its perpetrators sternly punished. The American mount, however, was a quite different matter. It had come to stay, and nobody thereafter thought of returning to the old cavalry seat in racing, with its erect posture. In its own way this was as big a revolution in racing as the discovery of gunpowder in warfare. It is undoubtedly true that the results are an immense improvement on those of the past, but aesthetically the disappearance of the old seat, with its dignity and grace in the rider as much as in the horse, is a great loss.

I have often been asked how the best horses of today compare with the best horses of the late nineties and the early years of this century. Are today's best really much superior to their predecessors? I personally have not the least hesitation in saying that great progress has been made in the past fifty years. And why not? If it had not been, racing, with its countless and elaborate methods of breeding and selection, would be senseless and time-wasting. The whole object of picking and choosing in mating horses is constantly to improve the breed by letting artificial selection assist natural selection. We who breed race horses firmly believe that the combination of these two, if it is carried out conscientiously and scientifically, can and does produce steady and marked improvement in racial characteristics and qualities. There is a time test not only of record performances but of average races over long but comparable periods of weeks in, let us say, 1914 and the present day. Statistically tested thus, there is no doubt that today's horses do run faster. The exceptional horse apart, the average speed has increased out of all recognition.

We are told that the horses of the past could sustain a gallop twice or three times as long as the ordinary course of today. The veterinary services in India too produced a crank of their own who maintained that the ordinary Indian horse—the Katty—is superior to the thoroughbred because he can jog along at a regular pace for miles and miles and miles without stopping. Well, what of it? We have bred for speed, and surely the answer to these croakers and cranks is that the English thoroughbred is not called on to sustain a six- or nine-mile gallop, or to keep going all day; he can sprint a few furlongs and then lie down and sleep—let the Katty horse amble away—and in that brief sprint he has done all the work that the other horse could have done, without the same long draw on his constitution and vitality. Whatever the distance, long or short, the thoroughbred will defeat the jogger because he has that extra vitality which will produce the effort needed. The race horse is bred for a highly specialized purpose, and he fulfills that purpose very well. The sheer facts sustain all the theories about breeding and selection and prove—it seems to me beyond the possibility of contradiction—that there is a steady and continuing improvement in the quality of the English thoroughbred race horse. Even if you compare the pictures of the horses of today and those of fifty years ago, you will see that the horse of today obviously looks faster, if there is anything in looks.

XI

Foreshadowings of Self-Government in India

OR SEVERAL YEARS, from the end of 1924 on, I took little part in
public life. In India the strength of nationalist sentiment grew
steadily throughout these years. The personal leadership and authority of Mahatma Gandhi in the Congress party intensified; the Nehrus,
father and son, and Vallabhai Patel were the only leaders approaching him in stature. There were periods of fierce conflict and sullen
repression; there were periods of comparative quiescence. The consciousness among Muslims that they must work out their own
destiny strengthened steadily. To Lord Chelmsford succeeded Lord
Reading; to Lord Reading, Lord Irwin,* who, as Edward Wood,
had been a Minister in Mr. Baldwin's first Government, a profoundly sincere and serious-minded man of deep religious convictions. Britain's promise of self-government by stages still stood out
as the crucial decision in Indo-British relations. Agitation increased,
as successive Governments seemed equally reluctant to take the first
steps toward implementing this promise.

Of these events and trends I was an interested observer but little
more. A full, active and eventful private and personal life engrossed
me. I went to India every year; my wife was settled in the south of
France; my son, Aly, his childish delicacy overcome, lived in England with his tutor, Mr. C. W. Waddington.† In the winter of
1923-1924 my wife and son came with me to India. My own interest in racing during this period was extremely active; my wife
followed my racing in France but not in England.

---

* Now Lord Halifax.
† Formerly Principal of the Mayo College at Ajmer.

In 1926 she fell ill, and was an invalid throughout that year. The doctors offered all sorts of diagnoses, ranging from indigestion to "nerves." Later in the year she was in a great deal of pain; and now at last the doctors paid some attention to her condition, and an operation for appendicitis was suggested. The operation was performed in December. It was discovered that she was not suffering from appendicitis. She seemed to make a steady recovery. But one afternoon I was out driving in the Bois, and when I went back to the hospital I was told that she had died during my absence. A small blood clot had escaped, traveled to her heart, and killed her. She was thirty-seven years old.

More than a year passed. Early in 1928 I proposed marriage to Mlle. Andrée Carron of Chambéry, Aix-les-Bains. I had known Mlle. Carron and her family for twelve or fourteen years, indeed since she was quite a young girl. She was thirty when I proposed to her. She hesitated for a long time before accepting me; and it was not until nearly two years later—December, 1929—that we were married at Aix-les-Bains. There arose a ridiculous legend—created and fostered by the newspapers—that I met her serving behind the counter in a chocolate shop whither I had gone to buy sweets. There was never a word of truth in it. What happened was this: when the news of our intended marriage reached the papers, all they knew was that I was going to marry someone called Carron from Chambéry. The reporters descended on Chambéry, looking for a Mlle. Carron. At last they found one—selling candy in a sweet shop.

"There she is," they said and scurried off to telephone their newspapers that they had discovered the Mlle. Carron whom the Aga Khan was going to marry.

The girl in the candy shop had never met me; she did not know me; my Mlle. Carron was someone quite different, who for several years had had a dressmaking shop in Paris with her sister, and she had never in her life had anything to do with chocolates. But the legend got away to a flying start, and the truth never seemed to catch up with it.

Ours was for many years a happy and well-knit marriage. We had one child, my second son Sadruddin, who was born on January 17, 1933. My wife went everywhere with me. In England in 1930 she was received by Their Majesties and was invited to luncheon at Ascot. She shared my social life actively and fully for many years.

Meanwhile I was being drawn back into political and public life. Lord Irwin, the Viceroy, in a momentous pronouncement, had shown Indians what—in the British view—was to be their ultimate goal in their constitutional evolution, but he had omitted to indicate with any precision the steps or the road to that goal.

"In view of the doubts which have been expressed," said Lord Irwin, "both in Great Britain and India regarding the interpretation to be placed on the intentions of the British Government in enacting the statute of 1919, I am authorized to state clearly that in their judgment, it is implicit in the Declaration of 1917 that the natural issue of India's constitutional progress as there contemplated is the attainment of Dominion status."

The two words "Dominion status" were to focus and bind Indian ambitions and aspirations for a decade and more, in an ever more forceful and dynamic drive toward independence; and in the end there emerged not one but two independent and sovereign states— Muslim and Hindu—the latter of which was, almost immediately, to throw away even the vestigial and nominal link of being called a Dominion and proclaim itself (as it had the constitutional right and ability to do) a republic within the Commonwealth.

In 1928-1929, however, all this was to be striven for. Congress met in Calcutta and prepared its own scheme for self-government and Dominion status; but it was marred by the fatal, obsessive flaw of all such Congress schemes to the end, that of underrating—indeed ignoring—Muslim claims to be considered as a nation within a nation. Muslim opinion was therefore alert. A Royal Commission —that classic British instrument for tackling a grave political or constitutional problem at home or overseas—was by now touring India, taking evidence in impressive quantities and with vast thoroughness; its chairman was Sir John Simon,* the great lawyer-poli-

* Now Viscount Simon.

tician, then almost at the zenith of his dazzling career; among its members was the pertinacious but personally self-effacing Mr. Clement Attlee, on whose knowledge of India this experience was to have a profound and lasting effect. The Viceroy had announced that after the Simon Commission issued its report it was intended that a conference should be held between the Government, the representatives of British India, and the representatives of the Indian states, in order to try to reach agreement on the way in which constitutional progress should be ensured.

It was decided therefore to hold an All-India Muslim Conference in Delhi at the end of 1928, to formulate Muslim views on the way in which Indian independence should evolve. I was asked to preside over this conference. It proved to be, I am convinced, one of the most important in the long series of such assemblies which marked the road toward total and final independence for the whole sub-continent. It was a vast gathering representative of all shades of Muslim opinion. I can claim to be the parent of its important and lasting political decisions. After long, full and frank discussions we were able to adopt unanimously a series of principles which we set out in a manifesto. They were as follows:

> In view of India's vast extent and its ethnological divisions, the only form of government suitable to Indian conditions is a federal system with complete autonomy and residuary powers vested in the constituent states.
> The right of Muslims to elect their representatives in the various Indian legislatures is now the law of the land, and Muslims cannot be deprived of that right without their consent.
> In the Provinces in which Muslims constitute a minority they shall have a representation in no case less than that enjoyed by them under the existing law (a principle known as weightage).
> It is essential that Muslims shall have their due share in the Central and Provincial Cabinets.

We agreed to concede a similar kind of "weightage" to the Hindu minorities in Sind and other predominantly Muslim provinces, but we insisted that a fair proportion of Muslims should be admitted into the Civil Service and into all statutory self-governing bodies. I myself demanded appropriate safeguards for "the promotion and protection of Muslim education, languages, religion, personal law and charitable institutions"—all causes for which, over years, I had fought as strenuously as I could. I also thought it right to warn my co-religionists and compatriots of the perils of being too easily taken in by Congress' protestations of undefined good will.

The principles which we had enunciated were henceforward to be our guiding lights in all our encounters with British or Hindu representatives and negotiators, with the Government of India or with the Congress party, in every discussion of schemes of reform and new projects for the administration of the country. We now had our code book, and we did not intend to deviate from it.

The unanimity of this conference was especially significant, for it marked the return—long delayed and for the moment private and with no public avowal of his change of mind—of Mr. M. A. Jinnah to agreement with his fellow Muslims. Mr. Jinnah had attended the Congress party's meeting in Calcutta shortly before, and had come to the conclusion that for him there was no future in Congress or in any camp—allegedly on an All-India basis—which was in fact Hindu-dominated. We had at last won him over to our view.

If India's political and constitutional evolution could be likened to a protracted and hard-fought chess contest (the analogy is imperfect, I know, for there were always at least three players in this game), then it may be said that the board had now been set for an especially crucial game, the pieces were in place, and there was a considerable lull while everyone thought out his next move. The Simon Commission set about the task of preparing its report. A General Election in Britain resulted in the resignation of Mr. Baldwin, and the formation by Mr. Ramsay MacDonald of his second Labor Administration; but although the Labor party were numerically the strongest, they did not command an absolute majority in the House of Commons and were dependent, as five years before, on Liberal support. The world scene changed rapidly and startlingly during 1929. The Wall Street crash ushered in the years of economic depression, the slump which was to send unemployment figures steadily mounting in practically every Western coun-

try and which was to lead desperate men—in Germany and elsewhere—to seek desperate remedies. The brief and deceptively sunlit
epoch of the 1920's was over; we were on the threshold of what
Sir Winston Churchill has described as "the terrible thirties."

I spent the first three months of 1929 in Egypt making a close
study of Egyptology, having as my guide and instructor Professor
Newbury, a distinguished Egyptologist, who accompanied me on a
tour of all the monuments of the Nile Valley right up to Abu Sim-
bal and back.

The British High Commissioner in Egypt was Lord Lloyd, whom
I had known well in India during his highly successful time as
Governor of Bombay. A strong-minded imperialist of the school of
Cromer and Curzon, George Lloyd was very shortly to come into
conflict with his Government at home and resign the post in which
he felt that he had lost their confidence. He was a man of remarkable intellectual gifts and great tenacity of purpose. Since he believed so fervently and with so deep and unswerving a passion in
the greatness of Britain's imperial destiny, it was perhaps a blessing
in disguise that he died early in the Second World War while still—
as statesmen are reckoned—a comparatively young man, for bitter
indeed would have been his feelings had he lived to see the final
hauling down of the British flag in India and the partition of the
subcontinent into the republic of Bharat and the eventual republic
of Pakistan.

To me personally he was the kindest and most generous of hosts,
but I could not help being uncomfortably aware of his unpopularity
with all sections of the Egyptian governing class. King Fuad, whom
I had known for more than thirty years and with whom I had been
in particularly close contact when the British Government sent me
on my mission to Egypt early in the First World War, made a
special point of asking me to call and see him. He received me in
private at the Abdin Palace. We were alone together for a long
time and we had a revealing, if saddening, conversation. The King
was already a sick man, though nobody realized the seriousness of
his malady. He wept openly at the way in which he himself was

rebuffed and neglected, and at the British High Commissioner's relentless refusal to permit him to have any effective voice in the governing of his own country.

"Lloyd," he said, "pulls the strings while the marionettes dance. Cromer turned Abbas Hilmi into a puppet. Lloyd is turning me into a corpse!"

At the Mohammed Ali Club, which was the great meeting place of Egypt's leaders, where they could talk, play their beloved cards, and canvass all their countless political and business schemes and plans, I heard—from one friend and acquaintance after another— the same story: Field Marshal Lord Allenby, for whose inflexible sense of justice they had a profound admiration, had made promises which had led them to expect increasing independence; but now they found that the "strings" which Allenby had reserved for the High Commissioner had been converted by Lloyd into iron chains —not, I may say, my own words but the precise phrase used to me by more than one Egyptian Minister.

Why had Lord Lloyd, who in India had been quite liberal and had always acted in the spirit as well as the letter of the constitution under which he governed, shown so different a face in Egypt? Why had he indeed acted not as a High Commissioner but as a Viceroy with plenary powers? May the answer not be that when he was in India as Governor of Bombay, the Montagu-Chelmsford constitution, whose principles he applied liberally and generously, limited home rule to certain clearly specified spheres of activity and administration, and within those well-defined limits there was neither need nor excuse for Lloyd to interfere? But in Egypt the glove came off his iron hand; for there the whole relationship was fluid and indeterminate, and there were no clear-cut lines of demarcation to divide and define the respective spheres of authority of the King and his Ministers and of the British High Commissioner. The Egyptians considered that their country was an independent sovereign state and that the King and his advisors were absolutely their own masters, not only in all matters of internal, executive, day-to-day control and administration of their country's affairs, but indeed in external relations, whereas the High Commissioner's function was merely to watch Great Britain's interests and see that Egypt took no action and joined no diplomatic combination hostile or injurious to Britain. George Lloyd, on the other hand, saw no clear definition of his powers or of those of the King and his Ministers, and he realized that if he did not keep a close watch and a firmly guiding hand, the whole team might get out of control.

In the summer of 1930 the Simon Commission issued its report. Its analysis of India's political history under British rule and of her contemporary situation was as masterly as it was lucid; it was however on the constructive side of its task that the Commission's report fell sharply short of the high expectations and hopes which its appointment had aroused. It particularly disappointed the Congress leaders, and their resentment of it was loudly and unequivocally expressed. Lord Irwin, the Viceroy, was on leave in England in the earlier part of 1930, and when he returned to India he announced that His Majesty's Government proposed to convene a Round Table Conference in London to consider the future of the country and to reform its constitution. The announcement came at a time of considerable tension, when a civil disobedience campaign, launched by Mahatma Gandhi, was at its height. It eased the tension for the time being; and the Viceroy was able to receive, in a calmer political atmosphere than had seemed possible a few weeks before, a representative delegation* to discuss the date and the personnel of the Round Table Conference and the question of an amnesty for political offenders jailed in connection with the civil disobedience campaign. Agreement, however, was not reached at this preliminary meeting; Mahatma Gandhi withdrew and refused to give any undertaking that Congress would attend the Round Table Conference. The Indian National Congress, in session at Lahore, passed a resolution in favor of a renewed resort to civil disobedience.

---

* The members of the delegation were Mahatma Gandhi, Sir Tej Bahadur Sapru, Pandit Motilal Nehru, Mr. M. A. Jinnah and Mr. V. J. Patel, then President of the Indian National Assembly.

The Viceroy pertinaciously maintained his hopeful, sympathetic and wise attitude. If Congress would not, at the outset at any rate, co-operate in the attempt to find a way out of India's political perplexities, the attempt would still be made. As many eminent and representative leaders of Indian political thought and feeling as possible—outside the ranks of Congress—would be invited. Mr. Nehru, in his *Autobiography* which was published in 1936 (when the whole issue of Indian independence was still unsettled), made some caustic observations about the personal qualifications of the delegates to the conference; in the longer perspective of history, however, it can be seen as a remarkable assemblage of men and women of widely differing background and outlook, all genuinely anxious to discover a peaceful and honorable path to the independence and self-government which had explicitly been proclaimed to be the objectives of Britain's rule in India.

The British representatives included the Prime Minister, Mr. Ramsay MacDonald; the Lord Chancellor, Lord Sankey; the Secretary of State for India, Mr. Wedgwood Benn*; and—representing the Conservative Opposition—Sir Samuel Hoare,† who was later, in some years that were crucial to India's destiny, to be Secretary of State for India; and Lord Reading, a Liberal leader and former Viceroy. The British-Indian delegation, of which I had been appointed a member, included Muslim, Hindu and Parsee representatives drawn from many shades of political opinion and other delegates representing numerous smaller communities; among the Muslims, Mr. M. A. Jinnah, Sir Mohammed Shaffi, Sir Zafrullah Khan and Maulana Mohammed Ali; and two women delegates, the Begum Shah Nawaz and Mrs. Subbaroyan; among the Hindus, Sir Tej Bahadur Sapru, the Rt. Hon. V. S. Srinivasa Sastri; Sir C. P. Ramaswami Aiyar, Sir Chimanlal Setalvad, Mr. M. R. Jayakar and Diwan Bahadur Rama Mudaliyar; among the Parsees, Sir Phiroze Sethna, Sir Cowasji Jehangir and Sir H. P. Mody. Mr. Ambedkar, himself born an "untouchable," represented the Depressed Classes; Sir Henry Gidney, the Anglo-Indian community. The rep-

* Now Lord Stansgate.
† Now Lord Templewood.

resentation of Ruling Princes was as impressive as it was stately, including as it did many of the bearers of the greatest and most famous names in Indian chivalry. The Maharajah Gaekwar of Baroda was their leader, and others with him were the Maharajahs of Bikaner, Patiala, Bhopal, Kashmir, Rewa and Jamnagar—better known perhaps to millions of British citizens as the unforgettable "Ranji" of cricket fame. The Princes were accompanied, many of them, by their Diwans—their Prime Ministers—who included statesmen of the quality and distinction of Sir Akbar Hydari and Sir Mirza Ismail, and other eminent men.

We assembled in London in the autumn of 1930. I had the honor of being elected leader of the Muslim delegation. We established our headquarters in the Ritz Hotel, where it has long been my custom to stay whenever I am in London. It is no formality to say that it was an honor to be chosen to lead so notable a body of men—including personalities of the caliber of Mr. M. A. Jinnah, later to be the creator of Pakistan and the Quaid-i-Azam, or Sir Mohammed Zafrullah Khan, for many years India's representative at numerous international conferences and first Foreign Minister of Pakistan, or my old and tried friend, Sir Mohammed Shaffi, one of the founders of the Muslim League.

The happiness of being thus chosen was for me one of the many joys of an exceptionally happy, as well as eventful, period of my life. It was the first twelvemonth of my marriage to Mlle. Andrée Carron, and I had also had the by no means negligible experience of winning the Derby with Blenheim.

Later, then, in this memorable year the full first Round Table Conference began with a formal inaugural session in the House of Lords, presided over by His Majesty, King George V. My colleagues then accorded me the further honor of electing me to be chairman of the British-Indian section of the conference, that is, of all the Indian representatives except the Ruling Princes, who had come, of course, as their own representatives and in their own capacity as the sovereigns of their various principalities and states.

The King, not long recovered from his extremely serious illness, made of his opening speech a most moving appeal to us all to contemplate the momentous character of the task to which we had set our hands.

"I shall follow the course of your proceedings," said the King, "with the closest and most sympathetic interest, not indeed without anxiety but with a greater confidence. The material conditions which surround the lives of my subjects in India affect me dearly, and will be ever present in my thoughts during your forthcoming deliberations. I have also in mind the just claims of majorities and minorities, of men and women, of town dwellers and tillers of the soil, of landlords and tenants, of the strong and the weak, of the rich and poor, of the races, castes and creeds of which the body politic is composed. For those things I care deeply. I cannot doubt that the true foundation of self-government is in the fusion of such divergent claims into mutual obligations and in their recognition and fulfillment. It is my hope that the future government of India based on its foundation will give expression to her honorable aspirations."

Other eloquent and stirring orations followed; and the conference, moving to St. James's Palace, settled down to its complex and formidable task. We achieved a surface harmony, but underneath there were deep and difficult rifts of sentiment and of outlook whose effect was bound to be felt from the outset. In order to understand this it is necessary to restate briefly the political situation and the state of Indo-British relations as they both stood in this autumn of 1930. The Simon Commission's Report advanced a scheme which denied central responsibility and also relegated the idea of a federation of India to a distant and undefined future. This could not really be satisfactory to anybody, for it offered, not a workable compromise, but an evasion of an existing—indeed a pressing—political conflict. For while the whole drive of the Hindu movement to self-government was concentrated on the idea of a strong central government and the establishment of an immediate democracy, conceived solely in terms of numbers, in which religious differences counted as such and as nothing more, Muslim opinion had crystallized steadily in favor of a distribution of powers from the center to virtually self-governing and autonomous provincial governments. Finally, no one had as yet evolved the conception of an All-India federation in which the states would be partners. Therefore none of the major parties at the conference arrived with any definite scheme—only with conflicting claims. The British Government, not unnaturally, was somewhat at sea when presented with what seemed to be a series of contradictory and irreconcilable claims and counterclaims.

The first essential task, as I saw it, was to find some way of bridging the gulf between the Muslim and Hindu sections of the British-Indian delegation. Only when we had achieved that bridge did it seem to me that we could offer to the British representatives our conjoint proposals for the constitutional development of India.

Pre-eminent among those whose efforts were devoted with zeal and enthusiasm to the same or closely similar ends was my friend, His Highness the Nawab of Bhopal. He was an outstanding figure among the Ruling Princes of his time—a devout Muslim, a man of driving energy and will power, of great physical strength, a sportsman and athlete and a first-class polo player. He was also a convinced Indian nationalist, eager to throw off India's semicolonial yoke and do away with her dependent status. He agreed with me entirely that if we of British India could not find ways and means of settling our own differences of opinion, we could not go to His Majesty's Government with any formulated set of demands; and this was leaving out of consideration altogether the protected states. From the first moment that we met at the Nawab's house, it was my deep conviction that this was what mattered most, which made me a champion of a Muslim-Hindu understanding about our ultimate view of an independent India—on the one hand, a truly confederate state or on the other, a state such as Canada in which the principal and overriding authority and power are reserved for the central government.

As a preliminary to reaching agreement with our Hindu colleagues we had to secure agreement inside our own Muslim delegation. At first several of the Muslim delegates, in particular Mr. Jinnah, were—as they had long been before the conference—suspicious of the idea of federation. Its dangers were, I well knew,

neither remote nor unimportant; to associate a growing democracy
with a number of states in which personal rule was the established
and, as it then seemed, inalienable custom might well be a risky as
well as complex innovation; and also there was the danger that
since the majority of Ruling Princes were Hindu, there might be a
serious diminution of the political influence of the Muslim community within the federation as a whole. However I was convinced
that whatever the temporary difficulties and risks involved in a federal scheme, it still offered the best and the most acceptable solution of India's political problems, that it offered an opportunity
which might never recur, and that if it required compromise to
make it effective, it would be a small price to pay for its obvious
and numerous advantages.

I am happy to think that when within the Muslim delegation we
had made our decision in favor of federation, Mr. Jinnah, who had
been its doughtiest opponent, was an inflexibly loyal and irreproach-
ably helpful colleague throughout all the subsequent discussions
and negotiations.

Since the Ruling Princes had signified their assent to some federal form of government, it remained now only to win the agreement of the Hindu representatives. I strove to convince them that
if they made the concession of accepting the principle of a fed-
erated and not a united India they—and we—would reap the harvest
of the benefits of immediate and large-scale political advancement
for the country as a whole. The guarantees which we asked consisted of a truly federal constitution; understandings that the Muslim
majorities in the Punjab and Bengal would not, by artificial "rig-
ging" of the constitution, be turned into minorities; the separation
of the Sind from Bombay and its establishment as a separate Province; the introduction of a full-scale system of constitutional government in the Northwest Frontier Province; and the assurance of
the statutory reservation of a certain proportion of places in the
Army and in the Civil Service for Muslims. If they gave us assurances of this character, we in our turn would offer them a united
front in face of the British. I even went further and offered, as a
special concession, unity of command under a chosen Indian

leader whose orders we would bind the Muslim community to accept. In his memoirs Sir Chimanlal Setalvad has referred to these offers of mine, and his evidence at least stands firmly on record that if the first Round Table Conference did not achieve all that was expected of it, and if, ultimately, not only was Dominion status not brought about but India had to be partitioned, some at least of the beginnings of these momentous happenings are to be found in the Hindu delegations' refusal to accept my offer. I am certain that Sapru and Sastri, in their heart of hearts, wanted to accept our Muslim proposals, but they were afraid of their Hindu colleagues and, above all, the influence of the Mahasabha.

I must formally record my solemn conviction that had my views been accepted then and there, later history would have taken a profoundly different course, and there would now have long since been in existence a Federal Government of India, in which Muslims and Hindus would have been partners in the day-to-day administration of the country, politically satisfied and contentedly working together for the benefit of India as a whole.

In a subsequent chapter I shall have occasion to refer to the continued stubbornness and intransigence of Hindu opinion, which at a much later date rejected the constitution offered it by the British Cabinet Mission. The formulation of this constitution, in outline and in principle, should have marked the beginning of the Round Table Conference, if the Hindu representatives, when we met them in the Nawab of Bhopal's house, had accepted my offer on behalf of the Muslims with the sincerity with which I put it forward.

That acceptance denied us, the rest of the first Round Table Conference was not of much essential or practical importance, since the foundation on which its deliberations should have been built was vague and fragile instead of strong and firm.

One successful step forward seemed then to be of great importance, but time and a train of great events have shown it to have been minor and transient. This was the Princes' announcement of their acceptance of the idea of federation. The British representatives at the Conference hailed it—perhaps not unnaturally from their point of view—as a significant and constructive advance, of real assistance in the task of securing a devolution of power from the United Kingdom Parliament to a so-called Indian Federal Parliament.

It gained in impressiveness from the fact that Lord Reading, leader of the Liberal party in the House of Lords, enfolded with the august aura of prestige which his status as an ex-Viceroy gave him, and strongly convinced as he was of the importance of a centralized responsibility in all major spheres of administration and executive authority, gave it his hearty if measured approval. To the Prime Minister, Mr. Ramsay MacDonald, it seemed salvation and success for the conference rather than the shipwreck which, so it appeared at the time, would have been disastrous. Mr. MacDonald's situation throughout the conference was complicated and delicate, though hardly unique, for it was the kind of situation which he frequently had to face in his career. At the height of his power he faced it with aplomb and adroitness, but it was difficult to disregard the fact that, despite all his diplomatic skill and finesse, he was not unlike the driver who has eight spirited horses in his coaching team and is aware that any couple can and probably will go off on its own and seek to pull the coach in a totally different direction from that which he intends.

To the Indian representatives at the conference Mr. MacDonald had to be—and was—our chairman, presiding with shrewd and benevolent impartiality over our deliberations, wise and venerated, our guide, philosopher and friend in the tricky mazes of democratic, constitutional procedure and theory in which we were having our protracted initiation. To his own party, burdened with office—in 1930, that year of dark foreboding and hints of the turbulence and the sorrow that were imminent—but without that support of a solid and unthreatened majority in the House of Commons which alone could ensure effectiveness and permanence to its decisions, he had to appear as the leader in the long crusade against out-of-date imperialism, obstructive vested interests, and the emancipator, the creator of Indian freedom and independence which he sincerely desired to be. In this role he was conscious that his was an advanced and most progressive view of India's problems and that he and his party were eager to travel swiftly the whole road to Dominion status, with few and minor reservations or restrictions. But the Conservative Opposition, whose patience he could not possibly afford to test too highly, was jealously watchful of Britain's imperial interests; and both in Parliament and in the Press the right-wing "die-hard" element of the Conservative party possessed powerful and authoritative citadels whence to challenge—perhaps to overthrow—him, if he too flagrantly disregarded their views.

In these circumstances it was perhaps inevitable that an especial atmosphere of hopefulness and optimism should envelop this, the conference's one major tangible achievement. Something, it was felt, above and beyond mere provincial autonomy had been established and ensured. The lawyers among us, like Sir Tej Bahadur Sapru, let themselves become zestfully absorbed in the details of what they then believed would lead to a serious and permanent advance along the road to Indian self-government. I must say that I in my heart of hearts was always suspicious that our work might not procure any real or lasting results because the great realities of India in 1930 were being forgotten.

It was forgotten that there were, first and foremost and all the time, fundamental differences between the Muslim and Hindu peoples that inhabited the subcontinent, and that these differences were most apparent between the Muslims of the two Northwestern and Eastern sections of India and the Hindu majority in the rest.

It was forgotten that the intelligentsia—although only ten per cent of the total Hindu population—numbered between forty and fifty million, and could not possibly be dismissed as "a mere microscopic minority." It was forgotten that they desired the British to quit India, bag and baggage, finally and forever; this was the aim for which they labored and strove, and indeed it was brought to pass in 1947. All the minutiae of an elaborate paper constitution, with all its cautious safeguards, its neat balancing of power by abstract and theoretical formulas which were to be embodied in it, seemed to them a pack of cunning and pernicious nonsense, a lot of irksome tricks by which all that the British seemed with one hand to give could be—and would be—snatched back with the other.

It was forgotten that the Princes, for all their wealth, ability, personal charm, prestige and sincere loyalty to the British connection, had in fact very little power or influence. They were not, of course, the sinister stooges that hostile propaganda often dubbed them, but both their actual authority and their capacity to sway opinion by their influence had been sapped in long years during which their subjects—and the Indian people at large—had come to realize that they were powerless, and incapable of holding an independent view or making an independent decision, if that view or that decision conflicted with the policy of the all-powerful British Residents. Thus gradually their support of the federal constitution—though it took in the British ruling class—was shown to possess very little reality, and to be a shadow without the substance of power.

By the time the second Round Table Conference assembled in the autumn of 1931 the world situation had changed vastly, and so had the state of Indo-British relations. The economic crisis, in all its sharpness and severity, had hit Europe and the United Kingdom. The collapse of the famous Austrian Credit-Anstalt Bank had led to a general and hasty restriction of credit and a long steep tumble in world trade. In Britain the number of unemployed mounted to a vast, grim total in the region of three millions; the publication of the May Report, an authoritative, officially ordered survey of the country's economic, financial and fiscal condition, which contained a number of recommendations for economy measures totally inacceptable to the majority of Mr. Ramsay Mac-Donald's Cabinet colleagues, precipitated a major political crisis. In September the King interrupted his annual and cherished holiday at Balmoral and returned to London, summoning to meet him the various leaders of the political parties. Thereafter a National Government was formed, charged with the task of dealing with the crisis; Mr. MacDonald was Prime Minister, supported by Conservatives and Liberals like Mr. Baldwin, Sir Austen Chamberlain, Sir John Simon and Sir Herbert Samuel. In the General Election which followed quickly on the formation of this government its supporters, mainly Conservatives and National Liberals, were returned to power with an overwhelming majority, and Labor representation in the Commons was reduced to "rump" propositions—almost the only ex-Ministers left in the House being Mr. George Lansbury, the veteran pacifist, and Mr. Attlee.

These changes could not but affect the second Round Table Conference; but, grave and preoccupying as were the events in which Britain and the British Government were involved, they did not cause its postponement. Meanwhile the patience and the considerable powers of persuasion of the Viceroy, Lord Irwin—"the tall Christian" as Mr. Mohammed Ali called him in an historic phrase —had prevailed and Mahatma Gandhi agreed to come to London. He went in his own personal capacity, but it was generally felt that, even if he did not come as the nominated leader and representative of Congress, his was the voice of authority and decision so far as the vast majority of Hindus were concerned.

We Muslims for our part hoped that Mahatma Gandhi, with his unique political flair allied to his vast personal prestige, would appreciate the fact (and act upon it) that to make a combined front of Hindus and Muslims would in itself be a major step forward, and that all would realize that it would offer an unparalleled opportunity for extracting out of the Round Table Conference a constitution which would be a genuine transference of power from British to Indian hands and which would give India the status of a world Power. Though Mahatma Gandhi could not possibly in 1930 have foreseen or hoped for anything like the final solution of 1947, he must, when he arrived, have hoped—as did most of us from the East at the Conference—that real power would be transferred, even if India and Whitehall were still linked by one or two silken strings.

Mahatma Gandhi arrived in London in November, 1931, as the sole representative of Congress. He was accompanied by the eminent Indian poet, Mrs. Sarojini Naidu. Our first meeting in our capacity as delegates to the second Round Table Conference occurred at midnight in my own room at the Ritz Hotel. It may be a suitable moment therefore to pause in my narrative and sum up my impressions and recollections of two truly remarkable personalities.

In one way or another I knew and was in touch with Mahatma Gandhi for more than forty-five years. I first heard of him about 1899 or 1900 when both he and I were actively concerned with the status and future of Indians in South Africa, a perennial problem which was to engage our attention across many years. At that time his philosophy was only beginning to coalesce, and he had not made the major personal decision of his life, which was the break with, and the turning away from, modern material progress. On and off we were in touch for the next ten or twelve years, usually on some facet of the Indian problem in South Africa. We were in London at the same time shortly after the outbreak of the First World War; as he had done at the beginning of the South African War he offered his assistance to the British Government for ambulance and field hospital work. Already he had, however, traveled far along his own mental and spiritual road, and I was aware that he had decided that salvation for India and for his fellow country-men lay in renouncing contemporary, industrialized and material-istic so-called civilization. I have given an account of our contacts at the time of the Khilafat agitation in 1920-1921; thereafter Mahatma Gandhi was, for the rest of his life, a major figure in world history.

I believe that both in Mahatma Gandhi's philosophical outlook and in his political work there were certain profound inconsistencies, which all his life he strove, without complete success, to reconcile. The chief, formative spiritual influences of his life were Christ, as revealed in the New Testament, Tolstoy, Thoreau, and certain ex-ponents of various forms of Hindu asceticism; yet he was not, in the ordinarily accepted sense, a pure ascetic; he had little patience and no sympathy with the merely contemplative life of the mystic totally withdrawn from the world, or with monks, whether Buddhist or Christian, who accept the rule of an enclosed order. If I may say so, I am convinced that Gandhi's philosophy was not re-nunciation of this world but its reformation, with mutual and associative human love as the dynamic spark in that reformation. Yet this involved for him a certain degree of renunciation. This

attitude toward the products of the industrial and technical revolution of our time was characteristically ambivalent. He believed
that all men ought to have the full benefits—in generally diffused
well-being—of the power over nature which science has put at
man's disposal. Yet he felt that, at man's present level of social
and spiritual development, if some individuals accepted these benefits, then the vast majority would be deprived of them and would
be both proportionally and absolutely worse off than before.

This ambivalence, rooted as it was in a profound mental and
spiritual contradiction, was always evident throughout his life, in his
relations with his nearest and dearest friends and in his teaching and
in his practice.

I remember that I once had a long conversation with him in
Poona after he had been gravely ill and had undergone an operation.
He was in bed at the Sassoon Hospital, where I went to see him.
His praise and his admiration for the hospital, for the British surgeon who had operated on him, for the consultants and the nursing
staff were unstinted. Yet he could not but feel that since such a
standard of treatment and attention could not be given to every
single one of the millions of India's population, it must be wrong
for it to be at his disposal in Poona. Just as much as everyone else,
however, he realized that it would be a crime to abolish the Sassoon Hospital—and everything which it symbolized and represented
—that its benefits must go to some, since they could not go to all,
but to whom? And yet, he felt, and yet, and yet . . . his philosophy
trailed off into a question mark that was also a protest.

There in his bed in that Poona hospital he faced the impossibility
of complete adjustment. It was this hard fact of incomplete adjustment, in the world as it is, which made him appear at some moments
"for" material progress, and at others "against" it. It gave some
critics cause to doubt either the sincerity of his Christian Tolstoyan
ideals or the efficacy of his activities on the world of practical politics
and economics. It would perhaps be more just as well as more
charitable to realize that Mahatma Gandhi was far from alone in the
contradictions and the conflicts of his inner and his outer life. Are
not such contradictions the very foundation of life for all of us, in

its spiritual as well as its material aspects; and if we seek to be of any use or service to ourselves and to our fellow men, can we do otherwise than live, as best we may, in the light of these contradictions?

Our last talk in 1945-1946 was in its way a reflection in miniature of the whole of Mahatma Gandhi's spiritual and intellectual life. Its setting and its circumstances illustrated, forcefully enough, the simple fact that in our world as it is we can never get away from contradictions. I had come to talk politics with Gandhi; since I was no longer actively a participant in Indian politics, I had to some extent come as a companion of my old and valued friend, the Nawab of Bhopal. Bhopal, Chancellor of the still existent Chamber of Princes, was a free lance in the Muslim ranks of the time, for he had not accepted the Quaid-i-Azam's conviction that only a partition of the subcontinent could give the Muslims what they wanted. I for my part still cherished some hopes that the full and final amputation could be avoided, if something on the lines of the constitution proposed by the last British Cabinet Mission could have been acceptable. Now I see clearly that I was wrong; amputation was the only remedy. Mahatma Gandhi and I talked of these matters; we talked of South Africa; then as I walked out, I changed the subject and asked: "What really is your opinion of Marxism— of Marx himself, of Engels, of Lenin and of Stalin?"

His answer was as characteristic as it was adroit: "I," he said, "would be a hundred per cent communist myself—if Marx's final stage were the first stage, and if Lenin's economic ideals were put immediately into practice."

If—there lay the contradiction. If, as Marx had laid it down, the state would "wither away" not as the last phase of the revolution but as the first; and if Lenin's economic axiom, "From everyone according to his capacity; to everyone according to his needs," could be put immediately into practice, then indeed the Marxist millennium would begin. I countered him with the orthodox Stalinist argument: the world as it is today contains capitalist-imperialist states, whose productive capacity is geared not to peace and utility but as a means to the possible end of aggressive and imperialist war; in such a world the communist state must be organized in its own defense; and how can there be a free society in which the state has indeed "withered away" without the essential preliminary phase of the world triumph of organized socialism?

"Well," said Gandhi, "let one country do it. Let one country give up its state organization, its police and its armed forces, its sanctions and its compulsions. Let one state really wither away. The happiness that would there prevail would be so great and so abiding that other countries would, for very shame, let their capitalist-imperialist societies and states wither away."

Mahatma Gandhi no more than anyone else could evade the contradiction that lies at the base of life in this epoch. We have constantly to put up with second-best and probably worse, since we cannot achieve our full ideal. Gandhi too realized this, despite his hope that mankind could attain Marx's final phase—a goal which, if it is ever attainable at all, will be reached by another route than an immediate short cut by way of selected portions of the lives of Christ, Mohammed and Buddha.

Mrs. Naidu, Gandhi's companion in his midnight conference with me at the Ritz that autumn night in 1931, was in her way hardly less fascinating a personality. She was one of the most remarkable women I have ever met, in some ways as remarkable as Miss Nightingale herself. Her home after her marriage was in Hyderabad. Although her original inclinations and her upbringing were extremely democratic, she was a poet. Her sensitive and romantic imagination was impressed by the originality and strangeness as well as the glamour of the character of the then Nizam of Hyderabad—the father of His present Exalted Highness— a gentle and timorous man, of a delicate and refined sensibility and sentiment, yet endowed with great clarity of vision, independence of judgment, and generosity and withal the possessor of a great heart in a sadly frail frame. He too had poetic aspirations, and some of his Urdu writings could indeed almost be dignified with the name of poetry. Mrs. Naidu sang his praises; but she herself was a real poet, who wrote strongly and tenderly of love and of life, of the world of the spirit and the passions. In that linking of tenderness and strength which was her nature there was no room for malice, hatred or ill-will. She was a vigorous nationalist, determined that the British must leave India and her destiny in the hands of India's children, yet her admiration for Western civilization and Western science—above all for English literature—was deep and measureless. Her proud freedom from prejudice she demonstrated at the time of the death of Rudyard Kipling. Kipling's out-and-out imperialism, the rigid limitations of his view of India's political capacity and potentialities—despite his recognition of their qualities of intelligence and fidelity—were inevitably at the opposite pole from Mrs. Naidu's outlook. Yet when he died Mrs. Naidu published a statement in which she paid her full and generous tribute of admiration to his genius—to the poet, the novelist, the unequaled teller of tales—making it clear beyond all argument that this recognition of the artist by the artist was utterly distinct from and unaffected by her profound and abiding dislike of his racial and political philosophy.

Such then were the notable pair who were ushered into my sitting room at the Ritz at midnight. We posed together for the press photographers, and then settled down to our conversation. I opened it by saying to Mahatmaji that were he now to show himself a real father to India's Muslims, they would respond by helping him, to the utmost of their ability, in his struggle for India's independence.

Mahatmaji turned to face me. "I cannot in truth say," he observed, "that I have any feelings of paternal love for Muslims. But if you put the matter on grounds of political necessity, I am ready to discuss it in a co-operative spirit. I cannot indulge in any form of sentiment."

This was a cold douche at the outset; and the chilly effect of it pervaded the rest of our conversation. I felt that, whereas I had given prompt and ready evidence of a genuine emotional attachment and kinship, there had been no similar response from the Mahatmaji.

Years later—in 1940—I reminded him of this. He said that he

completely recollected the episode. "I am very, very sorry," he said then, "that you misunderstood that answer of mine. I didn't mean that I was aware of no emotional attachment, no feeling for the welfare of Muslims; I only meant that I was conscious of full blood *brotherhood*, yes, but not of the superiority that *fatherhood* would imply."

And I, on my side, had only meant in that word "father" to show respect for the frailty of his age—not, of course, frailty in health or mental capacity—and not to hint at any superiority.

This unfortunate initial misunderstanding over words had more than a passing effect. For it left the impression, which persisted not only that night but throughout the Round Table Conference, that our attempts to reach a Muslim-Hindu entente were purely political and without the stabilizing emotional ties of long fellow citizenship and admiration for one another's civilization and culture. Thus there could be no cordiality about any entente we might achieve; we were driven back to cold politics, with none of the inspiring warmth of emotional understanding to suffuse and strengthen our discussions.

This preliminary talk did not take us far. Thereafter we had a further series of conversations—usually at midnight in my rooms at the Ritz—I myself presiding as host, and Mr. Jinnah and Sir Mohammed Shaffi negotiating on one side, and Mahatma Gandhi on the other. The story of these discussions is long and not, alas, particularly fruitful.

They were informal talks and no record was kept. I said little and left the bulk of the discussion to Mr. Jinnah and Sir Mohammed Shaffi, and to other delegates who from time to time took part, notably Sir Zafrullah Khan, Mr. Shaukat Ali and the late Shaffat Ali Khan. Much of the disputation vividly recalled Fitzgerald's quotation:

> Myself when young did eagerly frequent
> Doctor and Saint, and heard great argument
> About it and about: but evermore
> Came out by the same door as in I went.

Always the argument returned to certain basic points of difference: Was India a nation or two nations? Was Islam merely a religious minority, or were Muslims in those areas in which they were in a majority to have and to hold special political rights and responsibilities? The Congress attitude seemed to us doctrinaire and unrealistic. They held stubbornly to their one-nation theory, which we knew to be historically insupportable. We maintained that before the coming of the British Raj the various regions of the Indian subcontinent had never been one country, that the Raj had created an artificial and transient unity, and that when the Raj went, that unity could not be preserved and the diverse peoples, with their profound racial and religious differences, could not remain fellow-sleepers for all time but they would awake and go their separate ways.

However close therefore we might come to agreement on points of detail, this ultimate disagreement on principle could not be bridged.

The Mahatma sought to impose a first and fundamental condition: that the Muslims should, before they asked for any guarantees for themselves, accept Congress' interpretation of Swaraj—self-government—as their goal. To which Mr. Jinnah very rightly answered that, since the Mahatma was not imposing this condition on the other Hindu members of the various delegations attending the Round Table, why should he impose it on the Muslims? Here was another heavy handicap.

Our conditions were the same throughout: very few powers at the center, except in respect of defense and external affairs; all other powers to be transferred, and especially to those provinces in which there were Muslim majorities—the Punjab, Bengal, Sind, Baluchistan and the Northwest Frontier. We were adamant because we knew that the majority of the Muslims who lived in Bengal and the Punjab were adamant.

Mahatma Gandhi fully recognized the importance of having us in his camp. Who knows?—perhaps he might have seen his way to accept our viewpoint, but Pundit Malaviya and the Hindu Mahasabha exerted great pressure against us, deploying arguments based on abstract political doctrines and principles which, as the partition of 1947 proved, were totally unrelated to the realities of India.

As time went on the hair-splitting became finer and finer, the arguments more and more abstract: a nation could not hand over unspecified powers to its provinces; there was no constitutional way of putting a limit on the devices by which a majority could be turned into a minority—fascinating academic issues, but with little or no connection with the real facts and figures of Indian life.

In fairness I ought to mention one practical reform which did emerge from all our discussions and in the end contributed something to the settlement of 1947. This was the separation of Sind from Bombay and its establishment as a Province with a Governor and administration of its own. For at least thirty years previously the continued connection of these two had been an anachronism; its existence explains much of Sind's so-called backwardness, and the rivalry and the jealousy that arose between Bombay, the older city which ruled, and Karachi, the younger city which was ruled.

In the Province of Bombay the I.C.S. officials who attained the highest ranks of the service tended to have spent years in Marathi or Gujerati districts. Sind differed from other parts of the Province in race, language, religion and the physical shape of the land, and service in it required a quite different outlook, mentality and training. Sind had been neglected in matters like communications, roads and internal development, by an administrative center from which it was far distant and with which its only connections were by sea or across the territories of princely states.

A special committee was set up to consider the whole question of the separation of Sind. The Muslim representatives on it—of whom I was one—did not argue the case on communal lines; we urged that Sind be separated from Bombay as an act of common justice to its inhabitants, and on practical and administrative grounds. Apart from one or two members who represented Bombay and were anti-separation, our other Hindu colleagues supported us, and our proposal was carried.

The chairman of this particular committee was the late Earl

Russell, the elder brother of the present Earl, better known as Bertrand Russell. He was a lively and interesting personality, who had endured—and surmounted—the difficulties and the legal and social complications of a stormy marital career in his early life. He was a grandson of the first Earl—Lord John Russell, Queen Victoria's famous Whig Prime Minister. Born and reared in this inmost circle of the old Whig oligarchy of England, he was himself supremely unclass-conscious, endowed with a wonderful memory, richly stored, and with great gifts as a raconteur.

He died in the south of France not long after the end of the conference; the news of his death came as a shock, for I had looked forward to our friendship continuing and enriching itself for the rest of our lives.

One of his former wives, who lived not far from my own home at Antibes, was no less remarkable and original a character—the tiny, inimitable and indomitable Elizabeth, of *Elizabeth and her German Garden*. She maintained her passion for garden-building to the end. She lived not far from the country club and golf course at Mougins; she designed much of its landscape gardening and floral planning; and my wife, Princess Andrée, and I consulted her more than once about our own garden.

To return to the Round Table Conferences: in the end, their many long sessions achieved little. The Mahatmaji returned to India; the sum total of all our work was a vast array of statistics and dates, a great many speeches and little or no positive understanding. The second conference finished, all the delegates dispersed, and we awaited what was in fact the third Round Table Conference—it was officially known as the Joint Select Committee appointed by Parliament under the chairmanship of the Marquis of Linlithgow—to draw up the Indian Federal Constitution.

Meanwhile my ordinary life outside politics had continued tranquilly and eventfully. My wife, Princess Andrée, had throughout the exhausting and protracted sessions of the first two Round Table Conferences been of quite invaluable support and help to me. For the conferences had a circumambience of hospitality and sociability, parties, receptions and dinners innumerable, at which my wife was my constant, graceful and accomplished partner. In January, 1933, my second son, Sadruddin, was born in the American Hospital at Neuilly, just outside Paris. At the end of that year Princess Andrée paid her first visit to India with me, leaving our son in the south of France. We traveled all over the country, seeing most of the famous, beautiful and historical sights; stayed several days with the renowned old Maharajah of Bikaner; stayed in Calcutta as the guests of the Governor, Sir John Anderson*; went up to the hills for a time and traveled on to Burma. We were home in Cannes by April, 1934, delighted to be greeted by a much-grown, healthy, strong little boy.

Then I found myself fully back in political harness. The third of the series of Indian Round Table Conferences was upon us. On the British side there had been changes, consequent upon the formation of the MacDonald-Baldwin National Government. Mr. Ramsay MacDonald was still Prime Minister, but his support in the House of Commons came now from the enormous Conservative majority of which Mr. Baldwin was the master. This removed Mr. MacDonald from direct and close concern in our deliberations about India; consulted in all important matters he doubtless continued to be, but the effective decisions were, one could not help feeling, being made by the man in charge of the India Office. This, of course, was Sir Samuel Hoare, a sensitive, sagacious, broadminded and keenly intelligent statesman, who was acutely aware of the realities of our mid-twentieth-century world, and—so far as India was concerned—fully realized that the day of the die-hard imperialist was ended.

The Joint Select Committee assembled in London in the spring of 1934. The Chairman, Lord Linlithgow, was later to be Viceroy of India. The composition of the committee was as varied as it was strong. The British representation contained inevitably a heavy Conservative preponderance; the knowledge and experience of India of individual members varied in quantity and quality. Respected and influential leaders like Lord Derby and Sir Austen Chamberlain

* Now Lord Waverley.

were at the outset noncommittal; there were others who were frankly opposed to the whole idea of a federal solution to India's problems. India's representation was on the whole good; Mahatma Gandhi did not attend, but there was a sizable element of advanced Indian nationalism, drawn from outside the ranks of Congress. Looking back now on what happened in the course of this committee, I think I regret Mr. Jinnah's absence as much as that of the Mahatmaji. It was, I think, extremely unfortunate that we Muslims did not insist on having Mr. Jinnah with us; had he been a member of the delegation he might have subscribed to what I consider was the most valuable result of these Round Table Conferences.

This was the Joint Memorandum, which—for the first time in the history of Indo-British relations—put before the British Government a united demand on behalf of all communities, covering practically every important political point at issue. It propounded what would have been, in effect, a major step forward—the penultimate step indeed before Dominion status. By it we sought to ensure continuity in the process of the further transfer of responsibility. It was signed by all the nonofficial Indian delegates; it had been drafted by the delegation's brilliant official secretary and myself. It was a claim for the transfer to Indian hands of practically every power except certain final sanctions which would be reserved to the British Government. Had a constitution been granted along these lines, later critical situations—India's declaration of war in 1939, the problems which faced the Cripps Mission in 1942, and the final and total transfer of authority—might all have been much less difficult. Had this constitution been fully established and an accepted and going concern, it would have been in due course a comparatively simple operation to lop off those reserve powers which in our draft marked the final stage of constitutional devolution.

As I said in the course of evidence which I gave before the Joint Committee on the Government of India Bill:

"I accept the term 'Responsible Government,' though as an ideal my preference is for self-government either on the American federal plan or on Swiss lines leaving ultimate power through the Initiative, the Referendum, and perhaps the Recall. But the facts of the situation have to be recognized. . . . 'Responsible Government' must be our way toward evolving in the future some plan more suited to a congeries of great states, such as India will become, and I believe the way will be found in something akin to the American federal plan."

Despite all (as we thought) its merits, our Joint Memorandum was disowned by Congress, and therefore the British Government felt compelled in their turn to reject it. In its stead they brought into being the constitution adumbrated by the Government of India Act of 1935, which left far too many loopholes for British interference, and indeed actual decision, on matters which every Indian patriot believed should have been solely for India to decide—for example, India's entry into the Second World War. Its grossest failing was that it offered no foundation on which to build; Sir Stafford Cripps, during his mission in 1942, and Lords Alexander of Hillsborough and Pethick-Lawrence on their subsequent mission were halted by this unpalatable fact. Neither did the Act supply an impetus to any effort to bridge the rift between Hindus and Muslims; and in the testing times of 1942 and 1946-1947, the emptiness in the Act was glaringly revealed. By its reservations and by its want of clarity about the real meaning of Indian independence, the 1935 Act made a United India an impossibility. It had to be set aside and the effort made to build up Indian independence from scratch. Then it became harshly clear that Indian unity was impossible unless it were based on extremely wide federal, or confederate, foundations.

The second Cabinet Mission of 1947 did finally propose a constitution which would have maintained the unity of India, but at the price of handing over all ultimate power to the three confederate states of a Federal India. This was the sort of constitution for which our Joint Memorandum of 1934 could have naturally and steadily prepared the ground. Congress' attitude to this last effort was, to say the least, lukewarm; and it too fell by the wayside. In the end the only solution was that which occurred, and those strange Siamese twins—Muslim India and Hindu India—that had lived together so restlessly and so uncomfortably, were parted by a swift, massive surgical operation.

XII

Policies and Personalities
at the League of Nations

WITH the Joint Memorandum, and with the termination of the work of the Joint Select Committee in 1934, my own connection with Indian politics ended. However, I found myself striking out along a new line in public affairs and taking up new activities which were to be my main concern and interest in life from the early 1930's until the outbreak of the Second World War.

These developed from my close association at the India Office with Sir Samuel Hoare. He and I, in the intervals between our official discussions on the Indian problem, found ourselves more and more frequently exploring world affairs—in the 1930's an absorbing if formidable theme.

The curiously facile yet plausible optimism which had buoyed up the hopes of so many in the 1920's broke down rapidly; it gave place to an increasing and deepening anxiety. It is pitiable now to recall some of the illusions which were fostered in the years immediately after the First World War. I heard supposedly intelligent people, who habitually moved in circles which were considered to be well informed, remark, for example, that the war "had not impoverished but enriched the world and that its apparent cost had been more than met by a superior system of price control and economic adjustment." Only when the slump came was it realized that a war has to be paid for. As that realization dawned, it became harshly apparent that the world was lurching toward a new catastrophe.

Then as now there was no getting away from the question of Germany and the Germans. Today as we are all aware, the crux of Europe's difficulties and problems is to be found in Germany. There is indeed no hope of a real and abiding world peace without a final solution of the problem of Germany, to be achieved either by a frank and sincere understanding between Russia on the one hand and the Western Powers under American leadership on the other, or by the consolidation of a Germany allied with and integrated with Western Europe. Just as grimly the problem of Germany was with us in the 1930's; questions about where the Western world was moving, and of how it would work out its destiny, and the great issue of peace or war were quite inseparable from the question of what was going to happen to Germany.

Eighty million highly intelligent, industrious, efficient and well-educated people, cooped up in a comparatively small area between the Rhine and the Vistula, the North Sea and the Alps, with "colonies" of their kinsfolk settled outside the Reich's borders, in the Sudetenland, in Austria, and as far away as Rumania and parts of Russia, seeking unity yet conscious of a long history of religious and dynastic strife, constituted a permanent and enormous question mark in the very heart and center of Europe. Nor was it the only one of its kind. Fascist Italy loomed very large—Mussolini's imperial ambitions, his attitude toward Ethiopia and Albania, his talk of the Mediterranean as *"mare nostrum."*

Mussolini, for all his crimes and follies for which he paid in his ignominious fall and death, was in many ways a man of brilliant and powerful individuality. He achieved in the Italy of the period between the wars a political revival analogous in some respects to the Wesleys' religious revival in England in the eighteenth century. His revival did not touch every section of the populace—nor did Methodism. But many of its emotions suffused Italian society as a whole—far outside the ranks of the Fascist party itself. There was, for example, the longing for a place in the sun, the feeling that while nations like England, Spain and Portugal had built up vast daughter-nations overseas, Italy—Rome's successor and inheritor—banned from expansion in Europe outside the confines of her own peninsula, now had the sacred right and duty of renewing Rome's imperial mission overseas. Therefore there was a passionate concentration on Ethiopia—first to wipe out Aduwa's shame and, second and far more important, to build up in those high Equatorial lands (climatically so similar to many of the countries of South America) a vast European colony whose people might one day mingle their blood with that of the native Amharic aristocracy—as the Spaniards had mingled theirs with the Incas—reducing those whom they considered racially inferior to permanent helot or peon status.

Away in the Far East Japan was engaged in what came to be known as "the China incident"; the need of a policy of colonial expansion seemed imperative to her leaders; she was already deeply committed in Manchuria. To topics such as these, real, insistent and ugly as they were, Hoare and I found ourselves reverting again and again whenever we turned aside from the constitutional niceties of India's political development.

Hoare gradually became aware that from the moment India began to play a part—however limited—in international politics, I (so far as making any use of me was concerned) had been deliberately neglected and cold-shouldered by the Government of India. The reasons for this policy in New Delhi and Simla were not difficult to analyze; Hoare took their measure quickly enough. The exalted mandarins of the Indian Civil Service, that all-powerful and closely knit bureaucracy which governed India, had neither the desire nor the capacity to appreciate a man of independent position and views like myself, who had first-hand knowledge of a great many of these problems. They were painfully aware too that were I to be given any official diplomatic status and be therefore in a position to receive the Viceroy's instructions, I would not hesitate to make known to the Viceroy my own views and if necessary to criticize official policy, and that if I were overruled unreasonably, I should similarly have no hesitation in resigning and in giving my reasons for resignation fully and with conviction to both the Viceroy and the Secretary of State. If I represented India at any international conference, there would be no chance of my being a ventriloquist's dummy for officialdom. Officialdom therefore considered that I would be far more of a liability than an asset—after all, I might prove the officials to be wrong.

Not unnaturally the bureaucrats rationalized their distaste for me and their fear of me. They pointed out that I was a race horse owner, that I was an amateur of literature and the arts, that I had founded Aligarh University as a sectional, if cultural, institution, that since I was Imam of the Ismailis, my first loyalty would always be to my followers and therefore Government could not take the risk of employing me. The files in the Secretariat were, I daresay, heavy with minutes and memoranda about me; and they all added up to the one word "no." Sir Samuel Hoare saw through the whole elaborate façade and recognized it for what it was—arrant prejudice.

When arrangements were in train for the Disarmament Conference and the Indian delegation to the League of Nations was in process of being appointed, Sir Samuel Hoare took the whole matter up with characteristic energy and thoroughness, drew the Viceroy's attention to the fact that I had deserved more useful employment, and insisted that I be given a chance to serve India in the international field. Someone has used about me the phrase "Ambassador without Portfolio." The Secretary of State urged that it was high time for me to be given official status.

I think I may claim that I brought to my new task a mind fairly well versed in its main issues. My grounding in European as well as Eastern political and social history had been thorough. Ever since adolescence I had read widely and steadily. I was—and still am—a diligent student of the newspapers, and of those political magazines and quarterlies which, in Britain and France especially, give an authoritative and often scholarly commentary on all the main events and trends of our time. I had also for many years lived an active life in both national and international affairs.

Let me recall the international atmosphere of the spring of 1932, and some of the main international trends and factors. The U.S.S.R. was seeking to establish at least a superficial appearance of respectability. We know now that the internal situation in Russia, after the appalling disruptive efforts of the first Five Year Plan, was parlous. Stalin, by now sole master of his country's destiny, desired a period of relaxed external tension. In Litvinov he had a Foreign Minister who knew England well, who had an English wife, who had personal cognizance of the shrewdness and practical wisdom of British statesmanship and of the possibilities it afforded, if properly handled, of securing Russia her fit place in the comity of nations.

Litvinov was himself unaffectedly eager in his desire to promote the idea of his country's respectability, and to present her to the world as a thoroughly honest woman; the matron herself stood somewhat hesitant on the threshold—for reasons which became apparent later. However, social relations with Litvinov and with other members of his mission were at least possible. On my own initiative I broke the ice (somewhat, I suspect, to the surprise and secret amusement of my British colleagues, accustomed to the hesitations of previous Indian members of the delegation), and I gave a special dinner party in Litvinov's honor. His gratification was obvious. That dinner laid the foundation of a friendship which lasted as long as Litvinov was in Geneva; and it extended to embrace other Russian diplomats, who never failed in return to invite me to their social functions. Litvinov indeed began to appear in the role of a dinner-table diplomat and achieved his own quite real social success. My old friend, Baron Maurice de Rothschild, who had a beautiful chateau not far from Geneva, took to giving small informal luncheon parties, bringing together Litvinov and his colleagues with leading British and French delegates and with representatives of other countries.

The United States had disowned President Wilson and refused to join the League of Nations, and had proclaimed in sternly isolationist terms America's faith in her own destiny. But by 1932 the effects of the depression were being acutely felt all over the North American continent; the epoch of Harding-Coolidge isolationism was drawing to a close. The State Department had become increasingly aware that America could not afford to wash its hands of the rest of the world; it was decided that the Disarmament Conference offered a convenient method of exploring the long-unfamiliar international atmosphere of Geneva. Weimar Germany—unlike the

U.S.S.R.—was now a respectable member of the international fraternity, on terms of at least superficial equality with Britain and France. Had not Stresemann, Briand and Austen Chamberlain met in heart-stirring amity at Locarno, and had not Briand signalized the event with the tremendous oration which began "À *bas les cannons* . . ."?

In 1932 the key word was "disarmament." Disarmament was the concept to which so many high and noble hopes were pinned. Optimism still ran high: get the representatives of the nations around a table, agreeing in principle on disarmament, and let them work out the practical details of disarming—the melting down of the guns and the rifles, the scrapping of the battle cruisers, the limitations on the use and the armament of aircraft—and surely world peace could be made sure and stable.

Yet beneath this optimism there ran an undercurrent of doubt and fear. Were prospects as bright as many tried to believe? Was Weimar Germany all that she seemed to be? Ebert and Stresemann were gone; Brüning battled against a strange swirl of increasingly hostile forces, some of which were economic but many blatantly and violently political. Had all the effort that had gone into trying to woo Germany for democracy been in vain? Had the mountain labored and brought forth merely a negligible mouse?

A new word had come into current political phraseology: Nazism, which we were told meant National Socialism; it seemed a confused and extremely German version of Italy's Fascism, was already capturing the loyalty and the imaginative and romantic idealism of thousands of Germany's youth, and was associated with a man called Adolf Hitler.

Now the military adviser to the German mission in Geneva at this time was none other than General—later Field Marshal—von Blomberg, the man who later became chief of Hitler's *Reichswehr*, was Hitler's representative at King George VI's Coronation, and finally fell into disgrace in somewhat mysterious circumstances— allegedly because of his unsuitable marriage. This Prussian soldier and I established quite friendly relations. From him I heard a good deal about the men who were then trying to rule Germany—tiny

midgets, he called them contemptuously, who had stepped into
Stresemann's man-sized shoes. He was impatient with what he
thought their combination of doctrinaire liberalism and practical
incompetence in statecraft.

Such then was the troublous sea onto which I now was launched.
The Secretary of State's wishes prevailed in the Secretariat in New
Delhi. I was appointed a member of the Indian delegation to the
Disarmament Conference, nominally as second-in-command to Sir
Samuel Hoare, but to take charge as soon as he left. I was also ap-
pointed chief Indian representative at the 1932 Assembly of the
League. Thus began a phase in my public life which was protracted,
with little or no intermission, until Hitler's armies marched into
Poland and the fabric of world peace which the League strove so
hard to maintain was violently shattered.

The optimism that was prevalent in Geneva in 1932 was a mood
which I could not fully share. A more strenuous and a more realistic effort was needed, I felt sure, to bring about the fruition of
our hopes. As best I could, I sought to expound my own ideas and
beliefs in this new arena to which I had been summoned. I made a
speech of some length, and with all the earnestness that I could
muster, at the fourteenth plenary session of the League:

> We have found that armaments still hold sway and that the feeling
> of insecurity still persists. It is by no means certain that the war to end
> war has been fought and won. On the moral side we must set ourselves
> to remove the paralyzing effects of fear, ill-will and suspicion. On the
> material side it is absolutely essential that the nonproductive effort de-
> voted to warlike preparations should be reduced to the bare minimum. In
> distant India, no less than in Europe, the world war created a host of
> mourners and left a legacy of bitter tragedy. Over a million of my fellow
> countrymen were called to arms, of whom more than fifty thousand laid
> down their lives. India's own scale of armaments allows no margin for
> aggressive uses. The size of her forces has to be measured with reference
> to the vastness of her area and the diversity of her conditions. The fact is
> so often forgotten that the area of India is more than half that of the
> whole of Europe, and her population nearly one-fifth of that of the
> entire globe. There is a cry going up from the heart of all the peace-
> loving citizens of every country for the lessening of their military burdens,
> for a decrease of the financial load which those burdens impose, for the

security of civil populations against indiscriminate methods of warfare, and above all, for security against the very idea of war.

The words of many of us who, in those years, spoke out in the effort to prevent a Second World War have gone down the wind. But that is not to say that the effort was not worth making or that we were not right to make it. The vast palace in Geneva that housed the League of Nations is no longer put to the purpose for which it was built, but the United Nations Organization, which has arisen out of the ruin and the tragedy which we strove to avert, shows—by continuing our work in a new era and with new techniques—that we did not labor entirely in vain.

For the rest of the thirties the work of the League, and of its offshoot the Disarmament Conference, absorbed most of my time and my interest. I found myself in Geneva for months at a time, through many harassing and disillusioning happenings—Japan's aloof snubbing of the League, Germany's dramatic exit from it, and then the direct challenge of Mussolini's aggression in Ethiopia. Early in this period I cemented a close friendship with Mr. Arthur Henderson, the President of the Disarmament Conference. Henderson was perhaps one of the most remarkable statesmen who have come out of the British Labor Movement. He had been a conspicuously successful and much-liked Foreign Secretary in Mr. Ramsay MacDonald's second Labor administration, but he had not found himself able to support his leader in the rapid and dramatic change-over which resulted in the formation of the National Government. Therefore he retained the passionate and proud loyalty of Labor in Britain, but the immediate effect of his decision was to deprive him of power and of office. It was universally felt that it would be disastrous, for the world as for Britain, to lose his sagacity, his experience and his flair in the spheres of international affairs in which he had made so notable a mark. He was therefore appointed permanent President of the Disarmament Conference and until his untimely death he discharged his duties in this post—in face of much disappointment and a heartbreakingly uphill struggle—with courage and distinction. Our acquaintance ripened rapidly into a sincere and mutually affectionate friendship of great warmth. His mind and his achievements were as remarkable as his character was lovable. Like most of the Labor leaders of his generation, he was a genuine son of the people who from humble beginnings had made his way upward in the world to the high, onerous and lonely position which he occupied. He was modest and forthright, shrewd, imperturbable, quiet of speech, and of rocklike integrity. A labor leader of a younger generation, Mr. Morgan Phillips, has said that the origins of the British Labor movement are to be found in Methodism rather than Marxism; this was certainly true of Arthur Henderson, for he remained all his life a serenely devoted Methodist. His wife had been his faithful companion on his long and strenuous road; she was a woman of great sweetness and generosity of character, staunch and true and, in her own fashion, very wise.

Henderson was often my guest at my villa at Antibes; Bernhard Baron, the millionaire and philanthropist, would sometimes drive to Monte Carlo to spend an hour or two in the Casino, and Henderson would happily go along for the ride. When they reached the Casino, however, Henderson sat contentedly in the car, waiting till Baron came out again. Henderson was as steadfast as he was good, as selfless as he was courageous. We came to rely on each other for advice and support in the difficult and trying times through which we steered our way in Geneva.

The year 1935 was a memorable one. It was the year of Mussolini's attack on Ethiopia. It was the year in which the Government of India Act came into being—the last major piece of Indian legislation enacted by the Parliament of the United Kingdom until the brief, dramatic statute of twelve years later which ended the British Raj in India. It was the year of my great and good friend King George V's Silver Jubilee; and I fully shared the sentiments of gratitude, affection and loyalty with which his people so signally greeted the King and Queen Mary. For me it was Bahram's year, for during that summer that magnificent horse won the Two Thousand Guineas, the Derby and the St. Leger—the Triple Crown of the Turf, as the sporting journalists called this feat—the first horse to achieve it since Rock Sand, thirty-two years before.

I was able to be present at Epsom when he won his Derby—
Freddie Fox was the jockey—and of course I led him in after his
victory. I was immensely honored by being the guest (in company
with other members of the Jockey Club) of Their Majesties, the
King and Queen, at a celebration dinner at Buckingham Palace.
Queen Mary herself had ordered that the table decorations should
be in my racing colors, green and chocolate.

I was not in quite such happy surroundings when Bahram won
the St. Leger. By then I was back at my duties in Geneva. I can at
least however claim a record: I am sure I must have been the
only member of the Assembly of the League ever to be called
away to hear that his horse had won the St. Leger.

But the international scene by now was gloomy and its skies
were darkly overcast. The little, glimmering lights of peace and
hope which had been set burning since the end of the First World
War were going out, one by one. Exactly a fortnight before Mussolini launched his attack on Ethiopia, I spoke in the Assembly of
the League of Nations. The time had passed, I was convinced, for
smooth glib words. On my own and my country's behalf I spoke as
frankly and as gravely as I could:

> India is troubled by the League's lack of universality and by the great
> preponderance of energy which the League devotes to Europe and
> European interests. India is troubled by these dramatic failures, by the
> long-drawn-out and fruitless Disarmament Conference and by the fact
> that the rearmament of States members is in full swing. India's criticism
> of the League is directed to its shortcomings and not its ideals. The world
> is at the parting of the ways. Let wisdom guard her choice.

As 1935 drew to its close I went to Bombay to celebrate my
Golden Jubilee as hereditary Imam of the Ismailis. Half a century
had passed since I, a small, shortsighted, solemn boy, surrounded
by my bearded elders, had ascended the *gadi*. The climax of the
celebration was the ancient ritual of weighing me against gold. Earlier we had a special ladies' party at the Jamat Khana, at which my
beloved mother sat on my right and my wife on my left. The
actual weighing ceremony was both stately and heart stirring, evok-

ing as it did strong currents of reciprocal affection between my followers and myself.

Our rejoicings, however, were cut short by the grievous news of the passing of my old, staunch and good friend, the King-Emperor, George V, who died at Sandringham in January, 1936. I thought of all the years of our friendship, of the many tests and trials it had undergone in war and in peace, of his constant kindness and consideration to me in all matters great and small. The last word which I had had from him, indeed, had been a warm message of congratulation on my Jubilee. We immediately abandoned all further festivities out of respect to his memory, and I read out this brief statement to my assembled followers:

> I am deeply touched to hear the terrible news of the death of the King-Emperor. I have decided to stop all activities in connection with my Golden Jubilee celebrations, except the purely religious rites. We are in deep mourning. I myself will wear black clothes, and my people will wear their national mourning dress. The King-Emperor was not only a great ruler, but he was in the true sense a great man. His Majesty was always most kind to me personally. I am sure that the new King-Emperor will, with his knowledge of the world and of the whole Empire, be a worthy successor to Queen Victoria, to King Edward and to King George.

Although within a few brief months events had turned out sadly different, I do not for an instant regret or withdraw that last sentence of my statement. I had long known the attractive, brilliant and lovable man who acceded to his father's throne, that January day in 1936, surrounded by an Empire's loyalty and affectionate high hopes of a long and illustrious reign.

I first met him at York House, St. James's Palace in 1898, when he was a child of four. His mother, then Duchess of York, brought two little sailor-suited boys into the drawing room to shake hands with me—David and Bertie, as they were known within their family. The elder boy's vivid personality stamped itself instantly on my imagination; he had a look of both intelligence and kindness, and a limpid clarity of expression, which were most impressive. I still possess a photograph of the two boys as they were then, with their names written across it by their mother.

In the years that followed I encountered him often, in successive phases of that long and devoted career of patriotic public service of which the culmination was his accession to the Throne and to the duties for which he had so arduously prepared himself. I recall the shy, slim lad staying in Paris to learn French in his late teens, wondering (he who later in life was to become a devoted Parisian) "what my grandfather saw in Paris." I remember his early years as Prince of Wales. I remember the gallant young soldier, who strove in every way to evade Lord Kitchener's stern order that the heir to the Throne not be allowed near the front line. I knew the man whose spirit was stamped forever by the sense of slaughter and waste of those years of trench warfare, the man who has said so poignantly and so truly, in his own memoirs, "I learned about war on a bicycle"—endlessly trundling his heavy Army bicycle along the muddy roads of Flanders, to places like Poperinghe and Montauban and the villages around Ypres, the man who in after years in that annual ceremony at the Royal Albert Hall recited Laurence Binyon's "For the Fallen" with so rapt a sense of dedication and of loss.

I remember in the years after the First World War the "Ambassador of Empire" who ceaselessly traveled the Commonwealth and Empire and the whole world in the service of his country and his people. In the early twenties I met him more than once, strained and tired out as he was, during his extremely testing visit to India. At a big state banquet at St. James's Palace, given in honor of the then Crown Prince of Japan—the present Emperor—I sat next to the Prince of Wales. I remember his saying to me then that if Japan's request for the renewal of the Anglo-Japanese Alliance were refused—for this was the real reason of the Crown Prince's visit—the Japanese would never forgive us. His voice had not the robust, far-hailing quality that was in his father's and his grandfather's; his tone was in comparison with theirs always quiet and restrained, but he spoke with their earnestness, conviction and faith in the importance of what he said.

It was a commonplace of the 1920's to say that the Prince of Wales made friends wherever he went. That was no formal tribute but a simple statement of the truth. Why was it? What was the source of his immense and irresistible attraction, which won the sympathy and admiration of the masses no less than the respect of the powerful few? *The Times* correspondent who accompanied him on one of his many journeys found, I am convinced, the true explanation. The Prince of Wales, he said, was an artist. There lies the real secret of his temperament, of his tragedy as much as of his achievements; he was a born artist. He won the affection and the understanding of millions as only the greatest of artists can do, not by dramatic or thaumaturgic technique, but as a receiving and an "offering up" anew to and for others of that which he received from them and evoked in them. That is why all his state visits, with their numerous mass encounters, drained so much out of him. When he came back after a long drive through thousands of cheering people, the exhaustion which he felt had causes far deeper than the merely physical. He always was in profound nervous, mental and spiritual accord with those who so eagerly surrounded his slowly moving car.

In the early spring of 1936 I had my first audience with him after his accession. He was fully aware of my recent and current activities. He knew that for the past few years I had been India's chief delegate at the Disarmament Conference and at successive sessions of the Assembly of the League. He knew that I was gravely perturbed by the increasingly menacing state of world affairs; burdened—like so many of us who to any extent were behind the scenes in those years—by a deepening sense of the doom which we sought to avert; aware of the cancer at the heart of international, especially European, politics; alarmed too at what looked like American indifference and at the existence of what in those days we called Russia's Gunpowder Plot, her supposed plan to blow up capitalist civilization by a war in which the Soviet Union would take no sides but at the end of which she would appear as beneficiary and all-powerful arbitrator.

The Lords-in-waiting and the India Office officials who had come with me expected, I daresay, that I would have the ordinary perfunctory and brief audience. However, they cooled their heels for an hour and a half or more in the anteroom, while I underwent at the King's hands one of the most searching, serious and well-informed cross-examinations that I have ever experienced. I walked out at last filled with admiration not only for his knowledge, gleaned by his wide and deep reading of all the official and Cabinet papers which came to him, but even more for the seriousness of his outlook and the penetration of his insight.

During 1936 I met the King several times, at private cocktail parties and at luncheon in the houses of one or two close friends. At the bigger gatherings, even in the midst of flippant people, I was greatly struck with the King's utter lack of flippancy, his seriousness and his concentration on his duties. After my first audience and whenever I met him on these private and unofficial occasions during those months, he was accompanied by Mrs. Wallis Simpson, now the Duchess of Windsor. I found her as intelligent as she was charming, admirably well informed, devoid too of flippancy, and seriously and conscientiously striving to adjust her outlook to the King's. At two different houses I met them at luncheon, and on each occasion the only other person present, beside our host and hostess was my old friend—himself an ardent and persevering seeker after spiritual enlightenment—Philip Kerr, Marquis of Lothian.* Our conversation could not have been in its general tone more serious and more anxious.

Naturally neither the King nor Mrs. Simpson ever mentioned their personal affairs to me or in my hearing, but of course wherever one went in London that year, the whispers and the rumors abounded.

I have already mentioned a poignant conversation which I had had with Queen Mary on my return to London from Geneva. Later in the year, in July I think, a great friend of Queen Mary's told me that every day she wept bitterly when she thought of this hidden, unspoken catastrophe which loomed for her dearly loved son.

It was during this same critical period that Lord Wigram, when the two of us were lunching alone, said something which struck me greatly. "King Edward VIII," he said, "has it in him to be the

* Subsequently H. M. Ambassador to Washington; died 1940.

greatest King in the history of our country. With his charm and his personal prestige he can carry with him the whole population—regardless of class."

Lord Wigram, after all, spoke out of long and deep experience. He had been King George V's private secretary, in succession to Lord Stamfordham, and a calm, wise, loyal counselor and friend he was; but before he became a courtier he had been a serving officer in the Indian Army and then on Lord Curzon's staff when he was Viceroy. His equable and unimpassioned judgment seemed to me of considerable importance; yet I could see that, even as he spoke, he was mastering strong and extremely painful and anxious emotions.

By the autumn I was back in Geneva. The King spoke to me once on the telephone; our conversation necessarily was guarded; yet I was aware once more of the profound sadness and the complexity of the drama in his own life and in the life of the country, whose bleak climax was then so near. The swiftness and the completeness of the final irrevocable decision were utterly tragic.

Years have passed, and they have brought inevitably a new perspective to our view of those somber happenings of the first weeks of December, 1936. After King Edward VIII's abdication, his younger brother acceded as George VI. We are all now gratefully and gladly conscious of the magnitude of his selfless and steadfast service to his country and to the cause of human freedom in his sixteen years' reign, and of the immense, quiet goodness of his character, so like his father's.

George VI was blessed—as his elder brother was impelled to remark in the most poignant public utterance of his life—in a supremely happy marriage. His gracious Consort, now Queen Elizabeth the Queen Mother, was as persevering and as selfless in public service as he was, always at his side to sustain and support him through many testing years, which covered the dangers and the ardors of the Second World War and the postwar period of far-reaching social and economic change.

Now a beloved, charming young Queen reigns as Head of the Commonwealth. She brings to her task mental and spiritual qualities of the highest order, and it is already obvious that she has earned the deep loyalty and devotion of her peoples all over the world. She is sustained by the steadfast love of her husband; and her home, like that of her father before her, is a model of tranquil and affectionate family life. The omens are auspiciously set for a splendid new Elizabethan era in Britain's long, eventful history. The institution of the Crown in Britain and the Commonwealth has quickly and triumphantly survived its severest test; on this score therefore there is no reason for regret.

Yet considered as a human happening in its own right, apart altogether from its constitutional and political consequences, surely the story of Edward, Duke of Windsor and his Duchess is one of the very great love stories of all time. Set it alongside the imperishable, tragic and beautiful stories of Persian or Arabian legend, alongside the stories of Anthony and Cleopatra and of Romeo and Juliet, and does it not stand forth as perhaps the most moving of them all?

When I was discussing my religious views, I quoted the saying of the poet Hafiz to the effect that those who are not granted the grace and aid of the Holy Spirit to achieve direct communion with that Divine Presence in which we live, move and have our being, may yet attain blessed and pure felicity if they achieve the heights of human love and companionship—something not won lightly or easily, but the crown of a lifelong attachment, in which one human being devotes all that he has, knows and feels to the love and service of another.

Surely his former Majesty, King Edward VIII, who lost and sacrificed so much, has been granted, if not the supreme, at any rate the lesser and by no means unworthy, blessing and illumination of a durable and all-enfolding love.

I have one personal postscript to add to this sad yet stirring story. In the autumn of 1937 I was staying in Berlin at the same time as the Duke and Duchess of Windsor. I called on them and we had a long, extremely intimate and extremely revealing conversation. I was deeply affected by the obvious and transparently sincere loyalty and devotion with which the Duke talked of his brother, speaking of him always as the King; the whole tenor of his remarks was that of fidelity from a devoted subject to his sovereign. Later that year when I was in London I had an audience with King George VI; the ostensible reason for my being summoned to the palace was that I should give His Majesty an account of the interview which I had had with Hitler. Before I left, the King asked me, "You saw my brother?" I then told him the substance of the Duke of Windsor's conversation with me, and I stressed the warmth and the obvious sincerity of the Duke's loyalty. The King was clearly most deeply moved by his elder brother's willing and complete acceptance of the new situation—so moved in fact that I myself was equally stirred.

Can we sustain the peace, or must there in the end be war? This was the question with which we were faced at Geneva, year after year. To understand its intensity, and to understand the way in which each of us, as individuals or as representatives of our countries, strove to find our own answer, it is necessary to explore a good deal of the historical and political background. Munich has constantly been hotly attacked as a single, unparalleled and causeless act of appeasement, and Neville Chamberlain, the British Prime Minister, whose name is forever associated with Munich, who thought it his greatest triumph and found it to be his greatest tragedy, has been criticized in the most unmeasured and ferocious terms. Yet who are, in fact, the "guilty men," whom partisan propaganda so vituperatively pursued? What are the real reasons, not the superficial "blame," for Munich?

We must first probe far back into the story of Germany's relations with the rest of Europe. We must look afresh at that unfortunate, false, and unjust assertion, made at the end of the First World War and given explicit formulation in the Versailles Treaty, that Germany's and Germany's alone, was the war guilt. Whatever strict apportionment of guilt there should be, it is by no means all Germany's. Nearly half the responsibility was Russia's. What about the folly, the incompetence, the insane ambition and the revengeful self-satisfaction of a man like Isvolsky who, as Czarist Ambassador in Paris, said to me—not to me alone, for he said it to everyone he could—*"C'est ma guerre"*? What about the same idiot boast on the lips of Sazunov, that weak and foolish man who, despite all the warnings given him by abler men like Witte and Rosen, did not shrink in anticipation from a war that was to ruin his country, his Emperor and his own class?

However at the end of the war, to millions in the victorious nations, blinded by their own propaganda, Imperial Germany seemed a convenient scapegoat. Germany was branded as the only criminal. And then, almost before the ink had dried on the signatures to the Versailles Treaty, a significant development occurred in political thought. The intellectuals of the Left in Britain, profoundly affected by the limpidly persuasive writings of John Maynard Keynes, discovered that their consciences were troubled over Versailles' injustice, and over the admission written into it, above the enforced signature of Germany's representatives, that Germany alone was to blame for all the horrors and miseries of the First World War; and until Hitler came to power, they were very vocal in their criticisms of the 1919 settlement.

Doubts about not merely the wisdom but the morality of the Versailles Treaty were by no means limited to the highbrows of the Left. Many a conscientious political thinker on the Right—though perhaps more pragmatic, more inclined to see the issue in terms of power politics—had severe misgivings about the justification, at the price even perhaps of a war, of maintaining a *status quo* founded upon a falsehood. The constitution of the League of Nations, which formed part of the Versailles Treaty, was similarly questioned. Under this Constitution the League was endowed *in theory* with absolute authority to right all wrongs—"to break down this sorry scheme of things and replace it by something nearer heart's desire" —but, as familiarity with the actual processes of the League quickly made clear, its constitution was in fact so pliable that it was impossible for the League to right any wrong, however glaring.

The *status quo* had everything on its side. There was as much chance of achieving any real rectification of frontiers, any adjustment of conflicting national claims, through the League, as there would have been of successfully steering a bill providing for universal suffrage through the House of Lords of 1820. The ideologues of the immediate postwar era worshipped the constitution of the League, but like most idols it had feet of clay. It was, in fact though not in name, a repetition of Alexander I's Holy Alliance of 1815. It was Metternich's system, dressed up anew as democracy, freedom and—sacred word—self-determination. But it had been so adjusted that the "haves" among the nations had things all their own way, and the only hope for the "have-nots" of changing their inferior status lay either in sowing disunity among the "haves" or in building up their military power, sedulously and secretly, until they were able to launch direct and open aggression. This failing in the League was as durable as it was palpable. As I said later to Lord Halifax when he was Foreign Secretary, "You cannot make a silk purse out of a sow's ear."

Defects of this character could not long be hidden. The blood-stained Gran Chaco dispute between Bolivia and Paraguay was in a remote—and at the time strategically insignificant—region, but the difficulties it presented were real and grave, and those of us who had any share in reaching a fairly just solution of this problem were acutely conscious of them.

Then there arose the protracted Sino-Japanese trouble. Here the slate was, from the outset, the reverse of clean. At the conclusion of their successful campaign against Czarist Russia early in this century, the Japanese had built up a special and powerful position for themselves in Manchuria, from Port Arthur almost to the walls of Peking itself, under which China's sovereignty was still recognized but the country was administered and exploited by Japan as if it were a Japanese protectorate. The warlords of northern China had, in Bismarck's phrase, "a telegraph wire" with Tokyo —indeed a full and constant connection by telephone and radio as well. Though China was for years torn by internal strife, this relationship became more and more bitterly hostile as the extent and the determination of Japan's ambitions were disclosed. For a long time it was customary to talk politely about "the differences" between China and Japan; but they were in fact a war, to which we in Geneva strove to put an end.

From the League's point of view China's legal case was utterly unanswerable. Japan had no right in China except in the various concessions—the ports, railway lines, commercial depots, and bases—which she had received from China, or won from Russia to whom China had voluntarily given them. Her territorial pretensions, open or veiled, were without a shred of legal justification.

But when the League rebuked Japan and sought to intervene, it seemed to Japan's rulers that the pot was loudly calling the kettle black. Were they not, the Japanese argued, doing in the twentieth century precisely what countries like Britain and France had done in building up their empires a century or two earlier? They would not and could not accept the claim that, under the constitution of the League, a new world had come into being and with it a new international morality binding on all nations, under which the only way to effect any political change was through the League's elaborate, complicated and devious machinery. It was, in the Scriptural phrase, far easier for a camel to go through the eye of a needle than for Japan to procure *de jure* recognition by the League of her *de facto* position on the northern Asiatic mainland. The "haves" said No; it was only open to the "have-nots" to break through or to circumvent this wall of negatives.

When the Sino-Japanese dispute was brought before the League, I approached Sir John Simon, then British Foreign Secretary, on my own initiative and told him that I felt it was my duty as India's representative—*as an Asiatic*—to do all I could to bring about a direct understanding by conversations between China and Japan. Lord Simon has been bitterly assailed in many quarters, but he possessed—he still possesses—the mind of a statesman, not a bureaucrat. He saw immediately that although such a departure by an Indian representative, at a time when India was still without self-government, might seem unusual if unaccompanied by overt British support, the value of an Asiatic intermediary in a solely Asiatic dispute might be considerable. I was authorized to see what I could effect. I had several conversations with both Chinese and Japanese representatives. On one final occasion I got together the heads of the Chinese and Japanese delegations in a supreme effort to bring about an understanding; the three of us were actually photographed together.

However, a good deal more than the flash of a press photographer's bulb was required. The negotiations broke down. Subsequently hostilities in Asia were renewed on a large scale. The "China incident" became all-out war in Shanghai and in central China. Ultimately Japan left the League. Manchuria was separated from China, and the Japanese set up a puppet Emperor in Manchuria in the person of a scion of the old Manchu imperial dynasty, the man who, according to legitimist views, ought to have been Emperor of China. In central China conflict continued without cessation thereafter between the Japanese and the forces of General Chiang Kai-shek until, with Japan's attack on Pearl Harbor in 1941—the extension of the Second World War to the Far East.

Personalities as well as policies were of significance in those difficult years. I came to know many remarkable men in Geneva, as we battled with successive problems and crises. The first Secretary General of the League was Sir Eric Drummond*—an ideal man in a difficult, a well-nigh impossible, position. He was not only aware that there were two sides to any argument, he saw every question fully in the round. In my many conversations with him I began to appreciate the complexity and the far-reaching effects of every apparently small move or decision made by the League. It seemed that we were forever watching the widening ripples on the pool caused by the throwing of seemingly small pebbles. Yet I must not give the impression that Eric Drummond was in favor of immobility in international affairs, or of stubbornly preserving the *status quo*. No one, I daresay, had better appreciated the lessons of history than he; no one realized more clearly, for example, that—in spite of all that Alexander I and Metternich strove to establish—the European system established in 1815 had collapsed in something near chaos by 1830. Drummond had a flexible mind and highly developed powers of persuasion; I know that many a dispute that might have grown serious was settled in his office simply by his exercise

* Later the Earl of Perth.

of tact and sagacious foresight. However, his influence and authority were limited, for the tradition had transferred itself from the national to the international plane that permanent officials had no views of their own, and therefore as Secretary General he had no right to initiate policy on his own.

Brüning, the German Chancellor, was a forlorn, pathetic figure. A sincere Christian, a devout Roman Catholic, he was obviously beset, in the midst of our troubles, by a genuine Christian conscience, by his patriotism as a German, by the growing difficulties of keeping democracy afloat in Germany, by the mounting challenge of the Nazis, and by the increasing feebleness of the aged Hindenburg's attachment to the republic which had elected him as its President.

Beneš of Czechoslovakia was in his different way a no less tragic figure. He fully realized the dangers to which his country was exposed. More than once over a coffee or at luncheon he talked to me of his troubles and his difficulties. He knew that the German minority in Czechoslovakia had to be won over, persuaded to give up their Pan-German dreams and become loyal and sincere citizens alongside the other racial groups in the country; but he realized that a heavy price had to be paid for such an achievement. He continued, however, to pin high hopes to it. Yet whenever he went into the Sudetenland, to places like Carlsbad or Marienbad, he was faced with the limitations and the potential breakdown of his policy because the Czechs in those areas, although in a minority, strove to assert their superiority—politically and economically, and by the use of educational and linguistic barriers—to the German-speaking majority. His was a classic example of the way in which a well-meaning political leader cannot persuade his followers to carry out his express and sincere intentions.

Someone who was then embarking on his great career I encountered first in Geneva in those years—Mr. Anthony Eden. An immediate point of sympathy and understanding between us was that the subject in which he had taken honors at Oxford, immediately after the First World War, was Oriental languages; he had studied Persian and had known my very old friend Dr. E. G. Browne, the Orientalist and authority on Persian, who was Professor of Arabic. This shared friendship and our shared knowledge and understanding of, and fellow feeling for, Islamic literature, thought and philosophy, were special ties, uniting us more closely than the normal affiliations and social propinquity natural between a representative of the British Government and a representative of India at a meeting of the Assembly of the League. It has not been difficult for someone who has watched, as I have, the careers of so many eminent statesmen, past and present, to foresee Mr. Eden's ultimate and splendid destiny. Today I join my prayers with those of so many others that, when at length the great call comes and he takes up the highest position of all, he will have regained in full the health and the strength which, over past years, he has expended so generously in the service of his country and of humanity in general.

The next great crisis which faced the League was Italy's assault on Ethiopia in 1935. It presented an even more serious challenge than the Sino-Japanese dispute, for however aggressive Japan's actions were, there were explanatory, if hardly ameliorative, factors involved, which, as I have indicated, made it impossible for any of the Great Powers at least to regard that as a clean-cut case. All the various concessions, with all their legal equivocations about status, and (since the Japanese occupation of Korea) a common frontier along the Yalu River, were in themselves occasions for quarrels in which lack of diplomatic satisfaction could—and usually was—made the excuse for military action. The whole situation was morally indefensible, of course, but it had centuries of usage to sustain it and give it at least the superficial appearance of respectability.

Italy, however, possessed none of these opportunities or facilities for whitewashing her aggressive, imperialistic designs on Ethiopia. Italy's only case was one of naked need for living space for her ever-increasing population, if they were to remain Italian. Libya's possibilities of intensive and large-scale exploitation and colonization were few; fertile areas in this long stretch of the Mediterranean littoral were limited, and the desert was vast. Italy's surplus population seemed therefore faced with one of two possibilities. Either they could emigrate across the Atlantic to North or South America or to neighboring Mediterranean lands like Egypt, Morocco, Tunisia and Algeria, and be lost to Italy as citizens; or they could remain in Italy, millions too many for her limited soil to bear, with a standard of living far below that of any of their western European neighbors and thoroughly unworthy of the nation that had succeeded Imperial Rome.

Mussolini made no secret of his intentions. He made stirring speeches in towns and cities all over Italy, and his eloquence roused thousands to passionate enthusiasm and sympathy. At the diplomatic level he gave more than one warning, couched in terms, however, which were ambiguous enough for him to be able to interpret the silence with which France and Britain greeted them as consent, if not as direct encouragement to him. Whatever the shadowy background of the Duce's mental processes, there could be no ignoring the blatant openness of his preparations, throughout the summer of 1935, for the military conquest and annexation of the free, independent and sovereign state of Ethiopia, on pretexts which were flimsy in the extreme. The Ethiopians were faced with a tragic choice: either to accept an ultimatum from Mussolini or, rejecting it, to wage a hopeless war which could only end in total military defeat and subjection.

The League was thus thrust into a hopelessly difficult situation; and there developed that deep and catastrophic division of opinion in Britain and in France and indeed throughout much of the world, which was to persist with such unfortunate results until the outbreak of the Second World War four years later. In two countries, however, there was no chance for any division of opinion to show itself: the U.S.S.R. and Nazi Germany. Russian policy was simple and monolithic; Litvinov had proclaimed Russia's doctrine, "Peace is indivisible." Whatever weaknesses and drawbacks communist policy may possess, there has nearly always been about it a façade of logical unity between dogma and practice. The Nazis, of course, saw a superb opportunity to break up what remained of unity among the Powers that had been victorious over Germany in the First

World War and had sought to make their victory permanent by the guarantees written into the Versailles Treaty. They had the shrewdness not to proclaim their satisfaction too loudly; public opinion in Britain and France was therefore not alert to the hidden dangers in the German attitude, any more than it recognized the hidden dangers in Russia's expressions of shocked virtue.

In Britain confusion and irresolution were woefully apparent. There was the "realism"—grossly mistaken, as the naval history of the Second World War was to demonstrate—of old-fashioned imperialists like the late Lord Lloyd, then president of the Navy League, who argued that the Royal Navy had been so weakened by the years of disarmament and economic stringency that it could not risk being brought into the open conflict which severe and legitimate action against Italy's aggression would be bound to entail. Therefore the imperialists were opposed to any resolute policy.

Another school of thought argued that to annoy Italy would be— as the phrase went—"to drive her into the arms of Germany," and saw in this plea reason enough to submit to Mussolini's high-handedness. There were others who saw a practical political escape-ladder in what came to be known as the Hoare-Laval arrangements.

In Geneva there was a deep and widespread resentment and sense of humiliation at the easy success which apparently attended this shameless policy of aggression, on *condottieri* lines, with a twentieth-century technique in international relations and propaganda.

I saw my friend Mr. Eden and said to him: "If you want international politics to have a foundation of justice, if you want the League really to be what it is supposed to be, if you want to give it a chance to grow into a real society of nations, deciding matters of right and wrong among themselves, then here is an outstanding case which must be tackled. Here there is no valid excuse of any kind. There is no large Italian minority in Ethiopia deprived of their independence or their civic and economic rights. Here is a case of open and inexcusable aggression. And the remedy is in our hands. *All we need do is shut the Suez Canal.* Or if we must have sanctions, let them be applied to oil as well, and thus make them a reality and put some teeth into them. But I still think the best solution is a simple, unanimous resolution by the League to close the Canal."

Instead we found ourselves passing resolutions in favor of sanctions, which I found silly and futile. Yet ineffective as we knew them to be, we had to vote in support of them, for if we did not, we would seem to be condoning Italy's aggression; but the only sanction which would have achieved anything—the sanction of withholding petrol—was barred. I could foresee that it was inevitable from that moment on that there would come a bitter day when those of us who had once held such high hopes for the League would have to go to the Assembly and, with misery in our hearts, ask for the removal of sanctions. I saw too—and I have no hesitation in admitting it—that once the moment came for us to submit to the Italian conquest of Ethiopia, it would be much better for us to swallow our pride and our anger and do it with a good grace.

Here then was an important phase in the development of the policy and practice of appeasement. Here was an instance in which appeasement and conciliation of the aggressor were morally wrong; but once the Great Powers had appeased on this issue—a thoroughly bad and unjustified issue—there would follow the inevitable consequence that sooner or later we should have to stomach a new dose of appeasement, either in the matter of Japan in China, where there were loopholes both historical and juridical, or in the matter of some sort of German aggression, where there would be the pleas of oppressed minorities, of plebiscites demanding reunion, and a whole specious façade of legality and morality.

Was it, however, entirely specious? This was the grave and conscientious doubt which complicated relations with Germany both for individual nations and for the collective Assembly of the League—almost as soon as the Versailles Treaty was signed. Earlier in this chapter I have referred to the inevitable changes in mood and outlook toward Germany which occurred in opinion-forming and influential circles among the victorious Powers, most notably in Britain and to a lesser extent in the United States and Italy.

Now in general I greatly admire Britain and the British people, but my deepest admiration and respect I reserve for one abiding characteristic which they possess—the existence in a substantial and usually influential part of the population of an acutely sensitive conscience, which prevents their accepting as a national responsibility any unjust or violent act or policy however advantageous it may seem to the country's material welfare. No doubt in British history there have been phases of ruthlessness, violence and conquest; but has any healthy and virile race not passed through such phases in its long national life? It is fundamental to the British character and the British way of life that this voice of conscience is always heard; it may at the outset be still and small and belong only to a few, but in the end the majority has been persuaded by it. The naked code of the harsh struggle for existence, with its assertion that life is only maintained by the survival of the fittest, must in the British view be ameliorated by a still higher and nobler instinct—as the great Victorian scientist, Professor T. H. Huxley, said in a famous speech toward the end of his life. This quality of conscience has been far more persistently manifested among the British people and their cousins in the United States than among any other great nation that I know.

Among most of the human race this scrupulous conscience about external events is a personal and individual matter. In England it has long been a national possession; and this is true also of the United States. The cause of this phenomenon lies, I believe, in the influence of the Quakers; always numerically a fairly small minority, they have from the nineteenth century exerted a moral and spiritual influence out of all relation to their numbers. Through their connections with other nonconformist groups, this influence, even in the era of Britain's greatest industrial and commercial expansion at home and overseas, was diffused throughout the whole population, and the persistence and strength of its effect on British policy and actions have been remarkable.

During the 1920's the man who voiced these conscientious scruples about Germany most frequently and forcefully was Lloyd George. In the Press the campaign gathered strength and influence over the years, and it focused especially on the way in which Germany had been deprived of her colonies. J. L. Garvin and others made eloquent pleas for the return to Germany of one or more of the lost colonies. The British mind was never closed to the practical possibilities, as well as the abstract virtue, of such a step.

Now if in Britain there were these conscientious doubts about the wisdom of maintaining the *status quo* which had been imposed by the Peace Treaty, Germany's view of Versailles from the beginning was that it was a *Diktat*, which must be circumvented, challenged and finally overthrown by every means available to the German people. Germans in general believed neither that they alone had made the war nor that they were in fact defeated. Therefore as soon as Germany returned to the comity of civilized nations—long before the rise of Hitler—her attitude on all major questions should have been warning enough. Even the terms of the Locarno Treaty, for all the fervor and optimism with which they were acclaimed, were explicit only about the renunciation of war as a means of settling disputes in the west; German claims *vis-à-vis* Poland were left expressly undefined.

Not long after Locarno, Lord D'Abernon, the great British Ambassador in Berlin, who with his beautiful wife had long been among my dearest and closest friends, was staying in Monte Carlo when Stresemann came there. Lord D'Abernon asked me to meet Stresemann at a luncheon at the Hotel Metropole, at which, besides the three of us, the only other person present was Stresemann's secretary. Stresemann did not beat about the bush. He held that the postwar period had witnessed the establishment of certain general principles: the freedom of all European peoples to unite if they so desired and the right to self-determination of "colonies," racial minorities separated from their mother countries. He said that these principles had been applied to Jugoslavia, Italy and Czechoslovakia; and now, he argued, the implication of Locarno was that they must be extended to Germany by peaceful means. Locarno had fully and finally rectified the injustice of Germany's annexation of Alsace-Lorraine in 1871; henceforth Germany had no further claims in the west of Europe. Stresemann made no threats, and his arguments were based on grounds of justice and fair play.

"Rectification" was indeed the idea which for years obsessed Germany's statesmen and diplomats. At Geneva they canvassed it in and out of season. I recall from my own experience at least one instance of its being pushed forward regardless of the appropriateness of either time or place: a big official reception, with everyone in full evening dress, a stiffly formal occasion, when M. Tardieu, then leader of the French delegation to the Assembly, was, in full public view, relentlessly tackled by his opposite number on the German side.

The failure of the Disarmament Conference was an opportunity which the Germans exploited. In the thesis that the Versailles Treaty had been intended to be a step toward general and progressive disarmament among the nations, and that the Allies had broken the undertakings which they had then given, they found an excuse to rearm.

From 1933 on Hitler merely shouted what his democratic and nonrevolutionary predecessors had often said before, not in shy whispers, but in ordinary conversational tones. There was nothing particularly new in the substance of his demands; what was novel was the arrogant, aggressive and violent way in which he made them. His claims were as vague and as menacingly undefined as theirs had been, but he also made certain quite specific pronouncements. The last thing he wanted, he said, was another war. He would shed no more German blood. The German people had not recovered from the appalling bloodshed from the First World War. Such claims as he made, he said, were humble and reasonable. As I have said, in the autumn of 1937 I myself went to Berlin and saw him, not at the suggestion of the British Foreign Office, but with their full knowledge of what I was doing. By this time he had a fairly detailed list of demands: that an Austro-

German *Anschluss* should be permitted, if a plebiscite of the Austrian people showed a majority to be in favor of such a union; that the relations between the Czechs and the German-speaking community in the Sudetenland should be similar to those between Great Britain and the Irish Free State; and that Germany should have the right to a colonial empire, if not in the same territories as before, then in their equivalent elsewhere. He held that Germany had a moral claim to Tanganyika because African soldiers had fought valiantly on the German side, and therefore German rule must have been popular with them. He made no threat of going to war on this issue.

Six months later the whole picture had changed sharply. The Nazis had marched into Austria, and Hitler had been rapturously acclaimed in his native town of Linz and in Vienna. The Sudeten problem was no longer remote or academic. In the early summer of 1938 a major crisis occurred; Europe buzzed with rumors of a large-scale German mobilization along the Czechoslovak frontier; over a tense week end statesmen and officials were anxiously at work in embassies and foreign ministries. The crisis passed without a decisive flare-up, but it had indicated the depth and the malignancy of the disease from which Europe was suffering. Mr. Eden had resigned from the Foreign Office and had been succeeded by Lord Halifax, the former Viceroy. However, the Prime Minister, Mr. Neville Chamberlain, exercised a vigilant eye over foreign affairs; he, who—quite justly—had described the League's policy of sanctions against Italy as "midsummer madness," strove now with energy and sincerity to effect a practical easement of the difficulties and the dangers which beset Europe. He sought by finding specific solutions to specific problems to build anew, if necessarily brick by brick, a new structure of peace. The grievances of the Sudeten Germans were one such specific problem. Konrad Henlein, the Nazi leader and spokesman in the Sudetenland, visited England that summer and put his case to leading British statesmen. At Mr. Chamberlain's request and with the agreement of the Prague Government, Lord Runciman, a leading member of the Liberal party, an ex-Cabinet Minister of unblemished reputation and a long record of success as a negotiator on both the political and economic front, headed a small mission to Czechoslovakia in order to investigate the whole problem of the Sudeten Germans' future, and if possible to recommend a solution. Apart altogether from any military threat, Lord Runciman's mission was in no doubt as to what the result of a plebiscite in the Sudetenland would be.

A strong and influential current of opinion was running in England in favor of a radical but peaceful, just and permanent settlement of Germany's demands. Among those most closely concerned in the effort to achieve such a settlement was an old and intimate friend. By a coincidence two of Britain's outstanding Ambassadors in Berlin have been my dear and valued friends. I have already referred to Lord D'Abernon, whom I had known well since the early 1900's. Now the British Ambassador was Sir Nevile Henderson. He and I had first met, and had struck up a warm and lasting friendship, when he was a comparatively junior official in the British Embassy in Saint Petersburg in 1912. In Paris a few years later he and I were both members of the small, well-to-do, predominantly American set of agreeable, literary, artistic, sporting and cultured folk, whom I have mentioned earlier; and later again we had been in touch in Egypt. A quarter of a century after our first encounter he had reached the peak of his career as a diplomat, charged—as his own frank autobiographical record* has disclosed—with what could have been a uniquely important responsibility. He and I met several times after he had gone to Berlin. He assured me that sentiment in Carlsbad and Marienbad was overwhelmingly pro-German, having seen for himself on a visit there; he was convinced that a fair plebiscite would reveal a large majority in favor of unity with Germany.

Almost all the advice to which the British Cabinet hearkened was on similar lines. The bulk of the Conservative party supported the Cabinet. So did the City. In the Press the most powerful and influential support for a just and equitable settlement of Germany's demands—and of the demands of the people in the Sudeten-

---

* *Failure of a Mission*, by Sir Nevile Henderson.

land themselves—came from *The Times*. This great newspaper, in its recently published history of itself, has revealed with remarkable candor and forthrightness the part which it played in the whole Munich crisis. Contrary to a belief which has been widely held in Britain and abroad, there was no prompting by the Government of the attitude which *The Times* adopted. Geoffrey Dawson, then editor, and Robin Barrington-Ward, his assistant and eventual successor—both of whom are now dead—had themselves, by utterly independent processes of reasoning and judgment, come to the conclusion that it was not only politic but just and fair to seek to secure, if necessary by far-reaching concessions, a settlement with Germany, and they hoped that such a settlement would prevent the outbreak of a war.

There has of late been a curious shift of emphasis among those who defend Munich. It is fashionable to argue (as a correspondence in *The Daily Telegraph* in the summer of 1953 demonstrated) that Munich was justified, not on moral grounds, but on military grounds, as a strategic and logistic necessity imposed by Britain's weakness on land and sea and most of all in the air. This, I think, can be summed up as the "Munich-bought-much-needed-time" school of thought. This is a *post-hoc* thesis shaped to fit the pattern of subsequent events. It was not the argument which was deployed at the time. Then the case for Munich, as I heard it stated by members of the Government and by other champions of the settlement, and with all sincerity by myself, was proposed as a moral question and ran as follows: would Great Britain be justified in going to war to prevent the Germans of Czechoslovakia from declaring their choice by plebiscite, and in consequence to compel them to remain under Czech rule?

Looking back on it all now, I suppose that I was subconsciously influenced in favor of the idea of separating the Germans from the Czechs in the regions in which they were in a majority by my close personal connection with and understanding of the Muslim-Hindu issue in India, which afforded, on a much larger scale, an almost incredibly exact analogy. Here in miniature was what was to happen nearly a decade later in India. Konrad Henlein played at the time (though history was later to submerge him entirely) the decisive role which, in the Pakistan-Bharat issue, was Jinnah's.

Whatever the subconscious background to my conscious thought then, I had no doubt where I stood. At Geoffrey Dawson's invitation I wrote a *Times* leader-page article in unstinted praise of the agreement with which Mr. Chamberlain returned —in triumph and to a rapturous welcome, let it be remembered— from his last visit to Germany. I stand before history therefore as a strong, avowed supporter of Munich. And now, all these years later, after all the violent and troublous happenings since then, I say without hesitation that I thank God that we did not go to war in 1938. Apart altogether from any highly debatable question of military preparedness or the lack of it, if Great Britain had gone to war in 1938, the doubt about the moral justification of the decision would have remained forever, and doubt would have bred moral uncertainty about the conduct and the conclusion of the war. In the perspective of history Britain would be seen to have gone to war, not on a clear-cut, honorable and utterly unavoidable issue, but in order to maintain the *status quo* and to prevent a plebiscite by which a regional racial majority might seek to be united with their brothers by blood, language and culture.

An easy haze of forgetfulness enfolds many of the details of that period. An important, but frequently ignored, part of the Munich settlement as it was negotiated by Mr. Chamberlain was that there should be a plebiscite in doubtful areas in Czechoslovakia where the two races were mixed. In the subsequent turmoil of events this important provision was forgotten, and the plebiscite never happened; perhaps it can be argued that its result would anyway have been a foregone conclusion.

Perhaps, but I merely know now that I, like many others in that autumn of 1938, had the illusion that we were indeed going to have "peace in our time." Neville Chamberlain, who had brought this about, was our hero, and for a short time he was adulated as few statesmen have ever been before or since.

It was a tragically brief period. Hitherto Hitler had—whatever methods he had used to attain his ends—based his claims on the principle of self-determination as laid down in the peace treaties and in the constitution of the League of Nations. In the spring of 1939, however, he ripped off the veil of respectability. His forces entered what remained of Czechoslovakia, and the country was termed a "protectorate" of the Reich. Baron von Neuradt—a survivor from the pre-Nazi era—was sent to Prague as Protector to rule a country which had indeed been annexed and totally subjugated.

This destroyed in a single stroke the whole moral basis of Germany's case before history, and it united in a common resolution many who, in 1937-1938, had held very different views. There was now no doubt; there were no questionings. It was perfectly obvious to everyone—even to those who a year before had been the stoutest supporters of Munich—that Hitler's war in 1939 was a deliberate act of aggression. However, it was not only Hitler's war. The terrible fact is that it was the German people's war. This time the allocation of blame is correct. In the vast majority the German people were with Hitler in his attempt either to impose his "New Order," which was to last for a thousand years or to bring all European civilization crashing down in ruin with him in a final Wagnerian climax.

It is true that there were attempts to assassinate Hitler. But the only one that got beyond vague talk was the coup of July 20, 1944, which was the work of a group of senior Army officers and which very nearly succeeded. Even this effort—despite the sincere patriotism, the dignity and the courage under torture of the men involved—was not made until the Nazis' defeat was a certainty. Not one of the generals raised a finger in 1939, or in 1940 and 1941 when the Axis straddled the world. It needed the imminence of total defeat to convert them. If a genuine and consistent sense of responsibility had animated them, they would have plotted, not to avert the consequences of the war in 1944-1945, but to have prevented the war breaking out in 1939.

Someone may say: "A coup by a handful of soldiers would not have helped in 1939; the German people would have gone to war all the same."

If that is so—if offered all they demanded, the German people deliberately chose war instead of peace, aggressive conquest instead of shared prosperity—it is the most complete condemnation of Germany, the most complete justification of every act of retribution inflicted on her—the cutting off from the East, the loss of territory, the destruction of her cities.

The argument may be continued a stage further: "What about Danzig? That was a German city—why wasn't the principle of the plebiscite applied there?"

The answer is that Germany never wanted, never asked for an honest plebiscite in raising the Danzig issue or in any of her other claims on Poland. When Ribbentrop, Hitler's Foreign Minister, made his formal statement of those claims, how did he do it? Instead of taking any of the normal steps by which negotiations are ordinarily initiated, he summoned my friend Sir Nevile Henderson to witness a scene as tragic as it was futile. Rapidly and harshly, in German, he read his ultimatum to the Ambassador in the neurotic yet reckless way in which a criminal tries to arrange an alibi. He turned away abruptly without even handing Henderson the document to read. It was therefore as a criminal's alibi that Henderson interpreted it. The German mood in 1939 was a mood of criminal folly and a gambler's pride. To allege now that this was Hitler's war, the Nazis' war, the generals' war, the war of a handful, is an evasion of the truth. This was a war of the German people, for which the overwhelming majority must be held responsible, particularly the governing classes.

Is there a moral? Is there an explanation? I have come to believe this about the Germans: that in spite of all their great qualities, their ability, their capacity for hard work, their discipline, their intelligence and their passion for education, they are afflicted with a romantic, self-immolatory streak in their character which is never satisfied with mere success. Perhaps the Second World War was fought because other nations forgot about Wagner.

After 1870 Bismarck said again and again, "We are satisfied." Surely after 1938 that is what, in realistic terms, the German leaders and people should have said. Thinking in those terms, Neville Chamberlain believed that he had bought peace in our time. Instead, less than a year later he was saying in a sad, grave voice: "It is the evil things we fight against." Why? Was it not that Wagnerian, death-desiring streak which drove an allegedly civilized race into the most blatantly aggressive war ever launched? At least now no one on the Allied side can have a single twinge of conscience, a single doubt that we were justified in fighting. This was a righteous war.

My years of work at Geneva did not, I am glad to think, go unrecognized. In 1937 I was unanimously elected President of the League of Nations. When that year's session concluded I was asked to continue to hold the Presidency for another year, until just before the opening of the 1938 session. This was a rare honor and a responsibility, for mine would have been the duty of summoning a special session and presiding over it, had one been found necessary.

My work in this international field, and its crown and climax in my year as President of the League, had especially delighted my beloved mother. When I first went to Geneva she was over eighty, and she followed my work there with unflagging interest. Each year that I went to India we talked together as fully and as frankly about this as we had, throughout my life, shared our interests, our joys and our sorrows. For a very long time she retained her health, all her faculties, her keen zest for life and all its concerns, whether public and political or family and domestic. When the 1937 session of the Assembly ended, I went to my home in the south of France, with no reason to believe that my mother's health—she was by then in her eighty-eighth year—was causing any serious anxiety. Nor indeed was it, for she was maintaining her accustomed tranquil and happy way of life.

She had seen both my sons, Aly and Sadruddin, the latter of whom, as a little boy, was a special joy and comfort to her, both when she came to Europe and during a summer which he and his mother spent with her in the Lebanon. He bore, too, the name of my elder brother who had died in infancy, and this particularly rejoiced my mother's heart. She did not see her great-grandchildren, Aly's two boys, Karim and Amyn, but she knew all about them and she chose both their names, the younger bearing that of her brother who died as a young man in the 1880's. She had, as I have recorded, been present at my first Jubilee, and had been made especially happy by the congratulatory telegram sent by Lord Wigram, on behalf of King George V, just before the news of the King's death cut short our celebrations. Eager, affectionate, pious, alert to every new happening and new interest, my mother in her last years was someone who radiated a sense of joy and goodness among all who knew her.

It was at the end of 1937 that I had a cable from India saying that she had been taken seriously ill and bidding me hasten to come to see her. I flew to India at once, in the fastest aircraft of those times, which took three and a half days to reach Bombay.

All her life my mother had retained the habit of a Turkish bath. In each of our houses in India we had a regularly equipped Turkish bath, with dry, properly heated alcoves, the correct water system, and, as its climax, a hot pool and a small and very cold pool. My mother had a regular bath once a week, with all its traditional accompaniments of Turkish and Persian massage; she had a manicure and a pedicure, and in the Eastern fashion she had her hair dyed with henna. Coming from her bath one day in November she had a stroke; she recovered consciousness but thereafter her mental faculties were impaired and her memory was gone, except for brief periods of clarity and vision.

She was at our house at Malabar Hill. Her doctor—incidentally a descendant of one of my grandfather's original followers from Iran who had become a member of the Indian Medical Service—warned me that I must expect to find a great change in her. I was surprised to find that her physical health seemed excellent, but the mental breakdown—except for the moments of lucidity which I have just mentioned—was almost complete. I spent most of my time with her; and it was a great joy when occasionally she fully recognized me and talked to me.

All her long life my mother had been animated by one simple, sincere desire: that when the time came, she should die and be buried on Muslim soil, by which she meant a land ruled by a free, independent and sovereign Muslim government. To this was knit one more longing: that in death she should lie beside my father, whom she had dearly and deeply loved, and for whom her mourning from the moment of his death more than fifty years before had been as profound, as durable and as touching as Queen Victoria's for her beloved Prince Albert.

As soon as I could, therefore, I made preparations to have my mother taken to Iraq, where an independent Muslim government ruled, and where my father's body rested at Nejef near Kerbela. There were obviously considerable difficulties and problems about her journey thither. Medical advice ruled out air travel, though I have always believed that my mother, in spite of the various stops that the two-day journey to Baghdad would have involved, would have stood it better than the sea trip. However, it was by boat that she went to Basra and thence by train to Baghdad. I had been to Cairo in the meantime, and I flew back to Baghdad to find her at the house of a cousin of mine, Aga Mustafa Khan, close by the holy shrine of Kadhamin.

A few minutes after I reached her bedside, her eyes opened, and she recognized me. Then in the way that all true Muslims would ask, who seek to follow the Prophet's example and attain a safe and quiet journey from the midst of the living, she achieved peace and happiness and that final "Companionship on High" for which all yearn. In accordance with Ismaili tradition I did not accompany her body to its last resting place, but certain nephews and cousins laid her lovingly beside my father, and they were—as she had long and ardently desired—finally reunited.

Part Four

ം⸱ം

A NEW ERA

XIII

The Second World War

THE OUTBREAK of the Second World War meant for me the shattering of the hopes of a lifetime. The great Palace of the League of Nations at Geneva, which I had opened, was deserted and shuttered. Its emptiness and its silence were sharply symbolic. However, it was in Switzerland that I found myself in those late summer and early autumn days of 1939 when Hitler's armies swept over Poland, and Britain and France, for the second time in a generation, went to war against an aggressive and conquest-hungry Germany.

Although later in the war, when I was permanently resident in Switzerland, the Swiss Government—in the difficult and delicate conditions of the time—had to ask me to refrain from political activity of any kind, that provision was not in force in September, 1939. I was able therefore to address manifestoes to my followers everywhere bidding them give all the support and help of which they were capable to Britain and the British cause. There was, however, no occasion for diplomatic or political activity on my part such as I had undertaken in the First World War. No great Muslim Power was involved, as the Ottoman Empire had been involved. There was no Khalif; there was no proclamation of a *jehad*. My duties and my responsibilities were no more and no less than those of any other private citizen.

I had at that time a considerable number of horses in training and at stud. In the belligerent countries racing on any scale was obviously off for the duration and probably for a long time afterward. However, in 1939 Italy was not a belligerent. It occurred to me that

I might be able to negotiate a deal which would not be unhelpful to the Italian Government and—if I made a profit, as I hoped to do —would supply me with a considerable sum to invest in British War Loans. With my wife I went to Florence, and offered to sell all my horses to the Italian Government. I found that my offer had considerable support among people of standing, particularly those who wanted Italy to stay out of the war; Ciano himself, I have since discovered, was in favor of it. However, at the highest level, and on the edge of completion, the deal was forbidden by Mussolini himself.

To me this was a clear indication of Mussolini's intentions, for in addition to the large sum which I asked, I imposed two conditions, the money was to be paid immediately, but the horses were not to be delivered in Italy until after the end of hostilities.

Before I made this approach to the Italian Government, I had offered my stallions and mares to the British National Stud. In those days, I ought perhaps to point out, my son Aly had no share in the ownership of my stables, and I was therefore at liberty to do exactly what I liked without consulting anyone else. My terms in this offer were however very different from those which I later proposed to the Italian Government. For my whole stable, including Bahram, Mahmoud, and every race horse I had, I asked not one tenth of their real value, and less than a fifth of the price which I was on the verge of getting from the Italian Government. The Ministry of Agriculture however, for reasons best known to themselves, rejected an offer which I believe to have been unique and one which would also have been of enormous benefit to agriculture, one of Britain's most vital industries in peace and in war. To this day I have never understood this decision. They did not even bother to look in the gift horse's mouth.

In the winter of 1939-1940 I went to India, spending some months there seeing and staying in Delhi with the Viceroy, Lord Linlithgow. I gave him an account of the failure of my negotiations with the Italian Government. In April I went with my wife and my young son to my villa at Antibes in the south of France, as I had been accustomed to do for years. The cataclysmic events of May and

June, 1940, took me, like so many others, utterly by surprise. During my years at Geneva I had come to know many French statesmen, and always their confidence in the French Army's strength was so supreme and so unshakable that when French resistance collapsed along almost the whole front from the Rhine to the Channel, and the Nazi motorized divisions swept south and west across France, I was shocked and appalled beyond belief. When Italy declared war on the Allies, and the French Government, abandoning Paris as an open city, took refuge in Bordeaux, I saw that we were in peril of being trapped in a totally vanquished country. With my wife and my son I made my way as quickly as I could to Switzerland, by almost the last remaining door out of France before the end. My elder son Aly had taken a commission in a British Yeomanry Regiment and with official approval had been attached to the French, and he was at this time with their forces in Syria. My daughter-in-law, with her small boys, was in Cairo.

Neutral Switzerland was a haven, but for several years it was an isolated and solitary haven. I was barred from political activity; I was cut off from most of my contacts with the outside world; and these years saw the beginning of my series of grave illnesses. From the British Consul General in Geneva, Mr. Henry Livingston, and from his colleague in Zurich, I received a great deal of kindness and help in times that were difficult and trying enough for us all.

The origins of my illness lay several years back. From about 1935 I had been aware of certain troublesome internal symptoms, but various doctors whom I consulted did not take a particularly serious view of them. In Switzerland in 1940 I took the advice of a number of eminent surgeons; I underwent examination after examination, and the doctors' view grew graver and graver, with more than a hint that the tumor, which was the cause of the trouble, might be malignant. Its position was such, however, that they considered it dangerous to operate. Hemorrhages were an almost daily experience; I lost strength steadily and in consequence was greatly depressed. Only after the war, when I was able to go to Paris, did the great French surgeon, Professor François de Gaudard d'Allaines, operate on me and, removing the tumor, discover that it was nonmalignant. This however did not entirely end my trouble; of my subsequent bouts of illness I shall have something to say later.

Meanwhile during my enforced stay in Switzerland there was one profoundly important change in my private life. I have referred before to the differences between the Christian and the Muslim view of marriage and to the misunderstandings which arise. Whereas those brought up in the Christian tradition, with its sacramental concept of marriage, find it hard to understand the practical and contractual basis of the Islamic idea of marriage, for Muslims it is just as difficult to comprehend the laws in the West which compel the continuance of an unhappy marriage and insist on the artificial and arranged sin of adultery in order to bring to an end an association that has become insupportable and to permit both partners to make a fresh start in life.

Maritally my third wife, Princess Andrée, and I drifted apart, although our affection, our respect and our true friendship for each other were in no way impaired. In these circumstances by mutual consent we were divorced in a civil court in Geneva in 1943.

Thirteen months later I married my present wife, whom I had first met in Cairo and whom I had known for many years. I can only say that if a perfectly happy marriage be one in which there is a genuine and complete union and understanding, on the spiritual, mental and emotional planes, ours is such.

As a good Muslim I have never asked a Christian to change her religion in order to marry me, for the Islamic belief is that Christians, Jews—and, according to some tenets, Zoroastrians and reformed Hindu unitarians—may marry Muslims and retain their own religion. With no attempt on my part at influencing her mind, my present wife had already been converted to Islam while she lived in Cairo. Perhaps each of several motives and impulses played its part in her conversion: the quiet fervor of Muslim believers in their Friday prayers; the complete absence of snobbery, prejudice and racial pride that is fundamental to Islam's practice and preaching; and no doubt the serene, consolatory beauty—a beauty that seems spiritual as well as physical—of a mosque like that of Sultan Hassan in Cairo.

Our marriage came then at a time when I badly needed my wife's support and understanding. She has been my strong and gentle help and comforter through all my serious illnesses of recent years. I have at last been granted the real and wonderful haven of finding in and with my wife a true union of mind and soul.

My only political activity of any importance in the war years concerned the Allies' entry into Persia in 1941, with the double intention of opening up a less vulnerable line of communication with the Soviet Union than the route taken by the Arctic convoys to Murmansk and Archangel, and of preventing Persia's being used as a base for Axis intrigue and espionage against the Allies' position in the Middle East. This action, strategically necessary as it doubtless was, involved the deposition of that remarkable monarch, Reza Shah, and precipitated a long period of unrest, resentment and frustration in relations between Persia and the West which only reached (let us hope) its end in the events of August, 1953.

It may be timely, therefore, if I give a brief character sketch of Reza Shah, whom I knew well, before I describe the steps by which I attempted to ameliorate, on his behalf, the Allies' action in respect to his country. Reza Shah, although he had had his military education and training under Russian officers, was of pure Iranian descent, from the north of the country, a region whose peoples have not mingled their blood with the tribes of the south, nor with the Turkish tribes that settled in Persia in the epoch of the great migrations. The family name which he took, Pahlevi, indicates that he fully realized that his origin was pure Aryan Iranian.

I myself, as I have said, am closely related on both sides of my family to the preceding Kajar dynasty, whose beginnings were Turkish but whose blood, through the generations, had of course mingled extensively with that of the Iranians whom members of the dynasty married.

Reza Shah Pahlevi was a man of great stature, whose strength in his prime was moral as well as physical. A cavalry man by training, he rose rapidly—like Nadir Shah before him—by sheer ability, strength of character and superior intelligence, and became at length Minister of War under Ahmed Shah, the last Kajar emperor. With Ahmed Shah's encouragement he became Prime Minister and virtual dictator of Iran. His ambition was to make Iran a truly independent country, free of all *de facto* if not *de jure* suzerainty imposed from without, and free of constant Russian and British pressure and the clash of interests of these two countries. From all that I know of him I have long been convinced that he would have had no desire to seize the throne had Ahmed Shah shown even an ordinary interest in his country and in his duties as its sovereign.

Ahmed Shah's story was sad and not unfamiliar. He was an extremely intelligent young man, highly educated, with a wide knowledge of both Eastern and Western culture, and well read in history, politics and economic theory. But his intellect and his talents were corroded by a profound and pervasive pessimism. He did not believe that by effort, by intelligence and application—all qualities which he possessed—he could make his throne and his dynasty prosperous and stable. An indication of his strange indifference to the normal impulses of life was that, although he had children, he allowed his brother to remain heir apparent to his throne. I knew him well, both as a near relative and as a friend. We were on excellent terms and we met often. It was obvious, however, that he did not care about his crown, or rather he lacked any belief that he could achieve anything constructive with his destiny or do anything to improve conditions in his own country. He concentrated on providing for his children and his mother, and to a certain extent for his brother; he made shrewd investments in the United States, and carefully and steadily built up his private fortune. Adroit as he was in administering his personal affairs, he was equally despondent about his duties as Shah.

His end was untimely. He was enormously fat, and he determined to reduce his weight. He went to extremes, cut his weight down by half, and did his health irreparable harm. He was still quite a young man when he died in the American Hospital in Paris. But before that he had lost his throne. Again and again he was urged to go back to Persia; he disregarded every summons from his government and ignored the anxious advice of friends such as myself, and flatly refused to resume his duties. In these circumstances Reza Shah Pahlevi was fully justified, historically and constitutionally, in assuming the crown and the responsibilities which had been abandoned by the man in whose charge they had been set. And I therefore was one of the first to send him my homage and my prayers for a felicitous and prosperous reign.

Reza Shah was an able ruler, a patriot who suffered real torture to see his country perhaps the most backward of all the world's independent and sovereign nations. He was a shrewd and courageous modernizer. First, he set out to free Islam, as it was practiced in Iran, from the many superstitions and from the many semi-idolatrous ideas and practices which—contrary to the true tenets of our faith—had been fostered in Iran by the ecclesiastical lawyers, who thus kept the people ignorant, their own interests secure, and their power supreme. The Kajar dynasty, in order to conserve its own position, had allied itself with this bigoted semi-priesthood, and together they had discouraged the younger generation in Persia from going to Europe and America in order to equip themselves intellectually and technically in all that the industrial and scientific revolution had brought about. Reza Shah broke away from this, opened the doors of his country to the study of modern science and sent large numbers of Persian students to universities in Europe and America. He encouraged the education and emancipation of women and ended the horrible custom of purdah. He strove to foster national industries, especially carpet making which he restored to a high standard equal to the best traditions of the Saffevi period. In fact he was Iran's equivalent of Kemal Ataturk. But the long, deliberate obscuration, which had been the work of the Kajar dynasty and of their allies, made his task far more difficult than Ataturk's.

He passionately resented any attempt at interference in the internal affairs of his country by any foreign Power. No doubt in his dealings with both Britain and Russia he was helped by a number of factors: that the First World War had gravely weakened them both; that Britain's imperialist and expansionist ambitions and policies had dwindled almost to the vanishing point; and that Russia, absorbed in the consolidation of the new regime, in the Five Year Plan and the vast tasks of reconstruction allied to it, had no desire, for the moment, to resume the Czarist policy of expansion in Western Asia.

Therefore when the Second World War broke out, Reza Shah sought to keep Persia out of the conflict to the end, as did the rulers of other countries absorbed in their own internal problems. However, man proposes, but God disposes.

Until Germany attacked Russia in the summer of 1941, neutrality was not impossible for Persia. Thereafter however her position became increasingly vulnerable as its strategic importance grew. Even before the outbreak of war in the Far East and America's full-scale participation in the conflict, United States aid to the Allies was constantly growing in volume, and Lend-Lease untapped a vast source of vital military and other supplies, a proportion of which it was agreed to divert as soon as possible to Russia.

Access to Russia by any European route was, however, impossible. The Germans straddled every sea and land route. A certain number of ocean convoys were sent by the Arctic route, at an enormous sacrifice of British and American lives, and the cargo they gave so much to bring was received by the Russians grudgingly and without a word of thanks. The Chiefs of Staff were therefore determined to open up a less menaced and less costly road through Persia.

Reza Shah, proudly jealous of his country's hard-held independence, misled by the hitherto placatory attitude which he had encountered in both British and Russians and by the apparent depth and magnitude of Germany's military success, was totally uncooperative about offering to the Allies the facilities which they asked. In his view they implied the abandonment of Iranian neutrality.

The Allies at this juncture in the war were extremely hard-pressed. They could and did however assemble a sufficient show of military strength to overpower any Persian chance of effective resistance to their demands. A small force, sent from India, entered Persia; and I, far away in Switzerland, at once appreciated how gravely Reza Shah had jeopardized his own position. Through His Majesty's Consul General in Geneva, I therefore sought the Foreign Office's permission to communicate with him. I had some hope that, since our relations had always been very friendly not only at the time of his accession but consistently thereafter, he might listen to my advice. In a long telegram I implored him to realize that his throne was in danger and that if he persisted in this attitude of non-co-operation his own abdication would be compelled and Iran, instead of entering the war as an honored ally, would be forced in as a satellite. Alas, I do not know whether my telegram reached him soon enough to give him any time to reflect. I had had to wait for Foreign Office permission to send it. The pace of events in this crisis was rapid, and I fear that in all probability my telegram reached him too late, and his abdication had by then become inevitable. However, there is some consolation in the fact that—as I have subsequently been told by the man who was then his Court Minister, wielding great power—the second part of my cable, in which I begged him to come into the war on the side of the Allies, did have some effect. With the departure of the Shah, the people of Iran themselves could speak, the dynasty was saved and the present Emperor, Reza Shah's son, acceded peacefully. Reza Shah was sent into exile, first to Mauritius and thence to Johannesburg, where very soon afterward he died—doubtless of a broken heart.

The war years passed. Facilities for communication between Switzerland and the outside world were extremely restricted for a long time. I was able to send a rare telegram by courtesy of the Ambassador on great occasions, such as the substitute Derby, for example. Private telegrams to England took a fortnight or longer, and were often never received at all. I managed to hear that two of my horses had finished second and third in the Derby; and I also got the news that Tehran, which my son Aly had leased to me, was second in the 1944 Derby. Later in 1944, with the liberation of the greater part of France, news came through much more easily, and I heard at once of Tehran's victory in the St. Leger. Throughout the war these interests of mine had been in efficient hands; the father of my present agent, Mr. Nesbit Waddington, looked after my stud, and all my racing interests were supervised by Mr. Frank Butters in Newmarket. Gradually after the war I resumed my own day-to-day control of my stud and my race horses in training, and by 1947 the administration of them all was back in my hands.

Early in 1945 my long seclusion ended. The British Ambassador in Paris, now Lord Norwich, secured special French police protection for me; and my wife and I—in spite of the fact that a large part of the countryside was still fairly lawless, with German soldiers at large and armed bands marauding—got through to Marseilles without mishap. In Marseilles we were for a time the guests of the U.S. Army and of the commanding officer, General John B. Ratayo. From Marseilles we made our way in a British military aircraft to Cairo.

Although British G.H.Q. had been established in Cairo for all the Middle East campaigns from 1940 on and although a vast assemblage of British troops was in and around the city, it had been scarcely scarred by the war. Its social life as always was diverse, polyglot and many-sided. At the British Embassy there presided the last of the proconsuls, Lord Killearn, formerly Sir Miles Lampson, the man who earlier in his career had been primarily responsible for the Anglo-Egyptian Treaty of 1936. In and around the big houses, the hotels, the great new blocks of apartments in Gezira and the Garden City, a busy and exuberant social life ebbed and flowed. Anglo-Egyptian relations were in a phase of superficial correctness and amiability, overlying an increasing tension.

In Egyptian Court and political circles I had countless friends and acquaintances, including many members of the Royal Family. Three at least deserve, in my view, more than passing mention: King Farouk, whom I now met for the first time as a grown man; his Prime Minister, Nahas Pasha, and his Heir Apparent, Prince Mohammed Ali.

Prince Mohammed Ali and I have been friends for fifty-five

years. When I first went to London in 1898, he and I stayed at the same hotel, the old Albemarle in Piccadilly. He dined at Windsor Castle as Queen Victoria's guest either shortly before or after I had the same honor. By a curious and delightful coincidence, fifty-five years later, in Queen Elizabeth II's Coronation Year, he and I, who had been Queen Victoria's guests at dinner, in the same summer were her young great-great-granddaughter's guests at tea. Across this great stretch of time Prince Mohammed Ali and I have been firm and fast friends.

His is a fascinating and many-sided personality. A younger brother of the Khedive, he exerted for long a quiet, soothing but very powerful influence, largely behind the scenes, in Egyptian life and politics. He never married, since his view is (it has always been said) that his health has not been robust enough for him to feel justified in founding a family. Yet his energy and vivacity are as great as his spirit is sensitive and his intellect powerful. All his life he has been a devout Muslim; he has made the pilgrimage to Mecca; he is steeped in Islamic culture. Not long ago he wrote a series of pamphlets on Islam, its meaning and its spiritual message for mankind, many copies of which he asked me to circulate in Europe. He speaks several languages, ranging from Arabic and Turkish, through English, French and German and one or two more. His detailed historical knowledge of Egypt, whether in the time of the Mamelukes or in the era of his own great-grandfather, the conqueror Mohammed Ali, is truly phenomenal. His friends and admirers are legion, not only among his fellow countrymen and co-religionists but in Egypt's numerous foreign colonies and minority communities—British, French, Jews and Greeks and Copts. Outside Egypt he has earned respect throughout the Muslim East, in Europe and in the United States. All his life he has been a great admirer of Britain and of the British character and way of life, and a staunch supporter of Anglo-Egyptian friendship and understanding through many vicissitudes and disappointments. With the end of the monarchy and the establishment of the new regime in Egypt, he went into voluntary exile, without bitterness or resentment, wishing Egypt and her people under their new rulers continued and increasing prosperity, but feeling that he himself—being far advanced in years—lacked the strength to contribute his share. His palace, his famed and beautiful botanical gardens and his princely collection of *objets d'art* he has left in trust, to become after his death a national museum. Now in a green and tranquil old age he spends his summers in Switzerland and his winters on the French or the Italian Riviera. Long may he enjoy a peaceful retirement.

Nahas Pasha I first met when Egypt entered the League of Nations; he came to Geneva and I, as India's representative, entertained him. Much of his long-established success as a politician was due to his powers of oratory, to the spell of authority which he could exert over the masses of his fellow countrymen; these qualities however are scarcely visible when you first encounter him. By an odd irony, while he is likely to be remembered in history as a statesman who came into serious conflict with the sovereign whom he served, he is in fact an out-and-out monarchist. Madame Nahas has told me of the depth of the devotion which her husband felt for King Farouk, and with that devotion a strong conviction that the King would be best served by being constantly reminded of the limitations which hedged his power as a constitutional monarch. Now this is without doubt one of the legitimate duties of a Minister; but even in Britain—as Mr. Gladstone found in his long but severely formal association with Queen Victoria—an adviser who is forever telling a monarch what he or she must not do is not likely to be as popular with his sovereign as those who do not take quite so rigid or comfortless a view of their responsibilities. In Nahas Pasha this was not merely a superficial trait, but a fundamental principle on which he acted resolutely and without deviation. I myself have heard him say more than once: *"Le roi regne, mais il ne gouverne pas."*

Doubtless to a young and energetic sovereign like King Farouk it must have been irksome to have to accept advice so frequently. The King extended to his Prime Minister all the accustomed courtesies— I have often, for example, seen the two of them sitting side by side in the Royal box at the opera—but always one felt that behind the polite formalities there was a gulf which could not be bridged, with the King on his side nourishing a deep but unspoken resentment, and Nahas Pasha on his, a regret that his loyalty and his devotion were not appreciated.

And King Farouk himself? To me as to many others there will always, I think, be something enigmatic in this sad yet remarkable man's character. There are many baffling contradictions about him; yet back of them all there is great charm and a genuine and compelling simplicity. His father died when he was still a boy. His mother went abroad almost immediately and the young Farouk was deprived of the influence and the love of both parents. He was sent to England to be educated; yet he lived to all intents and purposes a prisoner in a vast country house, forbidden to go out and about and mingle freely with the people among whom he lived, under orders given by his father in the jealous fear that the boy might not grow up along the lines which he had laid down. He had no proper schooling, never went to a university, and spent only a few months attending the Royal Military Academy at Woolwich. There can, however, be no doubt as to his natural abilities. Like his uncle, Prince Mohammed Ali, he is an excellent and versatile linguist. But he has, I think, always felt hampered by the lack of the education which both his station and his talents merited. This developed in him an inferiority complex when he constantly found himself, as he was bound to do, in the company of highly educated as well as accomplished men of all nationalities; in compensation therefore he turned to a small coterie of inferior and ill-educated flatterers. Loveless in childhood and solitary, he grew almost morbidly afraid to be alone or in the dark or with time on his hands.

In this unfortunate background, I believe, lie the real reasons for the habits which have earned him criticism at home and notoriety abroad, for the gambling that has been so harshly reprobated and for the long, aimless hours wasted in seeking distraction in cabarets and night clubs. That they were wasted it is, alas, impossible to deny. Their sad and purposeless vacuity can be explained, if not excused, by his lack of discipline in childhood, and by the fact that nobody bothered to teach him that a man's chief capital is time, and that if he wastes time, he wastes his greatest asset which can never be recouped.

Against his defects I prefer to set his good qualities: his piety; as a good Muslim his aversion to alcohol (and this in spite of all that hostile critics have said of him); his courtesy and kindness especially to the poor, to humble *fellahin* and servants; and his patriotism and his pride in his country. This last I know to be a major trait in his personality. He is an Egyptian from the crown of his head to the soles of his feet, resenting hotly any suggestion, from any source, that Egypt and the Egyptians are or ever have been inferior to any country or people in the world; longing to recapture his nation's greatness at the time of Mohammed Ali and Ibrahim Pasha; and intensely proud of the farsighted ideals and achievements of his grandfather, the Khedive Ismail.

Each of us, it is said, is composed of many diverse and conflicting elements; seldom in one human being has the mingling been more complex and more contradictory than in this ill-starred yet amiable and talented King. Until late in his reign, when the worst of the damage had already been done, the uncertainties about the possibilities of the succession created in and around his Court an unhealthy atmosphere of stealthiness, intrigue and suspicion. His father occupied a throne left vacant because his cousin, the Khedive Abbas Hilmi, had been barred from it and because the other obvious claimant, the Sultan Hosein's eldest son, was not considered suitable by the Protecting Powers. He himself was an only son; until his second marriage, he had no son. There was a guarded uneasiness about the safety of his person, which in its way was just as insidious as direct and open fear of assassination.

His contests with his Ministers were protracted and stubborn. He himself believed, as his father had done before him, that Egypt's prime need was for firm and authoritative rule and guidance from the King. The Wafd, by far the biggest and most influential political party, strongly nationalist in sentiment but representative of big vested capitalist and industrialist interests, wanted to make him a rubber-stamp sovereign. They came into conflict again and again on numerous issues. There grew up as the King's instrument, or instruments, a group of politicians who looked to the King for their power and their promotion. At the times when the King and the Wafd could not get along together, it was one or another from this group, the King's Free Political party—as it was known—who would be called in to form a government which would last until the next major crises. In the Army too, it was said, the King used the same tactics, giving his favorites promotion, and thus incurring the unforgiving resentment of the officer class.

The Wafd's last sweeping electoral victory brought Nahas and his friends back into office, when the last possible permutation of politicians had been shuffled together against them and had failed. The King was deeply discouraged and took refuge in a sad and shoulder-shrugging pessimism. I met him on his last visit to Europe before his abdication, and I was immediately aware of a great change in him. He was enveloped in a mood of depressed fatalism, an atmosphere of "I cannot do what I wish—very well, let them do what they want," which in the long run was bound to contribute to his defeat and downfall. He had tried in his own way to help his people and improve their lot, and now he felt that he had failed. I was strongly reminded of Ahmed Shah, the last of the Kajar dynasty in Iran. King Farouk, like Ahmed Shah, had embraced a profound and defeatist resignation and had lost faith in his power to fulfill his duties and serve his people. Like the House of Kajar, the dynasty established by Mohammed Ali fell; and in both countries the power passed, not to the politicians, but to the military.

There is a forlorn and pitiable sadness about King Farouk now. Unlike his uncle and former heir, Prince Mohammed Ali, he must in the course of nature face a long life. What are to be his occupations? Where and how will he be able to build for himself a new existence in which he can find some self-respect and some usefulness to his fellow men? At present it is most distressing to see him on his course from European city to European city, rootless and without purpose; and the distress is sharpened by the knowledge that he had it in him—if he had had a proper education and proper guidance in his youth—to be a good and patriotic, perhaps a great, King of Egypt.

The sixtieth anniversary of my inheriting my Imamat and ascending the *gadi* fell in 1945. But in the troubled conditions at the end of the Second World War it was neither possible nor suitable to arrange any elaborate celebrations of my Diamond Jubilee. We decided to have two ceremonies: one, including the weighing against diamonds, in Bombay in March, 1946, and another five months later, in Dar-es-Salaam, using the same diamonds.

When the time came, world conditions were only just beginning to improve and travel becoming a little less difficult than it had been in the last months of the war. However, a magnificently representative assemblage of my followers gathered for a wonderful and—to me at least—quite unforgettable occasion. There were Ismailis present from all over the Near and Middle East; from Central Asia and China; from Syria and Egypt; and from Burma and Malaya, as well as thousands of my Indian followers. Many of the Ruling Princes of India honored me with their presence, as did senior British officials in this stormy twilight of the Raj. Telegrams and letters of congratulation showered in on me from all over the Islamic world, from the heads of all the independent Muslim nations, and from the Viceroy. I was a proud and happy man to be thus reunited with those for whom across the years my affection and my responsibility have been so deep and so constant.

I hope and believe that this ceremony, in its timing and setting, was in itself a completely effective refutation of a mischievous and trouble-making but minor story which a handful of evil people have recently put in circulation. Some busybodies have ferreted out the fact that in the 1930's I approached the Government of India and suggested that I might be given a territorial state and join the company of Ruling Princes. From the refusal of this request they have drawn the quite erroneous and absurd conclusion that I was offended, and that in resentment I abandoned all the principles and ideals which I had cherished throughout my life. Nothing could be further from the truth.

This is what really happened: it had long been felt among the Ismaili community that it would be desirable to possess a national home—not a big, powerful state, but something on the lines of Tangier or the Vatican—a scrap of earth of their own which all Ismailis, all over the world, could call theirs in perpetuity where they could practice all their customs, establish their own laws, and (on the material side) build up their own financial center, with its own banks, investment trusts, insurance schemes and welfare and provident arrangements. The idea of a territorial state made no particular appeal to me, but in view of the strength of Ismaili sentiment on the matter I made my approach to the Government of India. For reasons which I am sure were perfectly just and fair, the Government of India could not see their way to granting our request. The idea that they disapproved of me for having made it, or that I was hurt and disappointed by their refusal, is fantastic.

So far as I was concerned, the practical proof surely lay in the support, financial as well as in every other way open to me, that I gave to Britain's war effort from 1939 on; every penny that I could save or raise in London was invested in various war loans; and I know that neither the Bank of England nor the Treasury was unaware of the extent of such help as I was able to give.

So far as Britain and the British authorities in India were concerned, their help, their kindness and their consideration at the time of my Diamond Jubilee were unstinted. I am certain that we could never have held the celebrations at all if it had not been for the assistance and interest of Sir Stafford Cripps, then Chancellor of the Exchequer. All the authorities from the Chancellor down gave us every possible facility for the transport of the diamonds—accompanied as it had to be with vigilant security precautions—first to India and then from India to Africa. The Viceroy's personal message of congratulation was notable among the hundreds that I received, and it was exactly the same story a few months later in East Africa. There the weighing ceremony was honored by the presence of the Resident of Zanzibar, the Governors of Tanganyika, Kenya and Uganda, and no less important a person than the Secretary of State for the Colonies, Mr. Creech-Jones himself; and the whole time that I was in Africa I was most hospitably and graciously received and entertained by the Governors and by all senior British officials with whom I came in contact. I trust that this disposes of a false canard.

To the celebrations in India there was an extremely serious side. An amount equal to the value of the diamonds—more than half a million pounds—had been collected and was offered to me as an unconditional gift. I wanted this enormous amount to be used for the welfare of the Ismaili community throughout what was then undivided India. The specific scheme which I had in mind was a trust, along the lines which Ismailis have built up in Africa, of which I have already given some account, which is in essence not unlike the Friendly Societies that have made so valuable a contribution to British life. I hold that for a trading and agricultural community such as the great majority of Ismailis are an organization of this character, combining welfare with prudent financial advice, assistance, loans, mortgages and so forth, is much more important and much more suitable than an ordinary charity fund.

However, other opinions prevailed in India. Having handed back the money, with my advice as to its disposal, to the representatives of those who had subscribed it, I did not like to use my authority as Imam to make my advice mandatory. It was decided to set up a conventional charitable trust—a decision, I must emphasize, in which I had no share and no responsibility—and there was the outcome which I had feared and foreseen, for it is not unfamiliar in the East. Before the trust could get into its stride there was protracted and disastrously costly litigation between various parties among the Ismailis in Bombay. I still hope, however, that when the suits are settled, at least half the original sum subscribed will not have been spent on costs and will be available for charity among the Ismailis.

I myself have sometimes been criticized for not supporting and encouraging ordinary charities on a large scale—hospitals and dispensaries, schools and scholarships, and the usual run of charitable institutions and organizations. I am convinced that the Ismaili communities compose a special case. Many Ismailis are traders and middlemen; others are yeomen farmers, of the order of society known in Russian history as kulaks. Theirs is an intensely individualist outlook, acquired and fostered over many centuries. Welfare imposed from without is not in the pattern of their society. I am convinced that their first need is to learn to co-operate in their thrift and self-help, to extend what they practice in their families and as individuals to the community as a whole. This will not be achieved by the ordinary so-called charitable and welfare systems that are part of the fabric of existence in many European countries. Co-operation in banking and commerce, in the raising and lending of money, in building and in farming is, I sincerely believe, their path toward economic, social and cultural uplift, toward that better life for themselves and for their children which their talents and their virtues can secure.

The foundations have been well and truly laid in British East Africa and in Madagascar, and it is my earnest hope that by 1960 at least we shall have reached fruition in what I may call my worldly and material effort on behalf of my followers. In Egypt and Syria, in Pakistan, in India, Malaya and Portuguese East Africa the task will be more difficult. I am still at it however, and my Platinum Jubilee—to be celebrated in 1954-1955—offers, in my opinion, a superb opportunity to repeat in these areas the efforts which we have so successfully inaugurated in British East Africa.

India in 1946 demonstrated every symptom—in a critical and advanced stage—of that malady whose course it had been possible to foresee from the day of the promulgation of the Montagu-Chelmsford reforms almost thirty years earlier.

That sense of spiritual unity and of continuity, which in my youth and long before had sustained British rule in India and had given it its moral fiber and backbone as well as its outward manifestations of efficiency and thoroughness, was now finally sapped. That almost schizophrenic contradiction, which from 1917 on had eaten into the solidity and firmness of Britain's moral and practical position in India, was now exacting its inevitable and final toll. "Quit India," those two words so often chalked on walls in Calcutta, in Delhi and Bombay and every other big city, were no longer an agitator's scrawl; they now expressed a desire and intention. The British were going from India. Now the chief problem was the rate of departure—fast or slow. The only questions were when and how. Only a handful of Englishmen—well under two thousand in all— were now left in the Indian Civil Service; but power was still concentrated in their hands; and so long as they were responsible, not to the people of India, but to the Parliament and people of the United Kingdom, India was not free and self-governing.

The Second World War affected India far more closely and far more profoundly than its predecessor. The whole of Southeast Asia, including Burma, fell to Japanese conquest in the first six months of 1942; the tide of invasion lapped at India's borders; and Japanese bombers appeared—with remarkably little effect—over Calcutta. India raised and sent into battle, on the Allied side, forces numbering some two million, the largest volunteer army in history. The curious and false British theory about the martial and nonmartial races of India broke down utterly, and men from many regions in Bengal and the South served gallantly in combatant units. In the Middle East, in East Africa and in Italy, Indian Divisions were for years an integral part of the fighting forces of Britain and the Commonwealth. The enormous value of their contribution to ultimate victory, from the Battle of Keren to Marshal Kesselring's final withdrawal in northern Italy four years later, is written imperishably into the military history of the war. Indian officers, holding the King's commission, had demonstrated again and again their gallantry, their sagacity, their leadership, and their capacity to exercise high command. In the later phases of the war India was the essential base for the Southeast Asian campaigns of 1944-1945, under Lord Mountbatten's supreme command, which drove the Japanese in disastrous retreat down the length of Burma and which were a major contributory factor in Japan's ultimate defeat.

Yet in the whole conduct and strategy of the war India, as India, had no say at all. Many of her most distinguished political leaders languished long years in political detention. At the height of the war, in the spring of 1942, Sir Stafford Cripps headed a British mission

to India to try to work out—against the background of the titanic
problems of the time—a feasible scheme for realizing India's aspirations. The Cripps Mission failed, breaking itself against the harshest
rock of all—the fact that although British and Hindu representatives alike hoped to preserve the unity of the subcontinent (not
least so far as the British were concerned, in the conditions of
1942, the unity of the Indian Defense Forces), the price of
achieving that unity was one which no Muslim could accept, and
Muslim opinion by now had consolidated itself formidably under
the leadership of Mr. M. A. Jinnah, the Quaid-i-Azam. He made
it perfectly clear to Cripps that no constitution for a united India
which did not satisfy nearly one hundred million Muslims would
be accepted, and that their opposition to it would be broken only
by killing them; when they said "Death or Freedom," that was
what they meant.

After the failure of the Cripps Mission there followed more than
three years of political stalemate. The Bengal famine of 1943 revealed how slender and how fragile were the bases of India's economy. Lord Linlithgow was succeeded as Viceroy by Field Marshal
Lord Wavell. With the end of the war the political temperature
soared swiftly all over India. Throughout the whole of Asia there
was a surging tide of nationalist sentiment, an eager and insistent
desire to throw off the shackles of colonialism. Japan's conquests,
however detestable many of their military and social effects, had
achieved one momentous result: they had demonstrated, to millions
all over Southeast Asia, that their European masters were far from
invincible. Millions had seen an Asiatic nation challenge and hold
at bay for more than three years—in a huge area extending from
Korea to New Guinea and from the Assam border to the Central
Pacific—the combined might of the United States, Britain and the
Commonwealth, France and Holland. The lesson was too glaring
and too emphatic to be missed.

In India there was no talk now of a five—or ten—year
period of transition. The struggle would be real, immediate and
bloody unless self-government were granted, not in the future and
on terms laid down by Britain, but at once and on conditions

largely imposed by the people of India themselves. The most obvious symptom of the depth and magnitude of this feeling, visible to someone like myself returning after years abroad, was the hostility that had developed, not simply to Britain's political suzerainty, but to everything British—to the English language, to English habits and customs, to pipes and whisky-and-soda, to European suits and collars and ties, so that even Indians who had adopted these habits were in some areas in real danger. As the saying goes, this brought the situation home to one.

Britain for her part had no longer either the desire or the capacity to hold India against her will. Vastly weakened by the long strain of the war, her overseas investments expended, Britain, once the creditor nation of the world, seemed now to be in almost everyone's debt. Victory had been secured, but at the price of world leadership. At home her people faced a long period of economic stringency, of shortages, austerity and rationing; and even before the end of the Far Eastern conflict the Coalition Government, which had led the nation to victory, had broken up, and the Labor party had—for the first time in its history—attained power, with a big Parliamentary majority as well as office. Mr. Attlee, the new Prime Minister, had taken a close interest in India's problems since his membership of the Simon Commission fifteen or sixteen years earlier. In addition to its program of social and economic reform at home, the Labor party had pledged itself to end British imperialism overseas wherever it was able to do so. Independence for India had been one of the main planks in its platform for years. Where the wartime Coalition Government had failed, its successor, in the flush of vigorous optimism of its earlier years of office was determined to succeed. A Cabinet Mission, headed by Lord Pethick-Lawrence, the Secretary of State for India, and Mr. A. V. Alexander,* the Minister of Defense, set out for Delhi to consult with the Viceroy, the Commander in Chief and the Indian political leaders on the way in which power should be transferred.

The political leaders, with whom ultimately decision and authority rested, were four in number: on the Congress-Hindu side,

---

* Now Lord Alexander of Hillsborough.

Mahatma Gandhi, Mr. Nehru and Sardar Patel; on the Muslim side, Mr. Jinnah—the Quaid-i-Azam. On their agreement or dis-agreement, translated into economic and political facts, depended the future of the subcontinent.

The Quaid-i-Azam's brilliant and epoch-making career, so un-timely ended, reached its summit in these momentous years of 1946 and 1947. Now he belongs to history; and his memory, I am certain, is imperishable. Of all the statesmen that I have known in my life —Clemenceau, Lloyd George, Churchill, Curzon, Mussolini, Ma-hatma Gandhi—Jinnah is the most remarkable. None of these men in my view outshone him in strength of character, and in that almost uncanny combination of prescience and resolution which is statecraft. It may be argued that he was luckier than some—far luckier for example, than Mussolini, who perished miserably in utter failure and disgrace. But was Jinnah's success all good luck, and was Mussolini's failure all bad luck? What about the factors of good and bad judgment?

I knew Jinnah for years, from the time he came back from Eng-land to Bombay to build up his legal practice until his death. Mussolini, I met once only; and a memorable occasion it was—an afternoon in his box at the racecourse in Rome, when he harangued me for the best part of three hours, in very good English and curiously, for one who was such a "loudspeaker" in public, in a soft and gentle voice, but never once looking at the races or the people in the stands or on the course and never allowing me either to watch a race or open my mouth to argue with him. Yet between these two I detect one important similarity.

Each of them between his youth and his prime traveled from one pole of political opinion to the other. Mussolini made his pil-grimage from a socialism that was near-communism to the creation of fascism, from Marx to Nietzsche and Sorel. Jinnah in his earlier phases was the strongest supporter, among all Muslim political leaders, of Indian nationalism along Congress lines, with a unified Indian state as its goal; yet, in the final analysis, he was the man primarily responsible for the partition of the Indian Empire into the separate states of Pakistan and Bharat. He who had so long cham-

pioned Indian unity was the man who, in full accordance with
international law, cut every possible link between India's two halves
and—in the teeth of bitter British opposition—divided the Indian
Army.

Different in many superficial characteristics, different (above all)
in the success which attended the one and the failure, the other,
these two, Mussolini and Jinnah, both apparently inconsistent in
many things, shared one impressive, lifelong quality of consistency.
Each had one guiding light; whatever the policy, whatever the
political philosophy underlying it, it would be successful and it
would be morally justified so long as he was at the head of it and
directing it. In neither of them can this be dismissed as mere
ambition; each had a profound and unshakable conviction that
he was superior to other men and that if the conduct of affairs was
in his hands, and the last word on all matters his, everything would
be all right, regardless of any abstract theory (or lack of it) behind
political action.

This belief was not pretentious conceit; it was not self-glorifica-
tion or shallow vanity. In each man its root was an absolute certainty of his own merit, an absolute certainty that, being endowed
with greater wisdom than others, he owed it to his people, indeed
to all mankind, to be free to do what he thought best on others'
behalf. Was this not the same sort of supremely confident faith
which guided and upheld the prophets of Israel and reformers like
Luther and Calvin? In our own epoch we have seen at least two
other men who were animated by the same dynamic faith which
shakes the nations, and each—one for good and one for terrible
evil—was conscious of a cause outside himself: Hitler who dreamed
of a German-imposed New Order that was to last a thousand years;
and Mahatma Gandhi whose vision was of an India whose society,
economy and whole life would be based on certain pacifist, moral
principles, the objective existence of which meant much more to
the Mahatma than anything in himself. Britain's two leaders in
the two world wars were also men sustained by an irresistible and
buoyant self-confidence, but both Lloyd George and Churchill were
incapable of transgressing the limitations on the exercise of execu-

tive authority which are set by British life and by British civic, parliamentary, ethical and religious traditions and beliefs.

In the view of both Mussolini and Jinnah, opposition was not an opinion to be conciliated by compromise or negotiation; it was a challenge to be obliterated by their superior strength and sagacity. Each seemed opportunist, because his self-confidence and his inflexible will made him believe, at every new turn he took, that he alone was right and supremely right. Neither bothered to confide in others or to be explicit.

Mussolini traveled the long road from Marxism, not because of doctrinal doubts and disagreements, but because, in the world of Socialist politicians and theorists in which he spent his stormy youth as an exile in Lausanne, doctrines and theories were constant obstacles across the only path of practical achievement which mattered to him—practical achievement in which Benito Mussolini was the leader. When fascism first emerged as a political force in Italy, nobody knew what it was, nobody could define its principles or its program, for it had none. Mussolini simply said: "Let us have a party, let us call it fascist"—which meant anything or nothing. The party's only principle, its sole duty, was to do what its leader told it to do. And its leader believed implicitly—and went on believing for a long time—that everything the party did would be excellent, because everything was conceived and executed by Mussolini.

Throughout his career Jinnah displayed a similar characteristic. He would admit no superior to himself in intellect, authority or moral stature. He knew no limitations of theory or doctrine. The determined and able young barrister, who—against all the omens, without influence and without inherited wealth—triumphed within a few years despite entrenched opposition, became an Indian nationalist when he turned to politics. He joined Congress because he, like the Congress politicians, wanted to liberate India from British colonial and imperialist domination and because he believed that he himself could do it if he had a free hand. Yet in association with Congress he was a fish out of water. He worked to be the champion of Indian liberty, but his ideas of championship differed sharply from those of Congress' other leaders. He came back and rejoined those to whom he was linked by ties of race and religion. Nominally in the Muslim League of those days he was one leader among others, but he was unable to impose his beliefs and his policy, for the general tenor of Muslim thought ran strongly contrary to the convictions which he had held when he was in the Congress camp. He had worked hard and energetically for Congress; but, from his point of view, he was dogged by failure after failure. There was too deep a gulf between his concept of the duties and responsibilities of a political leader in a free society and those of the people with whom he worked. The instruments which he took up broke every time in his hands because it was impossible to reconcile policy as he conceived it with policy hammered out by compromise and negotiation in the committees and the councils of which he found himself a member. He met barrier after barrier and his frustration and his dissatisfaction deepened. His "point of no return" was, of course, the critical Congress meeting in Calcutta in December, 1928, dominated by the Nehrus, father and son. His disillusionment and disappointment there led him to the conviction that Muslims had no chance of fair and equitable treatment in a united India.

I here reaffirm that at the Round Table Conferences Jinnah played a loyal and honorable part as a member of the Muslim delegation. His work there, however, had not shaken his faith in his own means to his own end. The Muslims' sense of their own political needs and aspirations had been fortified and developed by years of discussion and negotiation with British officials and Congress representatives, and the Muslims very rightly followed and gave their full confidence to Jinnah.

In an era in which "no compromise" was coming to be the mood of something like a hundred million Muslims, Jinnah, the man who did not know the meaning of the word "compromise," was there to seize—not only on his own behalf but on behalf of those whom he was destined to lead—the chance of a lifetime, the chance perhaps of centuries. He embodied, as no one else could do, the beliefs and sentiments of the overwhelming majority of Muslims all over India.

Boldly therefore he came out and said: "We want a Muslim party. We want a unified Muslim organization, every member of which is ready to lay down his life for the survival of his race, his faith and his civilization."

But what program this organization should have, what specific and detailed proposals it should lay before its supporters, how its campaign should be timed and what form it should take, he would never say. What he intended, though he never said so publicly, was that all these matters be reserved for his own decision when the time came—or rather, when he thought the time came.

The Muslim League, as it emerged under Jinnah's leadership, was an organization whose members were pledged to instant resistance—to the point of death—if Indian independence came about without full and proper safeguards for Muslim individuality or unity, or without due regard for all the differences between Islamic culture, society, faith and civilization and their Hindu counterparts.

Jinnah gave always the same order to his Muslim followers: "Organize yourselves on the lines I have laid down. Follow me, be ready—if need be—to die at the supreme moment. And I will tell you when the time comes."

A few intellectuals who could not sustain this unwavering faith in Jinnah fell away, and their criticisms of him were a reiteration of the cry, "What, how, where and when?"

I myself am convinced that even as late as 1946 Jinnah had no clear and final idea of his goal, no awareness that he would, within a twelvemonth, be the founder of a new nation, a Muslim Great Power such as the world had not seen for centuries. Neither he nor anyone else could have imagined that fate was to put so magnificent, so incredible an opportunity into his hands as that which occurred in the crucial phases of the negotiations with the British Cabinet Mission, and gave him the initiative when Lord Mountbatten arrived. Pakistan was born: a new nation, with the fifth largest population in the world, of whom ninety per cent are Muslims. And it was the creation of an organization which had only one guiding principle: "Follow the leader."

Jinnah, as I shall shortly relate, made the right choice at the right moment. How different might Mussolini's end have been, had he, when the supreme moment came, chosen right instead of wrong. For him there waited a criminal's end, humiliation and ignominy. Jinnah, on the other hand, attained immortal fame as the man who, without an army, navy or air force, created, by a lifetime's faith in himself crystallized into a single bold decision, a great empire of upwards of a hundred million people.

When I reached India in 1946 these mighty events were in train. Although the principle of conceding to India immediate and total independence had now won universal acceptance in Britain, there still remained the great questions: was it to be a united India, with a single army, navy and air force, or was the subcontinent to be divided, and how complete was the division to be? There was still a faint hope too that some sort of understanding might yet be possible between the Muslim League and Congress, or—in terms of personalities—between the Quaid-i-Azam and the Mahatma. In such an understanding lay, of course, the answers to the questions which I have just enumerated.

The Chancellor of the Chamber of Princes, my old and dear friend, the Nawab of Bhopal, went with me to see Mahatma Gandhi, to explore the possibilities of reaching an understanding. There were also one or two other outstanding problems to discuss: for the Nawab, the future of the Ruling Princes and their states in a free India; for myself, the question of the Indian community in South Africa. In our two long conversations with him (the second of which terminated with the Mahatma's remarks on communism which I have quoted elsewhere) we came to the conclusion that there was no hope of a settlement between him and Jinnah. The Mahatma still firmly believed in a uninational India; Jinnah even more firmly held that there were two nations. I pointed out to the Mahatma that, having accepted the principle of the separation of Burma from India, he ought really to see that there was no reason why the Muslim lands of the Northwest and the Northeast should not be similarly separated, since they—like Burma—had only become part of a united India as a result of British conquest, and therefore the idea of their union with the rest of India was artificial and transient. However, I made no impression on the Mahatma; and I went away, leaving Bhopal to tackle the problem of the princes.

From Poona I went to New Delhi. I had conversations both with the Viceroy, Lord Wavell, and the Commander in Chief, Sir Claude Auchinleck. Both were fully convinced of the justice, as well as the necessity, of conceding Indian independence at once. Both, however, held firmly to the idea of Indian unity, doubtless because in the end the military facts meant more to them than the political facts. And the major military fact of 1946, in the vast region extending from the Persian Gulf to Java and Sumatra, was the existence of the Indian defense forces, above all of the Indian Army. It happened that both Lord Wavell and General Auchinleck* had had a great part, as Commanders in Chief in succession to—indeed in alteration with—each other, in building up the Indian Army, the Royal Indian Navy and the Indian Air Force to their magnificent and powerful condition at the end of the Second World War. They were especially aware of the value to Britain and the Commonwealth, to the Western Allies and to the United Nations, of the continued and unified existence of these superbly disciplined and well-equipped forces. They appreciated too the dangers that would loom if the Indian Army were divided. Not merely might the two armies of the successor-states watch each other across the frontier with jealousy and suspicion, but a perilous strategic vacuum would be created in a huge and important part of the world's surface. They endeavored therefore to find some solution which would preserve unimpaired the unity of the Indian Army. That they failed, and that all who strove with the same end in view failed, is a measure of the magnitude and resolution of the Muslims' determination, against every argument however powerful, every obstacle however stubborn, to achieve their just rights and full political, religious and cultural independence and sovereignty.

* Now Field Marshal.

My Diamond Jubilee celebrations accomplished, I returned to Europe. Physically, however, I was now in poor shape; my health broke down badly and put me out of action for many months. The successful operation carried out in Paris by Professor François de Gaudard d'Allaines relieved me of at least one cause of great anxiety; but it was many months before I was even partially able to resume my ordinary activities.

Meanwhile 1947 was India's year of destiny. The British Cabinet Mission made what turned out to be Britain's final offer and final proposal for a unified India. It was ingenious and—had unity on any terms been possible—it was constructive. It was a three-tiered constitution, combining the highest possible degree of sovereignty in the three great regions into which British India would have been divided—the Northwest and Northeastern areas predominantly Hindu—with an extremely limited concentration of essential power at the center, covering foreign affairs, defense and major communications.

Now Jinnah saw his chance and took it resolutely and unerringly. He announced his unconditional acceptance of the British scheme. In that one decision, combining as it did sagacity, shrewdness and unequaled political flair, he justified—I am convinced—my claim that he was the most remarkable of all the great statesmen that I have known. It put him on a level with Bismarck.

At this critical juncture when Jinnah stood rocklike, the Congress leaders wavered. With incredible folly they rejected the British proposals; or rather they put forward dubious and equivocal alternative suggestions, which so watered down the scheme that it would have lost its meaning and effectiveness.

However in Britain, as more than once at high moments in her history, there was found statesmanship of the highest quality to respond to Jinnah's statesmanship. Mr. Attlee had from the outset closely interested himself in the efforts to achieve a solution of India's problems. Now with a boldness almost equaling Jinnah's he accepted the basic principles for which we Muslims had striven so long. The long-ignored yet fundamental difference between the two Indias was recognized, and the recognition acted upon, quickly and resolutely. It was decided that India should be partitioned. One swift stroke of the pen, and two different but great nations were born. Lord Wavell, who had borne the heat of the day with modesty and magnanimity, resigned. The brilliant, still youthful, energetic and supremely self-confident Lord Mountbatten of Burma was appointed to succeed him, with a clear directive to accomplish, within a strictly limited period of time, the end of British rule and responsibility in India and the handing over of authority to the two successor states of Pakistan and Bharat.

Lord Mountbatten himself shortened the period of demission and devolution. August 15, 1947, was set as the date for the final and total transference of power. On every senior official's desk in New Delhi and Simla the calendars stood, in those last months, with the fateful day warningly marked. And on that day power was transferred; the two new nations took over the functions of government, and stood forth as independent, sovereign members of the Commonwealth.

The birth pangs which accompanied this tremendous process were, some of them, grim and painful. On these it is not my desire nor my purpose to dwell, nor on some of the consequent inevitable problems. About one great and far-reaching effect of the British withdrawal I must however make some comment. Rapid and virtually unconditional as the transference of power was, it left one major problem, one bad debt for Britain, for Bharat and, in a smaller degree, for Pakistan. Although the whole subcontinent of India, from the Northwest Frontier to Cape Comorin, used to be colored red in any ordinary little atlas, by no means was the whole of this vast area in fact British. Dotted about it were scores and scores of independent and individual states, governed by hereditary Ruling Princes, ranging in size from big countries like Kashmir, Hyderabad or Travancore to a few square miles and a township. With the consolidation of the British Raj their relations with it had been settled by treaty, under which Britain, as the Paramount Power, guaranteed their independent and autonomous status. An elaborate and carefully constructed protocol had been worked out between the Princes and the Raj. In the long and splendid reign of

Queen Victoria and in its aftermath in the opening years of this century, these complex and delicate arrangements had their own fittingness. In Britain and in India alike, a century ago, society was hierarchic. In the view of generations of able British administrators in India, the Princely Order corresponded not inexactly with the higher nobility in Britain. If in Britain the landowning and titled aristocracy had learned that their privileges and their possessions conferred on them special duties and responsibilities, a similar lesson and the practice that flowed from it were not impossible in India. Democracy on a basis of universal suffrage was only beginning to develop in Britain in those days; in India it was hardly the glimmer of a distant dream. In the vigorous moral climate of Victorian opinion, who could seem better suited to bear responsibility than those who were by inheritance endowed with privilege and power? In the high noon of Victorian liberalism therefore the relations between British officials and administrators and the Princely Order stood on a comprehensible and healthy foundation, and had about them much that was good and valuable.

Now that the whole remarkable phenomenon—illogical and anachronistic as it appeared in its later years—has vanished and is a part of history, it is both agreeable and salutary to recall some of its best facets, and some of its greater personalities. In my youth I was inevitably brought into contact with many Ruling Princes, and several of them—over and above those whose names have occurred from time to time in this narrative—became my lifelong friends.

The most eminent by far was the Maharajah Gaekwar of Baroda. I first met him in my earliest childhood, when my father was still alive; and during my adolescence I saw him whenever he came to Bombay. When I reached manhood we formed a friendship which lasted until his death, and was extended to his remarkable and talented Maharani, who, happily, is still alive.*

He possessed a sturdy independence of character, and the awareness that the honor and the dignity which he had inherited were not only his own personal right but attributes indissociable from the

* Vivid portraits of them both, thinly disguised as fiction, are to be found in Louis Bromfield's novel *The Rains Came,* of which there was a cinema version some years ago.

race and nation to which he belonged. For him India always came first. Neither family nor class nor creed mattered more than this simple, spontaneous and all-embracing loyalty.

A little over forty-five years ago, in the summer of 1908, he and I were the guests of the then Governor of Bombay, Sir George Clark, in Poona. One night, when everyone else had gone to bed, the Maharajah and I sat up talking to a very late hour. I have the clearest recollection of all that he said.

"British rule in India," he said, "will never be ended merely by the struggle of the Indian people. But world conditions are bound to change so fundamentally that nothing will then be able to prevent its total disappearance."

Then he added something very striking: "The first thing you'll have to do when the English are gone is to get rid of all these rubbishy states. I tell you, there'll never be an Indian nation until this so-called Princely Order disappears. Its disappearance will be the best thing that can happen to India—the best possible thing. There'll never be an Indian nation so long as there's a Princely Order. If Lord Dalhousie hadn't taken over half of India, abolishing or diminishing the sovereignty or territorial authority of scores of principalities, then perhaps something could have evolved along the lines of the German Empire, with considerable decentralization and local courts and capitals. But Dalhousie destroyed the possibility of the principalities ever becoming useful, federal, constitutional monarchies."

In view of what subsequently happened, was my old friend not as farsighted as he was eloquent?

Another of my good friends among the Princes was the great Maharajah of Kapurthala. His outstanding quality was his magnanimity. During his minority an uncle of his had been an active rival claimant to his titles and estates. When he came of age and was fully confirmed in his inheritance, the Maharajah was reconciled with this formidable opponent, not merely superficially or formally but with the utmost warmth and sincerity, inviting him frequently to his capital and entertaining him with as much affection as deference.

I recall one cheerful little anecdote which he told me about himself. In 1893 when he was quite a young man first visiting Europe,
he stayed for a time in Rome. One day King Umberto of Italy
called on him, unannounced. The King's manners were bluff,
abrupt and soldierly. As they entered the Maharajah's sitting room,
the King saw a number of photographs of beautiful women
displayed about the room.

The King barked gruffly, "Who are these women?"

"They, sir, are my wives."

The King swung round at him. "Well, I too have got as many
women as you. But there's this difference between us. I don't keep
'em together. I keep 'em in different houses. You keep all yours in
your palace."

Take him all in all, his culture, his impeccable taste, his sane and
balanced judgment, his vigorous and colorful personality, I believe
that the Maharajah of Kapurthala was, next to the Maharajah of
Baroda, the outstanding Ruling Prince of my generation. They
both, I think, possessed the political vision to have appreciated the
historical reasons for the disappearance of the Princely Order and
to have accepted it without bitterness or rancor. I do not think that
this would have been so easy for two other friends of mine, both in
their way admirable, talented and distinguished men: Ranjitsinhji,
the Maharajah of Jamnagar, that magnificent and lovable sportsman, one of the greatest cricketers of all time, a superb and generous host, but a man very conscious of his inherited rights and
duties; and the Maharajah of Bikaner, a Rajput of the Rajputs,
with a high and burning pride in his ancestry, for whom the passing of the Princely Order would have been very hard to bear.

But pass it did, in a series of swift and comprehensive decisions.
Pakistan—in the immediate attainment of independence faced with
countless momentous decisions—solved this particular problem
swiftly and well. Again it was the Quaid-i-Azam's achievement. He
who had had himself instantly proclaimed Governor General of his
new Dominion, was able, with his almost incredible clarity of vision,
his statecraft, and his practical, Bismarckian sense of "the best
possible," to effect on his own initiative an arrangement which was

not unsatisfactory to the Princes and made them a source of strength
to Pakistan.

India found the task more complicated and more difficult. Paramountcy was at an end. The treaties which the Princes had negotiated, first with the East India Company, then with the Crown,
lapsed with the withdrawal of the Paramount Power. Legally the
states reverted at once to being sovereign, independent countries. But
they were islands in the surrounding sea of the enormous new
nation of India. Lord Mountbatten, who at the invitation of India's
provisional Government remained as first Governor General during
a brief transitional period, wrestled to bring about a solution, deploying all his tact and persuasiveness. As Minister of the State
Department, Sardar Patel was massively determined that that solution should be satisfactory to the new India.

The situation which faced the Princes was not without its sadness, but it was inevitable. Few had governed badly or tyrannously;
taxation was usually lighter within their domains than in neighboring British India; yet their subjects secured, at this lower cost,
many of the benefits for which the taxpayers of British India supplied the revenue. By far the greater majority of the Princes were
amiable, honest, well-intentioned and gentle; but few of them had
been educated on modern lines to face the harsh and complex
problems of the contemporary world. Feudal in their outlook—often
in the best sense—but mentally and spiritually unadapted to the
swift transition from the bullock cart to the jet aircraft which is
our age, they were doomed by their estimable qualities as much as
by their limitations. Above all, the long years of paramountcy had
rendered them politically irresponsible. They were no more dependent on their own good behavior and good administration in
order to maintain their rule and their dynasties. In the background
stood always the Paramount Power. Extravagant and wasteful administration at the worst meant a few years of supervision by an
official sent down from Delhi; even scandalous misbehavior entailed
only the delinquent Prince's abdication, on pension, and the immediate succession of his heir. Secure in their privileges, yet without proper outlets for their abilities and ambitions, they tended to

lose the self-confidence and the capacity required for leadership, and their prestige dwindled in the eyes of their subjects.

When the moment of crisis came, when they found themselves without the Paramount Power, without its guarantees and without its limitations, they had—the vast majority of them—no alternative but to accept the terms which the Indian Union offered them. These on the whole were not ungenerous, provided each Prince took two important steps: first, authorized the immediate accession of his State to the Indian Union; and second, handed over political power. These done, they were assured of a great deal—large, tax-free emoluments; the retention of their private fortunes, their lands and their palaces, their honors and dignities. Almost all the Princes accepted with good grace; their States became part of the new India, and many, big and small alike, were merged to form great new provinces.

The exceptions were few but troublesome. Kashmir is an outstanding special case, in which a Hindu Prince, the vast proportion of whose subjects were Muslim, made a precipitate act of accession to India against the very first principles agreed at the time of partition. In Travancore the Maharajah and his Ministers made a brief stand on their legal and constitutional rights, but surrendered to pressure by the people of the State themselves. The Hyderabad issue was far less happily settled. The Nizam had the great good fortune to have as his adviser a man of the quality of Sir Walter Monckton. However, a fatal combination of weakness and obstinacy prompted him to refuse the settlement which was proposed by Lord Mountbatten on terms negotiated by Sir Walter, which would have ensured Hyderabad the last ounce of advantage in a helpless position. The results of this stubborn folly were disastrous. India took swift, stern police action, and disaster enveloped all Hyderabad's hopes and chances.

As the years pass, the immense effects of Britain's withdrawal from India—moral and spiritual hardly less than directly political —become more and more apparent. The decision and the act together constitute one of the most remarkable events in modern history. Beside Britain's voluntary and total transference of sovereignty to the successor states of Pakistan and Bharat, even Sir Henry Campbell-Bannerman's generous action in respect of South Africa pales into insignificance. Nothing on this scale has ever happened before, yet it is the culmination and the fulfillment of years of growth and struggle.

Much more remains to be accomplished, especially in the field of relations between Pakistan and Bharat. In the years since partition relations have inevitably often been strained and difficult; yet even the severest tension has been kept within bounds, and neither nation—however much sentiments may have become inflamed—has proceeded to extremes. Forbearance and reconciliation are not transient moods; they are qualities which have to be exercised, developed and strengthened.

When partition was imminent the veteran Madrassi statesman, Mr. C. R. Rajagopalachari, "Rajaji," who was later Governor General of India, made this wise and timely pronouncement: "If the Muslims really want to go, well, let them go and take all that belongs to them." There is the temper which ought to inform relations between the two peoples.

It proved impossible to sustain by compulsion an artificial unity. In separation there is a chance for understanding and magnanimity to grow. They are at first delicate plants; but if they are fostered carefully and wisely, and if their roots are deep, they will flourish. Membership of the Commonwealth supplies one intangible but important link between the peoples of Bharat and Pakistan. It is profoundly to be hoped that there will develop a neighborly understanding which may in time grow into an alliance. Peace, a shared prosperity, a shared and steady improvement in the standard of living for millions, are entirely in the interest of both. In the long run, as I firmly believe, the workings of fate on the Indian subcontinent will prove to have been beneficial, not evil. A relationship of mutual respect and good will between the two countries can—and let us hope and pray that it will—secure many years of happy and peaceful development and progress for millions in a vast and important region. Then the strivings of so many of us, Muslim, Hindu and British, through years of arduous toil, through periods of misunderstanding and bitterness, through difficulties now forgotten and crises long resolved, will in the end have had their abundant justification.

XIV

Postwar Years with Friends and Family

NEVER in my long life—I may say with complete honesty—have I for an instant been bored. Every day has been so short, every hour so fleeting, every minute so filled with the life I love that time for me has fled on far too swift a wing. A mind that is occupied, in health or in sickness, with things outside itself and its own concerns is, I believe, a perpetual source of true happiness. In ordinary prayer, as we in Islam conceive it, adoration of the beloved fills up every nook and cranny of the human consciousness; and in the rare, supreme moments of spiritual ecstasy, the light of Heaven blinds mind and spirit to all other lights and blots out every other sense and perception.

In recent years, since the end of the Second World War, I have had a great deal of illness—enough, I suppose, in its content as in its prolongation in time to have depressed me. I have undergone three major internal operations, two of them with what is ordinarily considered a fifty-fifty chance of survival. I have been laid low for months with severe heart trouble. Yet I have never been depressed. I can honestly say that my mind has constantly been occupied with things outside myself. There has been, for example, a great increase in Ismaili activities throughout the Islamic world with a swirl of new ideas and new schemes, with which I have been closely and actively associated. I have read a great deal; I have voyaged in my reading eagerly into the exciting new realms opened up by scientific discovery. The moment that I was well enough I went back to my old love—golf; and golf has brought me a renewal and an extension of the friendships and acquaintances that have meant much to me over the years. I think in this connection of the golfers whom I have known: the genial, warmhearted, openhanded Castlerosse, for example, with whom I played often in the years before the war— an able journalist, a witty and intensely entertaining conversationalist, at all times and on all occasions a boon companion; or my good and wise old friend, J. H. Taylor, who used sometimes to travel with me, who was often my guest at my home, whose pupil I was over many weeks and months—what a wonderful personality his is, with a mind ever open to delight in life and to curiosity about it—it is good to know that he is in excellent health and enjoying his well-earned retirement in his home at his native Westward Ho! I shall, incidentally, always be glad that among the game's professionals I came to know many men like J. H. Taylor, who were of sterling worth and in every way examples to all who met them.

Travel is another pursuit which, since the end of the Second World War, my wife and I have resumed with especial zest and joy —all the keener perhaps because it was denied to us in those dark years. We have returned to familiar places, discovering fresh charm and fresh beauties in them; and we have found delights hitherto unexplored. In Egypt we have tasted again the pleasure of Cairo that united, under its bright and limpid sky, so many civilizations, so many worlds; Luxor with its monuments; Aswan with its especial beauties of air and light; and Alexandria, the ancient and seductive, where memories of Greek and of Ptolemaic civilizations mingle in and alongside a big bustling modern Eypto-Levantine city and port. In India we have rediscovered the infinite beauty and wonder of that immense land—the high hill station of Darjeeling, for example, with its incredible sunsets and sunrises of rose and pink over the immense snowclad peaks of the Himalayas. And there is Lahore, whose mosques and other buildings are often so curiously ignored in favor of Delhi and Agra, even by those who know a great deal about Moghul and Indo-Saracenic history and art. In Europe, Rome the majestic and Venice the elegant and sophisticated, though they are both cities that I have long known and loved, have of late revealed to me new secrets and new enchantments in light, color and architecture.

All my life I have been a constant theatergoer, and, as I remarked in an earlier chapter, a devoted lover of the opera. Whenever I can, wherever I am, I go to every good opera within reach. One ray of light illumined for me the long, dark years of the war when I was confined in Switzerland and deprived of almost all contact with the outside world: the Municipal Theater in Zurich had a series of wonderful operatic seasons. Every year Kirsten Flagstad —the supreme singer among women as Caruso, to my mind, was the supreme singer among men—came to give her magnificent renderings of her great Wagnerian roles. Some of the best Italian singers too—Gigli and others—came each year to Zurich. There was an almost unique pleasure about these memorable seasons: the concentration of talent and genius in one city, the sensation of this beauty's enduring and surviving in the midst of so much that was barbarous and horrible, and the contrast of this intellectual and sensuous feast with our deprivations.

There are friends of mine, old and new, with whom I share this zest for life, this complete freedom from boredom. There is Elsa Maxwell, the mention of whose name brings a bubbling sense of happiness. Hers is a friendship, hers is a kindness, which I profoundly appreciate, for which I am ever grateful. She possesses a true exuberance, a boundless joy in living; to others she gives perpetual pleasure, and she is happy because she makes them happy. Elsa Maxwell, the best of friends and the most forgiving to her enemies—if such there be—stands out as an example and an encouragement to all who believe that social intercourse should be accepted and appreciated as one of God's good gifts to mankind, and not as a dreary obligation to be shuffled through when necessity arises.

A couple of friends whom I cannot forbear to mention here— since they have come so much closer to us since the war—have been my old racing trainer, Frank Butters, and his delightful, courageous wife. Their annual visit to us in the south of France was something to which, every autumn, we grew to look forward as one of the chief pleasures of next year's spring. Now alas, his health has so completely broken down that, though we go on repeating our annual invitations, Mrs. Butters has to refuse them. Greatly do we miss them both, but this sadness has not impaired our affection for two of the best human beings we have ever known.

A new good, kind friend made in the years since the war is Mr. Charles Grey, a member of the staff of the United States Embassy in Paris, a man of sweet and sunny temperament, gay, gentle and ever helpful. He is the embodiment of the French saying *"tout comprendre, c'est tout pardonner."* No one could be a better companion in joy or sorrow than Charles Grey, for he is another who realizes that friendship and social life are God-given, and that we ought to be thankful for them and accept them with joy and gusto and not with resignation or boredom. Elsa Maxwell, Charles Grey and I share one quality which I sincerely believe to be enviable: we don't know what boredom is.

During the 1953 Cannes Film Festival I met Miss Olivia de Havilland, the distinguished actress, a woman of subtle and interesting personality who seems to me to be in her own way, if I may say so, a seeker after truth. I believe that she is one of those fortunately gifted people who have an artistic and personal life of their own, full, busy and successful, and who are yet—in and through this active day-to-day life—sharply and constantly aware of the fundamental issue and problem of our world today, the enormous power that man has attained over physical nature contrasted with the still somewhat primitive limitations of his emotional and spiritual existence.

Another new friend—one of the few truly great individual and creative artists of our time—who is in his fashion a similar seeker after truth and a pilgrim in search of a reconciling wisdom amid the contradictions of today is Mr. Charles Chaplin, whom I first came to know in 1953. He and I have talked long and far into the night —of the dreams that lie near our hearts, of the puzzles that afflict and sadden us. That Chaplin is a rebel goes without saying—a rebel against the folly of modern society's impotence in the midst of such overwhelming material aggregations of power.

I will cite an example of the sort of thing which drives a mind like Chaplin's to distraction. A recent report of the World Food and Agriculture Organization stated, without equivocation, that the vast majority of human beings still live far below the hunger line, with consequences in waste, suffering, reduced productive capacity and shortened expectation of life too enormous to measure; and, as the report pointed out, at the same time the world's present ratio of food production (let alone the results of any improvements that would follow better methods of soil conservation, fertilization and farming) is sufficient to ensure a perfectly adequate diet for every human being alive if it were properly distributed.

Now if only some of the enormous capital investment all over the world which every year goes into totally unproductive and potentially violently destructive armaments could be expended in a single major productive project—let us say water conservation, in building dams and artificial lakes and providing irrigation schemes for the huge empty and desert areas of the world—the over-all agricultural output would be vastly and rapidly increased and the ordinary standard of living be raised thereby. This, which is a topic about which I have thought a great deal, I drew to Mr. Chaplin's attention, to discover that his views on it were just the same as mine.

His detractors have in the most unmeasured terms accused Mr. Chaplin of being sympathetic to communism. I discovered one aspect of communism which horrified him. Communist propaganda, as we all know, proclaims loudly from time to time Moscow's view that our two worlds, our two economic and social systems, can live peaceably side by side and maintain a system of exchange, not only economic but intellectual and cultural. Yet, as Chaplin argued fiercely, the communists have established the Iron Curtain, which prevents any real free exchange of ideas between the two worlds, banning utterly as it does a free interchange in writing and the other arts, unimpeded free and uncontrolled travel by students and tourists, and all the ordinary ways by which the people of one country or civilization get to know and comprehend the people of another. The only method, said Chaplin, by which the co-existence of our two systems would be possible, or could offer a natural and healthy solution of humanity's troubles and problems, would be to open all frontiers to travelers, with the minimum of passports, currency control and restrictions and with a free and full interchange of literature—academic, journalistic and popular as well as technical and scientific—from one end of the world to another, such as existed in the far-off, happy days before 1914.

Mr. Chaplin is interested in certain psychical and nonphysical phenomena, such as telepathy and its various derivatives. He quoted to me Einstein's demand that ten scientists should witness at the same time, and under precisely similar conditions, every case of this kind submitted before he would consider these manifestations proved. He and I agreed that the imposition of this kind of test would make all psychical research and experiment impossible, for these phenomena—and the laws under which they occur—are simply not at the beck and call of human beings.

I consider it a real privilege and pleasure to have met Mr. Chaplin and his beautiful and accomplished young wife. She comprehends and fully sympathizes with his ideals, with his mental and spiritual aspirations and satisfactions, and with the real suffering that the contradictions of our time cause him. I, who by the grace of God's greatest gift, am myself blessed with a wife who fully understands the joys and the sorrows of my mind and my spirit, can well appreciate the happiness which he finds in a domestic life very similar to my own.

For a time a famous and beautiful young star of the screen was my daughter-in-law—Miss Rita Hayworth, my son Aly's second wife. She is the mother of my granddaughter—whom I have seen only when she was a new-born baby.

Aly's first marriage—to Mrs. Loel Guinness, a young Englishwoman of beauty, charm, wit and breeding, born Joan Yarde-Buller, the daughter of Lord Churston—had had my full and affectionate approval. They were married in 1936, when Aly was twenty-five; I took my daughter-in-law, Joan, to my heart; and I had, and still have, a great affection for her. She bore Aly two fine sons, my grandchildren; these boys are now at school and in due course they will go to universities in America—the elder, Karim, who shows promise in mathematics, to M.I.T., we hope, and Amyn, probably to the Harvard Law School.

Their marriage remained perfectly happy until the end of the war. They were both in the Middle East, first in Egypt and then in Syria; Aly was in the Army and Joan was one of the many officers' wives who, at that time, were grass widows in Cairo. After the war they returned to Europe and Joan spent a year or two in East Africa with the children. However—and to my real sorrow—they drifted apart. Differences developed between them and they separated.

Not long after this, Aly went to the United States on business and there met Miss Hayworth. They were seen about a good deal together—and a blaze of sensational publicity enveloped them, with endless gossip and speculation. They came to see me at Cannes, and I asked them if they were really devoted to each other; they both said that they were, so I advised them to get married as soon as possible.

As soon as their respective divorce formalities were completed, they were married—but in circumstances of clamorous publicity such as we had never before experienced in our family. My own first wedding in India had been elaborate, yet its festivities were simple and unostentatious, but this was a very different matter. This was a fantastic, semiroyal, semi-Hollywood affair; my wife and I played our part in the ceremony, much as we disapproved of the atmosphere with which it was surrounded.

I thought Miss Hayworth charming and beautiful, but it was not long before I saw, I am afraid, that they were not a well-assorted couple. My son Aly is an extremely warmhearted person who loves entertaining, who loves to be surrounded by friends to whom he gives hospitality with both hands. Miss Hayworth was obviously someone who was emotionally exhausted with the strain of her work, which had absorbed her almost from childhood, and she therefore looked upon her marriage as a haven of peace and rest. Certainly for two people whose ways of life were thus dramatically opposed the collapse of their marriage was inevitable.

However, I must say that instead of tackling the matter frankly and openly, Miss Hayworth somehow got it into her head that either Aly or I myself might try to take her daughter away from her, indeed kidnap the child. Therefore taking the child with her, she ran away from my son in rather extraordinary circumstances.

Had Miss Hayworth taken a little care and trouble, she could have found out what in fact are the Ismaili religious laws and the code which governs all my followers and my family in these matters. Under this code the custody of young children of either sex rests absolutely with their mother, no matter what the circumstances of the divorce. Unless we were criminals, therefore, we could not even have contemplated taking the baby, Yasmin, from her mother. When they are seven, boys pass into their father's custody, girls into their mother's until puberty when they are free to choose. This code surely offered Miss Hayworth ample protection.

I was in India and Pakistan when the final crisis in my son's domestic life was developing. The moment I got back to Cannes— that very same night—Miss Hayworth, without having let me even see the baby, took her and ran away to Paris and then from Paris back to the United States. She has since, I understand, come back to Europe; but she has not brought the child to show her to her father's family.

The day that she was leaving with the child, a busybody in my employ telephoned to tell me what was happening and to ask what she should do about it. I answered at once that it was no affair of ours and that Miss Hayworth was fully entitled to take the child wherever she wished. She could surely have delayed her departure for Paris from Cannes and have let me see the baby.

Friends of mine and my lawyers have always maintained that I might have made a trust settlement or taken out an insurance for my small granddaughter's future. Their arguments, though well-intentioned, are mistaken. They have not realized that under Islamic law the custody of a female child, until puberty, rests absolutely with her mother. They have also forgotten that there is no way under Islamic law by which a child can possibly be disinherited by his or her father. Were my son Aly to die, he is not allowed to will away from his legal heirs more than one third of his property; two-thirds must go to his heirs, of whom his daughter Yasmin is one, and he cannot interfere with this provision in any way. Nor does Muslim law allow a testator to benefit one legal heir at the expense of another. Therefore, whatever happens to my son Aly, the child Yasmin is bound to get her proper share of any estate which he leaves. So long as capitalism and any system of private property survive, it is unlikely that Aly will die penniless; consequently, there is no particular urgency about making financial provision for his daughter.

A system of dowries and of marriage settlements is, I understand, developing in the United States, and doubtless when the child is of an age to contemplate marriage, either my son or I will arrange a reasonable dowry for her, in relation to the circumstances of the man she marries.

In conclusion, I can only hope that when next Miss Hayworth comes to Europe, she will bring her small daughter with her so that her father's family can see her and have the pleasure of making her acquaintance.

◆§ X V §◆

People I Have Known

THE PEOPLE whom I have met and known throughout my life stand out in my recollection more vividly and sharply than the dogmas that I have heard preached, the theories that I have heard argued, the policies that I have known to be propounded and abandoned. I have enjoyed the friendship of beautiful and accomplished women, of brilliant and famous men, who throng the corridors of my memory.

The most beautiful woman whom I ever knew was without doubt Lady D'Abernon—formerly Lady Helen Vincent—the wife of Britain's great Ambassador in Berlin. The brilliance of her beauty was marvelous to behold: the radiance of her coloring, the perfection of her figure, the exquisite modeling of her limbs, the classic quality of her features, and the vivacity and charm of her expression. I knew her for more than forty years; and when she was seventy the moment she came into a room, however many attractive or lovely young women might be assembled there, every eye was for her alone. Nor was her beauty merely physical; she was utterly unspoiled, simple, selfless, gay, brave and kind.

If Lady D'Abernon was pre-eminent, there were many, many others whose loveliness it is a joy to recall: Lady Curzon, now Countess Howe; Mme. Letelier, Swedish by origin, and almost from childhood a leading social figure; Princess Kutusov; the American, Mrs. Spottiswoode, who took London by storm during the Edwardian era, who married Baron Eugene de Rothschild, and—alas— died young, still in the pride of her beauty and her charm.

The most brilliant conversationalist of my acquaintance was

Augustine Birrell, now—I am told—an almost legendary figure in an epoch which has largely forgotten the art of conversation. Oscar Wilde I never met, for his tragic downfall had overwhelmed him before I first came to Europe. Strangely enough I had one chance of making his acquaintance after he came out of prison. My friend Lady Ripon was one of those who stood loyally by him after his disgrace. One day in 1899 I encountered her in the hall of the Ritz in Paris, and she invited me to dine with her and one or two others in a private room at the Café Voisins to meet Wilde; but unluckily an important previous engagement prevented me from accepting her invitation.

I have referred to my friend Walter Berry. He was one who could more than hold his own in any society however brilliant or accomplished. Another of a different epoch and from a profoundly different background was Dr. Hjalmar Schacht, the German financial wizard, who every time that I met him held a whole table enthralled.

I have known many women who allied great social and conversational talent to their beauty; notable among them were Mrs. Edwin Montagu and Lady Diana Duff Cooper (now Lady Norwich). My friend, Lady Cunard, was unique—the most complete personality that I have ever encountered. Another figure of legend whom I knew well was the Comtesse de Chevigny who was, as is well known, the original—or shall I say the chief original?—of Proust's Duchesse de Guermont. One of the most striking and memorable of the novelist's descriptions of her is at a great party in, I think, 1900. She looked worried and preoccupied, and when asked what was the matter, replied, *"La Chine m'inquiete."* And I reflect that more than once, in those far-off, seemingly carefree days before the First World War, I met the Comtesse de Chevigny and saw, across the dinner table, amidst all that brilliance and gaiety, that same sad and haunted expression. Had I asked her, would she have answered, I wonder, *"L'Allemagne m'inquiete"* or *"Agadir m'inquiete. . ."*?

Only recently, in the summer of 1953, I made the acquaintance of one of the most remarkable men of our time, an agreeable, shrewd and courtly old gentleman, the Sheikh of Kuweit, who is the personal embodiment of a truly astonishing romance—the romance of a sudden, dazzling rise to almost incalculable wealth. Kuweit's oil resources have only lately been tapped, but they are of tremendous richness. The royalties which the Sheikh derives from them suffice, at present, to enrich him and his little principality something like fifty million pounds a year. This sudden flood of wealth has come to what, until recently, was a small, frugal Arab state (though nominally under British protection it has always preserved its independence, and therefore its ruler ought to be designated as Sultan, not as Sheikh), whose population, through many centuries, had pursued their changeless callings as fishermen, tillers of the soil or nomad shepherds. Suddenly industrial need, with its accompanying exploitation and expansion, has enveloped them, bringing a swift and total revolution in their way of life and outlook.

It is particularly fortunate therefore that the Sheikh himself is a man of great wisdom, who allies an incredibly clear-sighted understanding of what this industrial and technical revolution means to a profound awareness of his own responsibilities. I especially delighted in his company because I found a kindred spirit, one whose mind had its full store of Arab and Islamic history and culture, and a steadfast appreciation of the spiritual unity of the Arab world which underlies its present divisions and miseries.

There is, I have often thought, a curious resemblance between the Arabia of today and the Germany of 1830: the many political divisions and subdivisions, minorities far dispersed and under foreign rule, the jumble of monarchies and republics, and withal the drive of a common language, a common culture and a common faith—and that common faith being Islam is sufficiently tolerant to embrace the Christian minority in its midst and admit them to a full share in Arab traditions, culture and aspirations. How will the Arab world evolve? Who can tell? But who, at the time of the Congress of Vienna, could have foretold the astonishing course of German history over the subsequent century?

The core of the Arab world is the high, central plateau of the

Arabian peninsula itself. Here Islam was born. Hence its vast tide of expansion poured out in the centuries after the death of the Prophet, that tide which carried Arab and Muslim culture across enormous area of the world—to India and China and Southeast Asia, to Byzantium, down the length of Africa, and deep into Europe, being stemmed only at Roncesvalles. Hence in succeeding centuries has come every great wave of Arab resurgence. Is the whole drive ended now? Few would dare say so with confidence. But given the conditions of today, and the domination of the world by science and technology, the Arab's future greatness must be spiritual and cultural. This is far more in keeping with Islam whose very meaning is "Peace."

For in Arabia vast and portentous processes of change are at work. After a series of violent and vigorous campaigns, during the years of the final decline and the Ottoman Empire's suzerainty over these regions, Ibn Saud consolidated his authority over a large part of the peninsula. The Kingdom of Saudi Arabia is his creation, and there can be no doubt that His Majesty King Abdul Aziz was one of the outstanding Arab personalities of recent centuries. The veteran Ibn Saud has sired a splendid brood of sons, numbering nearly forty, all tall, handsome, virile men—the modern counterparts of those bearded gallants who swagger through the pages of the *Arabian Nights*, causing strong men to tremble and maidens to swoon. Yet they cannot be dismissed as simple storybook characters; many of Ibn Saud's sons possess his redoubtable characteristics—whether in glamorous Arab dress or in European clothes—for they are as much at home in committee rooms, conference halls and the saloons of luxury hotels in London or in Washington as they are in their father's tents at Nejd.

For to Saudi Arabia the West has lately come, with the same all-embracing compulsive vigor as to Kuweit; the oil resources of the former are believed to be among the richest in the world. American enterprise is revolutionizing its economic existence. But the enormous power that this development brings is being used in a most enlightened and skillful manner, and it makes nonsense of the shallow propagandist allegations about the crushing effects of "economic imperialism." The United States is creating, in its dealings with Saudi Arabia, a new and profoundly significant pattern of relationships between so-called "backward" and "advanced" countries. There is the maximum of economic assistance and support, and exploitation of natural resources, with a complete absence of political interference. This outlook expresses itself in personal relations as well; it is a firm rule that if any American working in Saudi Arabia is discovered to have failed in courtesy toward the poorest Arab, he is at once sent home and forbidden to come back. There is thus being built up a sense of confidence, of good will and of mutual respect between the two peoples—and between individuals—which is of immense value both in itself and as an example to other nations who, whether under Point Four schemes or the Colombo Plan or any other of these world-wide arrangements, come into similar contact.

Whenever the state of my health has permitted, I have traveled widely since the end of the war. I have visited the two new independent nations that have succeeded the Indian Empire which I knew from my childhood; I have been to Egypt and East Africa, to Iran and to Burma.

Before the end of British rule in India one of the curious and erroneous opinions widely canvassed was that Indians lacked the capacity to govern themselves, manage their own affairs and play their full part in the councils of the world. Recent years have demonstrated the glaring falsity of this idea. Both countries have been particularly well served by their statesmen, high officials and diplomats; and their contributions to the work of the Commonwealth and of the United Nations have been many and valuable.

Bharat—though an assassin's hand struck down Mahatma Gandhi at a time when his country still badly needed him—has been devotedly served by many brilliant and patriotic men and women, notably Sardar Patel, Mr. Nehru and his talented sister, Mrs. Pandit. My own contacts with the new regime in Delhi are close and cordial, and I have been received there with great kindness and hospitality. We are all constantly aware of the immensely important part India plays, with increasing sureness and felicity of touch, in international affairs, seeking to provide a bridge of understanding between the West and a resurgent Asia in a fashion that is both courageous and sensible.

Pakistan faced at the outset a far harder task than her neighbor. In Delhi, Calcutta, Bombay and other cities there existed both the traditions of a strong and stable administration and the facilities— the staff, the buildings and the equipment—to maintain it. In Pakistan, however, everything, literally everything, had to be built from the very beginning. Typewriters, pens and paper and file covers hardly existed. Hundreds of miles separated East and West Pakistan. Neither had, in the ordinary sense, a capital city. Karachi and Dacca doubled and redoubled their size overnight; everything had to be built from the foundations up, and every ordinary facility of administration and government had to be established anew.

This vast task was undertaken with extraordinary skill and pertinacity. Pakistan was a going concern from the outset. Part of the genius of the Quaid-i-Azam was that, like the Prophet himself, he attracted into his orbit able and devoted people, and Pakistan has been served, throughout her brief existence, by men and women of the highest moral and intellectual caliber. They came from the ranks, not only of his previous followers, but of those who had been severely critical of his policy in earlier days. Their achievements have given the lie to all the croaking prophets who could foresee nothing but disaster for the young state.

First and foremost, of course, was the Quaid-i-Azam's sister, Miss Fatima Jinnah, who had been his companion, friend and helper for many years, who presided over his homes in London and Bombay, and later in his palace in Karachi and his summer home at the hill station of Ziarat. Miss Jinnah has much of the strength of character of her famous brother, much of his manner, voice, resolute bearing and appearance. Now, after his death, she is still prominent in public life, with a large and faithful following; and she acts as a zealous and vigilant guardian of the moral and political independence of her brother's God-given realm.

Ghulam Mohammed, the present Governor General, universally

admired and respected, is a former industrialist and a learned and devoted student of the history of Islam, its magnificent rise, its gradual decline and its present hope and chance of rising, phoenix-like, from the ashes of the past. A former distinguished colleague of mine at the Round Table Conference and the committees which followed, Zafrullah Khan, is at present Foreign Minister; and he brings to his herculean responsibilities sagacity, forensic ability and great experience in the field of international affairs.

There was too the Quaid-i-Azam's faithful and skilled hench-man, Liaquat Ali Khan, who was another tragic victim of the wave of violence and assassination which for some years swept the East. He is survived by his wife, in her own field of work and interests hardly less able and certainly no less devoted than her staunch and beloved husband. But Liaquat will long be missed; for surely if the Quaid had asked for an Abu Bakr, for a Peter, he could not have been granted a better one than Liaquat Ali Khan, whose qualities were not bright or showy but whose strength of character was solid, durable and of the utmost fidelity. He proved his worth in Pakistan's second stern testing. The Quaid's death, so soon after the foundation of Pakistan, strikingly resembled that of the Prophet himself who was received into the "Companionship-on-High" very soon after the triumph and consolidation of his temporal conquests. Similarly the Quaid did not live to preside long over the growth of the mighty child that he had fathered.

But Liaquat was in every way a worthy successor. Yet he who had been so near to the Quaid was himself soon to be struck down. Truly it may be said that he gave his soul to God. As life ebbed from him, his last words were: "No God but God, and Mohammed his messenger."

That is the stamp of a man whose achievement is the Pakistan of today. I think gladly of others: of Habib Rahimtoola, the brilliant son of a brilliant father, who had, as High Commissioner in London immediately after the formation of the State, a post of especial responsibility; of Mr. Isphani who, at the same critical period, represented his young country in Washington; of the present Prime Minister, formerly a very successful High Commissioner in Ottawa, who is the grandson of Nawab Ali Chowdry, a colleague of mine in the early days of the Muslim League; of Amjid Ali, for many years my honorary secretary who has rendered great service in the most onerous of charges; and of the other Mohammed Ali, a brilliant expert on economics and finance.

Most of these men are comparatively young in years, and they come from families with industrial and commercial rather than political or official traditions. Their zeal, their efficiency and their success in their new tasks have all been notable. Is not the explanation that they have been sustained by their patriotism, by their devotion to a great cause, and, above all, by their Muslim faith and their consciousness of immediate and permanent responsibility to the Divine?

My most recent, postwar visit to Burma was a particularly happy experience. As I have pointed out earlier, I took the step of advising my followers in Burma, a good many years ago, to identify themselves in every possible way with the outlook, customs, aspirations, and way of life of the people among whom they dwelt— to give up their Indo-Saracenic names, for example, and to take Burman names; to adopt Burman dress, habits and clothing, and apart from their religion and its accompanying practices, to assimilate themselves as much as possible in the country of their adoption. Now that the people of Burma have regained their independence, this advice of mine, and the full and faithful way in which my followers have carried it out, have borne fruit. My wife and I were received in Burma by the President and the Prime Minister and many other leading and notable personalities with the utmost kindness and friendliness. Burma is a beautiful country; her people unite a deep piety (in few other countries does the Prime Minister have to be begged not to retire from office and—as he longs to do—assume the saffron robe and the begging bowl of the mendicant monk) to gaiety, gentleness and intensely hospitable generosity.

They were especially happy days that we spent in Rangoon. The climax of the hospitality which we received was reached, perhaps, on the night that we were bidden to dine, in our own apartments, on Burman food specially prepared for us in the President's palace. At eight o'clock sharp two aides de camp and several servants arrived with an array which marshaled in all something like thirty courses. The Burmans are by no means vegetarians nor are they particularly ascetic in their diet. Most of the dishes were very, very rich and very, very nourishing. When they were laid out, we asked the aides de camp to join us. After a few courses we announced that we had finished.

"Oh, no," said the aides de camp, smiling in the friendliest fashion. "We have been specially sent to see that you try every dish."

Such hospitality was irresistible. On we battled as bravely as we could, on and on to the puddings, the bonbons and the sugared fruit. After all, I had lived in Victorian London and had attended the long, rich and stately banquets of that era, but never in all my life have I known a meal which in variety and subtlety of taste and flavor could rival that dinner so kindly given to us by the President of Burma.

Iran, the home of my ancestors for many centuries, I first visited in February, 1951, to be present at the wedding of His Imperial Majesty the Shah. Although the circumstances and the duties of an active and busy life had, by chance, prevented me from going to Iran until I was well past seventy, I have always taken great pride in my Iranian origin. Both my father and my mother, it will be recalled, were grandchildren of Fateh Ali Shah, who was a pure Kajar of Turkish descent, and the outlook and way of life of the home in which I was brought up was almost entirely Iranian.

Therefore to go to Iran was in a real sense a homecoming. It was made especially precious by the graciousness and the kindness we received as personal guests of the Emperor, and in the beautiful palace which Her Imperial Highness, Princess Shams, most graciously put at our disposal.

In Mahalat, which was long my ancestors' home, I was received by thousands of Ismailis from all over Persia. It was good to see that their womenfolk had all given up the *chaddur*, the Persian equivalent of the Indian purdah. Isfahan, which we also visited, is more old-fashioned. There we saw the *chaddur* frequently worn, and we encountered a good number of men wearing the long, high-buttoned coat that was customary under the rule of the Kajar dynasty. In Tehran the effects of Reza Shah's policy of modernization are numerous and visible. Iranians in general do not resemble any neighboring Asiatic people; in ordinary appearance many of them might be mistaken for southern Caucasians. And nowadays in the cities their adaptation of European—or allegedly European—dress and a somewhat forlorn appearance of poverty give them the down-at-heel look that one has seen in moving pictures about Russia.

Some of these appearances are, I think, misleading—especially the appearance of poverty. Weight for weight, man for man, the masses of Iran are certainly better off than the masses of India or China; and although their standard of living is obviously not comparable with that of Western European countries or America, they are in matters particularly of diet better off than the people of many Asiatic nations, living distinctly above, not below, the margin of subsistence.

One fact is clear above the welter of Iran's problems and difficulties: if the present Emperor now has, after all the stirring vicissitudes through which he has lately passed, a free hand and is able to choose his own ministers and advisers and is not hampered by conservatism on the one hand and individualism on the other, Iran will be able greatly to raise her economic and social standards and to support in far better conditions a considerably increased population.

I must not close this brief record of my recent doings and experiences without some reference to an incident a good deal less agreeable than most that have lately come my way. One morning in August, 1949, my wife and I left our villa near Cannes to drive to the Nice airport to catch a plane to Deauville. Our heavy luggage had gone on by road in our own two cars with our servants. My wife and I and her personal maid, Mlle. Frieda Meyer, were therefore in a car hired from a local garage. I was beside the driver, my wife and her maid in back. About two hundred yards from the gate of our villa the mountain road takes a sharp turn and another small road comes in at the side.

As we reached the intersection we saw another car drawn up across it, so that we could neither pass nor take the by-road. Three men, masked and hooded and extremely heavily armed—they had no fewer than ten guns among the three of them—jumped out and closed in on us. One of them slashed one of our back tires. The muzzles of their guns thrust into the car, one a few inches from my wife, another close to my chest. Fear, as one ordinarily understands it, did not bother any of us. I remember that I saw the hands of the man who was covering me trembling violently, and I thought with complete detachment: "That gun is quite likely to go off." My wife's maid, as she has often told me since, thought— again quite without agitation—"When is he going to kill the Prince?" And my wife at her side had no sensation of alarm or fear at all.

I said, in my normal tone of voice, "We won't resist; we'll give you what you want."

One of them snatched my wife's jewel box which she held in her lap. As they backed away toward their car he said, "Please be kind. Let us get away."

Then when they were just about to jump back into their car, I found my voice and my sense of humor.

"Hi, come back!" I shouted. "You've forgotten your *pourboire!*"

One of them ran back and I gave him the handful of francs which I had in my pocket.

"*Voilà le pourboire,*" said I.

"*Merci, merci,*" he said again and again, as he ran back to the other car.

We went home and telephoned the police at Lloyd's. Lloyd's dealt with our claim completely and generously. After almost four years had passed, six men were brought to trial in 1953, and three were convicted and sentenced. And that, I think, is all that need be said about an episode as unpleasant as, in my long experience, it was unprecedented.

➔§XVI§➔

Toward the Future

ALL MY LIFE I have looked forward. Large-scale prophecy, however, is as dangerous as it is easy, and true prophetic vision is rare indeed. It is a rarity more than ever marked in an epoch such as ours, in which science has placed in our reach material and natural powers undreamed of fifty short years ago. But since the human mind and the human imagination are as yet by no means fully equipped to master the immense forces which human ingenuity has discovered and unleashed, it is not too difficult to foresee at least some of the political and social reactions of nations as well as individuals to this enormous scientific and technical revolution and all its accompanying phenomena.

India, the country of my birth and upbringing, has been for centuries a land of extreme poverty, misery and want, where millions are born, live and work and die at a level far below the margin of subsistence. A tropical climate, aeons of soil erosion, and primitive and unskilled methods of agriculture have all taken their toll of suffering, patient, gentle but ignorant mankind. The Indian peasant has survived and multiplied but in face of the most ferocious and formidable handicaps. Many years ago, in my first book, *India in Transition,* I gave this account of the day-to-day life of the ordinary Indian peasant under British rule.

A typical rural scene on an average day in an average year is essentially the same now as it was half a century ago. A breeze, alternately warm and chilly, sweeps over the monotonous landscape as it is lightened by a rapid dawn, to be followed quickly by a heavy molten sun appearing on the

347

horizon. The ill-clad villagers, men, women, and children, thin and weak, and made old beyond their years by a life of underfeeding and overwork, have been astir before daybreak, and have partaken of a scanty meal, consisting of some kind or other of cold porridge, of course without sugar or milk. With bare and hardened feet they reach the fields and immediately begin to furrow the soil with their lean cattle, of a poor and hybrid breed, usually sterile and milkless. A short rest at midday, and a handful of dried corn or beans for food, is followed by a continuance till dusk of the same laborious scratching of the soil. Then the weary way homeward in the chilly evening, every member of the family shaking with malaria or fatigue. A drink of water, probably contaminated, the munching of a piece of hard black or green *chaupati*, a little gossip round the peepul tree, and then the day ends with heavy, unrefreshing sleep in dwellings so insanitary that no decent European farmer would house his cattle in them.

The Raj has gone, but in essentials the life and lot of the humble villager of rural India have scarcely changed since I wrote these words. Education, hygiene, welfare schemes, plans for village "uplift" have but scratched the surface of the problem, hardly more deeply or more efficiently than the peasant's own wooden plough scratches the sunbaked soil of India. Nor is the lot of his urban kinsman, working in one of the great and ever-growing industrial cities like Bombay or Calcutta, much better. At his factory, in his home, the Indian industrial worker endures, and takes for granted, utterly appalling conditions. From steamy, overcrowded mill or factory he trudges to the shanty or tenement, equally overcrowded, equally unhealthy, which serves him as his home. His diet, though more varied than that of his cousin in the country, is pitifully meager by any Western standard. Around him are the increasing distractions of a great city, but they have little meaning for him. His amenities are few, his luxuries nonexistent.

During the years of British rule it was relatively easy to shrug off responsibility for the economic *malaise* of India, to put all the blame on imperialist exploitation, and to say, "When we get our independence, then we shall put economic conditions right." The imperialists have gone; the period of alien exploitation is over. But can economic injustice be so easily righted? India's population is steadily and rapidly increasing, yet at the present rate—and in spite of all manner of schemes for soil conservation, irrigation, better use of land, intensive and planned industrialization—it is unlikely that more than half the natural increase in population can be economically absorbed. India's problem, like China's, is one of economic absorptive capacity. Pakistan's problem, since she has the empty but potentially rich acres of Baluchistan to fill with her surplus population, is less pressing. Doubtless in India, as in China, the extension of education and growing familiarity with the use of the vote and the processes of democracy will give rise to eager and energetic efforts to find political solutions to the gravest economic problems. Hundreds upon hundreds of millions of human beings in India and in China live out their lives in conditions of extreme misery. How long will these vast masses of humanity accept such conditions? May they not—as realization dawns of their own political power—insist on an extreme form of socialism, indeed on communism, though not on Soviet Russian lines and not under Soviet leadership? And may not that insistence be revolutionary in its expression and in its manifestations?

Yet in India, as well as in China, if every "have" in the population were stripped of wealth and reduced to the level of the lowest "have not," of the poorest sweeper or coolie, the effect on the general standard of living—the general ill-being—would be negligible. There are far too few "haves," far too many "have nots," in both countries for even the most wholesale redistribution of wealth as it now stands. Reform, to be real and effective, must strike much deeper. These are thoughts grim enough to depress anyone who possesses more than the most superficial knowledge of Asia's problems and difficulties.

There is one major political step forward which should be taken by the Governments of India and Pakistan, which would have a significant and beneficial effect on the life and welfare of their peoples. This is the establishment of a genuine and lasting *entente cordiale* between the two countries, such as subsisted between Britain and France from 1905 to 1914. Even more pertinent analogies are offered by Belgium and Holland, and Sweden and Norway. Here are two pairs of neighboring sovereign states, once joined and now separated. The separation of the Low Countries offers the nearest parallel since this was effected on the specific grounds of religious difference. I have earlier likened the Hindu and Muslim communities of the old Indian Empire to Siamese twins; as such they were, before they were parted, hardly able to move; now separate, surely they ought to be able to go along together as companions and friends, to their mutual benefit and support.

Here however it is for India with its far greater population, resources, and developed industries to show the same political judgment as Sweden showed toward Norway after their separation—that is to say—a final and sincere acceptance of the partition as desirable and in itself as at last opening the door to a real understanding between the two culturally different peoples of the subcontinent.

Even a small minority can make great mischief if it keeps up and repeats the political slogans of unity which may have had a sense at one time but which today can only prevent that good neighborly relation on which future co-operation in international politics depends.

In problems such as water, both east and west between the two republics of India and Pakistan, refugee property and other financial claims and counterclaims should be settled now in a way that the weaker country of the two shall not feel that it has been browbeaten and unjustly treated by its vast and powerful neighbor.

The problem of Kashmir should also be faced as an honest attempt to bring about by plebiscite, under international auspices, a final settlement on the basis of the triumph of the popular will. Were India to adopt consistently toward Pakistan the policy adopted by Sweden toward Norway, by Holland toward Belgium, not only for years but for decades, not only peace in Southern Asia but the full weight for international peace and good will will necessarily increase to an extent of which we at present can have little idea. The great role to be played as bridge between West and East beyond the frontiers of Pakistan and India can only be accomplished if and when these two neighbors are themselves capable of co-operation and such fair dealing toward each other as will convince the rest of the world that they have a claim to be listened to and seriously considered.

The alternative to an Indian policy of understanding and the encouragement of water and other economic needs of Pakistan, not only justly, but with free comprehension, can be that the neighbor will turn in other directions for alliances and friendships—the result of which must lead to these two neighborly powers, instead of looking outward and working for world peace, watching each other, ever on the look-out for danger and discord rather than for peaceful and economic independence and development.

I do not think that the countries of the Near East, with the possible exception of Egypt, face any population problems which, granted courage, resolution and ingenuity, should prove insuperable.

All that the people of countries like Iran, Iraq, Syria, the Lebanon, Yemen and even Saudi Arabia, need is knowledge—knowledge of new techniques, knowledge of engineering, knowledge of agriculture. They have room and resources enough. Science properly applied can repopulate their empty lands and make their barren spaces flourish; can plant cities, fertilize crops; can set up industries and develop their immensely rich mineral and raw material potentialities. Here there was once the Garden of Eden; historians and archaeologists have shown that this region was at one time fertile, rich and populous. So it can be again, if the powers and the resources available to mankind now are properly employed. The Arab lands have been devastated by centuries of folly, by waste and extravagance due to ignorance; the pitiful condition of their peoples today is a condemnation of their past. There is no need to look further than Israel to realize what courage and determination, allied to skill and urgent need, can achieve. The Arabs are no whit inferior to any race in the world in intelligence and potential capacity. A single generation's concentrated and devoted attention to the real needs of education for all, of scientific and technical as well as academic teaching, training and discipline, could revolutionize the Arab world. Self-help is better by far than grants in aid, and better than perpetual outpouring by the United States of its surplus pro-

duction. The Arabs' only danger lies in continued apathy and ignorance in a swiftly changing world, and in a social and economic outlook and practices unadapted to the challenging realities of our time.

I have little fear about the impact of the future of the British
Crown Colonies in Africa. We have seen the noble work of Great
Britain in West Africa. In East and Central Africa the problem is at
present complicated by the presence of a European settler population. I believe that there can be a healthy and satisfactory adjustment, provided all sections in these multiracial communities—indigenous Africans and immigrant Europeans and Asians—face the
simple, fundamental fact that they are all dependent upon each
other. No one section can dismiss any other from its calculations,
either about contributions to past development or about plans for
the future. The immigrant, be he European or Asian, has no hope
of prosperity without the Africans; the African cannot do without
the European farmer or the Asian trader, unless he wants to see his
standard of living fall steeply, and with it all hope of exploiting
and enhancing the natural wealth of the land in which all three
have their homes and must earn their bread.

To a Muslim there is one quietly but forcibly encouraging element in this situation. Wherever the indigenous population is Muslim, there is remarkably little racial antagonism or sense of bitterness
against the European, in spite of the European's obvious economic
superiority. Islam, after all, is a soil in which sentiments of this
sort do not take root or flourish easily. This is not a shallow and
fatalistic resignation; it is something much more profound in the
essence of the teaching of Islam—a basic conviction that in the
eyes of God all men, regardless of color or class or economic condition, are equal. From this belief there springs an unshakable
self-respect, whose deepest effects are in the subconscious, preventing the growth of bitterness or any sense of inferiority or jealousy
by one man of another's economic advantage.

Islam in all these countries has within it, I earnestly believe, the
capacity to be a moral and spiritual force of enormous significance,
both stabilizing and energizing the communities among whom it

is preached and practiced. To ignore Islam's potential influence for good, Islam's healing and creative power for societies as for individuals, is to ignore one of the most genuinely hopeful factors that exist in the world today.

But what of the recurrent, intractable issue of peace or war? Few epochs in recent history have been more devastating and disastrous than (to quote a phrase of Sir Winston Churchill's) "this tormented half-century." Is the long torment at last over?

I can only hope fervently, with all my being, that this is so; that the nations and their leaders are sincerely and actively convinced not only of the negative proposition that a Third World War would effect the destruction of civilization, perhaps indeed of humanity, but of its positive corollary that it now lies within men's power enormously and rapidly to enhance and increase civilization and to promote the material well-being of millions who now rank as "have nots." The only chance of nations and individuals alike among the "have nots" lies in the preservation of peace. Europe needs a century or more of recuperation after the agony and havoc that its peoples have endured, and recuperation means peace. The industrial and productive capacity of North America—the United States and Canada—already vaster than anything the world has ever seen, is increasing fast; North America needs markets; and markets mean peace. The underdeveloped countries, in Africa, Asia and South America, need over the years a vast and steady inflow of capital investment—to build and develop their communications, to exploit their resources, to raise their standard of living—and investment on this scale and to this end calls for peace. War, in face of such circumstances and so numerous and so imperative a series of needs, would be madness. But I must admit that if we look back at the history of the past fifty years, this has not been a consideration that has deflected the nations and their leaders from catastrophic courses. All the hardly won prosperity and security, all the splendid and beckoning hopes of the last quarter of the nineteenth century counted for nothing when the crucial test came. Pride and folly swayed men's hearts. The world's state today is the result of pride and folly.

As Germany did for so long, Russia now supplies the civilized world's great enigma, the riddle to which there seems no sensible or satisfactory answer. One factor in Russia's perplexing equation is obvious and known—the factor whose results can only be happy, peaceful and prosperous. The other—the perpetual "x"—is grim and incalculable. Long ago Lord Palmerston said that Russian history taught this lesson: the Russians must expand, and they will go on expanding until they encounter some force—a nation or a combination of nations—powerful enough to stop them. From its beginnings in the Grand Duchy of Moscow Russia has expanded steadily and remorselessly. Is expansion still the dominant motive in Russian policy? There are some somber indications that this is one of the many characteristics which Communist Russia possesses in common with Czarist Russia and that her appetite for expansion is still not glutted.

Yet why should this be so? Are there not other more peaceful factors at work? Russia's empty lands, within her own borders, are greater by far than those that opened up, decade after decade, in front of the pioneers who extended the United States from small, precarious beginnings along the Atlantic seaboard. Russia has no need of overseas colonies, no need, now that aerial communications have developed so swiftly and so powerfully, for those "windows on warm seas" which once mattered so much. Inside her own frontiers, if her leaders can be genuinely convinced that no one menaces the Soviet Union, that no one harbors aggressive, imperialist designs against her, her people may live at peace for centuries. Will these realistic and wholesome considerations carry the day, or will suspicion, blind hatred, pride and folly wreak new and more terrible havoc? As in the German people before the Second World War there was the dreadful, Wagnerian death-wish, driving a great and superbly talented nation to self-immolation, so is there in the heart of all men some dark, satanic evil still lusting for destruction? These are the stern riddles of our time, and each of us seeks his own answers to them.

But these issues and questions concern men in the aggregate, great bodies of men in national and racial groups. The biggest group, however, is only composed of the number of individuals in it. If it is possible to bring happiness to one individual, in him at least the dark and evil impulses may be conquered. And in the end may not the power of good in the individual prevail against the power of evil in the many?

I can only say to everyone who reads this book that it is my profound conviction that man must never ignore and leave untended and undeveloped that spark of the Divine which is in him. The way to personal fulfillment, to individual reconciliation with the Universe that is about us, is comparatively easy for anyone who firmly and sincerely believes, as I do, that Divine Grace has given man in his own heart the possibilities of illumination and of union with Reality. It is, however, far more important to attempt to offer some hope of spiritual sustenance to those many who, in this age in which the capacity of faith is nonexistent in the majority, long for something beyond themselves, even if it seems second-best. For them there is the possibility of finding strength of the spirit, comfort and happiness in contemplation of the infinite variety and beauty of the Universe.

Life in the ultimate analysis has taught me one enduring lesson. The subject should always disappear in the object. In our ordinary affections one for another, in our daily work with hand or brain, most of us discover soon enough that any lasting satisfaction, any contentment that we can achieve, is the result of forgetting self, of merging subject with object in a harmony that is of body, mind and spirit. And in the highest realms of consciousness all who believe in a Higher Being are liberated from all the clogging and hampering bonds of the subjective self in prayer, in rapt meditation upon and in the face of the glorious radiance of eternity, in which all temporal and earthly consciousness is swallowed up and itself becomes the eternal.

INDEX

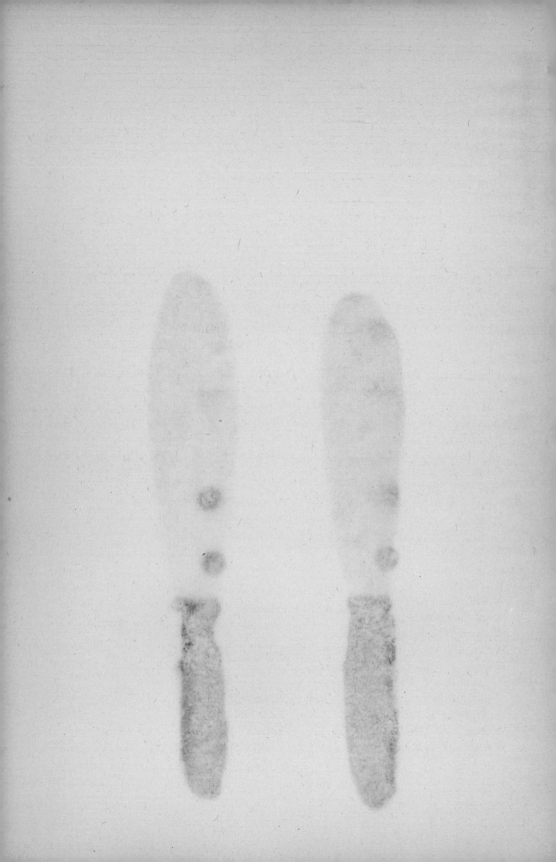

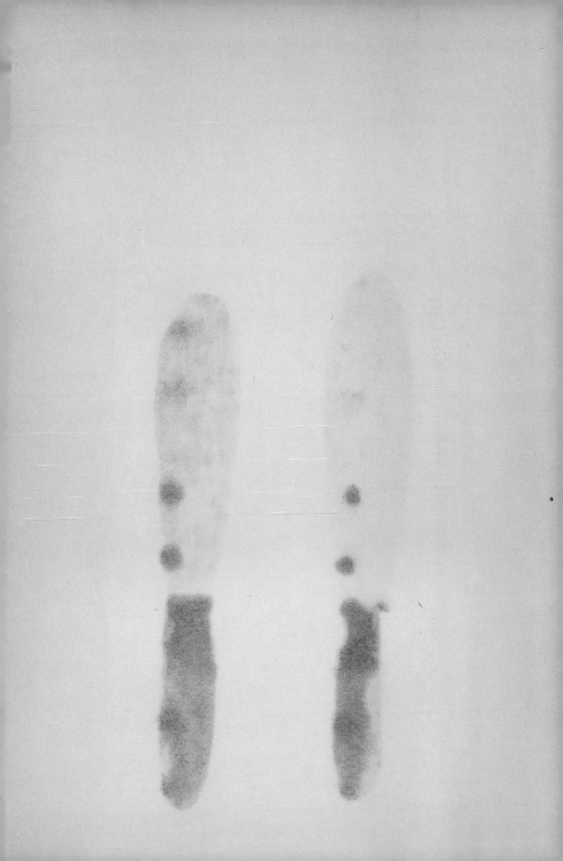